NINTH
EDITION

SOCIAL STUDIES IN ELEMENTARY EDUCATION

JOHN JAROLIMEK
WALTER C. PARKER

University of Washington, Seattle

Macmillan Publishing Company
New York

Maxwell Macmillan Canada
Toronto

Maxwell Macmillan International
New York · Oxford · Singapore · Sydney

Editor: Robert Miller
Cover Illustration: Dave Cutler
Production Editor: Stephen C. Robb
Art Coordinator: Peter A. Robison
Text Designer: Susan E. Frankenberry
Cover Designer: Thomas Mack
Production Buyer: Pamela D. Bennett
Illustrations: Maryland Cartographics, Inc.

This book was set in Palatino and Helvetica by Carlisle Communications, Ltd. and was printed and bound by Arcata Graphics/Halliday. The cover was printed by Phoenix Color Corp.

Macmillan Publishing Company
866 Third Avenue
New York, NY 10022

Macmillan Publishing Company is part of the
Maxwell Communications Group of Companies.

Maxwell Macmillan Canada, Inc.
1200 Eglinton Avenue East, Suite 200
Don Mills, Ontario M3C 3N1

Library of Congress Cataloging-in-Publication Data
Jarolimek, John.
    Social studies in elementary education / John Jarolimek, Walter C. Parker.
    —9th ed.
        p.   cm.
    Includes bibliographical references and index.
    ISBN 0-02-360571-5
    1. Social studies—Study and teaching (Elementary)—United States.
    I. Parker, Walter.   II. Title
LB1584.J3 1993
372.83′044′0973—dc20   92-5501
                                                                          CIP

Printing: 2 3 4 5 6 7 8 9   Year: 3 4 5 6

Preface

Each year thousands of women from Latin America, Asia, the Middle East, and Africa come to the United States for a few days' visit and then quietly return to their homelands. Why do these women migrate to the United States in such large numbers only to stay for a few days or a week? To vacation? To attend a conference? To visit relatives or friends? No. These women come because they are pregnant, are near the end of their term, and want their child to be born on American soil, thereby qualifying the infant for United States citizenship. The practice is actually illegal, but it is nearly impossible for authorities to enforce the laws that prohibit it. Thus, these expectant mothers are willing to go to great expense, enormous inconvenience, discomfort, and considerable risk, to give their child that most precious of gifts—citizenship in this land of freedom and opportunity. What an astounding contrast with many of us who are already here and take our citizenship for granted!

For the children of these mothers and all others who are born in this country, American citizenship, or more correctly, United States citizenship, is legally their birthright. But is legal citizenship all there is to being a responsible and participating citizen? We think not; and in this book we argue that citizenship in a democratic society requires the individual to have a functioning familiarity with certain knowledge, skills, and values. Moreover, while the individual citizen's *rights* are constitutionally guaranteed, there are no such assurances that the individual citizen will face up to his or her *responsibilities*. For the latter to obtain, citizens must be taught those behaviors and attitudes that are prerequisite to this broader concept of democratic citizenship in a free society.

The role of the elementary school teacher in this process is critical. Except for the family, no other social agency or institution shapes the life of the young child as profoundly as does the elementary school. It is during these formative years that children are the most flexible and most receptive to the basic learnings that are the foundation stones of responsible citizenship. The evidence is overwhelming that the teacher is the essential ingredient in a child's getting a good education. It is the purpose of this book to help prospective teachers build professional knowledge and skills that are known to contribute to a quality education in social studies and citizenship.

Since this book was last published, there have been incredible changes in the international community of nations. Today it is impossible to get a wholly accurate political map of the world! Some newly formed nations are enjoying independent status that they may not have had for several hundred years. Those that are experimenting with democratic political and economic institutions and processes are looking to the democracies of the Western World as their models, and often look first to the United States for direction and guidance. The children who now fill the classrooms of America will be major players in the exciting domestic and global events in the next six to eight decades.

In revising this book, we have been mindful of this changing world in which we live and of the many changes occurring in education itself. The integration of learning is a major concern of many teachers today, and we have introduced a new chapter on the subject. Additionally, we have infused the concept of integration of learning throughout the text. Readers will find a much heavier emphasis on cooperative learning than was evident in earlier editions. Sections on concept learning have been expanded; there is a more extended treatment of the use of biographies; and we present new perspectives on assessment, particularly authentic assessment. A change of major proportions in this edition is the emphasis on multicultural education, flowing from the rapidly shifting demographics of school populations.

With this ninth edition, I am pleased to introduce as coauthor Professor Walter C. Parker of the University of Washington College of Education. Professor Parker's background of classroom teaching, university-level teaching, social studies curriculum consulting, research scholarship, and authorship is of immense value to this book. He is one of the authors of the Macmillan/McGraw-Hill social studies series for the elementary and middle school grades. Professor Parker has been active in social studies work nationally and internationally and is well known in social studies professional circles. His rich experience brings fresh perspectives and insights to this text, and I am extremely pleased to welcome him aboard as a colleague and coauthor.

The authors thank Kenneth C. Schmidt, University of Wisconsin-Eau Claire; Jay A. Monson, Utah State University; and JoAnne Buggey, University of Minnesota, who reviewed the previous edition and offered helpful suggestions for the current edition.

The authors are indebted to a number of individuals who kindly assisted in procuring photographs and artwork. We wish to express our sincere thanks and appreciation to them: Gay Campbell, Tacoma School District, Tacoma, Washington; Carol Hamilton Cobb, Gateway School, Metropolitan Nashville, Tennessee, Public Schools; Carey Deckard, The University of

Texas Institute of Texan Cultures at San Antonio, San Antonio, Texas;
Alberta Sebolt George and Marguerite E. Haley, Old Sturbridge Village,
Sturbridge, Massachusetts; Judy Glickman, Macmillan/McGraw-Hill
School Division, New York, New York; Catherine H. Grosfils, Colonial
Williamsburg Foundation, Williamsburg, Virginia; Don Hodel, Seattle Public Schools, Seattle, Washington; Tarry Lindquist, Mercer Island School
District, Mercer Island, Washington; Terri Malinowski, Northshore School
District, Bothell, Washington; Sylvia Soholt, Lake Washington School District, Kirkland, Washington; and Stacey Williams, Southern Oregon Historical Society, Medford, Oregon.

We also wish to express our thanks and appreciation to Mildred Fleming
Jarolimek for her expert technical assistance in the preparation of the
manuscript and in the production of the book.

John Jarolimek

Contents

List of Lesson Plans

Color Inserts

I

ORIENTATION TO SOCIAL STUDIES EDUCATION

1 | The Social Studies Curriculum

"I love to teach! When I work with my kids in the classroom and imagine their kicking around this planet until 2060, it blows my mind! I do my best teaching in social studies because it is there that I can challenge the students to really think about the exciting world in which we live. I want them to leave my class feeling good about themselves and about the fantastic future that can be theirs . . ."

Such enthusiasm for teaching social studies is characteristic of good elementary school teachers. Indeed, elementary and middle school teachers *need* to have a sense of vision of the future for the children they teach. Users of this text will be teaching a part of the human family that is destined to be in charge of the affairs on this planet during the next six to eight decades. Seated in the classrooms of today's teachers are many children who, as senior citizens, will help this nation celebrate its Tricentennial anniversary! This, of course, presumes that there actually will be such an event. Whether this nation survives to its Tricentennial and beyond depends in no small measure on how well the forthcoming generations of schoolchildren are instructed in the responsibilities of democratic citizenship. All of this is meant to suggest that teachers of elementary and middle school children have a heavy responsibility for the future of the children they teach and, indeed, for that of the nation.

When the public school movement developed momentum in the 1840s, the idea was to educate a citizenry that could meet the challenge of self-government. To enhance their economic opportunities, people were at that time moving in large numbers to the big cities and to the open lands of the West. The vastness of the country and the isolation of many areas resulted in regional dialect differences that were creating problems of communication. Communities were becoming more and more heterogeneous with respect to wealth, religion, ethnicity, and national origins. The society needed a "glue" to hold it all together, and reformers of the time saw the common school as just the vehicle to do the job. The term *common school* was used not to mean ordinary, but to mean that it was to be a school for everyone's children. One reformer of the time described *common* as "the air we breathe in common." The schools were to be free, they were to have a common curriculum, and they were to serve all the children of all the people.

The establishment of the free public school system in this country was a clear statement that the nation believed that it could not have a population of uneducated people. That is to say, education of the masses was perceived as a public good. We see many of the same kinds of concerns being expressed today. The National Commission on Excellence in Education proclaimed in 1983 that we were "a nation at risk" because the education that young Americans were receiving was not adequate for the kinds of challenges they would face as citizens in the modern world.[1] What the Commission said — and what several other study groups since then have said — is that a quality education is the key to this society's future. Without a collective intelligence afforded by a rigorous school curriculum, the chances are slim that the United States can solve its myriad social problems, retain its competitive edge, or contribute in wholesome ways to the planet's future.

SOCIAL STUDIES AND CITIZENSHIP EDUCATION

Concerns about deficiencies in education ordinarily focus on basic literacy on the one hand, and on the highly specialized, technical knowledge and skills that are marketplace oriented on the other. But the education of free people for life in a democratic society needs to go far beyond teaching for simple literacy and developing useful job skills. This society places high value on individual decision making, on social participation, on self-determination, and on citizen participation in the determination of public policies. But how can citizens involve themselves in these processes if they are not informed about the issues and have no commitment to the society's values and principles? The question answers itself. It is social studies education that must take seriously the challenge that gave birth to public education in this nation a hundred and fifty years ago: namely, to educate citizens who are willing and able to face up to their responsibilities as a free people. No other area of the school curriculum is as specifically charged with citizenship education as is social studies. Such an education should prepare the student of today to become "an informed person, skilled in the processes of a free society, who is committed to democratic values and is able, and feels obliged to participate in social, political, and economic processes."[2]

---

[1]*A Nation at Risk: The Imperative for Educational Reform.* Report of the National Commission on Excellence in Education (Washington, DC: U.S. Department of Education, 1983).

[2]Walter Parker and John Jarolimek, *Citizenship and the Critical Role of the Social Studies,* NCSS Bulletin No. 72. (Published jointly by Washington, DC: National Council for the Social Studies, and Boulder, CO: ERIC Clearinghouse for Social Studies/Social Science Education, Social Science Education Consortium, 1984), 6.

Research from the behavioral sciences tells us that in large measure human beings *learn* to become who and what they are. One does not inherit the culture through genetic transmission; the culture has to be transmitted through teaching and learning from one generation to the next, or it is lost. It is significant that all human societies make provisions for the young to learn the social and cultural imperatives that characterize that society's particular way of life. In this way, the society perpetuates itself; it provides for social continuity. Through education, the individual becomes acquainted with the mainstream or common culture.

Life in modern societies is so complex and the need for knowledge and skills is so great that the family is simply not able to teach children and youth all that they need to know. Accordingly, schools assume a major responsibility for the transmission to the young of certain knowledge, skills, attitudes, and values that are deemed to be important. The entire school curriculum shares the responsibility for citizenship education, but social studies has historically occupied a unique role in contributing to that process.

A publication of the National Council for the Social Studies defines social studies as an important component of the school curriculum:

> Social studies education is a basic subject of the K–12 curriculum that (1) derives its goals from the nature of citizenship in a democratic society that is closely linked to other nations and peoples of the world; (2) draws its content primarily from history, the social sciences, and, in some respects, from the humanities and science; (3) is taught in ways that reflect an awareness of the personal, social, and cultural experiences and developmental levels of learners; and (4) facilitates the transfer of what is learned in school to the out-of-school lives of students.[3]

The major mission of social studies education is to help children learn about the social world in which they live and how it got that way; to learn to cope with social realities; and to develop the knowledge, attitudes, and skills needed to help shape an enlightened humanity. Social studies focuses specifically on citizenship education, which means learning to participate in group life. The outer edges of that participation for today's child is the global community.

In a democratic society based on individual freedom and citizen participation, citizenship education, and, therefore, social studies education, is directed toward the attainment of two quite different, and sometimes contradictory, ultimate ends. The first has to do with *socialization* and the other with *social criticism*. As a society, we have to depend on individual citizens to "do the right thing" most of the time. Through socialization, citizens internalize values and attitudes that cause them to behave willingly in accordance with prevailing expectations and norms. This is an essential requirement of orderly social life.

---

[3]National Council for the Social Studies, *Social Studies Curriculum Planning Resources* (Dubuque, IA: Kendall/Hunt, 1990), 20.

Here we see citizenship taught through direct participation. The "city," named after fourth-grade teacher Kathy Strawn, is a town built of used refrigerator boxes recycled to become condos, a hair salon, a bank, a post office, a gift shop, etc. Each one encloses a student's desk. The city simulation provided student opportunities to learn of the many facets of community life and to exercise civic responsibilities. "The focus is on citizenship, cooperative decision making, and contributing to the economy through gainful employment," Mrs. Strawn told an interviewer. "Everyone has responsibilities."

(Photos by Carla Anderson, Northshore School District.)

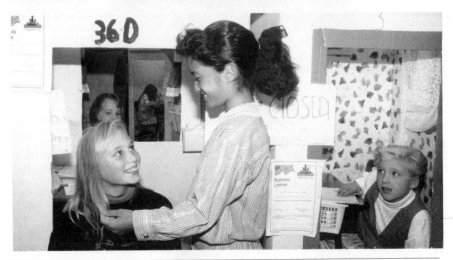

But citizenship in a democratic society also carries with it the obligation to be critical of the system itself, in order that basic rights and freedoms can be sustained and extended to all citizens. Indeed, the exercise of social criticism defines a free society. Doing the "right thing" includes speaking out against laws that are unjust, local or national policies that are wrong-headed, and working tirelessly, when needed, on behalf of the common good.

There is a fragile balance between teaching for socialization on the one hand and teaching for social criticism on the other. For example, we want citizens to respect the law, but we do not want them to be intimidated by the law or by those who enforce it; we want citizens to support elected officials, but we do not want them to follow blindly the leadership of demagogues. A major dilemma for a democratic society and for citizenship education in such a society is how to socialize children in ways that ensure social tranquility without repressing the necessary dissension that must, on occasion, be unpleasant and not socially acceptable.[4] The elementary and middle school teachers who sow the seeds of citizenship in the hearts and minds of children have a responsibility to keep these two dimensions of social studies education in proper balance.

GOALS FOR THE SOCIAL STUDIES

There are numerous goal statements for social studies education. The National Council for the Social Studies (NCSS) has issued statements that deal with the role of the social studies, as have many school districts and state departments of education. All of the fifty states require the teaching of certain elements of social studies. The following are typical examples of what is expected of social studies education:

Knowledge and Information Goals

Learning about

1. The world, its geography, its people, and their cultures.
2. The history, geography, and cultures of the United States.
3. The neighborhood, community, and home state; how people live and work there; how they meet their basic needs of life; how they interact and depend on each other.
4. The legal and political systems of the local community, the state, and the nation.
5. The world of work and an orientation to various careers.
6. Basic human institutions, such as the family, education, and the economy.

---

[4]James P. Shaver, Professor and Associate Dean for Research, College of Education, Utah State University, Logan, Utah, discussed in correspondence with the authors.

7. How people use and misuse the earth.
8. The problems and challenges that confront people today in the realm of social living and human relations in the local, state, national, and international arenas.
9. The basic social functions that characterize all societies such as producing, transporting, distributing, and consuming goods and services; providing for education, recreation, and government; protecting and conserving human and natural resources; expressing esthetic and religious drives; communicating with others.

Attitude and Value Goals

1. Knowing the common values of this society as defined in the historical documents of the republic, by laws of the land, by court decisions, and by the religious heritages of this country.
2. Being able to make decisions that involve choices between competing values.
3. Knowing the basic human rights guaranteed to all citizens.
4. Developing a reasoned loyalty to this country.
5. Developing a sense of respect for the ideals, the heritages, and the institutions of this nation.
6. Developing a feeling of kinship toward human beings everywhere.

Skills Goals

Social Skills

1. Living and working together; taking turns; respecting the rights of others; being socially sensitive.
2. Learning self-control and self-direction.
3. Sharing ideas and experiences with others.

Study Skills and Work Habits

1. Using maps, globes, charts, graphs, and other graphic and pictorial materials.
2. Locating and gathering information from books, the library, and from a variety of other sources and special references.
3. Making reports; speaking before a group; listening when others are reporting; listening to and following directions.
4. Reading social studies materials for a variety of purposes, e.g., to get the main idea; to locate a particular point or fact; to predict outcomes; to detect author bias; to compare and contrast.
5. Organizing information into usable structures such as outlining; making charts; making time lines; classifying pictures or data; arranging ideas, events, or facts in a sequence; taking notes; keeping records; and preparing summaries.
6. Conducting an inquiry on a problem of interest.

Group Skills

1. Working cooperatively to organize information and plan group work.
2. Assuming various roles in small groups such as being chairperson, secretary, or group member.
3. Participating in a group discussion; leading a discussion.
4. Participating in group decision making.

Intellectual Skills

1. Defining and identifying problems; relating prior experiences to a present inquiry.
2. Forming and testing hypotheses; drawing conclusions based on information.
3. Analyzing, manipulating, and interpreting data.
4. Thinking critically; distinguishing between fact and opinion; learning to separate relevant from irrelevant information and to recognize bias in persuasive materials such as advertising, political statements, and propaganda.
5. Inferring cause and effect relationships.
6. Reasoning dialogically—comparing and contrasting differing perspectives; arguing both for *and against* one's initial opinion.
7. Recognizing value components in decision making.

Creative thinking and problem solving are associated with the American ethos, and Americans have taken pride in being stereotyped as creative problem solvers. Accordingly, teaching procedures that are presumed to enhance thinking abilities of students have received a great deal of attention from educators in this century. One of the consistent goals of social studies education has been that of developing in children those attitudes and skills that enable them to be independent thinkers and problem solvers. This means, among other things, that children need to develop a healthy skepticism about things and events in the world. Good problem solvers have a curiosity about what they see going on around them. They develop a questioning attitude. They are adept at figuring out new ways of doing things.

The ultimate outcome of education is, of course, to prepare individuals to make decisions, to make judgments, and to lead lives that are qualitatively superior to those who are uneducated. This involves intellectual processes that we define by the summarizing term "critical thinking." The person who has had the advantage of education should be able to apply appropriate criteria in order to distinguish between what is true and what is not, what is better than something else, what enhances the human condition and what does not, and what is morally uplifting and what is not. These kinds of discriminations in quality are what schools and education are supposed to equip individuals to make. If there were no *qualitative* differences between the lives of persons who went to school and those who did not, society would have little need for schools. This is not to suggest that schools are always successful in achieving such goals, only to emphasize that they must continue the effort. When social studies programs identify critical thinking as a goal toward which teachers should encourage children to strive, such programs are contributing to the overall, general goals of education.

TEACHING METHODS RELATED TO GOALS

Some goals are achieved through the encounters with subject matter whereas others are achieved through the *process* of the study itself. For example, to learn about the history of their country or the geography of the home state or about life in another culture, children must deal with the subject matter appropriate to those topics. On the other hand, to learn the skill of using the encyclopedia, children must be involved in the use of that reference. Similarly, to learn to inquire, they must engage in investigative searches. To learn cooperative work skills, they must be involved in group-work processes. Soundly based social studies programs build content and process learnings simultaneously. Much of social studies teaching is directed toward the achievement of more than one objective at the same time.

There is good teaching and poor teaching of social studies today, just as there always has been. A social studies program can be no better than the teacher who implements it. We know that social studies education is seriously flawed when large numbers of students find it uninteresting or even boring. Lack of student interest has been noted numerous times by observers and researchers. In an article in *Social Education*, Fred M. Newmann discusses this problem as one of "student disengagement," which implies more than simply a lack of interest.[5] It suggests that the student removes herself or himself intellectually and psychologically from what is going on. It is as if the student says—and evidently many do—"I could not care less."

Student interest in social studies seems to follow a declining curve, with the most rapid drop following fourth grade. Children find the activity-oriented social studies program of the primary grades interesting and engaging. It is when social studies begins to be more abstract, more book driven, and less related to the life of the child that the students begin to drop out psychologically. Doubtless the problem could be rectified considerably by more inspired teaching. In classrooms where we find children highly motivated and interested in learning social studies, we find teachers who are teaching the subject with genuine enthusiasm. But whatever contributes to it, student disengagement constitutes a serious problem for

---

[5]Fred M. Newmann, "Priorities for the Future: Toward a Common Agenda," *Social Education* 50 (April/May 1986): 240–50.

social studies. It would be nearly impossible to achieve the goals of social studies education if the students find the program dull and lacking in any relevant connection to their lives.

CURRICULUM CONTENT AND SEQUENCE

Although most elementary and middle schools include history and the social science disciplines in their social studies programs, they do not ordinarily conduct separate courses in geography, history, economics, political science, or the other social science disciplines. The usual organizational format is one that combines components from more than a single field to form an interdisciplinary or integrated study around some topic of interest. Significant subject matter from related disciplines is *infused* in the instructional program. For example, a sixth grade class might study the topic "Crossroads of Three Continents—The Middle East." In such a study, geography would be essential, as would history, economics, and government as well. Doubtless, too, religious concepts would be included because this area of the world was the birthplace of three of the world's major religions.

Most schools are introducing basic concepts from history and the social sciences and related disciplines in the early years of the elementary school although they may not always be labeled as such. When children are studying the local landscape and are learning how to map it, they are dealing in a simple way with geography. When they learn about the need for rules and laws, they are beginning to understand ideas from political science; and when they study about life in early times, they are having their first brush with history. It is not the purpose of the elementary school to teach the social science disciplines apart from their relevance to social reality. They should be taught in ways that will help children build an understanding of the social and physical world in which they live.

The social studies program should be built on what the child already knows. This means that, in introducing topics or units for study, the teacher will need to explore with the children the extent of their prior knowledge of the subject. Some knowledge will come from their experiences outside of school through television, movies, peers, travel, and contact with adults. Some will come from school experiences in earlier grades. Social studies programs should take advantage of that background of knowledge.

Each year there will be study units and topics that are consistent with the emphasis suggested by the district curriculum for that grade. Ordinarily, topics that are concrete and familiar to the child such as the school, family, neighborhood, and community are placed in the primary grades. Topics that are more remote in space and time, such as the home state, the nation, and foreign cultures, appear in the middle and upper grades. It should be noted, however, that newer programs expand the world of the child early and rapidly. For example, even in the primary grades it is not unusual to find children studying family life as it takes place in many parts of the world. Teachers often begin a study by focusing on aspects of a topic that are familiar to the children, such as their own homes, schools, and families; then the study is expanded to include those same institutions in other cultures. The movement from things that are close to those that are far away and back again is common in social studies programs today.

Curriculum specialists often talk in terms of the "scope and sequence" of a social studies program. The "scope" of the program refers to the substantive content—the subject matter, skills, values, attitudes, and beliefs—that the program is to include. The "sequence" has to do with the order in which the various components are to be presented. In recent years there has been a revival of interest in scope and sequence documents at the state and local levels.[6] The National Council for the Social Studies has published a planning document that can be useful to local schools in building their social studies programs. It includes guidelines for the social studies curriculum, criteria for excellence in social studies, questions for reviewing and evaluating the social studies curriculum, and three model scope and sequence statements. The following is one of the scope and sequence models included in the council's document:

RECOMMENDATIONS OF THE NCSS TASK FORCE ON SCOPE AND SEQUENCE

Kindergarten—Awareness of Self in a Social Setting

Grade   1—The Individual in Primary Social Groups: Understanding School and Family Life

Grade   2—Meeting Basic Needs in Nearby Social Groups: The Neighborhood

Grade   3—Sharing Earth-Space with Others: The Community

Grade   4—Human Life in Varied Environments: The Region

Grade   5—People of the Americas: The United States and Its Close Neighbors

Grade   6—People and Cultures: The Eastern Hemisphere

Grade   7—A Changing World of Many Nations: A Global View

Grade   8—Building a Strong and Free Nation: The United States

Grade   9—Systems That Make a Democratic Society Work: Law, Justice, and Economics

Grade 10—Origins of Major Cultures: A World History

Grade 11—The Maturing of America: United States History

Grade 12—One-year course or courses required; selection(s) to be made from the following:

Issues and Problems of Modern Society

Introduction to the Social Sciences

---

[6]Wayne L. Herman, Jr., "Development in Scope and Sequence: A Survey of School Districts," *Social Education* 52 (September 1988), 385–88.

An institute staff member demonstrates some of Mexico's food traditions at the *jacal* or Mexican kitchen in the Mexican area of the Institute of Texan Cultures. Such an experience combines the study of history with cross-cultural education. The University of Texas Institute of Texan Cultures is an exceptionally fine instructional facility that has a special exhibit area for each of the ethnic and cultural groups that have contributed to the state's development. Although this Texas facility is unique, all communities have some resources, however modest, that can be useful in studying the local community and home state.
(Photo courtesy of The University of Texas Institute of Texan Cultures at San Antonio.)

The Arts in Human Societies

International Area Studies

Social Science Elective Courses: Anthropology, Economics, Government, Psychology, Sociology

Supervised Experience in Community Affairs

Local options[7]

This model also provides three optional programs for grades six through twelve.

What follows is a list of *representative examples* of topics and units taught at the grade levels indicated in schools across the nation. The examples

[7]National Council for the Social Studies, *Social Studies Curriculum Planning Resources* (Dubuque, IA: Kendall/Hunt, 1990), 25–29.

should *not* be construed as a model curriculum. What is represented here will not be precisely the same as that found in any specific school program; the teacher will need to consult local curriculum sources to find out what is required.

··············· EXAMPLES OF UNIT TOPICS FOR EACH GRADE LEVEL

Kindergarten   Kindergarten programs ordinarily deal with topics that help to familiarize children with their immediate surroundings. The home and school provide the setting for these studies. With some kindergarten children it is possible to include, in a simple way, references to the world beyond the immediate environment.

Learning About Myself

Rules for Safe Living

Learning How My Family Buys Goods and Services

Working Together at School

Continents and the Globe

People Change the Earth

Grade One   Grade-one studies are based in the local area, such as the neighborhood, but provision is often made to associate the local area with the larger world. A major criticism of first-grade units in particular and primary units in general has been that they have tended to be too confining and that their content has been thin. Units should provide for easy transition from the near-at-hand to the faraway and back again at frequent intervals—when it is established that the backgrounds of children warrant such movement. Neighborhood and community services can be stressed in this grade.

The Shopping Center

Families at Work

Great Americans

A Japanese Family (comparative study)

Scarcity and Demand

Families: Size and Structure

Families and Their Needs

Dividing the Work

Grade Two   The grade-two program provides for frequent and systematic contact with the world beyond the neighborhood. Through the study of transportation, communication, food distribution, and travel, the children begin to learn how their part of the world is connected to other places on earth.

Suburban Neighborhoods

Transportation and Communication: Our Links to the World

Rural and Urban Communities

Where and How We Get Our Food

People Work Together in Communities

How Neighborhoods Change

Grade Three The grade-three program often emphasizes the larger community concept: what a community is, types of communities, why some communities grow though others do not, how communities provide for basic needs. Many programs include an outside community for purposes of comparison. Schools are giving a great deal of attention to the large, urban community at this grade level.

Our City's Government

Food for the Community

Keeping Cities up-to-date—Change

Communities at Home and Abroad (comparative cultures study)

Life in Early American Settlements

Why a City Is Where It Is

The Parts of a City

Natural Surroundings and People's Actions

Grade Four In grade four the world as the home of people, showing various geographical features of the earth along with variety in ways of living, is often stressed. These studies help children understand some of the adaptive and innovative qualities of human beings. Home-state studies are popular in grade four; often they are included to meet legislative requirements. Comparative studies are commonly recommended.

Historical Growth and Change of the Home State

The Pacific Northwest (regional study)

Deserts of the World (regions)

Others Who Share Our World (comparative cultures study)

Kenya and Its African Neighbors (comparative study)

India, a Society in Transition (comparative study)

Regions Make a World

Grade Five Almost everywhere the fifth-grade program includes the geography, history, early development, and growth of the United States. The program may focus on the United States alone or on the United States and Canada or on the United States, Canada, and Latin America. The latter option makes the fifth-grade program a heavy one. The fifth-grade emphasis should be coordinated with the eighth and eleventh grades in order to revisit difficult concepts (e.g., democracy, pluralism).

The American Land

The Native Americans

European Colonization

Independence and Democracy

Slavery and the Civil War

An Early American Mining Community

The Industrial Revolution

Civil Rights and the American Dream

One Nation; Many Heritages

Grade Six   The sixth-grade program may include the study of Latin America and Canada or of cultures of the Eastern Hemisphere. Both of these patterns are in common use. A major limitation of sixth-grade programs is that they attempt to deal with too many topics. Often this results in a smattering of exposures without developing significant depth of understanding. The same criticism applies to the seventh grade. Stronger programs emerge where teachers carefully select a few units that are representative of basic concepts that have wide and broad applicability. For example, a class need not study all the Third World nations in order to gain some understanding of the problems of newly developing countries.

WESTERN HEMISPHERE EMPHASIS

Cooperation in the Americas

The Prairie Provinces

Three Inca Countries

The Saint Lawrence Seaway and Its Effect on Canadian Growth

The Organization of American States

EASTERN HEMISPHERE EMPHASIS

Ancient, Classical, and Medieval Civilizations → MICHAELANGELO

The Birthplace of Three Religions

The former Soviet Union

Eastern Europe in Recent Times →

Great Discoveries

The Renaissance and Reformation → ⋆ DAVINCI

Empires and Revolutions

The People's Republic of China

Grade Seven   The nature of the seventh-grade program depends on the content of grade six. Either Latin America or culture regions of the Eastern Hemisphere are popular choices for this grade. Some schools are developing exciting programs in anthropology in grade seven. World geography is also included in some districts as are studies of the home state.

Rise of Modern Civilization

Africa: Yesterday, Today, and Tomorrow

The Home State: Democracy and Pluralism

Public Issues of our Times

World Resources: Who Has Them? Who Uses Them?

The Age of Technology—Its Effects on People

Environmental Problems

Themes of Geography

The Future of Planet Earth

Grade Eight   The study of the United States and of the American heritage is widespread in grade eight. The program usually stresses the development of American political institutions and the development of nationality. The approach typically consists of a series of units arranged chronologically. The fifth and eleventh grades also include elements of American history. Defining the emphasis for each of these grades and differentiating appropriately among them in terms of content and approach is necessary in order to ensure depth and breadth of understanding.

Mapping the Americas

Natives and Colonizers: Cultures and Conflicts

Creating a Democracy

A Divided Nation

Birth of an Industrial Giant

Immigration and the American Dream

Hot and Cold Wars

The United States in the World Today

THE CHILDREN WE TEACH: DEMOGRAPHIC CHANGES

As recently as a generation ago, an elementary school teacher would quite probably face a classroom in which the children were remarkably similar in appearance. Children were required to attend their neighborhood elementary school, and because neighborhoods were not racially integrated, neither were schools. Neighborhoods tended to be segregated along socioeconomic variables as well, resulting in a consistent similarity among the children of the people who lived there. Children with disabilities were not a part of the regular classroom because they were placed in special education classes. Indeed, the *appearance* of homogeneity masked individual differences among children to such an extent that researchers had a difficult time convincing teachers that they needed to be concerned about individualizing learning programs for students.

All of this, of course, has changed in recent years. Federally mandated racial integration of schools, busing, immigration, social mobility, increased integration of housing, differences in birth rates between white and nonwhite groups, social legislation, integration of students with disabilities and an increased concern for social justice are among the factors that have contributed to the changing demographic pattern of the nation's schools. So completely have these changes overtaken the schools that today it would be difficult to find a classroom anywhere in America that is wholly homogeneous with respect to the ethnic, racial, cultural, and religious backgrounds of its students. Today's classrooms consist of aggregates of children that are incredibly diverse, and that diversity translates into monumental challenges for the teacher, especially in the area of the social studies. We will discuss briefly three dimensions of that diversity that have a direct impact on social studies and citizenship education: (1) poverty, (2) changing family life, and (3) ethnic and cultural diversity.

Poverty

In 1964 President Lyndon B. Johnson's War on Poverty legislation was enacted, yet more people in this country are poor today than they were when the Johnson antipoverty program went into effect. According to a report issued by the *Phi Delta Kappan* in 1990, "nearly 20% of all children under the age of 18 are poor."[8] For preschool children the figure is nearly 25 percent, which means that the number appears to be increasing for the school-age groups of the future. Because these data are based on the nation as a whole, the number in specific areas or pockets of poverty may be as high as twice or three times the national average.

It is nearly impossible to overstate the debilitating effects of a lifestyle of poverty on young children. Poverty generates feelings of destitution, helplessness, and despair. Associated with a life of poverty are such other social problems as crime, child abuse, delinquency, drug addiction, alcoholism, gang life, prostitution, unemployment, and social alienation. Poverty has been described as a cyclical phenomenon in that it extends and recycles from one generation to the next. Recent research indicates that (1) brain growth is enhanced if stimulated by interacting with a rich environment;[9] and (2) children who suffer extended malnutrition during prenatal and early years may suffer long-term and perhaps irreversible intellectual deficiencies. Children of poverty are in jeopardy on both counts. Moreover, a child cannot function normally in school if he or she is hungry, cold, sick, or is frightened much of the time.

Changing Family Life

In a recent article, the Director of the Center for Demographic Study, Harold Hodgkinson, makes the astounding assertion that "the 'Norman Rockwell' family—a working father, a housewife mother, and two children of school age—constitutes only 6% of U.S. households today."[10] He goes on to point out that every kind of "atypical" family increased in number

---

[8]Sally Reed and R. Craig Sautter, "Children of Poverty," Kappan Special Report, *Phi Delta Kappan* 71 (June 1990): K3.

[9]Renate Nummela Caine and Geoffrey Caine, *Making Connections: Teaching and the Human Brain* (Alexandria, VA: Association for Supervision and Curriculum Development, 1991): 27–29.

[10]Harold Hodgkinson, "Reform Versus Reality," *Phi Delta Kappan* 73 (September 1991): 10.

during the 1980s, whereas married couples with children declined. The situation is such that *almost half* of the nation's children will spend some time being raised by a single parent before they reach age eighteen. Frances Smardo Dodd reports on two national surveys conducted in 1988 and 1990 indicating that as many as 15 million children representing 20 percent of the elementary school-age population are what have come to be called "latchkey kids"—children who are on their own before and after school until an adult returns home from work.[11] In 1990, for every male head of a single parent household, there were 4.32 female heads, a figure slightly higher than in 1980.

The realities described in the foregoing paragraph have a great impact on the home life of children. Very often single parent households have limited disposable income. The amount and quality of time available for child–parent interaction is necessarily shortened, especially during school days. Housing options are ordinarily limited for a single parent, especially if that parent is a female. The pressure to meet basic day-to-day needs adds to the stress—and often guilt—experienced by the parent in such circumstances.

Ethnic and Cultural Diversity

During the past three decades, significant social trends have resulted in dramatic changes in the ethnic and cultural composition of school populations. Among these trends are (1) a decrease in the birth rates among Caucasion women; (2) an increase in the birth rates among African American and Hispanic women; and (3) an abrupt rise in immigrants entering this country from Latin America, Asia, and the Middle East. Reporting on the results of the 1990 U.S. Census, *The New York Times* called attention to changes in the racial makeup of the nation:

> The racial complexion of the American population changed more dramatically in the past decade than at any time in the 20th century, with nearly one in every four Americans having African, Asian, Hispanic or American Indian ancestry. In 1980, one in five Americans had such minority backgrounds. . . . In New York, minority residents make up about 31 percent of the population, up from 25 percent in 1980.[12]

The Center for Immigration Studies has concluded that the number of legal immigrants that came to this country between 1981 and 1990 exceeded the alltime record of 8.7 million recorded for the decade 1901–1910. At least two-thirds of the world's immigrants come to the United States, most coming from South America and Asia. As many as 80 to 100 different home languages are spoken by schoolchildren in cities such as Los Angeles and New York and other ports of entry to the United States. As a result of these

[11]Reported in *Education Week*, October 16, 1991, p. 12.

[12]*The New York Times*, March 11, 1991, pp. AI and B8. Cited in the "Report of the Social Studies Syllabus Review and Development Committee," Albany, New York: The State Department of Education, June 1991, 14.

trends, American teachers today face classrooms that are a diverse collection of individuals representing a variety of ethnic and cultural heritages.

The effects of these trends are more apparent in some sections of the country than in others, but hardly any community in America is wholly immune from significant demographic shifts. The terms *minority* and *majority* are not always accurate descriptors when applied to present-day school populations. For example, Harold Hodgkinson reports that in the thirty largest school districts in the nation today, the *minority* is a *majority.* The same applies to the schools of three states: New Mexico, Mississippi, and Hawaii. In five states—California, Louisiana, Maryland, North Carolina, and Texas—minority enrollments are over 40 percent. Because of the low birth rates among white women and the enormously high immigration of nonwhites in recent years, the prediction is that shortly after the turn of the century, one out of every three adult Americans will be nonwhite.[13]

Implications for What and How We Teach Social Studies

For children of poverty and for those whose nurturing needs may not be attended to adequately by their home environments, the teacher is limited in what he or she can do. Yet, there are numerous cases of individuals, some who became prominent Americans, who were products of precisely such environments, but who gained inspiration and hope from some caring teacher who helped them turn their lives into ones of responsible, productive citizenship. It is doubtless true that for many children, the only caring adult they encounter in their lives on a daily basis is their teacher. The teacher needs to realize that he or she is in a position to greatly influence and shape the lives of children who are victims of poverty and unstable homes. Some teachers have made a remarkable difference in the lives of children who were heading in the direction of crime and self-destruction. One former youth gang member said, "There was one person I'll never forget. It was a schoolteacher who had a lot of interest in kids. She taught me how to read and write. She was probably the most important person in my life."[14]

Teachers who make a difference are the ones who see the potential for success in all children. Such teachers set challenging but realistic expectations and provide a strong supportive environment for students. They think less in terms of learner deficits than they do about student possibilities for success. These teachers help students sense a linkage between their school experiences and their lives outside of school. In this way, students learn that their schoolwork can both help them cope with conditions in the larger society and help them achieve meaningful life goals for themselves.

---

[13]Harold Hodgkinson, "The Context of 21st-Century Civics and Citizenship," in *Citizenship for the 21st Century*, ed. by William T. Callahan, Jr. and Ronald A. Banaszak (Bloomington, IN: ERIC, 1990), 23–32.

[14]Kirkland Police Department, "Gang Awareness," Kirkland, WA, 1991, p. 2.

After reviewing the research on cultural diversity for the *Handbook of Research on Social Studies Teaching and Learning*, Geneva Gay concludes that "the primary message from previous research on cultural diversity and learning for social studies is that cultural socialization affects how students learn."[15] Having been sensitized to that, however, the teacher is still left with the challenge of figuring out precisely *how* the cultural milieu in which the child is reared will affect his or her learning of social studies. Some suggestions can be provided, but the research does not support sweeping generalizations concerning learning styles that can be applied to all children simply because they come from a specific ethnic or cultural group. Individual differences within groups are often as large or larger than mean differences between groups.[16]

Keeping in mind the cautions cited in the foregoing paragraph, we here suggest a few guidelines that the teacher can apply in teaching social studies from a perspective of cultural and ethnic diversity. The most important responsibility that the teacher has is to develop a classroom environment that respects and supports the unique backgrounds of all children.

1. Integrate diverse cultural perspectives into the total social studies curriculum. Do not rely solely on special days, weeks, or months (such as Black History Month in February) to do an adequate job of providing a multicultural education.

2. Be sensitive to the fact that much of the social studies curriculum is anchored in Western European traditions and history, whereas many of today's schoolchildren have personal "roots" that reflect other cultural traditions.

3. Keep in mind that multicultural education is supposed to serve the learning goals of *all* children, not only those who come from visible ethnic minorities. Also, the presence or absence of a culturally diverse school population should not be confused with the development of a multicultural *curriculum*. A predominantly white middle- or upper-class student body requires a multicultural curriculum every bit as much as a diverse student body.

4. Multicultural education should focus mainly on the life and culture of the people of our own country. It is important, of course, for students to learn about the people of other lands, too, but such global studies serve different purposes from multicultural education.

5. Expand the knowledge base of social studies to illustrate the contributions of many cultures of American life. Traditionally, nonwhite, non-

---

[15]Geneva Gay, "Culturally Diverse Students and Social Studies," in *Handbook of Research on Social Studies Teaching and Learning*, ed. by James P. Shaver (New York: Macmillan, 1991), 154.

[16]John O'Neil, "Making Sense Out of Style," *Educational Leadership* 48 (October 1990): 7; Lynn Curry, "A Critique of the Research on Learning Styles," *Educational Leadership* 48 (October 1990): 50–56.

Western immigrants have been expected to assimilate into the dominant white, Western culture. That is still the expectation, but it is obvious from what we see around us that, to some extent, the dominant culture is also assimilating aspects of non-Western cultures.

6. Be alert to the fact that the language and learning styles of culturally different children *may not* be in harmony with what is expected by the school. Recognize that the personal values of some children may not be compatible with the typical competitive goal-seeking learning strategies found in most schools.

7. Explore the use of various forms of cooperative learning formats that may be more appropriate than individual study strategies with culturally different learners.

8. Be aware that little things that show sensitivity mean a lot to children, as, for example, pronouncing the child's name correctly.

Additional and more detailed teaching suggestions for multicultural education are provided in chapter 8.

Commentary

We have emphasized changing demographics because of the impact of these changes on school programs and most especially, on social studies education. It is important that the reader is *not* left with the impression that these realities are presented as problems and deficits. It is true that teachers today are challenged as perhaps never before to help all children to learn and to practice democratic citizenship and to become contributing members of society. But it is out of this diverse mix of humanity that our nation has in the past gained much of its strength, and America continues to be nurtured by the diversity of its people. This comes about not by promoting the separateness of individual ethnic groups but by opening avenues of opportunity for all to contribute in significant ways to the emerging American culture.

The teacher is urged to look at individual children for what they are and what they bring to the classroom, rather than to rely on generalizations and labels as clues to indicate how children are supposed to behave and learn. For every child who fits a particular stereotype, many more do not. Not all children from poor families do poorly in school. Not all Hispanic children thrive on cooperative learning, and not all students of northern European ancestry find individualistic or competitive learning to their liking. Most children from one-parent families are well-adjusted youngsters and have successful school records. High school honor rolls clearly show that many minority students have high scholarship and that those students are not always of Asian heritage. Most importantly, all of these children are citizens who will one day be eligible to vote and hold public office, and who will share in all of the rights and privileges of adult citizenship. The future of the nation demands that *all* children be well prepared for their roles and responsibilities as citizens of a free society. That is what social studies education is all about as this twentieth century ends and a new one begins.

SOCIAL STUDIES AND THE COMMON CULTURE
● ●

The education of children always assumes that they are being prepared for some kind of social context as adults. Teachers prepare children for adult statuses and roles that are at the present time unknown. The mental images that teachers have of the future are usually an extension of the world of today; that is, we assume that children will need about the same knowledge and skills in the future that the adults of today need. Futurists have repeatedly called attention to the limitations of such assumptions. In a world in which change seems to be the only reliably predictable constant, teachers of social studies are still expected to engender in children a strong attachment to those traditional beliefs and values that have characterized this nation from its beginning—liberty, justice, equality, human dignity.

It is in the social studies that the public purposes of education can be best served. Through social studies, teachers have a major responsibility to help children learn those components of the *common* culture that constitute the social and cultural heritage of this nation. It is these learnings that acquaint citizens with the rituals of our culture and give us a sense of identity as a nation committed to realizing the ideals of "liberty and justice for all." These ideals have always been important to social studies education but have recently received widespread public attention because of interest in *cultural literacy,* a concept that has been widely discussed in educational circles since the publication of a popular book dealing with that subject.[17]

During the 1980s, a great deal was said about cultural literacy. Developing cultural literacy has to do with identifying and learning a body of essential knowledge and skills needed by an individual to function in a culture. Language would be an obvious and perhaps most important example. But presumably there are other learnings that are a part of the common culture that everyone who is schooled is expected to know. Such common knowledge and skills facilitate communication between and among citizens and would solidify the society around a common body of information and values shared by all. It is argued that this is more important in the United States than in many other countries because of the diversity of cultural legacies from which this nation has derived. Many of these learnings would fall in the social studies curriculum simply because of its emphasis on historical knowledge and its basic concern for democratic citizenship.

Although many may find the idea of a common core of information, values, and skills to be taught to all students mildly attractive, problems arise in identifying the specifics of such a plan. There is little agreement on what items constitute the core learnings needed for cultural literacy, nor even on who should put together such a list. The lists that have been

---

[17]E. D. Hirsch, Jr., *Cultural Literacy: What Every American Needs to Know* (Boston: Houghton-Mifflin, 1987); "Special Feature: Cultural Literacy," *Educational Leadership* 45 (December 1987–January 1988): 63–77.

generated by scholars and intellectuals have immediately been painted with the brush of elitism. Other lists, if developed at all, would doubtless not be found acceptable by scholars and intellectuals. The issue continues to be a matter of discussion and controversy by the profession in this last decade of the century.

In the past fifteen years, this nation has celebrated its bicentennial, it has honored the centennial birthdate of the Statue of Liberty, and has paid tribute to that remarkable document of freedom, the U.S. Constitution, on the 200th anniversary of its ratification. Most recently it has commemorated the 500th anniversary of Columbus's first voyage to the Americas. All of these events and countless others at the state and local levels throughout the land have stirred the hearts and minds of Americans everywhere. Conditions have rarely been more favorable to channel these public attitudes toward improved civic education.

In a great many ways, the importance of civic education, meaning particularly social studies education, is being reaffirmed. Americans care deeply about their country and its future. They want schools to have strong

The computer has not created the revolution in education that some had earlier predicted, but it can be a helpful tool in teaching social studies through the use of drill and practice programs, by developing and using databases, by doing simulations and games, and by having students prepare spreadsheets and graphics. *(Photo by Carla Anderson, Northshore School District.)*

offerings in those subjects, skills, and values that will ensure the nation's survival. This is not likely to be accomplished by nationally prominent educators writing reports about educational reform. Rather, it will be done by teachers and other educators, in concert with parents, at the local and state levels who care deeply about the students they teach and about the future of our communities, our nation, and the human family.

DISCUSSION QUESTIONS AND SUGGESTED ACTIVITIES

1. Try to recall two or three specific things you learned when you were in the elementary or middle school that would fit in each of the three sets of goals presented in this chapter. Are these things still worth learning by children in school today? Why or why not?

2. Do you think it would be a good idea to have a *national* social studies curriculum? What would you see as the advantages and limitations of such an arrangement?

3. The text stresses the importance of teaching for more than one objective at the same time. In each of the following situations, identify at least one additional objective that could be achieved concurrently.

   a. First grade: Children are learning how the local environment changes in appearance with the seasons.

   b. Third grade: Children are learning how goods and people are moved in and out of their community.

   c. Fifth grade: Children are learning the major geographical features of North America.

4. The education codes of most states stipulate the amount of time that is to be spent on social studies each week. This might be expressed in clock hours per day, per week, days per week or term, or some other standard unit of measure. These minimum time requirements are usually different for primary, intermediate, and upper grades. Check local sources to find out if there are such requirements, and, if so, what they are.

5. Decide when in the day's schedule you would prefer to teach social studies and provide a rationale for your choice.

6. Examine the list of skills given in this chapter. Which of these skills are also included in other areas of the school curriculum, and which ones fall entirely within the social studies? Suggest ways that social studies and other curriculum areas might be combined for purposes of instruction in skills.

7. Visit the educational materials collection in your campus library, and examine a few social studies curriculum guides from school systems throughout the country. Include the curriculum guides for your state

and community. Indicate the extent to which these documents incorporate ideas discussed in this chapter.

8. Study the scope and sequence of a major publishing company's social studies textbook series. To what extent does the grade-by-grade sequence of subject matter follow the NCSS model given in this chapter?

9. What are your views concerning the relative emphasis that should be given to *socialization* as opposed to *social criticism* at the elementary or middle school level? Provide examples of teaching practices that would encourage one or the other of these two thrusts of social studies education.

10. Examine the NCSS scope and sequence recommendations reprinted in this chapter. If you had the responsibility of designing a scope and sequence, which topics would you include that are not on the task force list? Which topics on the task force list would you not include in your scope and sequence? Are there topics you would place in a different grade? Explain.

11. In many parts of the world—the former Yugoslavia and Soviet Union, Spain, the Middle East, and even Canada—ethnic tensions and rivalries have been a serious obstacle to building nationhood. Why has this not been a problem in the United States? Could it become one? Explain.

12. Become familiar with the magazines *Social Education, Social Studies and the Young Learner, The Social Studies, Instructor, Learning: The Magazine for Creative Teaching,* and *Early Years.* Learn what they have to offer the teacher in the social studies. Locate one or more teaching ideas from these journals, and make plans to apply them in a classroom.

13. Talk to your instructor and/or your supervising teacher about local and state councils for social studies. Arrange to attend one of their meetings.

14. What are some ways you might create a classroom environment that is hospitable to the cultural backgrounds of all of your students?

SELECTED REFERENCES

ATWOOD, VIRGINIA A., ed. *Elementary School Social Studies: Research as a Guide to Practice.* NCSS Bulletin No. 79. Washington, DC: National Council for the Social Studies, 1986.

BARBER, BENJAMIN. *Strong Democracy: Participatory Politics for a New Age.* Berkeley, CA: University of California Press, 1984.

BRAGAW, DONALD H., and H. MICHAEL HARTOONIAN. "Social Studies: The Study of People in Society." *Content of the Curriculum,* Ronald S. Brandt, ed., ASCD Yearbook. Alexandria, VA: Association for Supervision and Curriculum Development, 1988, chapter 2.

Butts, R. Freeman. *The Morality of Democratic Citizenship: Goals for Civic Education in the Republic's Third Century.* Calabassas, CA: Center for Civic Education, 1988.

Callahan, William T., Jr., and Ronald A. Banaszak, eds. *Citizenship for the 21st Century.* Bloomington, IA: ERIC, 1990.

Dewey, John. *Democracy and Education.* New York: Macmillan, 1916.

Jenness, David. *Making Sense of Social Studies.* New York: Macmillan, 1990.

Kaltsounis, Theodore. *Teaching Social Studies in the Elementary School: The Basics for Citizenship.* 2d ed. Englewood Cliffs, NJ: Prentice-Hall, 1987, chapter 3.

Knapp, Michael S., Brenda J. Turnbull, and Patrick M. Shields. "New directions for Educating the Children of Poverty." *Educational Leadership,* 48 (September 1990): 4–8.

Kozol, Jonathan. *Savage Inequalities.* New York: Crown, 1991.

Levy, Tedd, ed., and William M. Alexander, Conrad F. Toepfer, Jr., Michael G. Allen, John H. Lounsbury, and Bill Honig. "Making a Difference in the Middle." *Social Education,* 52 (February 1988): 104–22. (Special section on social studies in the middle school.)

National Commission on Social Studies in the Schools. 1989. *Charting a Course: Social Studies for the 21st Century* (Washington, D.C.: author).

National Council for the Social Studies. *Social Studies Curriculum Planning Resources.* Dubuque, IA: Kendall-Hunt, 1990.

Parker, Walter C. *Renewing the Social Studies Curriculum.* Alexandria, VA: Association for Supervision and Curriculum Development, 1991.

Parker, Walter, and John Jarolimek. *Citizenship and the Critical Role of the Social Studies.* NCSS Bulletin No. 72. Washington, DC: National Council for the Social Studies, and Boulder, CO: ERIC Clearinghouse for Social Studies/Social Science Education, Social Science Education Consortium, 1984.

2

Teaching Subject Matter and Related Skills

Chapter 1 introduced the goals of social studies curriculum and instruction. They are ambitious goals, but democracy is an ambitious way to try to organize a society. Because social studies education is aimed at democratic citizenship, its goals emphasize both knowledge and participation. Citizens need to *know* much from the fields of history and geography as well as the social sciences. Without rich and interrelated ideas drawn from these disciplines, citizen participation can be ignorant, even dangerous. We are told that "those who do not remember the past are condemned to relive it."[1] But knowledge is not enough; popular sovereignty requires citizens to *use* knowledge to create society day by day—to solve social problems, reduce international tensions, employ people in meaningful work, and reduce damage to the natural environment, to name just a few of the daunting tasks of citizenship. Democracy is never "done"; popular sovereignty is daily labor.

In this chapter and chapter 3, we will examine teaching procedures that are used to achieve social studies goals. We address subject matter and related skills here. Chapter 3 explores methods for value, moral, and character education.

Picture this: A teacher notices that her third-grade children are confusing *continents* with *countries*. She knows this is a difficult distinction, made no easier by the similarities in the words themselves. She gathers students around several maps and deftly focuses their attention on the characteristics causing the confusion. Involving each child in one way or another, she builds their collective understanding of both ideas and guides them through an exercise in which they practice distinguishing the two.

Watching such a teacher, the observer might think, "Anyone could do that!" It is true that the more adept the teacher, the easier the process

---

[1] Attributed to the philosopher George Santayana.

appears to be. It is only when the novice attempts to emulate the master's behavior that the complexity of teaching becomes apparent. At this point, frustration can overwhelm the beginner. Even seasoned professionals can be tried to the limits by new situations, students with whom they have not "clicked," and subject matter they have not themselves come to understand fully. But there are proven routes for meeting the challenges of elementary school teaching, and we examine some of them here.

How one goes about teaching should have something to do with the nature of what is to be learned. For instance, many skills require children to participate actively on a firsthand basis in the process of learning them. Cooperative learning skills are of this type; no amount of reading about group skills or listening to someone explain them will make the learner proficient in their use. On the other hand, if one wants to learn about European settlements in the Americas, reading might be the best way to achieve that objective.

How one goes about teaching should also have something to do with the characteristics of the person doing the learning. A well-presented series of technical, lengthy lectures on the U.S. Constitution, for example, might be wholly appropriate for a college course in American history. But no matter how well they are presented, such lectures would be inappropriate for fifth graders studying the same topic; we can do some things with some groups that we cannot do with others.

Knowing this is just one piece of the knowledge base that distinguishes the more from the less experienced teacher or, more precisely, the expert from the novice teacher.

The techniques and strategies used in teaching social studies, therefore, have to be considered in terms of the goals of the program, the objectives to be achieved, and the maturity of the learners. If we want children to gain information, this can be achieved through reading, viewing, discussing, and other procedures that involve the transmission of information. These are referred to as *expository* teaching strategies. If we want children also to develop critical habits of thought, to search for information independently, to be able to form hypotheses and test them, we use *inquiry* teaching strategies. If we want children to learn to work with each other, to plan together, or to apply what they are learning as they are learning it, we would use *activity* teaching strategies. *Demonstration* strategies can be a part of any of the others and would be used to improve the communication process through showing, doing, and telling. What is called discovery learning is a variation of inquiry. Various modes of teaching are discussed in detail in other sources.[2]

Beginning teachers are usually most comfortable starting with an expository strategy. The teaching environment can be controlled sufficiently well

---

[2]See, for example, John Jarolimek and Clifford D. Foster, *Teaching and Learning in the Elementary School*, 5th ed. (New York: Macmillan, 1993), 133–52.

A volunteer shows students the proper way to make adobe bricks on the Back 40 of the Institute of Texan Cultures in San Antonio. Direct experience, such as this, adds a rich measure of detail and involvement to the learning of concepts. Skillful teachers are careful, however, to help children connect firmly the experience to the concepts they are to form. Here, the concepts may be *shelter* and *human-environment inter-action.*
(Photo courtesy of The University of Texas Institute of Texan Cultures at San Antonio.)

to reduce management concerns to a minimum, the objectives can be made specific, the children's study materials can be preselected by the teacher, and the process can be entirely teacher directed. First encounters with teaching social studies should be short—20- to 30-minute episodes—and involve teaching a simple concept or skill. This initial teaching experience might be based on the textbook, with heavy reliance on the suggestions presented in the teacher's manual that accompanies the book. After a few experiences of this type, the novice will have gained some confidence in the teaching role, will know how to evaluate responses, and can begin to add variations, such as increased use of visual material, discussion questions, and followup activities.

Having achieved a backlog of successful teaching experiences in the expository mode, the teacher might plan a demonstration. Some aspects of map or globe use would serve well for this purpose. Followup work to the demonstration might be individualized, by giving children some choice in what they will do. This can be succeeded by a class discussion of the individual followup activities.

While doing this type of rather formal teacher-directed expository teaching, the teacher will ask informational questions requiring children to do little more than recall what they have read or observed. The teacher is not concerned with much beyond the literal comprehension of what has been taught. With increased experience and confidence, the teacher should begin asking some questions that require children not only to remember information but to analyze and manipulate it in some way. These higher-order questions should not be ones that can be answered simply by recalling factual information but should require children to respond to such queries as "Why?" "How do you know?" "If that happened, how do you explain . . .?" "Can you summarize . . .?" "What conclusion can we come to?" "What other problems does that raise?"

These questions will gradually lead the teacher and the class away from exposition and in the direction of inquiry. In time, children will be raising questions and problems themselves and will speculate about their solutions. These hunches will be converted into hypotheses that result in searches for information, which will necessitate the wide use of resources, individualized assignments, and a variety of interesting learning activities. At this stage the teacher is well on the way to developing professional maturity in the use of teaching techniques and strategies in social studies.

TEACHING CONCEPTS AND GENERALIZATIONS

In everyday parlance, the term *concept* is used to mean *idea*, as when someone says, "My concept of leisure is not the same as yours." In social studies the meaning is the same: concepts are ideas. Social studies concepts often embody an elaborate meaning that evolves with experience and learning over a period of years. Sometimes a child's initial understanding of a concept includes misconceptions that in later years must be corrected. Consider a kindergartner's concept of *history,* for example, or *freedom* or *money,* compared to an eighth grader's or a twelfth grader's. Let us explore in some detail the meaning and implications of concepts for teaching and learning social studies.

The Nature of Concepts

If asked to tell what a village is, most adults would probably say something along this line: "A village consists of a group of persons living in a rural area in a cluster of homes smaller than a city or a town." For most purposes this is an adequate definition to make communication possible. But *village* had a much more elaborate meaning for the Indians of British Columbia, as explained in Margaret Craven's novel *I Heard the Owl Call My Name*. On the boat trip north, the young priest, Mark Brian, recalls what his bishop had told him about the village:

> The Indian knows his village and feels for his village as no white man for his country, his town, or even for his own bit of land. His village is not the strip of land four miles long and three miles wide that is his as long as the sun rises and the moon sets. The myths are the village and the winds and the rains. The river is the village, and the black and white killer whales that herd the fish to the end of the inlet the better to gobble them. The village is the salmon who comes up the river to spawn, the seal who follows the salmon and bites off his head, the bluejay whose name is like the sound he makes— "Kwiss-kwiss." The village is the talking bird, the owl, who calls the name of the man who is going to die, and the silver-tipped grizzly who ambles into the village, and the little white speck that is the mountain goat on Whoop-Szo.

> The fifty-foot totem by the church is the village, and the Cedar-man who stands at the bottom holding up the eagle, the wolf and the raven! And a voice said to the great cedar tree in Bond Sound, "Come forth, Tzakamayi and be a man," and he came forth to be the Cedar-man, the first man-god of the people and more powerful than all others.[3]

This is a superb example of a concept because it illustrates so well the richness and depth of meaning that can inhere in a single word label. It also illustrates how vital experience is in developing such meanings. It is doubtful if anyone who did not actually grow up in the village culture of these Indians could understand and appreciate the full meaning of *village* as they conceptualize it. Yet the novelist does very well in conveying the meaning by skillfully building word images for us of things that are familiar because they come out of our own background of experience.

As we have said, concepts are ideas. But what are ideas? They are abstract categories or classes of meaning. Ideas are abstract because they are removed from specific instances. For example, *island* is the word label for a geographic phenomenon consisting of land completely surrounded by water. Kauai is one specific example of such a set of conditions. There are thousands of other specific examples of the concept *island*. But to know that Kauai is an island (that is, a body of land completely surrounded by water) is not to know very much about that beautiful outcropping of land in the Pacific. To early Hawaiians, *Kauai* had a meaning closely akin to that

---

[3]Margaret Craven, *I Heard the Owl Call My Name*, (New York: Doubleday, 1973).

of *village* to the Pacific Northwest Indians. Concept definitions, therefore, tell us only about those qualities or attributes that a group of examples *has in common*. They do not tell us about the unique features of particular examples. The concept—the idea—refers to the attributes shared by all examples.

The human intellect makes use of this system of classifying, categorizing, and organizing the vast amount of specific perceptual data with which it deals. Trees having certain attributes are *evergreen*; others having different attributes are *deciduous*. Some groups of animals are known as *mammals*; others, as *reptiles*; and others, as *birds*. A certain form of government is called a *democracy*; another, an *autocracy*. This ability and inclination to classify perceptions of reality into groups having common qualities is what is meant by conceptual thought. Conceptual thought makes it possible to manipulate reality intellectually; that is, one can figure out complex problems "in one's head." This is a distinctly human quality.

Concepts *always* have to do with meanings; words are simply their labels. Concepts may deal with concrete places, objects, institutions, or events such as these:

mountain	flood	valley
plateau	dairy	ocean
home	island	Chinese
country	famine	harbor
state	community helpers	desert
producer	political party	consumer goods

Concepts may also be more or less abstract ways of thinking, feeling, and behaving, such as these:

adaptation	freedom	responsibility
democracy	justice	cooperation
tolerance	fairness	rights
honesty	liberty	equality
loyalty	interdependence	conflict
culture	free enterprise	legal system

The meanings of these concepts can be developed by description or by definition, providing the descriptions or definitions or both are rooted in the experiences of the learner—that is, in something that is already known. This means that if we are to develop new concepts or extend the meanings of those partially understood, it is critical to link them to prior experience and knowledge.

Social studies material is literally loaded with concepts. For example, a student might encounter the following paragraph in a social studies textbook. The concepts have been italicized here to call attention to them:

> San Francisco is a *leading cultural, industrial,* and *distribution center* of the *West.* It is also the *leading seaport* on the Pacific Coast. People from *many lands*

have *migrated* to San Francisco. Therefore, the *people* of this *city* are of varied *ethnic backgrounds.* This reflects itself in the many *languages* one hears spoken in San Francisco. It also explains the *ethnic cuisines* offered by its *hundreds* of fine *restaurants.* Today *thousands* visit this *city* each year for *business reasons.* Others come as *tourists.* The *waterfront* is especially *fascinating,* but the *city* has many *museums, bridges, markets, galleries, cable cars,* and *squares* for visitors to *enjoy.* The unusual *geography* of San Francisco has made much of its *architecture* known *worldwide.* Thus, a combination of *interesting* features makes San Francisco a *favorite city* to visit.

If one tries to simplify this paragraph by substituting alternate words for those that are italicized, one finds that it cannot be done and still convey the same meaning. This example illustrates that concepts carry much of the meaning of social studies.

The Nature of Generalizations

Let us return to the village concept cited earlier and ask the question: What can we say about the relationship between the village and the people who live there? Several things could be said, of course, but the following will serve our purpose:

The village embraces the total culture of traditional Pacific Northwest Indians.

This statement expresses a relationship between the concepts *village* and *culture.* Such relationships are called *generalizations* and are expressed as declarative statements. Because generalizations are relationships between two or more concepts, they are summarizing statements that have wide applicability. They can be transferred to many situations. For example, the generalization cited does not apply only to one village but to *all* villages of traditional Pacific Northwest Indians. That is what makes it a generalization. The generalization "All human societies have a culture" has even broader applicability. It would apply to *any* human society anywhere in the world.

Generalizations are similar to concepts in that they, too, help the individual order the physical and social environments. Rather than being represented by a single word or expression, however, generalizations are usually expressed as declarative statements. The following are examples of generalizations often found in social studies. Notice how each expresses a relationship between concepts embedded in the statement.

1. New inventions lead to change in ways of living.
2. As human beings interact with the physical environment, both they and it are changed.
3. Because the peoples of the world are interdependent, the behaviors of one group of people affects the lives of the other groups.
4. Families are a primary means of socialization in all cultures.
5. Written laws clarify the rules by which a society operates and promote fair and equal treatment of its members.

6. The survival of a multicultural society relies upon most citizens agreeing to a core of commonly held values (e.g., justice, equality, liberty).
7. Great and small historical events rarely have a single cause.
8. Compromise is necessary in most situations because continuous conflict has severe consequences.

Teaching Concepts to Young Learners

Social studies concepts and topics can be studied at various levels of complexity. Kindergartners and first-graders often study the family and family life. Yet a graduate student working on a doctorate in sociology or anthropology might take an advanced seminar on the same subject. The United States Supreme Court struggles with the meaning of justice in a complex case, yet children in the elementary school learn about the meaning of "liberty and justice for all." How does a teacher go about setting the complexity of subject matter, concepts, and generalizations and present them in ways that make sense to children? The following are suggested:

1. Define concepts in terms familiar to young children. For example:

CONCEPT	FOR A YOUNG CHILD THIS MEANS
Justice	Being or playing fair
Laws	Rules
Equality of opportunity	Seeing that everyone gets a turn
Cooperation	Working with others
Responsibility	Doing your part or doing your duty
Democracy	Majority rule plus civil rights

2. Select subject matter with which children can identify. This does not mean that topics selected for study must be physically close to them. Children can study about things far away that are psychologically close to them. On the other hand, things that are physically close may be psychologically remote. The lifestyles of families who live across town, for example, may be as unfamiliar to a child as those of people halfway around the world.

3. Rely on diagnostic approaches to teaching. That is, find out what children already know. It is especially important when teaching concepts to anchor them in a child's experience. Such experience may be direct or vicarious, real or represented in some way, but one way or another, new ideas must be linked to students' prior knowledge. This usually can be accomplished through informal class discussions in which children respond to open-ended questions the teacher has prepared in advance. For any concept, ask students to think of several examples and then tell why they are examples. By listening to the examples students suggest but, more importantly, to the *reasons* they give, teachers can diagnose children's present knowledge of a concept and plan accordingly.

We assume that students have learned a concept when they can summarize the attributes shared by all of the concept's examples. But there are other indications of learners' understanding of concepts. For example, they can distinguish examples from nonexamples (a nonexample is any item that has some but not all of the attributes the concept requires). Students who have learned a concept thoroughly can produce (find, create, describe) new examples, distinguish examples from nonexamples, and correct nonexamples. When students have learned the concept *village*, for example, they can:

- summarize what all villages have in common (summarizing)
- write a story about a village they invent (producing)
- distinguish villages from cities and suburbs (distinguishing)
- describe the changes the state capital would have to undergo to become a village (correcting a nonexample).

Concept Learning: Three Strategies

Teachers can help students learn concepts by designing lessons that focus directly on concept development. In this section, we describe three strategies. The first, called "concept formation," has students systematically

Here we see middle school students from Seattle getting firsthand experience in sheep shearing at the local fair. These children could not possibly have gained the same level of understanding of the concepts related to this process simply by hearing or reading about it.
(Photo by Greg Bickel, Seattle Public Schools.)

build the summary in their minds as they compare and contrast three or four examples.[4] The second is the time-honored "list, group, and label" strategy.[5] The third, called "concept attainment," is a deductive version of the first strategy. The teacher tells students the critical attributes of a concept and then helps them work with examples and nonexamples.

Strategy One: Concept Formation.   A fifth-grade class is studying the concept *democracy*. The teacher, Kenneth Bailey, has asked diagnostic questions such as these: What is democracy? Is the United States a democracy? Why? What persons do you think of when you think of democracy? In this way, Mr. Bailey learns that students have no concept of democracy save vague notions of voting and majority rule. With this information in hand, he builds an introductory concept-formation lesson on *democracy*.

First, he knows he should assemble three or four examples of democracy. These will be the building blocks of the concept. He decides to use the governments of the United States, Mexico, and Canada, because the textbook has information on them. For the fourth example, he wants something less "bookish," more experiential; accordingly, he selects the democratic classroom meeting his students have each Monday afternoon.

Using the concept-formation strategy, students will build an understanding of democracy "from the bottom up" by studying each example and then comparing and contrasting them. Similarities among examples are the critical attributes of the concept *democracy:* In the United States, Mexico, Canada, and Mr. Bailey's classroom meetings, the majority rules (laws are made by all citizens or their representatives), minority rights are protected, and laws are written down. These are the three attributes students eventually should summarize under the name "democracy." Is the resulting concept as complex as the one formed by college political science majors? Of course not, but it would be quite an achievement for fifth-grade children. Here is the teacher's plan for achieving this result.

Studying Multiple Examples.   Mr. Bailey creates a data-retrieval chart that contains the four examples down the left and Focus Questions across the top (see Figure 2-1). These questions focus students' attention on the critical attributes.

Mr. Bailey instructs his students to use this chart to record information they find on each example. He gives them some time in class to work with the information in their textbooks and complete the chart. He directs them to finish the chart as homework.

Noting Differences.   The next day, after verifying that all the needed information on the four examples has been gathered and recorded, Mr. Bailey asks students, "In what ways do these four governments differ?"

---

[4]Walter C. Parker, "Thinking to Learn Concepts," *The Social Studies* 79 (March/April 1988): 70–73.

[5]The listing-grouping-labeling strategy was developed by the late Hilda Taba and her associates in research related to concept learning in social studies.

FIGURE 2-1

A data-retrieval chart for the concept *democracy* as developed by Mr. Bailey for his class.

FOCUS QUESTIONS			
EXAMPLES	Does the majority rule? How?	Are minority rights protected? (describe)	Are laws written? Where?
United States			
Canada			
Mexico			
Class meeting			

Noting Similarities. He then asks, "In what ways are these four governments all alike?" He records their responses on the chalkboard for use in the next step.

Summarizing. He then instructs students, "Take a few minutes now to jot down a summary of these similarities in one, complete sentence. Let's begin the summary with, 'These are all ways of governing that. . . .' " Now students compose their own definition of the concept. Mr. Bailey takes time to allow for sharing, and gives students feedback. Students then compose a second draft, taking more care to include all the critical attributes of *democracy* in their summaries.

Labeling. He then asks, "What is a word you might use to describe governments like these? Be creative—invent a word if you like. Make sure it captures the essence of this kind of government." After eliciting several nicknames, Mr. Bailey tells them that the conventional label for this kind of government is *democracy.* He takes some time to examine with his students the etymology of this Greek term.

Guided Application: Classifying. Now that students have constructed in their minds a rough idea of *democracy,* it is time to reinforce, extend and refine it through a powerful application activity called classifying.

Classifying requires students to recall the critical attributes of a concept and, moving to higher-order thinking, determine whether those attributes are present in a new situation. The new situation is bound to be different from the examples studied initially to form the concept; accordingly, students need to decide if any of the differences really matter as far as the concept is concerned. In this way, a concept is not formed only to remain unused in the mind. Rather, learners are asked to regard a concept as "portable" knowledge that can be taken with them and used to make sense of new situations. There are several varieties of this time-honored activity. Here we give the basic form and two variations:

a. *distinguishing examples from nonexamples.* Mr. Bailey gives students information about two or three other governments (China's; Denmark's; Japan's) and asks them to decide which of them, if any, is a democracy. He asks them to write down their reasons and calls on several students to share their decisions and reasons.

b. *producing examples.* He directs his students to get into teams of four and together create a fictional example of a democracy. He asks them to imagine themselves shipwrecked on an island with no chance of rescue; hence, they must create a society from scratch. He reminds them to look back at their summaries to be sure the example they create has each of the attributes all examples of democracies must have.

c. *correcting nonexamples.* Mr. Bailey tells students that he will describe several organizations, all of which are nonexamples of *democracy.* The students' task is to describe the changes that would be needed in order to make each of them into examples of the concept. First, he describes a modern military dictatorship and asks them to make the needed changes that would render it a democracy. After students have accomplished this task satisfactorily, Mr. Bailey describes a little league baseball club and, finally, a monarchy. Students again are asked and helped to make the needed changes.

Incorporating Cooperative Group Work.   At step one in concept formation, students can be placed in cooperative teams of four students each. Each member of the group takes responsibility for gathering information on one of the four examples. Sherry takes Mexico, Jamal takes Canada, Mei takes the classroom meetings, and Rena gets the United States. Because one member of every other team is studying the same example, these students get together in an "expert group" to work on their example together. Every team member thus leaves his or her team to work with other students responsible for the same example. Eventually, experts return to their teams where they teach their example to teammates. In this way, everyone studies all examples—which is crucial for concept formation: remember, a concept is a summary of attributes shared by all examples.

For *noting differences* through *labeling,* it is a good idea to work with the whole class as Mr. Bailey did. But for *classifying,* teams can again be convened to work through the three activities.

Strategy Two: Listing, Grouping, and Labeling.   Imagine a primary grade class that has just returned from a field trip to a supermarket. Now, back in the classroom, the teacher asks the children to list as many things as they can remember having seen in the supermarket. As they name items, the teacher writes them on the chalkboard—for example, eggs, bread, beans, meat, butter, checkout person, stock clerk, watermelons, candy, store manager, dog food, ice cream, and so on.

After completing the process of listing what they saw, the teacher asks the children to examine their list to see if certain things on the list seem to go together. That is, can these items be put together in groups that have something in common, as, for example, milk, butter, cheese, cream, and yogurt? They catch on to this activity quickly, and soon they are suggesting which items can be placed in the same group. Having placed items that seem to go together in the same group, children are then asked to think of names or labels for these groups. In the foregoing example, a name for that group would probably be "dairy products." The children should develop a name or label for each of the groups.

This listing-grouping-labeling strategy can be used in many ways to teach concepts in social studies. Here are a few additional examples:

1. Suppose a visitor from another country spent a day at our school; what would he or she see?
2. What did you see on the walk through the neighborhood?
3. What are all the ways goods and people can be moved from one place to another?
4. How many things can you list that are manufactured in our city (or state)?
5. What items are sold in a department store?
6. What are things human beings can do that no other creatures can do?
7. What natural resources do we depend on in our everyday life?

This strategy is particularly useful in situations in which learners have made many observations in a short period of time and need to sort out what they experienced into meaningful categories.

In using this strategy with young children, the teacher may have children find examples of the concept in pictures from old magazines. Or the teacher may have a collection of magazine pictures that illustrate examples of the concept and have children group the ones that seem to "go together." Children can then suggest word labels for these groups.

Strategy Three: Concept Attainment.   A sixth-grade class has been studying the economic development of nations in the Third World. The teacher, Ms. Rush, wants her students to develop the concept *modernization* and helps them do so in the following way. Note that she does not give them examples to study and then lead them to a discovery of the concept based on the examples' shared attributes; rather she *tells* them the attributes and then provides examples and nonexamples. She begins by writing the concept label and critical attributes on the chalkboard:

MODERNIZATION INVOLVES

1. The application of technology to the control of nature's resources.
2. The use of inanimate sources of power and energy.

3. The use of tools to multiply the effects of human energy expended.
4. A high per capita production output.

The teacher then explains the meaning of each of the four attributes by using large pictures. That is, she shows the class specific examples of modernization—situations in which technology is applied to the control of resources, where inanimate power and energy sources are used, where tools multiply human energy, and where the per capita production is high. As children raise questions, these are discussed and issues are clarified. The teacher then provides the class with a series of pictures in which modernization, as defined by the particular attributes, is *not* evident. Again, these are explained and discussed, and questions raised by children are answered.

Having satisfied herself that the children understand the attributes that indicate modernization, the teacher presents the class with another set of pictures, but this time the *children* must identify examples and nonexamples of modernization and tell why or why not each is an example. These pictures are discussed in detail. The teacher then provides the class with back issues of *National Geographic* and asks them to find picture examples and nonexamples of modernization and to tell why each is or is not an example. Finally, the teacher evaluates the children's ability to understand the concept by having them identify examples and nonexamples from a new set of pictures.

This strategy is less inquiry oriented than the other two, but it does, nonetheless, present opportunities for search and discovery. In this case, the teacher provides the attributes of the concept in advance rather than having learners define them in the process of study. In summary, Ms. Rush:

1. Identified the label for the concept (modernization).
2. Provided the major attributes (or critical characteristics) of the concept.
3. Provided examples that illustrated the presence of the attributes.
4. Provided nonexamples in which the attributes were missing.
5. Presented examples and nonexamples and had the children identify the attributes and had them tell why or why not each was an example.
6. Had children find examples and nonexamples on their own.
7. Evaluated their ability to use the attributes in identifying examples and nonexamples.

Concept Extensions

These three concept-learning strategies help learners form initial ideas of all kinds of phenomena—people (e.g., civil rights reformers; explorers), places (continents; countries), events (national holidays; cultural festivals), skills (composing summaries; cooperating in small groups), systems (democracies; civilizations), and so on. The concepts children build as a result of such strategies are necessarily incipient; that is, they are *beginning* understandings because they contain only a small number of examples, and each example may not have been examined in great detail. For this reason, expert teachers have in their repertoire strategies that help students extend and elaborate concepts after they have been formed initially. These strategies have the effect of building a second and third layer of understanding atop the first. Further, they help learners to correct misconceptions formed earlier.

In refining their concept of democracy, for example, children should learn that their classroom is not really a democracy, though it operates according to some democratic principles. Generally, though, school governance is out of their hands. However, when Mr. Bailey convenes a democratic classroom meeting on Monday afternoons, then for the duration of that meeting the classroom becomes an example of democracy.

Return to the Examples.   This is the easiest way to extend the meaning of concepts. It involves having students return to the examples they studied initially to build the idea, only now to learn about them in greater depth. Returning to Mr. Bailey's *democracy* lesson, three committees might be formed to write biographies on the founders of democracy in the United States, Canada, and Mexico respectively. A fourth can gather information and stories related to the first town meetings in colonial America and use this information to advise classmates on the conduct of their own democratic classroom meetings.

Additional Experience with Classifying.   Classifying of any sort should strengthen a concept after its initial formation. This is so because classifying requires learners to recall the attributes of the concept over and over again, each time applying them to a slightly different set of information. This higher-order thinking process should result in a flexible understanding of the concept that can be used in various situations.

Any of the three kinds of classifying explained under the concept-formation strategy (strategy one) is effective, but perhaps *distinguishing examples from nonexamples* best promotes the elaboration of a concept. When children have formed an initial understanding of modernization, for example, they are ready to apply it to the examination of any country in the world, on any continent, deciding if the society in question is "modern" according to the attributes they have learned.

In the primary grades, teachers can provide children with experiences in classifying through the use of pictures. For example, magazines such as *Better Homes and Gardens, Sunset, Family Circle,* and others have many pictures that relate to the subject matter of the primary grade social studies program. Teachers can have children peruse these to find examples of things that seem to "go together." These can be cut out by the children, mounted on cards, displayed in appropriate clusters, and discussed. Of course, this same procedure can be used to have children identify examples and nonexamples of concepts being studied.

Forming and Testing Hypotheses.   An intermediate-grade class has been introduced to the the concept *advertising*. Sensing that the children's understanding is still quite weak, the teacher selects the following strategy to extend and strengthen it. First, children are asked to search for as many different examples of advertising as they can find. This search uncovers newspaper and magazine advertisements, classified ads, radio and television commercials, billboards, signs on transit buses, signs in public buildings, direct mailers, catalogs, and others. These various methods of advertising are discussed in terms of their purpose; the audience to which they are directed; the extent to which they are local, regional, or national; and the nature of the appeal. This leads the class to speculate on the value of advertising. Who benefits from advertising, and how do they benefit? Out of this discussion the children develop the following hypotheses:

1. Advertising helps consumers because it informs them about new products and their prices.
2. Effective advertising tries to create wants for products whether they are needed or not.
3. Local advertising has a more direct effect on sales in local stores than does national advertising.

The children begin searching for information that would support or refute these hypotheses. Much of their information gathering is done outside of school by interviewing consumers, local merchants, and representatives of advertising agencies. This process forces them to explore further such related subconcepts as needs and wants, promotion, audience, client, account, market, layout, impact, theme, and sales appeal. In time, they are able to form some tentative conclusions relating to their hypotheses, but their searches suggest other hypotheses that need exploration. The entire process provides the children with a thorough familiarity with the concept of advertising from several different perspectives.

In one form or another, the procedure just described is frequently used in teaching social studies concepts. What takes place is the following:

1. Learners are provided with extended, direct, firsthand exploratory experiences.
2. Terms and subconcepts related to the main concept are explained, and their meanings are developed as a natural extension of the study.
3. Children discuss ideas relating to the main concept and are encouraged to speculate about explanations of perceived relationships. These speculative statements become hypotheses to be tested.
4. An information search is made to test the hypotheses.
5. Tentative conclusions are drawn, which give rise to other hypotheses, and the search continues.
6. Through extended study and firsthand experiences, the meaning of the main concept is extended and refined.

Whatever strategy or strategies the teacher elects to use, the important point is that student *experiences* are the building blocks of concept learning. Moreover, to develop the depth and breadth of meanings that inhere in concepts, learner experiences need to be many and from varied contexts. This cannot be achieved by having students memorize definitions or learn meanings of concepts as given in glossaries or dictionaries. Such definitions are meaningful to learners *after* they have been introduced to concepts through direct experiences as exemplified by the strategies discussed in this chapter.

Developing Generalizations

Generalizations are relationships between two or more concepts that are usually expressed as declarative statements. Four different types of generalizations are relevant to social studies education:

1. A supermarket sells all food products needed by consumers.

This is a *descriptive* generalization. It could have been a concluding statement made by the children who were using the first strategy described in the prior section on concept development. It describes in summary form the relationship between the supermarket and the food needs of consumers.

2. Advertising the price of merchandise results in more comparative shopping by consumers.

This is a *cause-and-effect* generalization. It might have been developed by the class studying advertising in the second strategy described in the prior section. "If-then" statements are usually generalizations of this type.

3. Misleading or false advertising takes unfair advantage of consumers and is illegal.

This generalization is a statement of a *value principle*. It, too, might have evolved in the study of advertising described earlier. Generalizations of this type constitute the guidelines by which individuals govern their actions, and many have been handed down through the ages in the form of proverbs or wise statements for good living.

4. The capacity of a nation to modernize depends on its natural resource base, the quantity and quality of its labor force, the amount and kinds of capital available to its industry and agriculture, and the institutions, attitudes, values, and habits that determine the effectiveness with which these economic resources are used.

This generalization is a *universal law* or *principle* and is highly abstract. These generalizations are often used as the organizing frameworks for the social sciences and for social studies curricula. Such a generalization may have been the focus of the study of modernization discussed under concept development strategies. The possibility of the children arriving at such a generalization themselves is, indeed, remote, and it is probably inappropriate to expect them to do so.

Teaching Generalizations

It should be clear that generalizations are expressed as summarizing statements. That means that they will usually come near the ends of study sequences. For example, in the strategies for concept development described earlier, the children should be involved in stating generalizations that illustrate relationships between concepts. When generalizations are introduced at the beginning of a study sequence, they should be used as hypotheses to be confirmed or rejected in the process of study. This might occur in the following way:

> The teacher says, "Many people believe in the law of supply and demand, which states, 'Scarcity of goods results in higher prices whereas an oversupply of goods drives prices down.' How might we go about finding out whether this is true of the things we and our families buy daily?"

At this point the search begins to test the validity of the generalization the teacher has provided as a working hypothesis.

Generalizations, like concepts, have to be developed out of the experiences of children. It is essential that students understand the concepts in the generalizations in order to grasp the meaning of the relationship being expressed. For this reason, it is not appropriate for learners simply to memorize generalizations. Generalizations that are memorized but not understood are of no value in gaining meaning from new situations where the relationships expressed in the generalization apply.

Many adults can recall a picture displayed by a teacher or a textbook photograph that was used to illustrate a *desert* or a *bridge* or a *skyscraper* or an *island* or some other social studies concept that was unfamiliar to them at the time. Forever after, whenever that concept enters the individual's consciousness, he or she retrieves a mental picture of the exact illustration that was used when it was first presented! If we are to teach for a wide application of ideas, that is, for *generalized knowledge* that can be useful in new situations, children must be given as many broad and varied experiences with ideas as is possible. They need to view the ideas in a variety of contexts. Citing single examples should be avoided whenever possible because this presents too narrow an experience for the child. When pictures or illustrations are used, several should be presented. Assessments of children's understandings should not be cast in the exact context as presented in the instruction but should be placed in new settings. The teacher needs to ask frequently such questions as these: "Where else do we see this happening?" "How is this like or different from the problem we discussed at news time?" "Can you give another example of that?"

It cannot be assumed that children will apply knowledge from one situation to another if left unaided by the teacher. A skillful teacher will pave the way for transfer to take place and, in so doing, will be teaching un-

These children are learning many facts about panning for gold by actually doing it. This experience will be long remembered. With help from a skillful teacher, the children will use these facts to build important ideas. To which concepts and generalizations might this experience be linked?
(Photo courtesy of the Southern Oregon Historical Society.)

derstandings with wide application. In the teaching of concepts and generalizations, the need is not to repeat, drill, and practice. Rather, it is to enable the learner to encounter the idea in many settings, each slightly different from the other.

THE ROLE OF FACTS

The practice of having children learn factual information in social studies has been subject to considerable criticism by educators. These critical comments often have been misunderstood to mean that factual information is unimportant. Actually, factual information is crucial to the understanding of concepts and generalizations because it provides the supporting detail and the elaboration that make them meaningful. For example, let us say that a child reads this generalization: "The l ɔlihood of the people of this region depends on the seasonal cycle of rain to make their crops produce their maximum yield." This statement has meaning only if one has specific information needed to answer such questions as "Which crop?" "How much is a maximum yield?" "How much rain is needed?" "When does the rain come?" "What do the people do with their harvested crops?" These specifics will not be long remembered, but they are critical in understanding the larger ideas that children are expected to learn. Teaching for concepts and generalizations without being concerned about the supporting specific facts results in shallow learning.

Unfortunately, there is not a list of facts that all children should learn in social studies, nor is there even a satisfactory set of criteria that the teacher can use in making decisions about which facts should be learned. Thus, the teacher's judgment is critical in determining the specific facts children are expected to learn. In exercising that judgment, the teacher will want to consider such matters as (1) whether the factual information is needed to elaborate on or explain main ideas, (2) the extent to which it is frequently used in ordinary living, (3) whether the information is likely to remain important for a long period of time, and (4) whether the information is an important part of the *common culture* and is therefore something all people are expected to know.

TEACHING SOCIAL STUDIES SKILLS

The systematic and sequential development of skills is of utmost importance to children because skills are the tools with which they continue their learning. Consequently, inadequately developed skills tend to retard learning in many areas of the elementary and middle school curriculum, particularly in the social studies. Inadequate achievement in the social studies can, in many cases, be traced to poorly developed reading skills, inability to handle the vocabulary of the social studies, inability to read maps and globes, poor work-study skills, inability to use reference materials, or underdeveloped language skills. Therefore, a well-balanced program in the social studies needs to provide for systematic and planned instruction to ensure the development of these skills.[6]

Skill implies proficiency, the capability of doing something well. To have a skill is ordinarily taken to mean that a person is able to respond more or less habitually in an efficient way. Skills are commonly classified as motor, intellectual, and social.

All skills have two characteristics in common: They are developmental and they require practice if they are to be mastered. To speak of skills as

---

[6]For an extended list of social studies skills, see National Council for the Social Studies, *Social Studies Curriculum Planning Resources* (Dubuque, IA: Kendall/Hunt, 1990), 36–37.

being developmental means that they are learned gradually over a period of years. They are never really learned to completion although there usually comes a time when the learner has mastered them sufficiently for most purposes. However, one could continue refining these skills throughout one's lifetime. Thus, teachers should not assume that skills are taught and learned only once in some particular grade. All teachers need to assume some responsibility for the teaching and maintenance of social studies skills.

No amount of explanation or meaningful teaching will make children proficient in skills. They must practice and use the skills they have learned in order to build proficiency. This does not mean repetition or drill in the traditional sense, where a response was repeated over and over in exactly the same way. Instead, it is hoped that children will practice skills with the intention of improving. This also does not mean that skills would be practiced wholly out of their functional context, although there might be occasions when this would be necessary. In the ordinary study of a topic, there will be numerous opportunities to practice skills in the daily work-study activities of the class. In this way, the children improve their skills as they develop their understanding of concepts and subject matter. Skills are learned more effectively when they are closely related to actual situations in which they will be used.

Procedures in skills teaching are fairly clearcut. The learners should first understand what is involved in the skill, how it is used, and what it means. Providing a good model of its use is helpful at this point. Second, the learners need to work through a simple use of the skill under careful teacher guidance. This is essential to verify that they understand what is involved and are making a correct response. Third, they need additional practice in increasingly complex variations of the skill, applied in functional settings. Children need to use the newly learned skill in solving problems, thus demonstrating its value as a learning tool. Finally, they need continued practice in its use over an extended period of time to maintain and improve facility with the skill.

Teachers who help children develop skills do not depend entirely on incidental teaching of them. Rather, the skills are carefully identified, systematically taught, thoroughly practiced, and widely used. This principle applies to such intellectual skills as critical and reflective thinking, coming to valid conclusions based on evidence, evaluating sources of information, and interpreting data as well as to work-study and group-process skills. These steps, along with an example of their application, are provided in Figure 2-2.

For purposes of focus and clarity of analysis, in the treatment of teaching methods, skills teaching is often discussed in a separate section. This separation should not suggest to the teacher that skills are taught or learned outside a content (i.e., subject matter) framework. The content connection is most obvious in the case of work-study skills such as finding information, arranging information in usable forms, using maps, globes, and

FIGURE 2-2

Example of Steps in Teaching a Skill Applied to the Use of the Directory of a Newspaper

STEPS IN TEACHING A SKILL:

STEP 1   Make sure children understand what is involved in performing the skill. Show them how it is used. Provide them with a good model of the skill in operation.

STEP 2   Break the skill into components and arrange them sequentially. Develop the teaching sequence step by step, having the children do each component as it is presented and explained. Supervise carefully to make sure their responses are correct.

STEP 3   Have the children perform a simple variation of the skill under your close supervision. This is to ensure that they are performing the skill correctly.

STEP 4   After it is established that the children are performing the skill correctly, provide for supervised practice, using simple variations that ensure success.

STEP 5   Gradually increase the complexity of the variation of the skill, and begin having children apply the skill in situations in which it is useful. Continue this procedure until the desired level of proficiency is achieved.

STEP 6   Continue to practice the skill at regular intervals, largely through functional application, in order to maintain and improve performance.

EXAMPLES OF APPLICATION OF EACH STEP:

Step 1   Secure a newspaper, preferably a Sunday edition, and show how difficult and time-consuming it is to find some bit of information if one has to leaf through the entire paper to find it. Have children try their hand at finding items without using the newspaper directory. Show how easily one can find information with the aid of the directory.

Step 2
a. Make sure children know how to use the dictionary and the encyclopedia prior to teaching this skill.
b. Acquaint children with various sections of the newspaper: general news, classified ads, sports, editorials, weather, and so on.
c. Teach children the specialized vocabulary associated with the newspaper: vital statistics, obituaries, market quotations, masthead, dateline, syndicated, and so on.
d. Teach children what items are included in the various categories listed in the directory, and how they are arranged. For example, what is included in the Arts and Entertainment section, how are the classifieds organized, and how does one find out what arrangement is used?
e. Provide a newspaper for each member of the class, and have the children locate easy items using the directory. Such items might include the television schedule, sports, and the comics. Supervise to make sure everyone is performing the skill correctly.

Step 3   Follow Step 2 immediately with an exercise requiring children to locate items making use of the directory. Supervise and assist as needed. Check responses.

Step 4   Assign children to find information in the next day's newspaper. This should be done on their own without teacher supervision. Check responses.

Step 5   Bring to class copies of a different newspaper from the one used thus far in which a slightly different directory format appears. Assign children to find information in this paper without your assistance to see if they can transfer and modify their skill from one situation to another. Check responses.

Step 6   From time to time have children make use of the directory to locate needed information. Observe the accuracy and extensiveness of use of the directory.

graphics, and organizing information. Such skills have no purpose outside of a subject-matter setting. But the integration of content and skills applies to intellectual skills and group-work skills as well. Processes such as problem solving, critical thinking, inquiry, and decision making must have a content framework if they are to be taught with integrity. Teachers should not set out to teach these important processes without giving ample consideration to the subject matter in which they are to be used.

LEARNING AND TEACHING RESOURCES
FOR CONTENT AND SKILLS

Children cannot learn content and content-related skills without valid sources of information. In recent years, a multimedia approach to social studies has been strongly encouraged, but the textbook remains the most widely used information source for children in social studies. The practice of using basic textbooks is often criticized because of their misuse. The challenge to the teacher is to learn how to make enlightened use of textbooks and to broaden the information sources available to children.

As we examine the potential of various media useful in teaching content and skills, we must be ever mindful that it is the *teacher* and not the media who produces exciting programs for children. The artistry of the teacher is enhanced when the necessary materials for creative teaching are easily available. But it is a mistake to assume that a generous supply of instructional materials will ensure inspired and creative teaching. It is the interaction of a talented teacher and a wide range of appropriate media that generates superior social studies programs.

Information sources for the social studies can be grouped into two categories: (1) reading materials and resources (textbooks, encyclopedias, references, computers, magazines, pamphlets, newspaper clippings, travel folders, classroom periodicals, and similar printed material) and (2) nonreading materials and resources (pictures, films, filmstrips, recordings, field trips, maps, globes, and community resources of all types). Together they provide the information base for social studies programs.

In the selection of any instructional resource, the objectives to be achieved should be uppermost in the mind of the teacher. The particular resource or material selected should be the one that will move children most effectively in the direction of those objectives. In short, instructional aids, materials, and resources are used to achieve specific purposes. The teacher is encouraged to use a wide range of instructional media for any or all of the following reasons:

1. Not all children learn in the same way; different media are able to appeal to the learning styles of different learners.
2. The reading ranges among children who are randomly selected to form classroom groups are great, averaging three to five years in the lower grades and five to ten years in the middle and upper grades.

3. Each of the media has peculiar strengths and limitations in the way it conveys messages.
4. The impact of a message is likely to be stronger if more than one sensory system is involved in receiving it.
5. Material to be learned varies greatly in its abstractness and complexity.
6. The use of a variety of media has motivating and interest-generating qualities.
7. Teaching modes that stress inquiry and problem solving require extensive information searches and sources.
8. Different sources may provide different insights on the same subject; there may be discrepancies or inaccuracies that go undetected if a single source is used.

Instructional materials need to be evaluated carefully before, during, and after they have been used. It is not a good policy to use any and all materials simply because they are available. The quality of the material or resource should be a primary consideration in deciding on its use. Maps that are out of date, films that are of poor quality, pictures that are inaccurate, or field trips that are poorly guided, for example, might better not be used at all.

The maximum value of any instructional resource requires skillful use on the part of the teacher. No instructional material is entirely self-teaching—all require a teacher to set the stage for learning to take place. A first-rate textbook in the hands of an unimaginative teacher can be devastating to the social studies program. The same book used by another teacher can become one of the most valuable resources available to the class. Materials of instruction can be no better than the teachers who use them.

Textbooks

The policy of school districts that calls for furnishing free of charge the same basic textbook for every child in a class is based on the legal principles of equal treatment and equality of opportunity. For this reason, textbooks are widely used and will doubtless continue to be widely used for years to come. It is apparent from their widespread acceptance that most teachers, especially those in grades three and above, perceive the textbook as a valuable teaching tool in social studies. It is important, therefore, for the beginning teacher to learn how to make the best use of these books.

Textbook development has tended to be consistent with changes in curriculum and teaching methods. Modern textbooks are attractive, inviting, a pleasure to look at and to read. There is better use of maps and visual materials; some social studies textbooks for elementary grades boast of at least one illustration on every page, many of the illustrations in color. Multiple authorship is common, with at least one author being a specialist in elementary education. This has served to retain high scholarly accuracy as well as to refine and improve the format and reading level of the books.

Significant changes are apparent in the treatment of racial and ethnic groups and of women. In general, there has been substantial headway in presenting social reality more accurately in modern social studies textbooks.

Social studies textbooks almost always present problems of reading difficulty even though they are written at a level that is suitable for the average reader. The reason for this is that these books are designed to deal with substantive content, and this means that the terms and concepts relating to that subject matter must be used in explaining the ideas presented. For example, a book may be treating a topic such as *trade and commerce*. This subject cannot be meaningfully presented without including at least some of the following concepts and terms: *cargo, tariff, import, duty, international markets, ports, interdependence, hold, tonnage, trade, freight, shipping, stevedore, merchant, commercial, barge.* If these terms are eliminated from the selection to simplify the reading task, it is no longer an essay on trade and commerce. It is the complexity and frequency of concepts that often make reading social studies textbooks difficult, and there is no way this problem can be overcome entirely. An easy-to-read textbook is probably not a good social studies text because its purpose should be to provide information rather than be a simple storybook.

Textbook authors assume that the teacher will guide and direct children in their use of the book. Textbooks are highly condensed and factual presentations and are written with the thought that teachers will supplement and enrich the presentation through the use of other materials. Moreover, texts are not meant to be entirely self-instructing, and if children use them without guidance from the teacher, much of their value may be lost. This is especially true of accompanying visual material in the form of pictures, maps, charts, cartoons, graphs, and study helps.

Textbooks are written to be used as information sourcebooks and are not intended to become the social studies curriculum. They can be used in a variety of ways, and individual children may make different uses of the same book. For one child it may constitute a reading resource, for another child the illustrations may be more valuable, for a third child the map materials may be needed, and for a fourth child it may be a source of ideas for additional study. Similarly, different teachers may choose to make different uses of the same book, depending on their skill, experience, or method of teaching. Teachers are encouraged to make such differential use of textbooks rather than to "cover" the content uniformly and require children to "master" all the facts presented.

If the teacher keeps in mind that no single book can meet adequately the reading needs of all children in the class, the textbook can be a useful tool in teaching social studies. Four of the most common uses of the textbook are for (1) exploratory reading; (2) gathering data related to the topic; (3) map, chart, graph, or picture study; and (4) summarization of learning.

What does a teacher look for in selecting a textbook? From the teacher's point of view, the most important criterion would seem to be *usability*. The book has to fit the teacher's style of teaching if it is to be used well. This means that the text has to be constructed in such a way that it lends itself to flexible use. A book that can be used in only one teaching mode or stresses only one approach to social studies is generally less useful than one that can be adapted to a variety of teaching modes. Readability always has to be an important consideration, and it is significant that one of the frequent criticisms of social studies texts is that they are hard to read. Good social studies texts include study aids; such study aids should facilitate learning the content and skills and, at the same time, encourage good study habits.

Many good social studies textbooks are available today. Some are better suited for certain purposes than others. Some more accurately reflect current curriculum developments than do others. Those who are charged with responsibility of making the selection should develop their own criteria for evaluating textbooks in social studies, but they will probably want to look critically at the following points:

1. *Authorship*—to ensure scholarly accuracy as well as suitability for use with elementary schoolchildren in terms of interest and appeal, reading gradation, and curricular consideration. How is the author identified with elementary school social studies?

2. *Treatment of Content*—to ensure adequate treatment of important concepts in sufficient depth as opposed to highly descriptive factual accounts or storybook approaches to significant content. Is subject matter selected from a broad range of sources, including history, the social sciences, the humanities, and science? Does the book provide readers with a global perspective? Is there a good balance in the treatment of objectives dealing with subject matter, skills, and values and attitudes? Are topics presented from diverse cultural perspectives? Does the book present realistic representations of societies both in prose and in illustrations? Does the book deal with ethnic minorities and women in a realistic way? Is there evidence of stereotyping or tokenism or both in the illustrations?

3. *Format and General Appearance*—to ensure an interesting and appealing book of proper size with good-quality binding and suitable type size. Are illustrations functional or simply decorative?

4. *Organization*—to ensure the book's harmony with the existing curricular pattern and see that it meets the needs of the instructional program within which it will be used. Is the book organized in a way to encourage good study habits?

5. *Visual Materials*—to ensure colorful, accurate illustrations of sufficient number and size. Are these related to the text or included only to enhance the attractiveness of the book?

6. *Instructional Aids*—to ensure their being an integral part of the text itself and of such nature as to be genuinely helpful to the teacher. Do study aids help explain and extend the meaning of important ideas?

7. *Literary Quality*—to ensure that the book is as well written as it can be consistent with the basic purposes of a textbook.

Other Learning Resources and Media

The numerous resources and media in addition to textbooks that contribute to a vital social studies program for children are discussed in context in other sections of this text. For example, the use of maps, globes, charts, cartoons, posters, and graphs is singled out for attention in chapter 6. Other resources are discussed in connection with the teaching of history, geography, and other topics throughout the text.

Computers in Social Studies

The use of computers in education has been promoted so vigorously that it is estimated that, by the end of this decade, microcomputers will be a part of the instructional media of all schools. It is presumed, therefore, that the preservice preparation of teachers will familiarize them with the basic knowledge and skills needed to operate a computer, an ability currently referred to as *computer literacy.* In the social studies, as in other curricular areas, the challenge to the teacher is to integrate the use of this new technology into the ongoing instructional program of the classroom.

One of the major differences between the computer and other instructional media is that the computer has the capacity to *interact* with the student. The computer does not simply present the material to be learned as is the case with a film, filmstrip, or a recording. The computer requires the operator to *do something* in order for the process to proceed. This interactive characteristic of computers necessitates the active involvement of the learner. This has many implications for the pacing of instruction and for individualizing learning. For example, with conventional instructional materials, the program of what is to be learned is fixed. Only the time allowed to complete it can be varied from one student to the next. The computer, however, has the capacity to diagnose an individual learner's knowledge of the subject or skill, to call up a program appropriate for the learner, and to adjust the complexity of the presentation accordingly.

In the social studies, the contribution of computer-assisted instruction (CAI) falls into the following four categories:

1. Using the computer to obtain needed information (data). There is a growing number of collections of data, known as *databases,* many of which are relevant to social studies. These databases will one day include most, if not all, of what is now found in libraries, government document centers, encyclopedias, and other information collections. The new CD-ROM technology (Compact Disc-Read Only Memory) is making all this possible today. This is a durable disk about five inches in

diameter that can store the equivalent of at least 220,000 pages of text, including music, animation, speeches, maps, and photographs.[7]

2. Using the computer to practice and apply social studies skills such as map reading, graph reading, chart interpretation, thinking, and problem solving. Simulated "town meetings" are available, too, that engage students in discussion and decision making related to public issues. The emphasis in the classroom use of computers should be to develop conceptual understanding and problem-solving competence.

3. Using the computer for tutorial assistance in providing a sequential program for the development and elaboration of concepts and knowledge that all students are expected to learn. These are essentially courses of study that have been programmed for the computer. So-called *courseware* is available for such social studies topics as the Constitution, basic economics, and United States history, but most courseware has been geared to the secondary school level.

This is a rapidly evolving field, so the teacher is advised to use the most current lists and reviews of available computer resources. These can be found in two periodicals published by the National Council for the Social Studies, *Social Education* and *Social Studies and the Young Learner*. School libraries ought to carry both of these. In chapters 5 and 14 of this text, we review samples of the many interesting software programs now available for helping to teach history, civics, and geography.

DISCUSSION QUESTIONS AND SUGGESTED ACTIVITIES

1. Select three unit topics from the following list, and provide examples of five concepts that might be included in such units. Then, using two or more of the concepts you have identified, write a generalization that expresses a valid relationship between them that is relevant to each of the topics you have selected.

   People Change the Earth (K–8)

   School Living (K)

   Families and Their Needs (1)

   The Shopping Center (2)

   Life in the City (3)

   Our Home State (4)

   The Westward Movement (5)

---

[7]Joseph A. Braun, Jr., "Media Corner," *Social Studies and the Young Learner* 4 (September/October 1991): 25–29.

Crossroads of the World: The Middle East (6–7)

Colonial America (8)

2. Interview individually four or five children from a grade in which you have a special interest to determine their understanding of selected social studies concepts. Use a straightforward procedure and everyday concepts. For example, you might ask, "What does the term *prejudice* mean to you? Can you give me some examples of prejudice?" (or use *history, justice, cooperation, democracy, long ago, the future,* or geographical terms such as *environment, plateau,* or *rain forest*). These interviews will provide you with firsthand knowledge of what it means to transform an otherwise complex idea into a form that is sensible for elementary schoolchildren. Write up your findings to share with classmates, parents or, perhaps, potential employers.

3. Select a grade of your choice. Suggest units for that grade that would make use of two of the six concept teaching/learning strategies discussed in this chapter. Select one from the strategies for helping students learn an initial concept and one from the extension strategies.

4. What are the essential differences between how one teaches concepts and how one teaches skills?

5. Use the left side of Figure 2-2 and apply each of the points to a skill of your choice for a grade in which you have a special interest. Share your example with others in class.

6. Provide examples of content and content-related skills that you believe are important for citizens to know, using the criteria listed in this chapter. Why do you think there is such widespread disagreement over what is essential knowledge that all citizens should know?

7. Today the individual citizen has access to information sources that are almost unlimited in the scope of knowledge they can provide. Does this increase or decrease the individual citizen's need to accumulate and store information in his or her own brain? Should the availability of information influence decisions about what is taught in school? Discuss and provide examples to support your points.

8. What are your reactions to the following?
Ms. Dickens always insisted that students understand details. Some children even knew entire passages by heart. Those who were able to write such memorized answers to the questions on her tests were the ones who were given high marks.

9. Select a children's social studies textbook for a grade of your choice. Does the book identify important concepts that students are expected to learn? Where do these appear? Does the book provide any exercises that would help the reader learn concepts and skills?

10. Assume that a teacher were allowed to choose *not* to use a social studies textbook and made such a choice. What provisions would need

to be made for children to get the basic information they need? Would this be easier to do at some grade levels than others? Explain.

SELECTED REFERENCES

BARELL, JOHN. *Teaching for Thoughtfulness*. New York: Longman, 1991.

BECK, ISABEL L., AND MARGARET G. McKEOWN. "Toward Meaningful Accounts in History Texts for Young Learners," *Educational Researcher* 17 (August/September, 1988): 31–39.

BEYER, BARRY K. *Developing a Thinking Skills Program*. Boston: Allyn and Bacon, 1988.

BROWN, W., AND EDWARD L. VOCKELL. *The Computer in the Social Studies Curriculum*. Santa Cruz, CA: Mitchell, 1989.

CAINE, RENATE NUMMELA, AND GEOFFREY CAINE. *Making Connections: Teaching and the Human Brain*. Alexandria, VA: Association for Supervision and Curriculum Development, 1991.

MARTORELLA, PETER H. "Knowledge and Concept Development in Social Studies." In James P. Shaver (ed.), *Handbook of Research on Social Studies Teaching and Learning*, 370–84. New York: Macmillan, 1991.

MARZANO, ROBERT J. ET AL. *Dimensions of Thinking: A Framework for Curriculum and Instruction*. Alexandria, VA: Association for Supervision and Curriculum Development, 1988.

NOVAK, JOSEPH D., AND D. BOB GOWIN. *Learning How to Learn*. Cambridge: Cambridge University Press, 1984.

PARKER, WALTER C. "Teaching an *Idea*." *Social Studies and the Young Learner* 3 (January/February 1991): 11–13.

RESNICK, LAUREN B., AND LEOPOLD E. KLOPFER, (eds.) *Toward a Thinking Curriculum: Current Cognitive Research*. Alexandria, VA: Association for Supervision and Curriculum Development, 1989.

3 | Value, Moral, and Character Education

A class of elementary school children has been studying a unit on the early history of the United States. As a culminating activity, the children have prepared a series of dramatic skits that are being presented to their parents. We enter the classroom as the children, dressed in appropriate costumes, are dramatizing the origin of our country's flag. A committee headed by George Washington is meeting with Betsy Ross in her home. The time is June 1776, scarcely a month before the signing of the Declaration of Independence. The place is Philadelphia. George Washington speaks first.

G. Washington: Mrs. Ross, now that we are soon to be an independent nation, we will need a flag for our country. George Ross is a member of our committee and an uncle of your late husband. He told us that you sew very well; that you would be able to make our new country's flag.

B. Ross: I would be honored to try, General Washington. It is true that I am a seamstress, but I have never made a flag before. What did you have in mind?

G. Washington: We brought a design with us. The flag should have red and white stripes. Thirteen of them. One for each state. It should also have thirteen stars on a blue background.

B. Ross: I see your stars have six points, General Washington. I think stars with five points look better.

G. Washington: Well, you do what you think is best, Mrs. Ross. The flag will have to be approved by the Continental Congress. The Congress does want the flag to have the colors red, white, and blue. We will check back with you in a few weeks. Goodbye, Mrs. Ross.

B. Ross: Goodbye, General Washington.

Each year skits such as the one just described are repeated in hundreds of classrooms throughout the country—Pilgrims celebrating the first Thanksgiving, a meeting of the Iroquois League, a wagon train family along the Oregon Trail, rancho life in early California, plantation life in

61

antebellum days. How does one evaluate these activities in terms of social studies education? Although the dramatizations may be based on actual historical incidents, the details of the representations are probably inaccurate. Is that important? Should teachers involve children in them? What purposes do such activities serve?

From a strictly pedagogical point of view, these activities have two important values. First, they are highly motivating for children. Children enjoy being involved in plays and pageants, and their natural interest in dramatic play can be used as a powerful vehicle when used in school learning. Second, the use of a dramatic activity to recreate a situation under study gives children tangible purposes for doing their information gathering. The children do their research to be able to recreate the situation as accurately as possible through dramatic representation. In the process they accumulate important background information about the subject under study.

But beyond their usefulness as teaching vehicles, activities of this type make a lasting impression on the affective development of children. When asked to recall their elementary school social studies program, adults most often mention experiences that were distinctly affective—a skit on George Washington's birthday in one of the primary grades, a play about Harriet Tubman and the Underground Railroad in the fifth grade, or those moving stories of courage and bravery that some teacher read to the class. These experiences are important because they provide ways for children to become acquainted with those common values, attitudes, and ideals that go into the making of our national character. They also provide important foundations for the moral and character development of children.

The attachment to and internalization of common core values by individual members is an essential requirement for stable social life in a society. In a society with such a diversity of cultural legacies and origins as ours, the task of educating children in these common values and attitudes becomes both more challenging and more critical than it is in a more culturally homogeneous society. In a diverse society, the core values serve as the moral bonds that unite individuals and make of them a community. The process of socializing children for life in the common culture begins in the home but is continued and extended in the school, particularly in social studies education. Such education involves inculcation of values and related beliefs, the development of character, and the moral development of children. The dramatizations and skits described earlier call attention to those values and human traits that society likes to see in its citizens.

THE LANGUAGE OF AFFECTIVE EDUCATION

Affective education is a generic term that includes a variety of educational activities associated with the development of feelings and emotions. The well-known taxonomy of Krathwohl, Bloom, and Masia describes five levels of objectives in the affective domain: receiving, responding, valuing, organization, and characterization.[1] Affective education includes the study of the arts and humanities but is also related to the development of a system of values, attitudes, and beliefs, to the development of character, and to moral development.

(handwritten margin note: important)

Values can be defined as standards that individuals and social groups use to judge the worth of some behavior or some thing. Values are criteria that can be applied in making decisions. Values are associated with those things we perceive to be right and desirable. Values define for us what is worth striving for, what is preferred, what constitutes worthy life goals, what may be worth sacrificing one's life for. Values are abstract conceptions and, therefore, cannot be observed directly. We assume the influence of certain values by the way one behaves. Raths, Harmin, and Simon suggest seven criteria for defining a value, all of which must be present:[2]

(handwritten margin note: repeating shows the value is instilled)

1. *choosing freely* (This means that the individual is not coerced, pressured, or unduly influenced by others in making the choice. Choices made because they are suggested by the teacher or parents or as a result of peer pressure are not ones that are freely made.)
2. *choosing from among alternatives* (To make a choice, one must have available at least two options. If there is only one option, and the individual is required to participate in the activity, there can be no choice.)
3. *choosing after thoughtful consideration of consequences* (This requirement rules out decisions made on impulse or on the "spur of the moment" because such choices cannot be said to represent one's values. Value-based decisions are arrived at thoughtfully with a full knowledge of the consequences insofar as they can be determined in advance.)
4. *prizing and cherishing* (This means that the person is pleased with the choice that was made.)
5. *affirming* (Because the individual is pleased with the choice, he or she says so. The affirmations are made freely and publicly.)
6. *acting on choices* (This is based on the ancient truth that actions speak louder than words. People act in accordance with what they value.)
7. *repeating* (When behavior is value based, it is consistent, and the individual will repeat it. Such behavior can be reliably predicted. For example, if an individual "loves to read," he or she will not read just one book but will continue reading many books throughout his or her lifetime.)

In terms of orderly social life, it is essential that most members of a society embrace those core values on which there is general consensus and lead their lives in accordance with them. It is important to note, however, that there is a big difference between knowing the *content* of social values

---

[1]David R. Krathwohl, Benjamin S. Bloom, and Bertrum B. Masia, *Taxonomy of Educational Objectives—Handbook II: Affective Domain* (New York: David McKay, 1964), 95.

[2]Louis E. Raths, Merrill Harmin, and Sidney B. Simon, *Values and Teaching: Working with Values in the Classroom*, 2d ed. (Columbus, Ohio: Charles E. Merrill, 1978), 28–29. Explanations in parentheses are not quoted material.

Beliefs & Commitment

and leading one's life in correspondence with them. The term *beliefs* often appears in the literature of affective education. Beliefs can be defined as *commitments* to certain values. There is a direct connection between one's belief system and one's commitment to specific values.

An *attitude* is an inclination or a predisposition to respond in a particular way. Attitudes are based on one's values and beliefs. To say that one has a "prejudiced attitude" is redundant, because an attitude is a prejudice, but it may have positive or negative value connotations. Thus, if educational programs are targeted to reduce racial prejudice in society, the programs have to be geared to deal with attitude changes in learners. This means that such programs will need to deal fundamentally with changing learners' values and beliefs related to various racial groups.

Moral development has to do with educating children in modes of conduct that are desired by society. Although the term *morality* is sometimes defined narrowly to mean only sexual behavior, it is a much broader concept. While there are moral values related to sexual behavior (we value commitment over promiscuity, for example), there also are moral values related to political participation (one should), stealing (one should not), racial prejudice (it should not be tolerated in oneself or others), and so on. Moral development includes not only knowing which values are accepted by the social group but also living accordingly. When we speak of people being faced with a "moral dilemma," we refer to situations in which the person is forced to choose between two alternatives, both of which may be right but in either case the unselected option results in unpleasant consequences. For example, a man might be presented with an opportunity for a well-paying job on an oil rig in the North Atlantic. As a father of four children, he has had erratic employment in West Texas for the past three years and he is deeply in debt. He badly needs the money that he could earn on the North Atlantic job. But if he takes it, he has to agree to a two-year assignment. He is deeply devoted to his family, and a two-year separation from them would be heartbreaking for him and for his wife and children. Should he take the job? Clearly, this conflict in his personal values must be resolved if he is to make a decision with which he will feel comfortable.

The test of one's moral maturity comes in the everyday choices in day-to-day living. Most people have no problem with those choices that are clearly wrong or clearly right. But it is in the gray areas that one is confronted with genuine moral dilemmas. Moreover, the strength of one's moral conduct is not known unless it is put to the test. The person who lives in a protected environment, sheltered from the necessity of making moral choices, may lead a virtuous life because he or she has not faced the need to consider alternatives and, therefore, is never confronted with a genuine moral challenge.

true!

The term *character* is a summarizing concept that speaks to an individual's reputation as one who embraces those values and beliefs cherished by society and who has the moral strength to live in accordance with them.

Character education has been a consistent goal of public school education in this century, much of it falling in the purview of social studies. These programs represented affirmative efforts to promote certain moral virtues and traits such as truthfulness, self-discipline, consideration for others, and trustworthiness. Earlier efforts used direct methods of instruction, focused on specific character traits, and used instructional resources that carried strong moral messages. More recent efforts stressed indirect teaching strategies with more subtle moral and ethical instruction. In general, programs in character education have not received enthusiastic support from the social science intellectual community mainly because historically these programs have relied on indoctrination and exhortation rather than inquiry, analysis, and informed choice.

VALUES EDUCATION

Values education is concerned with both *general* values and *personal* values. Such values as liberty, justice, equality, honesty, consideration for others, individualism, human dignity, responsibility, and truthfulness are examples of general values on which there is consensus. This does not mean that everyone has the same values or interprets them in the same way. But there is general agreement that such values reflect the basic orientation of the society. These values are a part of our political and religious heritages. They are incorporated in our great historical documents and in our legal and judicial systems. They are apparent in our folklore and in our literature. Individuals who lead exemplary lives that reflect such general values are extolled as national heroes.

If children are to be socialized in accordance with these general values of society, they must be provided with examples of behavior that illustrate these values in action. That is, young people need to have encounters with idealized types–persons who illustrate by their way of life the values that society rewards and likes to see in its citizens. It is because these general values are internalized by the majority of citizens that orderly social life can take place. We expect our fellow citizens to behave in ways that are predictable and consistent with the basic premises inherent in those values on which there is general consensus. Law enforcement agencies are provided to protect society from the minority of persons who cannot or will not live in accordance with the general values embraced by the majority. But no police force could possibly monitor the behavior of all citizens if they were not willing to comply voluntarily with the accepted rules of the society.[3] We are able to enjoy social order because a large majority of citizens have internalized general values on which there is accordance.

---

[3]The chaos that has prevailed in Lebanon, and in several other Middle Eastern countries, in recent years is not precisely an example of this point, but it does illustrate vividly what happens to a nation when there is an absence of social order.

Children should not wait until middle and upper grades to begin learning about the democratic way of life. Carol Hamilton Cobb, recipient of the Elementary School Teacher of the Year Award from the National Council for the Social Studies in 1985, routinely has her *kindergartners* vote in local and presidential elections. On the left, Mrs. Cobb helps children complete their voter registration cards in the classroom. We then see children voting at two polling places in the school building.

Photos courtesy of Carol Hamilton Cobb, Gateway School, Metropolitan Nashville, Tennessee, Public Schools.

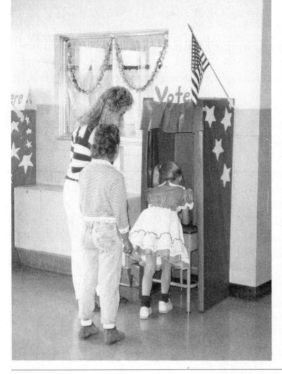

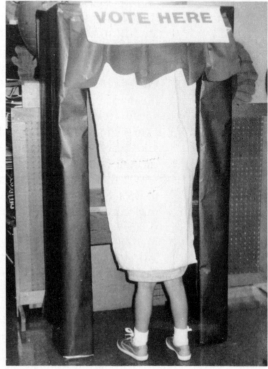

Lesson plan 1 on page 68, dealing with symbolic values, provides a good example of a lesson based on general values. General values are promoted through social studies in the following ways:

1. Daily life in the classroom that stresses consideration for others, freedom and equality, independence of thought, individual responsibility for one's actions, and the dignity of individual human beings.
2. The study of the history and development of this country stressing the ideals that inspired it and showing that a continuing effort is needed to move reality closer to those ideals.
3. The study of biographies of individuals whose lives reflect the general values of the nation.
4. The study of law and the legal and justice systems.
5. The celebration of holidays that reinforce values and ideals associated with the holiday.
6. Thoughtful analysis of the meaning of such statements as the Pledge of Allegiance, the Preamble to the Constitution, and the Bill of Rights.
7. Building awareness of situations that are not in accord with values to which this society is committed.
8. Cross-cultural studies to illustrate differences in values from one society to another.

As we move from general values to *personal* values, the role of social studies becomes considerably different and, to some extent, less clear. Personal values are those values that influence the decision making of individuals in their own personal lives. To some extent they represent individual interpretations of general values, that is, the integrating of general values in the personal life of each individual. However, they do refer simply to what individuals like or want to do — preferring films to television, blue to yellow, bicycling to jogging.

Modern life involves an incredible amount of choice making: how to spend our time, what career to choose, what clothes to buy and to wear, where to live, what brand products to buy, what hobbies and leisure-time activities to pursue, and how to spend our money. The list could go on and on to include literally every facet of our lives. In each of these decisions, there are probably no absolutely right and wrong choices in the sense that basic general values are being compromised by either choice. Rather, these decisions are expressions of individual preferences. When selecting an automobile, one person buys a blue Ford sedan; another, a yellow Chevrolet stationwagon; and a third, a red Dodge Caravan. To ask which is *right* is inappropriate because right and wrong in the absolute sense are not issues in such choice making. This is really what personal values are all about — choice making concerning our personal lives.

It should be obvious that the social studies program cannot promote personal values in the same way that it can promote general values. What social studies *can* do is to help children think about the choices they make in terms of a values framework. This is often referred to in current literature as *values clarification* or the "process of valuing." Raths, Harmin, and

Lesson Plan 1

Topic:	Symbolic messages
Grade:	Six
Time:	One class period
Objectives:	Children will deduce certain information about a country from symbols placed on its coins. Children will relate the symbols to basic values of that country.
Resources:	At least one coin for each child, preferably coins or facsimiles of coins, from several different nations.
Lesson Development:	**TEACHER:** Boys and girls, for the past few days we have been studying the use of signs and symbols. At the close of our discussion yesterday we came to an important conclusion. What was it? **CHILD:** We said that we could tell what people considered to be important to them by the symbols and signs they use on their buildings. **TEACHER:** Yes. Now today you will have a chance to test that idea in a slightly different way. Each of you will be given a coin to use. Study the coin carefully and see how many things you can tell about the country just from what you see on the coin. Coins are distributed to the class. After they have had time to make their observations, ask the children what they have concluded. As these are presented, write them on the chalkboard. Have each child tell *why* the conclusion was made. Pass the coins about for other children to inspect. Items such as the following may surface in this discussion:

Simon suggest that if adults seek to help children in the process of valuing, they should

1. Encourage children to make more choices and to make them freely.
2. Help them discover alternatives when faced with choices.
3. Help children weigh alternatives thoughtfully, reflecting on the consequences of each.
4. Encourage children to consider what it is that they prize and cherish.
5. Give them opportunities to affirm their choices.
6. Encourage them to act, behave, live in accordance with their choices.
7. Help them be aware of repeated behaviors or patterns in their life.[4]

Children need experiences in which they are confronted with a conflict of values, both of which are attractive, but a choice has to be made between them. These choices are between or among "goods" rather than between or among something that is desirable and something that is not. Similarly, the choice is *not* between options that are illegal, unethical, or contrary to social

---

[4]Raths et al., *Values and Teachings*, 38.

These people believe in God.

They want (or believe in) liberty.

They are able to read their language.

Men must be more important than women in this country.

They construct large buildings.

They speak more than one language.

It is an old country.

They have a queen (or king).

They are a peace-loving people.

They are proud of their wars and war heroes.

They want people to be courageous.

Side 1

Followup: Imagine that the United States is planning to issue a new coin and there is a contest to get the best design. You decide to enter the contest. The rules are these:

1. Write down two ideas that best describe what people in our country think are important to them.
2. Think of and draw symbols that could be used on a coin to show these two qualities.

Side 2

norms. Value clarification exercises that probe the sensitive, personal, psychological space of youngsters present serious psychological and ethical problems and are not recommended for use with elementary school children.

Almost any subject, topic, situation, or picture can be used to explore values. Questions of the following type are suggested to elicit value responses for discussion:

classroom scenarios it's our daily life that's real life hard

1. If you return someone's lost billfold, do you think you deserve a reward?
2. Do you think you would like a job like that?
3. How would you like to live in such a place?
4. If you won a cash prize of $100, what would you do with it?
5. How did you feel when you read that paragraph?
6. If you could change *one* thing about this community to make it a better place to live, what would you change?
7. If the principal dismissed everyone at noon today and you could do anything you wanted this afternoon, what would you choose to do?
8. What do you think are the three most important qualities of a person who is president of the United States?

9. Can you name three decisions about which you think you ought to have something to say? Why do you think you should have something to say about these decisions?
10. Can you think of some person you really admire? Why do you admire that person?

Expressing value preferences is a normal part of everyday life. Everyone makes choices based on values several times each day. Valuing exercises simply build an awareness of the value dimension of the choices we make. In the day-to-day work of the class, the teacher can use many situations to build such a consciousness of values and thereby get children to think more deeply about what is important to them.

MORAL AND CHARACTER EDUCATION

Educational goals having to do with moral and character education have been an important component of the educational enterprise even before the founding of the republic. Indeed, efforts to achieve such goals were more apparent in the practices of public schools in the nineteenth and early twentieth centuries than they are today. American schools were not unique in this regard. Edward A. Wynne refers to this practice as the "great tradition" and points out that, "The transmission of moral values has been the dominant educational concern of most cultures throughout history."[5]

The public schools of this nation operate as secular rather than religious institutions, and, consequently, the source of moral authority has had to be found in such imperatives of social organization as social order, justice, and the concept of the social contract. As a result, conventional approaches to moral and character education have focused on specific virtues and character traits to be developed. Historically, moral messages were conveyed to children through direct instruction, using stories or case studies to illustrate the harsh consequences that flowed from violations of the moral code. Although the presentations were made within a secular context, it is obvious that what was being transmitted was a code of Christian ethics and virtues.

This method of moral and character education was dealt a serious blow by research conducted between 1928 and 1930 by Hartshorne and May and published as a book entitled *Studies in Deceit*.[6] These studies reported that character education as conducted in schools had little effect on the moral behavior of individuals as measured by objective tests of honesty, service, altruism, and self-control. The findings led the researchers to conclude that it was the situation that confronted the individual that made the difference

---

[5]Edward A. Wynne, "The Great Tradition in Education: Transmitting Moral Values," *Educational Leadership* 43 (December 1985–January 1986): 4.
[6]Hugh Hartshorne and Mark A. May, *Studies in Deceit* (New York: Macmillan, 1928).

in the kind of moral choice that was made. Following the publication of the results of these studies there was something of a thirty-year hiatus in moral and character education in public schools.

Alternatives to the traditional methods of moral and character education have emerged in recent years. The search for effective ways to inculcate basic values that lead to desirable moral conduct and character, and, at the same time, doing so in ways that do not compromise democratic principles, continues to the present time. The strategies that have received the most attention in recent years have taken two directions: one focuses on some variation of value analysis; the other builds on the "stage theory" of moral development. The value analysis thrust is best illustrated by the work of Raths, Harmin, and Simon dealing with value clarification and the valuing process, discussed in the previous section of this chapter. The research of the late Lawrence Kohlberg and his associates is the most widely cited example of work dealing with stages of moral development.[7] Though promising, these procedures have not been sufficiently well developed—nor accepted—to be given an unqualified recommendation as strategies for moral and character education.

Moral Reasoning

Kohlberg and his associates theorized that people's ability to reason about right and wrong moves through a sequence of developmental stages. At succeeding stages, an individual will grapple in more mature ways with moral dilemmas. In the earliest stages, moral reasoning is characterized by attention to the immediate consequences of behavior. It is wrong to do something if you get punished for doing it; the same action is right if you do not. For example, cheating is wrong when you get caught; it is right when you get away with it. In higher stages, social approval guides moral reasoning. "What will the neighbors think?" and "What will my friends (family; coworkers) think?" become the most important questions when considering what action to take. Also, strict obedience to laws and rules for their own sake is paramount. The question "Why should you obey the law?" is, therefore, answered with circular reasoning: "Because it's the law."

At the highest stages, one's reasoning shifts again, this time to principles. Now, right and wrong are disentangled from what friends or family may think, even from law and from the norms of acceptability in one's own ethnic group. One's moral allegiance, instead, is directed toward *principles.* When someone really understands the principle of equality, for example, he or she may take a stand against racial or gender prejudice even though friends and neighbors practice it routinely. People capable of reasoning at the principled level can for the first time in their lives fully comprehend principled documents such as the *Declaration of Independence* and the *Bill of*

---

[7]Lawrence Kohlberg, *The Philosophy of Moral Development: Moral Stages and the Idea of Justice* (New York: Harper & Row, 1981).

Rights, and they can understand when it is right to break the law, as did Thomas Jefferson, Rosa Parks, Mohandas K. Gandhi, and countless other reformists: when the law is wrong. But how did these people *know* when the law was wrong? They knew because they had achieved a level of moral maturity with which they could perceive those principles of fairness—those "inalienable rights"—against which the law could be judged. As Mark Twain said, honor is more difficult to master than the law.

According to stage theory, teachers can help children to develop from lower to higher stages of moral reasoning by engaging them in discussions of moral dilemmas. The dilemmas should be those that emerge from school life, from classroom incidents involving cheating, stealing, or lying, for example, or from differences of opinion regarding the fairness of play-ground rules and procedures. Teachers should listen carefully to children's reasoning and encourage them not merely to express their opinions but to give the reasoning behind them, to examine the values implicit in reasons given, and to listen carefully to opposing arguments.

These discussions should be separated from normal classroom routines. Doing so highlights the fact that instruction *per se* has ended for the moment and that a moral discussion among the students will be held. This can be accomplished by having children move to a special seating arrangement (a circle or a double semicircle are best), appointing a discussion leader (the teacher can serve in this role in the primary grades), and clarifying the issue that will be the focus of the discussion.

Of course, conducting successful meetings of this sort requires the teacher and students to lay the groundwork—to identify discussion skills and norms and to practice them; and to reflect back on the meeting at its conclusion, noting its strengths and weaknesses and planning how to improve the discussion the next time around. Chapter 13 treats discussion in greater detail.

Caring.   Feminist scholars Carol Gilligan and Nel Noddings have extended Kohlberg's theories in critically important ways.[8] They have argued that moral reasoning is only one facet of moral development, albeit an important one, and that it alone paints only part of the picture. The part it deals with is abstract and detached from a basic fact of human existence—relationships. The other part of the morality picture has little to do with abstract reasoning or with principles but everything to do with basic human relating, with caring for one another.

On this view, the primary aim in life is not fairness, though that certainly is important. The primary aim, rather, is caring and being cared for. "A life meeting this aim," writes Noddings, "is—despite pain, deprivation, and trouble—filled at least occasionally with joy, wonder, engagement, and

---

[8]Carol Gilligan, *In A Different Voice* (Cambridge, MA: Harvard University Press, 1982). Nel Noddings, *Caring: A Feminine Approach to Ethics and Moral Education* (Berkeley, CA: University of California Press, 1984).

Why "push" children into more mature decisions?

tenderness."[9] Teachers can lead discussions of moral dilemmas in which they try to prompt children into more mature ways of reasoning, to be sure, but they should couple this with carefully constructing a caring environment. This means many things, of course, but it includes modeling for children what it looks and sounds like to care for others, children and adults and pets alike. It means helping children to see the origin of classroom rules in caring. As well, it means "attributing the best motive" to children—assuming that a child's intentions were good even when she or he has done something bad. Making this assumption is a basic act of kindness on the teacher's part, and generally it should be communicated to the child directly. For example, the teacher might take aside a student who has cheated, beginning not with a reprimand or punishment, though these may well come, but with caring, saying, *I know you want to do well.* Likewise, a student who has called another student a cruel name can be taken aside, and the conversation can begin with, *I know you mean to treat others as you want to be treated yourself.*

Direct and Indirect Approaches to Moral Education

The transmission of knowledge and skills is most commonly facilitated through *direct* methods of instruction. The material to be taught is identified, appropriate objectives are specified, and the instruction proceeds step by step toward the attainment of the objectives. Because these procedures work so well in teaching knowledge and knowledge-related skills, we assume that they work equally well for character and moral education. This, however, is not the case. In character and moral education, we are not concerned only that the individual knows social values and can deal with them intellectually. We are concerned fundamentally that the individual's *conduct* reflects those social values. And as every teacher and preacher should know, there is a world of difference between the two. Because one knows what to do and how to behave, it does not necessarily follow that the person will act accordingly. All of the world's great religions admonish their faithful not to kill, steal, lie, and cheat, but people continue to kill, steal, lie, and cheat as they have done for thousands of years. Surely the people about whom the late William V. Shannon wrote are well informed about social values, yet these are not reflected in their character nor in their moral behavior:

> The hollow men are everywhere—on the television screens and in the pulpits, in the banking and brokerage houses, in board rooms and sports arenas. Their distinguishing marks are faces distorted by greed and actions disdainful of law and limits.
>
> Rival preachers struggle for control of lucrative television programs. On Wall Street, speculators bribe investment bankers to obtain inside information

---

[9]Noddings, *Caring*, 174. (Also the following quotation, this paragraph.)

on pending deals. The governor of Texas admits he and fellow trustees bribed youth to play football in defiance of rules. A former Secretary of the Treasury admits he set up a bank in the Bahamas to handle hot money and evade his income taxes. If America goes under, some Edward Gibbon of the future will write our epitaph: 'In the midst of plenty, they died of avarice.'[10]

Because knowledge does not necessarily lead to more ethical and moral behavior, it does not follow that direct instruction on ethics, values, and morals is useless. It means simply that direct instruction is limited in its effectiveness in changing such behavior. Character education and moral development are complex processes that must include many opportunities to experience what is being taught. Eventually the individual must *want* to behave in the expected way; he or she must *willingly comply* whether anyone is watching or not; he or she must *feel uncomfortable* when not behaving in accordance with the value; he or she must have a conscience that guides behavior.

The kinds of learning experiences needed to internalize values that lead to improved ethical and moral behavior should take the form of *indirect* instruction. This has to do with engineering an environment that elicits the desired behavior. There is obvious wisdom in such simple sayings as "values are caught rather than taught" and "actions speak louder than words." Rather than relying only on verbal instruction and precept, indirect strategies instruct by example, by inference, by modeling, by emulating, by imitating, by identifying, by imagining, and by observing. That is why the selection of teachers is so important, especially in the elementary and middle school years. These adults are expected not only to instruct children in knowledge and skills but to provide *examples* and *models* of good character and moral conduct. The classroom and, indeed, the entire school environment should exemplify those values, beliefs, and attitudes that the social studies program expects to see reflected in the conduct of the children who attend it.

The story is told of the person who was so struck by the play *1776* as a statement about freedom and democracy that she was moved to say that all Americans should be *forced* to see it! This is an example of the kinds of inconsistencies we often see in practices related to civic and citizenship education. Is it proper to use undemocratic methods to inculcate the basic social values of a democratic society? The answer to that question depends on the maturity of the learners that are being instructed.

In academic circles, there is a strong bias against anything that smacks of indoctrination. The term "to educate," we are told, is a derivative of a Latin word meaning "to lend out" or "to draw out." Thus, education is a process that *draws out* from the learner, not one that puts something in. Indoctrination and inculcation are, accordingly, not acceptable procedures if one is to "truly educate," especially to educate for life in a democratic society in which individual choice making is a cherished value. Although

---

[10]William V. Shannon, *Boston Globe*, April 5, 1987.

understanding or sensitivity

this perception of education seems attractive from a philosophical point of view, it does not easily convert into a plan of action for the conduct of character and moral education of young children.

The problem here is that a considerable amount of socialization, which is the foundation of character development and moral education, must take place *before* the child is capable of understanding the rationale for moral principles.[11] Teaching normative behavior and developing a sensitivity to what is perceived as right and wrong conduct simply cannot be postponed until the child has reached the "age of reason." The young child will not learn how to act and will not learn how to make judgments about the appropriateness of conduct unless there is adult intervention. The socialization process must begin early in the life of the child and a certain amount of inculcation or indoctrination of norms and values is inevitable. The teacher or the parent, however, must guard against being too heavy-handed in such teaching so as not to destroy the inclination to be critical and must not carry it on too long. As children mature, they need to develop some sense of ownership of the social values they are being asked to internalize. For example, they need to develop the attitude that it is *their* classroom, *their* school, and *their* community, that they are an important part of it, and that what happens there affects them directly. When they share in this investment in their surroundings, they are not apt to think of themselves as outsiders who are simply passing through someone else's "turf." It is at these more advanced levels that children need to think through reasons and rationales, and to have the opportunity to resolve moral dilemmas appropriate to their age level. Thus, in the end, we want children to be socialized into the moral values on which there is general consensus, while at the same time to cultivate their capacity for thoughtful criticism.

THE LEARNING CONTEXT

When it comes to values, beliefs, attitudes, moral, and character education of children, one cannot escape the importance of a social context and the human teacher. Subject matter and skills can often be learned effectively through reading or by means of computer instruction or other sophisticated media. Working with classmates often facilitates the achievement of academic learning goals, but it is not critical to their attainment. Children who live in geographically remote regions may be home schooled and learn the basic subject matter and skills very well. But the kinds of learnings with which this chapter is concerned really need to be taught and learned in a social setting under the guidance of a human teacher. It is the teacher who is responsible for establishing the kind of classroom environment that

[11]Jean Piaget et al., *The Moral Judgment of the Child* (New York: The Free Press, 1965).

[handwritten margin notes: Bottom line / Consistency + / express expectations up front //]

embodies the values that children are expected to learn. It is the teacher who ensures that human relations in the classroom honor and respect the dignity and worth of all human beings. It is the teacher who provides the day-to-day adult model of democratic values in action. And it is the social setting of the classroom environment that provides the laboratory in which values and morals are nurtured and in which the child's character takes shape.

RELIGION AND THE SOCIAL STUDIES

[handwritten margin notes: this would not be sensitivity understood by am value to others followed]

"The schools' silence on religion results in failure to tell students the whole story of human civilization," says a recent publication of the Association for Supervision and Curriculum Development.[12] In keeping with the mandate of the First Amendment, the schools have been diligent in their effort to maintain a separation of church and state. Some observers believe that schools have been overly zealous in removing religion from the schools. As a result, religion is treated as though it does not exist as an important force in shaping the affairs of human beings and their cultures. The First Amendment prohibition is against teaching doctrinal religious beliefs; it does not disallow the *study* of religion as a phenomenon of culture.

Religion is always associated with the inculcation of values and with moral education. Thus, when schools engage in values and moral education, they are, to some extent, invading the domain of religious and family responsibility. Such teaching can easily become controversial because of what is presumed to be the ultimate source of truth and moral authority. Even though it is undoubtedly true that many—perhaps even most— public school teachers have deeply held religious convictions themselves, the public school is a secular institution. Thus, the extent to which it can teach that the affairs of human beings are somehow influenced by the hand of God is limited. Schools do not and, by law, must not promote a religious belief system. When schools engage in problem-solving or thinking activities that are based on values such as human dignity and rationality, rather than on mandates from God, they are judged to be promoting a philosophy of *secular humanism*. Certain religious groups have taken schools to task for teaching "the religion of secular humanism," claiming that this is in violation of the First Amendment. School authorities take the position that schools are simply following a well-established system of validating knowledge using the methods of modern-day science.

The procedures used by schools to teach various aspects of thinking are almost always based on an empirical problem-solving model. Although the process did not originate with the prominent American philosopher and

---

[12]*Religion in the Curriculum.* A Report from the ASCD Panel on Religion in the Curriculum (Alexandria, Virginia: Association for Supervision and Curriculum Development, 1987), 27.

Lesson Plan 2

Topic:	People of Prominence
Grade:	Five
Time:	Variable—three to five class periods
Objective:	Children will develop an awareness of the qualities and traits that characterize persons of prominence.
Interest Building:	Have children list as many names of "famous people"—living or dead—as they can think of in five minutes. Then have them discuss their lists in terms of what the individuals did to make them famous. Do a quick check on the number that were political figures, war heroes, sports figures, etc. Have children speculate on why these particular individuals became well known, whereas most of their contemporaries did not. Tell the class that over the next few days they will study the qualities and traits of famous people more carefully.
Lesson Development:	Have a wide selection of biographies of prominent people available for children. Ask each child to choose one biography to read. The books are to be read in the next week, and children are to answer the following three questions:

1. What did you admire about the person?
2. What qualities did the person have that made him/her come to the attention of others who knew him/her?
3. What did the person do that made him/her famous?

At the completion of the assignment, have children discuss their ideas with classmates in groups of four. Have them try to find qualities or traits that were common to each of the persons about whom they read. Have each group report findings to entire class and discuss. |
| **Summary:** | Generate a list of qualities that (1) applied to all; (2) applied to some; (3) applied to a few; (4) applied to none. Discuss reasons for differences. Solicit individual reactions in terms of how they might apply some of these qualities to their own lives. |
| **Materials:** | Biographies of prominent persons at a reading level suitable for the class, to be secured from the school library.

Ideas for Additional Lessons:

1. Familiarize children with several well-known fables. In groups of four or five, have children dramatize the fable as it was originally written. Then have the children develop another skit illustrating an application of the message of the fable to some aspects of modern life. Discuss.
2. Have children develop a running list of proverbs. Place each proverb on an index card and post on the bulletin board. (*Example:* "The nail that sticks out gets hammered, " "A rolling stone gathers no moss," "Where there's smoke, there's fire," "When pulling weeds, be sure to get rid of the roots.") Have children discuss those they find especially interesting and have them generate examples of applications in ordinary living. Relate the discussion to specific values or moral messages being conveyed in the proverbs. |

educator, John Dewey, he popularized it and brought it to American education through his writing and teaching. This helps explain why critics of the schools even today point to Dewey as the person most responsible for bringing secular humanism to the public schools. It was out of the Dewey book, *How We Think,* that have come the five basic components of problem solving: (1) problem identification; (2) hypothesis formation; (3) data gathering; (4) testing hypotheses in terms of evidence (or data); and (5) drawing conclusions based on evidence.[13]

Conclusions based on scientific problem-solving procedures are accepted tentatively on information available at the time the investigation is made. This leaves the door open to further refinement of explanations and conclusions—or even different explanations or conclusions—at a later time when more information may become available. This procedure stresses the *probability* of something's being true in terms of evidence rather than being true in the *absolute,* unchanging sense. This means that there are no areas closed to further investigation, obviously a point of conflict with those who embrace other ways of knowing. It has also caused some critics to claim that today's schools are teaching so-called New Age practices and beliefs such as moral relativism, guided imagery, progressive relaxation, meditation, and visualization.

those are, of the "religions" of today.

Scientific problem-solving procedures are exceedingly powerful weapons in the battle against ignorance. It is no exaggeration to say that knowledge breakthroughs that have made possible modern science, technology, and medicine can be attributed to this system of thinking. But the method has also given rise to some of the most bitter conflicts among schools and parents and communities. Some parents object to the questioning of authority and to the idea of the tentativeness of knowledge. To put it simply, some believe that there are at least a few absolute truths that must be accepted as "givens," and that the authority supporting those truths should not be questioned, especially by children. The conflict becomes most severe if parents perceive the school's teaching as jeopardizing the child's belief in God as the ultimate authority.

Teachers cannot ignore the fact that a large segment of our population believes that revealed truth is a legitimate way of knowing—that is, that God revealed truth to human beings either through written accounts (such as the Bible or the Koran) or through holy persons who were especially commissioned to make these truths known to others. It does not matter in the slightest what the teacher's personal views on this matter are; the fact is that seated in the public school classrooms of this nation are hundreds of thousands, perhaps millions, of children who, to some extent, are taught the validity of revealed truth, and to fail to take this into account in school instruction is a mistake.

Where, then, does this leave the teacher who is serious about wanting to teach critical thinking and other intellectual skills to students? Does this

---

[13]John Dewey, *How We Think* (Boston: D.C. Heath, 1933), 106.

mean that teaching for independent thinking must be done only passively or clandestinely and that it cannot be pursued affirmatively as an instructional goal? Certainly not; but the teacher needs to know that the matter remains an *issue* in education. This means that it is the context of the local school community that will govern the guidelines to be followed in teaching thinking and problem-solving procedures. The matter will continue to be discussed and debated by professionals and laypersons in the years ahead. Meanwhile, it is the responsibility of public school teachers to help children develop ways of thinking that characterize an educated and thoughtful citizenry. At the same time, teachers must be sensitive to the fact that there is so much about which we know so little; for many people, ways of knowing other than scientific problem solving appear to be more appropriate in dealing with those unknowns. The individual's right to embrace other paths to those unknowns must be respected.

Quite apart from the connection of religion with values and moral education, the study of religion as a social phenomenon constitutes a legitimate area of inquiry for social studies. Indeed, studying religion and its impact on the lives of people is likely to become more widespread in the years ahead.[14] Religion has had and continues to have a tremendous impact on history, human affairs, and the humanities. We need go no farther than the daily news to learn about present-day religious conflicts in Northern Ireland, the Middle East, India and Sri Lanka. The challenge to teachers will be to make religion a natural part of the social studies topics studied and to deal with the subject sensitively. This means that teachers will need to become knowledgeable about the various religions of people studied, and how the lives of those people are affected by their religious beliefs. Closer to home, today's teachers will also need to know more about the diverse religions embraced by the families of the children in their classrooms.

DISCUSSION QUESTIONS AND SUGGESTED ACTIVITIES

1. In recalling your own elementary and middle school social studies experiences, what values did your teachers stress? What activities do you remember that were particularly values oriented? Would such activities be worthwhile for today's children? Why or why not?

2. The use of plays and pageants is sometimes criticized, or even ridiculed, because such activities are not consistent with what the critic perceives as the true mission of schools. Do you think such criticism is soundly based? Discuss.

3. As you think about the world in which today's children live, can you think of situations they encounter or experiences they have that either

---

[14]Carol Chmelynski, "Religion Makes a Comeback in the Classroom," *School Board News* 22 (November 12, 1991): 8.

reinforce or contradict character traits being promoted by the social studies program? What implications do you see in this for the teacher?

4. Examine report cards used by schools in your area. How do they report to parents on the learnings discussed in this chapter? If a checklist of traits is used, are the items stated in a negative or a positive way? Is the emphasis on building conformity or independence?

5. Select a nontext children's book that might be especially useful in illustrating a general value. Explain why you selected the one you did. Develop a set of values-oriented questions you would want children to respond to after they have read the book.

6. Why do you think parents often react negatively when the school deals with the development of personal values in children? Suggest guidelines that a teacher can use to handle personal values in ways that are educationally and ethically acceptable.

7. What values are being promoted when children engage in activities that symbolize patriotism, such as saying the Pledge of Allegiance? What are the advantages and limitations in using symbolic exercises to promote values?

8. What indicators might a teacher look for to determine whether his or her work with children in the area of moral and character education is being effective? Do this for a grade in which you have a special interest.

9. Think about your own K–12 social studies experience as a student in terms of how your teachers handled the role of religion in the lives of people. Would your experience validate the quote that began this chapter's discussion of religion? What are *your* views on how the subject of religion should be included in social studies units?

10. Think of episodes in American history that are interpreted differently by various ethnic, cultural, or special-interest groups. Explain how differing values influence these interpretations. Is it possible to establish the validity of differing interpretations of what is presumed once to have been an objective reality?

SELECTED REFERENCES

ASSOCIATION FOR SUPERVISION AND CURRICULUM DEVELOPMENT. *Moral Education in the Life of the School.* Alexandria, VA: author, 1988.

BENNINGA, JACQUES S., ed. *Moral Education and Civic Education in the Elementary School.* New York: Teachers College Press, Columbia University, 1991.

BYRNES, DEBORAH A. "Children and Prejudice." *Social Education* 52 (April/May 1988): 267–71.

CARTER, ROBERT E. *Dimensions of Moral Education.* Toronto: University of Toronto Press, 1984.

GILLIGAN, CAROL, *In A Different Voice.* Cambridge, MA: Harvard University Press, 1982.

HAYNES, CHARLES C. *Religion in American History: What to Teach and How.* Alexandria, VA: Association for Supervision and Curriculum Development, 1990.

HOFFMAN, ALAN J., AND NANCY L. HOFFMAN. "Today's Tarnished Sports Heroes: Implication for Ethics-Based Instruction." *Social Studies and the Young Learner* 1 (September/October 1988): 14–18.

JOHNSTON, MARILYN, AND CAROL LUBOMUDROV. "Teachers' Level of Moral Reasoning and Their Understanding of Classroom Rules and Roles." *The Elementary School Journal* 88 (September 1987): 64–77.

LICKONA, THOMAS. *Education for Character.* New York: Bantam, 1991.

MURPHY, DENNIS F. "The Just Community at Birch Meadow Elementary School." *Phi Delta Kappan* 69 (February 1988): 427–28.

NODDINGS, NEL. *Caring: A Feminine Approach to Ethics and Moral Education.* Berkeley, CA: University of California Press, 1984.

NYBERG, DAVID. "Teaching Values in School." *Teachers College Record* 91 (Summer 1990): 595–611.

PARKER, WALTER C. "Why Ethics in Citizenship Education?" *Social Studies and the Young Learner* 1 (September/October 1988): 3–5.

PATE, GLENN S. "Research on Reducing Prejudice." *Social Education* 52 (April/May 1988): 287–89.

PHI DELTA KAPPAN 69 (February 1988). This issue of the journal presents a special section on emerging developments in character and moral education in the elementary school.

REIMER, JOSEPH, DIANA P. PAOLITTO, AND RICHARD H. HERSH *Promoting Moral Growth.* New York: Longman, 1983.

4 Preparing Teaching Plans for the Social Studies

Midway through her interview for a position as fourth-grade teacher, the school district representative asked the candidate, "Tell me, Susan, are students still required to prepare detailed plans for social studies units in connection with their methods course?" Susan assured the interviewer that her methods course instructor had required the students to plan social studies units in considerable detail and to assemble examples of related instructional materials as well. She explained that students were also required to prepare plans for shorter instructional episodes, including daily lesson plans.

"I thought the requirement was pretty demanding when I took the course several years ago," the interviewer continued, "but it proved to be very helpful to me when I started teaching the following year." The interviewer's experience and Susan's, too, are not very different from those of most prospective elementary and middle school teachers. School district authorities expect that the teachers they hire will be prepared to plan well for teaching social studies. Few teachers can plan and teach social studies completely on their own, unencumbered by forces beyond their own specific situation. In most cases, planning and teaching are influenced by a variety of factors, agencies, and organizations at the national, state, and local levels.

In the United States, education is legally under the jurisdiction of the various states. School programs, therefore, are not subject to the scrutiny and supervision of the federal government. Nonetheless, social studies education is influenced at the national level by federal social or fiscal legislation (or both), by projects funded by the Department of Education that may encourage certain procedures or emphases, by textbook and standardized test authors and their publishers who sell to a national market, and by national lay organizations whose special interests are aligned with social studies education. In the 1980s, the reports of several national commissions and study groups that surveyed the status of American education have been influential in shaping the policies and directions of education. As was noted in chapter 1, national professional associations also speak to the nature of the social studies curriculum of the schools.

The largest and most significant professional association for social studies is the National Council for the Social Studies. This organization has given leadership and direction to social studies planning at the national level. Its committees study problems relating to the social studies on a continuing basis. Its journals, *Social Education* and *Social Studies and the Young Learner*, and its numerous other publications have been widely circulated and have proved to be valuable aids to teachers and curriculum planners. Membership in the National Council for the Social Studies is open to anyone who has an interest in any of the facets of the social studies at any teaching level.

State governments have the legal responsibility for directing educational programs of public schools. Typically, one finds certain curricular requirements relating to social studies in state education codes. These range from mandating the teaching of United States history and the Constitution to requiring the observance of state Admission Day. State education agencies often have a state framework for social studies that provides guidance to local districts in developing a philosophy and rationale, selecting subject matter for various grade levels (scope and sequence), recommending teaching procedures, and selecting instructional materials. In practice, state agencies have delegated much of their responsibility for education to local school districts.

Much choice making in curriculum is left to local districts. With site-based management on the rise, more of these decisions are likely to be made at the school level. The feeling that the schools belong to the people of the local community and that schools should serve local needs has long been fundamental to educational planning in this country. Social studies programs must be tailored to the experience and background of children who live in a specific attendance area. State and national influences presumably ensure attention to common societal goals that are necessary for national unity; local influences should ensure that the children living in the area are well served by the social studies program.

As teachers design social studies programs, they should be mindful of the influences at the national, state, and local levels. It is helpful, for example, for the teacher to be familiar with the social studies guidelines and position statements published by the National Council for the Social Studies. Likewise, the teacher ought to know what is required by the state framework for social studies. The teacher should consult the local curriculum guide before the planning process begins.

TYPES OF TEACHING PLANS

In most instances, the school district will supply a curriculum guide, a list of suggested topics, a curriculum framework, a textbook, or some directive that provides the teacher with guidance as to which topics or units are to be included in the curriculum. Often teachers can exercise limited choices within the established guidelines. It is not uncommon to find some topics required, some optional, and perhaps some to be chosen by the teacher. A teacher must be familiar with district expectations and assessment policies in order to plan appropriately.

Thorough planning will not ensure successful teaching, but it will do much to give the teacher a margin of confidence that will enhance the possibility of more effective teaching. Many experienced teachers make use of three types of plans for the social studies: (1) unit plans; (2) short-range plans focused on a single topic, main idea, or skill; and (3) daily plans. The long-range plan, usually referred to as a *unit* or a *unit of work,* covers a period of six to ten weeks, during which time the class studies some broad topic on an ongoing basis. The unit plan is a way of organizing materials and activities for such an extended study. A unit might be thought of as a *depth study.* The following are examples of topics that would be suitable for parcels of work called *units:*

Living in Our Community

Families Around the World

The Exciting World of Lewis and Clark

The World of the Big City

Life in Early America

The Middle East—Crossroads of Cultures

Not all social studies instruction needs to be organized around comprehensive units of the type described. Many topics can be adequately covered within a week or two. These can often be sandwiched in between the larger units. Such topics, which call for short-range plans, might be organized around subject matter that is timely or is of special relevance to a class. They might consist of unconventional subjects or topics on which there is not an abundance of learning resources for children to use. The following are examples of topics suitable for such shorter blocks of work:

Winners and Losers in the Election

Danger Spots in Our Home

Caring for Pets

Getting Information from Maps

Workers and Their Wages

Getting Your Money's Worth

Who Is the Me I See?

It is also possible to plan a large unit of work as a series of sequentially related miniunits of the type described here. When this is done, however, the teacher will want to provide some ongoing activities to give continuity to the larger study.

The third type of teaching plan is that which the teacher actually uses in doing the teaching. It is what is usually called a "daily lesson plan" and is really the teacher's "trip map" through the lesson. Such plans should extend and continue the instruction from one class session to the next. Naturally, these specific teaching plans are developed within the context of the more extended unit of study. Separate and discrete plans that do not tie into some larger framework are not recommended because of the resulting fragmentation of the topics studied. Plans should move the process of learning sequentially and continuously over a period of time.

Textbook-Based Plans

A textbook-based plan is one that is developed in advance by the teacher, who often relies on the textbook or other curriculum documents in determining the nature and content of the program. If children help in the planning, they do so minimally and usually in matters that do not alter the basic content and emphasis. That is, they might exercise some choice concerning individual activities to be performed but would not suggest alternative topics to be studied. Reliance on the textbook as the prime information source is complete. Variations in requirements to accommodate learner differences would include varying the lengths of assignments or varying the amount of time needed to complete them. All children deal with the same basic subject matter.

If we follow a teacher through the steps in planning and teaching social studies in this way, we would observe that the teacher

1. Surveys the text to find out which units are included and decides how to apportion the amount of time available to each one. The recommendations of the textbook authors may be used in making these decisions.
2. Studies the teacher's guide accompanying the text to find out how the program is organized and what major goals and objectives are stressed. These goals and objectives may be accepted as appropriate for the program.
3. Uses the teacher's guide for teaching plans and learner activities.
4. Uses additional resources and activities for enrichment, for extension of learning, and for individualizing learning. Some of these are suggested by the teacher's guide, including those provided by the publisher of the text series as supplementary materials such as workbooks or "blackline" masters. *on a regular basis*
5. Evaluates learnings as suggested by the text and teacher's guide, focusing mainly on informational learnings, basic concepts, and related skills.
6. Uses formal teaching procedures consisting mainly of question and answer, some discussion, an occasional pupil report, and map making; there is infrequent use of drama, art, music, or construction activities.

Topic or Subject-Oriented Plans

A planning approach based on a topic or subject has some of the same characteristics as the one just discussed, but the reliance on the text is not

these plans seem to have a lot to do y! the age of the child

as complete, more of the teacher's influence is apparent, and it is not so thoroughly preplanned and teacher directed. Children are more involved in planning, and there is greater use of a wide range of instructional materials and activities. The formality that characterizes the textbook-based approach is missing. Learners feel freer to voice their own opinions and views on issues. Interactions are more along the lines of discussion as opposed to question-and-answer procedures. The teacher is sensitive to the individuality of children and provides for variations in ability and motivation. Children may be involved in expressive activities such as construction, art, music, role playing, and simulation games. This is not an altogether child-centered approach, yet it is not one that is wholly teacher directed either.

If we follow a teacher through the steps in planning and teaching in this way, we would observe that the teacher

be more

1. Examines the curriculum guide and the textbook to find out what topics and units are expected to be included in the program.
2. Establishes broad goals and objectives for the year; takes into consideration those suggested by the curriculum guide and textbook teacher's guide, but makes her or his own.
3. Tentatively selects topics to be studied; consults the teacher's guide and curriculum guide in this process, selects some that are suggested, omits others, and adds some. These topics may be modified as the program develops and as learner interests and capabilities are better known.
4. Decides on the sequence of units selected and time allotment for each, taking into account holidays, seasons of the year, and so forth.
5. Uses some teaching suggestions from the teacher's guide and curriculum guide but develops many of her or his own ideas for learning activities and teaching procedures.
6. Develops and uses learning packets, self-paced materials, learning centers, and learner contracts; also, individualizes learning through use of small groups.
7. Plans for and uses many instructional resources in addition to the textbook. This includes pictures, packets, library books, films, filmstrips, recordings, and artifacts.
8. Uses a variety of informal assessment techniques and devices such as discussion, observation, student conferences, teacher-made tests, checklists, and experience summaries.
9. Maintains a relaxed instructional pace but stays close to teacher-learner planned treatment of the topic.

Child-Centered Plans

Some teachers prefer to plan the social studies program cooperatively with children, deriving the subject matter and skills from the interests and concerns of the children. Although it requires considerable preplanning by the teacher, the program itself is not structured in advance, as are the other two approaches that have been discussed. Study units and learner experiences

It is imperative that children learn safety procedures associated with the school bus. This photo shows the use of a talking robot, "Barney the Bus," to capture the attention of these kindergarten children. What in-class followup activities would you suggest be undertaken after the children have encountered "Barney the Bus"?
(Photo by Carla Anderson, Northshore School District.)

are planned jointly by the teacher and the children in terms of their interests and backgrounds. Thus, the unit emerges under the guidance of the teacher, who relies on learner initiative and interest. Children help decide what they will study. They raise questions about the information they are interested in getting and search out relevant sources. They plan ways of working, activities in which they will engage, and ways of sharing ideas with one another. Children are encouraged to become involved in assuming responsibility for what they are to learn and how they will go about learning it. *The boundaries between the various school subjects and skills are blurred; indeed, the social studies units may serve as the integrating center for the total elementary school curriculum.*

If we follow a teacher through the steps in planning and teaching in this way, we will observe that the teacher

1. Formulates broad goals and objectives for the year in terms of anticipated social and intellectual development of the children.

2. Studies learner backgrounds; develops an awareness of the social milieu from which children come.
3. Prepares motivating or facilitating questions dealing with social issues and topics to arouse learner interest.
4. Provides books, artifacts, displays, visuals, construction materials, and other items to generate interest and curiosity.
5. Encourages children to suggest topics for study and to suggest possible questions and problems for exploration.
6. Guides children in exploratory information searches.
7. Assists children in developing an in-depth study of topics and problems selected; plans are refined and/or modified as the study progresses.
8. Individualizes the program in accordance with learner interest and ability using interest centers, individual study contracts, individual study materials, projects, and activities.
9. Closely relates social studies work to reading, language arts, mathematics, science, art, music, and drama.

PLANNING INSTRUCTIONAL UNITS

One must conclude from the foregoing discussion that the way units are planned and taught varies greatly from one teacher to another. For one, the unit may be no more than a chapter or a section of the textbook that deals with a single topic. For another teacher, the unit may be a comprehensive study that incorporates subjects, skills, and activities from all the rest of the school curriculum. One teacher may structure the unit in advance by thorough preplanning; another may plan the unit as the study evolves. Two teachers working on an identical topic at the same grade level may have their classes deal quite differently with it. The same teacher might handle the same topic differently with different groups of children. What follows is a description of the essential components of a comprehensive unit plan. The reader should understand, however, that a great deal of individual teacher judgment and decision making go into the planning and teaching of social studies units.

Making a Survey of Available Instructional Resources

If a school district includes particular topics in the social studies curriculum, it will ordinarily provide the necessary instructional resources. The amount of such resources that are available will vary, however, from no more than a basic textbook to a generous amount and variety of multimedia. As an initial step in planning, the teacher should inventory the availability and the adequacy of learning resources for the unit to be studied. What the teacher finds will have a direct bearing on how the unit will be planned. Whereas instructional materials should not entirely determine the social studies program, the availability of essential instructional resources necessarily affects the teacher's planning.

Much difficulty is avoided in securing and using instructional materials when teachers plan well in advance what they will need. Books, recordings, pictures, films, and filmstrips must be requested early enough to ensure their arrival at the time they are needed. Usually, instructional resources must be ordered, reserved, or even secured before the unit begins.

Establishing Objectives

Social studies instruction is almost always concerned with the attainment of multiple objectives. Facts, concepts, generalizations, principles, and general knowledge are derived from the encounter with the subject matter. Skills are learned during the process of study, including many of those discussed in chapter 1. Affective outcomes deal with attitudes, values, and feelings that are important in studying most social studies topics. It is not likely that all the outcomes of a study will be formally defined by the teacher. Many outcomes are realized as side effects, meaning fortuitous learnings or unpredicted extensions of learnings associated with the unit.

We restrict our attention here to those few objectives that the teacher singles out for special attention. These are objectives that the teacher perceives to be the major purposes of the study. Our concern is not with those serendipitous outcomes that emerge as children read, interact with their teachers and with each other, prepare and give reports, and engage in various other activities. This is not to say that these latter outcomes are not important, only that it is not possible to know what they are to be in advance of the study.

Instructional objectives should be stated in ways that make clear what children are supposed to *learn*. This will enable the teacher and the learners to see more clearly how instructional activities relate to the purposes of the study. Insufficient clarity of objectives is likely to lead to the performance of activities that have neither purpose nor meaning. It makes little sense for teachers and children to try to solve a problem when no one seems to know what the problem is.

Objectives may be framed as broad, general statements that describe what it is the children are expected to learn. The following are examples, selected from several different units, of such descriptive objectives:

As a Result of a Study of This Unit Children Will

- Learn the use of simple research skills associated with gathering information.
- Understand that certain basic needs must be satisfied if human life is to be sustained.
- Realize that decisions are based on one's value orientation.
- Learn to work cooperatively in small groups, respecting the rights and feelings of others.
- Understand the interdependent relationship between geographical regions.
- Develop the skill of orienting a map to directions.
- Gain a knowledge of vocabulary associated with the legal system.

- Learn how advertising aids both the consumer and the producer.
- Learn to formulate and test causal hypotheses relating to community development.

These examples would provide purpose and direction for a study. Many teachers are comfortable with descriptive objectives of this type. Although they are general, they are, nonetheless, specific enough to communicate what the main concerns of the study are to be. Such objectives need further clarification, but most teachers prefer to make these statements more specific and explicit at the time the material is actually taught.

Another way to state objectives is in terms of specific observable learner behavior. Such statements are referred to as *behavioral objectives.* Prior to the time the instruction takes place, the teacher frames statements of expected student performances that are predicted to occur as a result of the proposed learning experience. These predicted performances are so precisely stated that their achievement could readily be assessed by an objective observer.

In order to achieve this degree of precision, teachers must use language that leaves no doubt as to what is wanted. Verbals such as "to comprehend," "to know," "to realize" are not well suited for this purpose because they do not specify what the learners are *doing* that would convince an impartial observer that the children do, indeed, "comprehend," "know," or "realize." Stems that are more suitable for behavioral objectives are these:

to name	to explain why
to choose	to identify
to illustrate	to cite
to provide examples	to define
to write	to locate
to place in order	to use

Examples of behavioral objectives are these:

As a Result of a Study of This Unit Children Will Be Able to

- Identify four different types of structures people use for homes.
- Provide five examples of consumer fraud.
- Locate a specific reference book in the library.
- List the main ideas in a passage of social studies prose.
- Show that they know how to use the index to find factual material in the textbook.
- Match causes and effects in an exercise relating to labor-management conflicts.
- Define the essential characteristics of the concept *region.*

The use of behavioral objectives has accompanied the growing concern for accountability in education. Advocates of behavioral objectives claim that such objectives encourage precision in teaching and learning by

WHEN FORMING OBJECTIVE ASK THIS Question ?!?

focusing on observable learner performance. They would argue that unless the child can actually do something to show what has been learned, that one can only speculate about whether or not learning has taken place. They argue, further, that unless the teacher can define what is to be learned in terms of the child's intellectual or physical behavior, it cannot be assumed that learning has actually occurred. The issue boils down to the question, → "What can the child *do* that he or she could not do prior to the instruction?" In this framework, it is learner behavior that provides convincing evidence that intended learning has or has not taken place.

Those who do not favor the use of behavioral objectives say that many significant outcomes of social studies instruction, or any instruction, for that matter, do not lend themselves well to behavioral definition. For example, who can say precisely what happens to a child while reading an exciting account of life on the frontier? How does one define such learning behaviorally? Should it be the same for all learners? Besides, there is the question of whether or not such a degree of precision serves any useful purpose. Another argument against the use of behavioral objectives is that the practice encourages the narrowing of the instruction to those objectives that can easily be defined behaviorally, thereby neglecting other important learnings that cannot be so defined or that are difficult to manage in behavioral terms. Additionally, opponents claim that the use of behavioral objectives tends to fragment the social studies curriculum into bits and pieces of content and skills rather than to encourage the integration of learnings into larger wholes.

Perhaps there is a midposition that suggests a limited use of behavioral objectives for those components of social studies that lend themselves well to definition in terms of observable learner performance. For example, certain work-study skills would be of this type—reading maps, using references, gathering data, interpreting graphs and charts, reading for a specific purpose. Some content-related objectives can also be stated behaviorally, such as arranging events in a sequence, relating effects to causes, drawing a conclusion based on data, providing examples and nonexamples of concepts, and so on. In the case of social, intellectual, or affective learnings that cannot be easily defined behaviorally, the teacher may want to state instructional objectives in descriptive terms as illustrated previously. The types of objectives used will depend on local requirements and on teacher preference. Because there are philosophical differences among competent professionals as to the appropriateness of behavioral objectives, this is an issue that individual teachers will need to resolve for themselves.

Whatever form the teacher uses to state objectives, it is important to stress that the objectives should indicate clearly what it is the children are *expected to learn,* not what they will do. For example, the following are *not* appropriate instructional objectives because they simply describe procedures and activities that will be used by the children presumably to learn something that remains undefined:

The children will view a film.

The class will work in small committees.

The children will draw a map of the local area.

The class will discuss individual projects.

Children will make a model of a harbor.

Children will role play workers in a shopping center.

Selecting and Organizing the Subject Matter

When teachers are asked what they are doing in social studies, they often respond by naming the title of the unit or topic under study, as for example, "We are studying Japan (or Canada, Mexico, the Community, and so forth)." The presumption is that this response will communicate the nature of the study. The fact is, however, that the title or topic of a unit tells us little about the focus of the study, the concepts being developed, the relationships being established, or the conclusions reached, if any. Any topic can be studied from several different perspectives. Part of the task of organizing subject matter, therefore, deals with establishing the focus of the study and determining which particular main ideas and concepts will receive priority.

Many social studies programs and most of the modern textbook series organize subject matter around basic ideas from history and the social science disciplines. These are usually called major generalizations, basic concepts, key ideas, or other similar designations, depending on the preference of the district. Examples of such ideas are listed in the chapters of this text where the disciplines are discussed.

There is some variation in school district policies, but typically elementary and middle school teachers have only a limited amount of freedom to select the subjects and topics to be included in the social studies curriculum. Topics and units are either designated by the school district curriculum guide, or the district has adopted a textbook series that pretty much determines the subject matter and skills to be included. Teachers do, however, have a considerable amount of latitude in deciding how those topics will be developed and what ideas will be singled out for emphasis. It is those ideas that really determine the specific subject matter. An example will illustrate how this comes about.

Let us say that the fifth-grade curriculum guide calls for a unit on Canada. The guide also indicates what the emphasis is to be and the major generalizations that are to provide a focus for this unit:

CANADA: LAND GIANT OF THE WESTERN HEMISPHERE

This unit should provide children with a comprehensive view of Canada as it is today. This does not mean that historical information will be excluded, but simply that the stress is to be interdisciplinary with an emphasis on contemporary life. The unit should treat Canada as a whole rather than focus on a particular small sample of Canadian life and culture. Whereas the similarities between the United States and Canada should be studied, it is important to present Canada as a nation distinguished by its own nationality and culture. Some emphasis must be placed on how it is different from the United States. The longstanding tradition of cordial relations between the United States and Canada should also be stressed. The following generalizations should emerge as a result of the study of Canada:

1. The physical features of an area influence settlement patterns and transportation routes. (geography)
2. Maintaining an ethnic identity is important to most members of a cultural group. (anthropology)
3. The use of available resources depends on the nature of the economic system, the values of people, and their level of technology. (economics)
4. The early history of a country has a definite bearing on the present culture of its people. (history)

How does the teacher go about selecting subject matter about Canada that will be in accord with the focus suggested by the curriculum guide? One option available to the teacher is simply to teach whatever is included in the children's textbook. If the textbook treatment is in harmony with the focus suggested and the teacher makes enlightened use of the books, this is not an altogether undesirable procedure. We would like to think, however, that the teacher will be able to develop a more imaginative approach and, in the process, make better use of the text and other learning resources that are available.

The basic question here is this: What is it that children are expected to learn about Canada that is consistent with the suggested emphasis? Or, what are the main ideas about Canada that will receive attention in this unit?

To respond to this question, the teacher should do some self-study with the thought of selecting six to eight major ideas to be included in the unit. The public library, *The World Almanac,* encyclopedias, and the instructional materials in the classroom can be used for this purpose. Let us assume that the teacher has done this research and decides that the following *main ideas* will be developed in the unit:

1. Canada is a country with a unique northern geographic location.
2. Canada is a large, regionally divided, and diverse country.
3. Canada is a highly industrialized and technologically advanced country.
4. Canada is an urbanized country, rapidly becoming a nation of city dwellers.
5. Canada is an exposed country, open to a multitude of external cultural, economic, and political influences.
6. Canada is a multiethnic country with two predominant linguistic groups.[1]

---

[1]CONTACT, No. 60, Canada Studies Foundation, 252 Bloor Street West, Suite 3-390, Toronto, Ontario M5S IV5, Canada. December 1983.

After the teacher has selected the main ideas, such as those listed here, it is possible to identify the essential related concepts and the specific subject matter, as shown in Figure 4-1.

Thus far we have discussed subject matter selection only in terms of informational outcomes—that is, cognitive objectives. But what about skills, attitudes, and values? How do they fit into the picture? Objectives that deal with skills, attitudes, and values are structured around the subject matter, too, and are developed concurrently with informational objectives. Unless the curriculum guide specifically indicates which skills, attitudes, and values are to receive attention—and usually it does not—the matter is left to the judgment of the teacher.

In the example of Canada, it is reasonable that map and globe skills would be a necessary part of main ideas numbers 1 and 2. All the main ideas will require information searches that will provide a way to teach and apply research and inquiry skills. The teacher will doubtless plan activities that require the children to use group-work skills. Attitudinal outcomes can hardly be ignored because the curriculum guide states explicitly, "The longstanding tradition of cordial relations between the United States and Canada should also be stressed." Values will come into the study as children begin to examine the tradeoffs involved in Canada's becoming an urbanized country, exploiting its resources, assimilating its native people, and maintaining an official bicultural position.

The use of a planning format such as the one shown in Figure 4-2 can be helpful for the coordination of information, skills, attitudes, and values objectives. The essential point is that it is around the basic subject matter that all these objectives are achieved. If a careful job is done in completing the four cells above the double line (Figure 4-2) *for each of the main ideas included in the unit, the task of selecting resources and activities will be made easier.*

Beginning the Study

Building and sustaining the interest of children in a topic are continuing responsibilities of the teacher, but are especially important when beginning a new unit of study. This involves more than simply getting started. It requires arousing the curiosity of the youngsters, exploring some of the possibilities for study presented by the topic, and, in general, setting the stage for learning to take place. In advance of the time the unit is actually undertaken, the teacher should post material in the room that will arouse interest in the anticipated study, and the relationship of the new topic to previous work should be indicated. There should be books and other appropriate materials in the room through which the children may browse. Materials can be brought to class that stimulate the thinking of the children. All these activities and others, which the imaginative teacher will use, serve to create interest and will help cause the children to want to learn more about the topic. Through procedures such as these, the children have an opportunity to discover the new material gradually and will be ready to engage in productive teacher-guided planning.

FIGURE 4-1

Essential Cognitive Elements of a Unit on Canada

Main Ideas	Essential Concepts	Subject Matter Synopsis
1. Canada is a country with a unique northern geographic location.	Arctic Latitude Coastline Heartland Natural boundary Political boundary	Location and size of Canada along with its dominant physical features, unique natural regions, and climatic characteristics; population distribution; location in terms of other nations of the Northern Hemisphere
2. Canada is a large, regionally divided, and diverse country.	Regionalism Prairie Maritime Offshore Province	Brief history of Canadian development; political and natural regions; occupations of its people; regionalism as a social, economic, and political factor in Canadian life
3. Canada is a highly industrialized and technologically advanced country.	Natural resources Minerals Raw materials Technological change	Development of Canadian resources for export and domestic use; rise of Canadian industry; transportation and communication systems in Canada
4. Canada is an urbanized country, rapidly becoming a nation of city dwellers.	Metropolitan area Trading center Manufacturing center Urban environment	Move toward urbanism with cities gaining in their influence over the lives of all Canadians; problems associated with urban sprawl and urban renewal: Toronto, a case study
5. Canada is an exposed country, open to a multitude of external cultural, economic, and political influences.	Foreign investment Nationalism Cultural influence	Influence of foreign investments in Canadian industry and agriculture; the American presence; cultural influences from the United States; influence of immigration on Canadian development
6. Canada is a multiethnic country with two predominant linguistic groups.	Ethnic group Bilingual Bicultural Heritage Minority Cultural mosaic	Historical background of Canadian bilingualism; effect of bicultural life on social, political, and economic decision making; status of native people in Canada

FIGURE 4-2

This form can be used in developing unit plans. Notice that it consists of four components: (1) the learnings to be achieved; (2) the references and resources to be used; (3) the activities to be performed; and (4) how to relate it to the rest of the curriculum.

SOCIAL STUDIES UNIT PLANNING

Unit Title _____   **Date** _____

Main Idea to Be Developed: Key Concepts and Terms: Focus Question:	Related Skills:	Related Attitudes and Values:	Questions to Stimulate Reflective Thinking:
Text References: Supplementary References: Audiovisual Resources: Community Resources:	Oral and Written Language Activities:	Dramatic Activities:	Construction Activities:
	Related Curriculum Activities (Science, Math, Art, Music):		

Some teachers use dramatic representation successfully in the initial stages of the unit. Let us assume that a primary class is beginning a unit on transportation. The teacher suggests that the children show through creative dramatics what the workers at an airline terminal do. The children become excited about this and want to start immediately, which the teacher allows. Under the teacher's guidance, they begin to plan and to play the representation, but they soon discover that they do not really know enough about the situation to present it accurately. They do not know who the workers are at the terminal, let alone what each worker does. Now they have identified a problem they can understand and can go about their research and problem solving with genuine purpose. The children's purposes have to do with getting information to do the dramatic play whereas the teacher's purpose is to have them learn basic ideas about the airport and to learn important related skills. Although the example given applies to a primary grade, the procedure can be used at any level.

Other activities can be used in a similar way to motivate work, to develop purposes, and to give children reasons for doing the things they do. The projects are important in that they provide a child-oriented vehicle for learning. Construction activities are often used in this way. If an individual or a class is to build something, they have to learn what goes into it, how it functions, and how it is or was used. One has to be careful, of course, to make certain the time taken in such endeavors is justified by the learnings that result.

Properly understood, this phase of unit development consists of a *group* or *series* of experiences rather than a single experience. Sometimes teachers plan to initiate a unit through the viewing of a film. A film may be used in the introductory stages of a unit, but this experience should be supported by many others of the type previously described. In one sense, this unfolding process is continued throughout the unit in that each new learning is a readiness for the next.

Developing the Study: Problems, Experiences, or Activities

A distinguishing characteristic of a good elementary or middle school teacher is the ability to engage children in an interested way in activities that help them achieve important learnings. One unfortunate practice in teaching social studies is that of using activities without relating them to social studies purposes. This applies to traditional activities, such as reading textbook assignments and giving reports, as it does to the more informal activities such as committee work or some type of expressive experience. Activities are means to ends—they are used to help children learn something. It is thus imperative that the teacher define the objectives and know clearly what the children are supposed to learn *before* deciding what activities are to be used. If the planning format shown in Figure 4-2 is used as suggested, this will not be a problem because the upper portion dealing with objectives is completed before the activities are selected. As decisions are made concerning activities, the teacher must also select the information sources that will be used by the children. These can be listed in the space provided, as shown in Figure 4-2.

Good unit development always makes provision for the involvement of children in planning instructional activities. This is in keeping with attaining and maintaining student interest. Having them participate in planning can do much to overcome the feeling that they are only "doing assignments for the teacher." Such participation assists in clarifying objectives of learning for the children and allows them to identify psychologically with the unit activities. The many values of such planning have been well documented, and it is now generally recognized as sound teaching procedure by good teachers everywhere.

Teachers should plan with children many of the specific learning tasks undertaken in the unit: listing questions on which information is desired, making charts of what to do, finding and listing sources of information, appointing committees, reporting progress, pooling suggestions, and making plans for a construction activity. A fifth-grade teacher and her class summarized their plans for part of a unit on colonial New England as shown on page 100.

In general, the development of a unit consists of a sequence of procedures, each one emerging from the preceding one. In its simplest form, this pattern might be described as follows:

1. *Problem identification* and related information gathering; problem-solving activities such as reading, interviewing, listening, viewing, collecting, using references, doing map work.
2. *Application* through expressive activities such as discussing, illustrating, exhibiting, dramatizing, constructing, drawing, and writing.
3. *Summarizing, generalizing,* and *transferring* to new situations resulting in identification of new problems of a more complex nature; the cycle is then repeated.

This procedure includes both intake and expressive activities. Children not only take in knowledge but also must act on knowledge so obtained. Moreover, they must generalize and apply their knowledge to new problems and situations.

As the unit moves into the development phase, each class period should provide for three instructional operations: (1) readiness, (2) work-study, and (3) summary and evaluation. Teachers usually begin the social studies instructional period with the entire class in one group. At this time the previous day's progress is reviewed, plans for the day's work are outlined, and work objectives are clarified. The children then turn to their various tasks while the teacher moves from one child to the next or from one group to another, guiding, helping, clarifying, encouraging, and suggesting. The teacher will terminate the work period sufficiently early to assemble the entire group once again to discuss progress, to evaluate work, and to identify tasks left undone that must be continued the next day. As the

·················· JOBS IN A COLONIAL NEW ENGLAND TOWN

Each of us will select a different job from New England town life.
Each of us will find out what skills and responsibilities each person has.
Each of us will share our role with the others in the class by dressing up like the person, showing something one might have created or used, making a bulletin board or diorama, or preparing a dramatization.

Some of the jobs in a colonial New England town are:

candlemaker	homemaker–mother
blacksmith	merchant
weaver	shipbuilder
farmer	minister
schoolteacher	fisherman
miller	barrister
carpenter	tanner
slave	doctor
watchman	innkeeper
printer	cooper

What We Will Want to Find Out About Our Jobs

1. What skills did the person need?
2. What training was necessary to do the job?
3. How much money did the person make?
4. How was the person paid?
5. How many people will need the services?
6. How does the job relate to other jobs in the community?
7. What special equipment or resources did the people use in their job?
8. Would you like to have done this job or performed this service?

children complete their various work projects and are ready to share them with the class, time will be arranged for them to do so. On some days the children may spend the entire period sharing, presenting reports, discussing, and planning. Other days may be spent entirely in reading and research or on worksheets the teacher has prepared because of a special need of the class. And on other days part of the group may be reading while others are preparing a mural and still others are planning a report.

The need to take time at the end of the work period to summarize what has been learned or to review work that has been accomplished should be underscored. Having a clear understanding of the objective or purpose of a learning activity and having knowledge of the progress go hand in hand. Unless the teacher spends some time crystallizing what has been accomplished or learned, the children may work for days without feeling that they have learned anything or that they are getting anywhere. Some teach-

A TALL TALE ABOUT

Paul Bunyan

Paul Bunyan was so big that everything he did had huge results. Even a little mistake caused huge problems. There was the time on a cold winter day that he almost caused a terrible flood. He spilled a huge tank of water that he was carrying back from the Great Lakes.

Paul spilled so much water that many homes and farms were in danger of being washed away. So he grabbed a shovel and started to dig a huge ditch to hold the water. He dug the ditch all the way to the Gulf of Mexico.

As Paul dug, he threw the dirt from the ditch to the west. People say that this ditch became the Mississippi River. They say that the dirt made the Rocky Mountains.

• Multiple Perspectives for Enriched Meanings

With Paul Bunyan's help, children are introduced to major landforms. Tall tales captivate children and round out units involving, in this case, geography.

"A Tall Tale About Paul Bunyan," **the World Around Us,** Grade 3 Student Text, p. 34, Macmillan/McGraw-Hill School Publishing Company.

Tr. #1900(3) **Sioux Indians Buffalo Hunt in Summer** (Photo by Robert E. Logan). Courtesy of the Department of Library Services, American Museum of Natural History.

The Scene at the Signing of the Constitution of the United States (Howard Chandler Christy). Courtesy of the Architect of the Capitol/U.S. House of Representitives Collection.

Paintings, like literature, can deepen children's understanding of most historical topics and should be part of most social studies units. Here, George Catlin captures the wonder of a buffalo hunt, the founders of the United States hammer out the rule book called the Constitution, and Diego Rivera shows natives working precious metals for Spanish rulers.

Napotec Civilization (Photo by Robert Frerck). Courtesy of Odyssey Productions/Chicago.

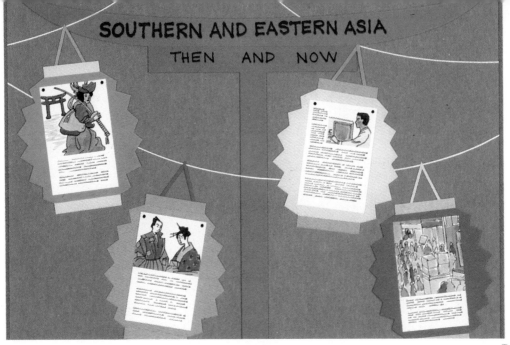

Southern and Eastern Asia bulletin board, **the World Around Us: World Regions,** Teacher's Edition, p. 421-B, Macmillan/McGraw-Hill School Publishing Company.

Bulletin boards bring the classroom environment and the topic of study into harmony. They deserve a central place in unit planning. Here, two time-honored themes are sampled. Above is a *then and now display,* here applied to Southeast Asia. Below is a *geography* display focused on Sub-Saharan Africa. Note the three sections. Both themes can be adapted to any society or continent being studied.

Sub-Saharan Africa bulletin board, **The World Around Us: World Regions,** Teacher's Edition, p. 383-B, Macmillan/McGraw-Hill School Publishing Company.

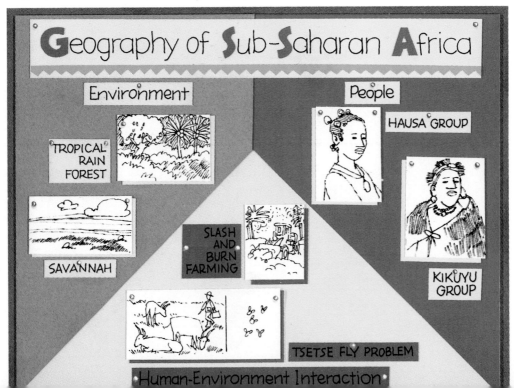

ers find it worthwhile to place these daily summaries on charts that serve as a log of the unit work as it progresses. Such logs are helpful in the culmination and may also be useful in evaluation activities associated with the unit.

The work-study or problem-solving phase of the unit is handled somewhat differently in the primary grades than it is in the middle and upper grades. Although children of all ages need many firsthand experiences to extend their understanding of social studies concepts, the older child has a greater familiarity with the world of things and people and can, therefore, profit from vicarious experiences to a much greater extent than the primary-grade child. Furthermore, the older child can make use of reading as a tool for learning in the social studies whereas the young child is less able to do so. The physiological and psychological makeup of the primary-grade child makes necessary the use of learning activities that involve the child actively in firsthand experiences. (See Figure 4-3.)

The following are a few examples of learning activities for all grade levels:

LEARNING ACTIVITIES

Sharing

Mr. Johnson's second graders were studying their seashore community. Using a sandbox and things that each of them had gathered or collected with their families, they created a model of a seashore. The boys and girls talked about what they had brought and where their items had come from. They discussed whether or not the items were natural or artificially constructed.

Construction

Ms. Smather's class studied early people and constructed tools and utensils with sticks, rocks, and vines they gathered in nearby wooded areas. Each child demonstrated the use of the implement.

Experimenting

Ms. Womble secured samples of various grains—oats, corn, barley, wheat—while studying agriculture with her class. The children compared the appearance and taste of each type of grain and then planted some to compare germinating time and appearance of the first shoots.

Listening

In Mr. Potts's class, the focus of study was the American Indian. In motivating the children, Mr. Potts read an Indian legend and asked them to decide what the Indians valued in their lives, using the legend as a clue to their value system.

Discussion

Ms. Perkle's sixth-grade class had a current events time, and a child brought an article from the evening paper telling about the sale of United States grain to China. A discussion that weighed the advantages and disadvantages of this action to the American people followed.

Written Language Experience

Ms. Thomas's class had written letters to their grandparents asking them to share their recollections of earlier schooldays. Those grandparents who lived nearby were asked to visit Ms. Thomas's classroom.

Dramatic Activities

During their study of Indonesia, each of the children in Ms. Monroe's class created a shadow puppet. In small groups they dramatized situations from Indonesian life. .

Art Experience

In a first-grade class the children made a trip to a farm. On their return they painted a mural showing the animals, equipment, people, and buildings they had observed.

Field Trip

A day was spent at a fair during the study of the state. The children noticed what products were displayed and what their region of the state had contributed.

Processing

During a study of colonial history the class divided into groups to make soap, dip candles, bake bread, churn butter, make dyes, and weave.

Some of the unit activities will involve the entire group whereas others will be individual or small-group endeavors. In carrying out this part of the unit, the teacher should make certain that each child knows what is expected. Classrooms operating in this way are places where children are doing things; consequently, they will be moving about, asking questions, and communicating with one another; and a generally informal but task-oriented atmosphere will prevail.

Evaluating Learning

Throughout the study the teacher and the children should make frequent evaluations of how well the unit is progressing. This is *formative* evaluation conducted to diagnose student learning difficulties and to improve teaching and learning. Much of this day-to-day evaluation is, and ought to be, informal. The teacher sees children working well or poorly and adjusts the instruction accordingly. The teacher can also sense whether or not children

FIGURE 4-3
Learning Activities for Social Studies

Type of Learning Activity	Examples	Purposes Served

Research	Reading
	Writing
	Interviewing
	Notetaking
	Collecting
	Map work
	Reporting
	Using references
		To
		  Gather information
		  Practice information-gathering skills
		  Answer questions

Presentation	Telling
	Demonstrating
	Illustrating
	Dramatizing
	Exhibiting
	Announcing
	Giving directions
	Pantomiming
	Relating events
		To
		  Share ideas with others
		  Practice communication skills
		  Clarify ideas
		  Encourage initiative
		  Apply information

Creative experiences	Writing
	Sketching
	Illustrating
	Sewing
	Soap carving
	Manipulating
	Comparing
	Drawing
	Modeling
	Painting
	Constructing
	Singing
	Dramatizing
	Imagining
		To
		  Express ideas creatively
		  Encourage creative abilities
		  Stimulate interest
		  Extend and/or enrich learning

Appreciation	Listening
	Viewing
	Describing
	Reading
		To
		  Develop attitudes and feelings
		  Provide valuing experiences
		  Extend and/or enrich learning

Observation or listening	Observing
	Visiting places of interest
	Viewing pictures or films
	Listening to recordings
		To
		  Gather information
		  Build observation and perceptual
		   skills
		  Compare and contrast

FIGURE 4-3
(*continued*)

Group cooperation	Discussing Sharing Helping one another Doing committee work Conversing Asking questions	To Develop group-work skills Use socialization skills Engage in larger projects
Experimentation	Measuring Demonstrating Conducting experiments Collecting	To Clarify complex procedures Develop inquiry skills Gather information
Organization	Planning Outlining Holding meetings Discussing Summarizing	To Clarify relationships Prepare a plan of action Organize ideas
Evaluation	Summarizing Criticizing Asking questions Reviewing	To Clarify direction and purpose Assess progress toward goals Modify plans

are interested in what they are doing. Through observation and feedback, the teacher can gauge the extent to which progress is being made toward the achievement of objectives. An appropriate, short teacher-made test can be used to check how well specific areas of content and skills have been learned. Much of the informal evaluation that takes place on a day-to-day basis involves the children themselves. They should be encouraged through discussion to take stock of their work individually and as a group. Evaluation of learnings, therefore, should not be associated only with the conclusion of a unit, but should be an important part of the ongoing instruction. Of course, the end of a unit provides a time to examine the extent to which the overall objectives have been achieved. This is *summative* evaluation and both informal and formal evaluation procedures are appropriate for this purpose. (See chapter 15.)

Concluding the Study

As a class nears the end of a unit, the teacher should plan a series of activities that encourage children to summarize what they have learned. This might involve opportunities to show what they have done or to share interesting things they have learned with other classes in the school or with their parents.[2]

---

[2] The idea of a "sidewalk fair" in a local shopping mall could be a good outlet for sharing what has been learned with others. See Barbara Hatcher and Mary Olson, "Sidewalk Social Studies," *Social Education* 48 (September/October 1984): 473–74, 485.

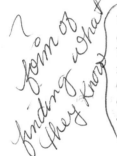

What is important about closing a unit of study is the opportunity to discuss conclusions, evaluate what has been learned, identify what children found to be of especial interest to them, and identify areas where additional study is needed. Concluding activities should include a suggestion of various interesting facets of the topic that were left unexplored and about which the children may wish to read and study independently. Concluding activities can and should serve as bridges to new intellectual pursuits.

INCORPORATING THINKING SKILLS

The usual assumption is that the development of thinking skills flows naturally as a result of the acquisition of knowledge. The belief is widespread that if one is well informed, the application of that knowledge to the solution of problems will pretty much take care of itself. Consequently, educational programs often emphasize the accumulation of information rather than a concern with its application. If there is a concern for application at all, the feeling is that it should come later, after there has been a period of knowledge accumulation, in high school or college or as an adult. Research indicates that this procedure is based on faulty assumptions and that knowledge accumulation and knowledge application go hand in hand and are part of the same process we call thinking.[3]

The process of thinking consists of a series of subskills, and, like any other skills, they must be practiced if they are to be applied with any degree of proficiency. These subskills can be identified as follows:

1. Identifying problems and questions for study.
2. Making inferences and drawing conclusions from data.
3. Making comparisons.
4. Developing hypotheses.
5. Using evidence to test hypotheses.
6. Planning how to study a question or a problem.
7. Getting data from a variety of sources.
8. Predicting possible outcomes.
9. Deciding what evidence is needed in studying a problem.
10. Deciding what evidence is relevant to the study.

These skills must be incorporated in the ongoing work of the class if learners are to develop proficiency in their use. Occasional special lessons on inquiry are not in themselves adequate for building competence. Of course, not all these subskills will appear in social studies lessons every day. During a period of a few weeks, such as that of a study unit, one should see balanced and systematic attention being given to them.

---

[3] See Barry K. Beyer, "Teaching Critical Thinking: A Direct Approach," *Social Education* 49 (April 1985): 297–303.

Special instructional materials that are inquiry based are helpful, but not essential, to engaging children in inquiry. Any of the standard materials can be used as sources of information, including textbooks. What is different when thinking is stressed, however, is the way these materials are used. The usual assumption regarding instructional material is that it includes essential information that must be learned. Nowhere is this more evident than in the use of textbooks. Textbook content often *becomes* the curriculum. In teaching for thinking, the textbook is a data or information *source*, and it should be used along with other information sources.

Not all social studies teaching need be, nor even should be, inquiry oriented. The teaching mode selected must be consistent with the objectives to be achieved. If the purpose is to convey information to children or to teach a skill, exposition and demonstration are often more effective and efficient teaching modes than is inquiry. If the purpose is to teach thinking and problem-solving skills, however, an inquiry strategy should be used.

Almost any topic selected for unit study can be shaped to meet the requirements of an inquiry episode. However, topics that are to some extent controversial and problematic are best because they are consistent with the nature of inquiry. That is, there is clearly something to inquire about, and the outcome may still be in doubt. Subject matter and topics relating to current affairs, law and justice, the environment, energy, intergroup relations, economics, and geography are a few that lend themselves well to inquiry. As an example, the following case could be used as the basis for an inquiry into certain aspects of the legal and justice systems:

FARMER INDICTED IN ELK-KILLING CASE

Kenneth Reed was indicted in Sheridan District Court Tuesday on five counts of killing elk, a protected species in this state. Reed, a local farmer, did not deny killing the elk, but said they were damaging the grain crop he needed to feed his dairy herd.

Reed said that the animals began damaging his crop in midsummer and that he had repeatedly asked the Fish and Game Department to do something about it. Through his attorney, Reed said that he had contacted the department "at least a dozen times" by telephone. He also said that he sent three letters to the department warning that if something were not done, he would shoot the animals. Reed insists that he was justified in killing the elk to protect his property.

It is expected that the case will come to trial this fall. If found guilty, Reed could be sentenced to one year in jail and fined $1,000 on each of the five counts.[4]

This case raises some interesting legal questions relating to the right to protect one's property. Because television programs often show individuals using firearms to protect their property or themselves, children may

---

[4]This is a fictitious case, although in 1975, in a case much like this one, a Minnesota farmer was found not guilty by a district court jury.

Problem-Solving Behavior

Ms. Carroll's class is discussing problem solving in relation to their study of early societies. To increase their understanding of this concept further, she divides the class into groups of four and gives each group a carambola (any food that is uncommon—jicama, plantain, cherimoya, kiwi, and so on, would do).

> Ms. Carroll.   Pretend you are an early person and you have just found one of these fruits while food gathering. You do not know what it is because you have never seen one like it before. You are not sure whether or not you can safely eat it. In your group, discuss what decisions you can make concerning this "find" and the consequences of each decision.

The groups discuss this question, and then Ms. Carroll has each group present its decisions to the class. They conclude there are three options, and Ms. Carroll writes them on the chalkboard.

Decision	Consequence
1. Do nothing; pass it by.	1. Might lose a good and needed food source.
2. Test it by eating it.	2. Could become sick or could even die if it is poisonous; *or* could be a tasty nutritious food.
3. Develop some way of testing it before eating it.	3. Would take time but would be safe.

> Ms. Carroll then continues: Suppose you made decision no. 3. In your group, develop a plan of action you could use to test whether or not you could safely eat the newfound fruit.

The children develop plans that involve testing the food on nonhuman subjects. These plans are discussed and compared with modern-day practices in testing food products, new drugs, and medical practices. This discussion raises many issues related to the use of human subjects for experimental purposes.

Ms. Carroll concludes the inquiry by asking the children to speculate on
1. The risks of trial-and-error behavior.
2. How such risks can be reduced.
3. Alternatives to trial-and-error, problem-solving procedures.

have distorted ideas about the legal aspects of protecting oneself or one's property. Some of the issues raised by this case are these:

1. Why might the person be found not guilty in this case even though the specific action—that is, killing the elk—is clearly against the law in that state? Why should such a finding *in one case* not be interpreted by citizens as encouragement to break the law any time they think it is unfair or does not apply to them?

2. How does the fact that Reed had contacted the Fish and Game Department several times, without any apparent results, have any bearing on the outcome of the case?
3. Do individuals have the right to "take the law into their own hands" when appropriate officials refuse to or are unable to take corrective action?
4. Would the outcome of this case most likely be different if the trespassers were people instead of elk?

Intellectual skills such as critical thinking, reflective inquiry, problem analysis, and creative problem solving should not be taught outside a related subject-matter context. That is, to think critically or reflectively, learners must think about *something*. These are not processes that can either be taught or learned in isolation. Therefore, as the teacher is planning the social studies unit, some provision needs to be made to include instruction on and the application of critical thinking and other intellectual skills in order that they be perceived by the learners as a natural extension of what they are studying. This can be done by using the planning format suggested in Figure 4-2. Notice that space is provided in the upper right corner of the form to list questions to stimulate reflective thinking.

PLANNING FOR EFFECTIVE QUESTIONING PROCEDURES

In using reading and writing activities, in conducting classroom discussions, and in challenging children to do critical and reflective thinking, the teacher will make frequent use of questions. Questioning strategies are among the oldest and most widely used methods of conducting instruction. The teacher uses questions to clarify procedures, to determine whether children understand what they are to do, to find out whether additional explanation is required, to get feedback on the effectiveness of a demonstration or explanation, and so on.

Questions may also be used to check the child's comprehension of concepts, generalizations, or subject matter. Often such questions require the learner to reproduce or recall factual information that has been read or discussed in class. Research of classroom-teacher behavior through the years shows that teachers use a high percentage of questions of this type.[5] These questions are sometimes referred to as "lower-level" because they involve simple recall and memory rather than higher-order mental operations such as application, analysis, synthesis, interpretation, sensing cause and effect, or evaluation. So-called "lower-level" questions can be easily identified because they usually begin with who, what, when, and where.

[5]Arthur L. Costa, "Teacher Behaviors that Enable Student Thinking," *Developing Minds: A Resource Book for Teaching Thinking*, ed. Arthur L. Costa (Alexandria, VA: Association for Supervision and Curriculum Development, 1985), 125–37.

These questions are important, especially in checking reading comprehension or to ascertain that children are familiar with facts essential to the topic. The problem is that there is a tendency to overuse such questions, with a corresponding lessened use of other questions that do require higher-order thought processes. In terms of the development of intellectual skills, the most important questions to ask are those that require elaborative, reflective responses. These higher-level questions often begin, "Why . . ." "How . . ." "How do we know . . ." "Show that . . ." "If that is true, then . . ." The difference between the two is clearly illustrated by the example based on the narrative "Ellis Island" on pages 112–113.

These higher-level questions serve two general purposes relating to thinking skills. One is that they trigger mental operations that are in accord with a problem-solving discovery learning format. For example, what mental operations are involved if the teacher asks the question: What is the most important reason for a small population in the area? Before responding, the child has to (1) analyze the situation, (2) consider all of the reasons that might apply, (3) evaluate each in terms of its importance, and then (4) select the one considered to be most important. Mental operations of this type characterize higher-level, or reflective thought processes. Simply recalling a "correct" response is not adequate—the information has to be processed intellectually: analyzed, synthesized, applied, interpreted, evaluated, and so on. Thus, appropriate questions are essential in building reflective habits of thought.

Reflective or "thought" questions also serve the purpose of teaching the child improved habits of study. If the only kinds of questions encountered are based on recall of factual information, the child learns to study in accordance with such objectives. The child may not learn how to apply information or even to process it in terms of broader intellectual outcomes. For example, without such experience, a child may attach the same degree of importance to a trivial incident as to a major concept or a profound generalization. Also, problem solving requires the ability *to ask* appropriate questions, and children cannot develop this skill unless they encounter such questions in their study.

For what purposes are questions used in social studies? Examples of some of the more common purposes are provided in Figure 4-4.

It is apparent that there is overlap among some of the categories of questions listed in Figure 4-4. For instance, a question for independent study might also be used to check comprehension, to analyze component elements, or to draw conclusions. The object of these examples is to show that questions can be used for many different purposes, not that the categories are mutually exclusive.

To improve questioning techniques, the following suggestions are provided:

1. Consciously reduce the number of factual recall questions asked. These are usually questions that begin with "Who?" "What?" "Where?" and

FIGURE 4-4
Types of Questions used in Social Studies and Examples of Each

1. **To establish procedures.** Examples:
   a. Does everyone have a copy of the map?
   b. Are you looking at the lower part of the picture?
2. **To analyze component elements.** Examples:
   a. How many steps are involved in the process?
   b. What land features are most important to the occupations of the people who live there?
3. **To check comprehension or general understanding.** Examples:
   a. Where was the first settlement made?
   b. What were the reasons for moving to a new location?
4. **To interpret data.** Examples:
   a. Why is there such a difference in climate between Rome and Boston even though they are on about the same parallel of latitude?
   b. Which income groups are hardest hit by a sales tax on food? Why?
5. **To predict outcomes.** Examples:
   a. What other products are likely to be affected by increased prices of steel?
   b. If everyone worked only four days a week, what businesses might be expected to grow?
6. **To probe for additional information.** Examples:
   a. Who can tell a little more about why the law was passed?
   b. Does this mean that one could not enter that country without a visa?
7. **To clarify meanings of learner responses.** Examples:
   a. Who can give an example of how daylight saving time benefits people?
   b. I am still not sure I understand your explanation of "duty-free." Is "duty-free" the same as tax-free?
8. **To explain something.** Examples:
   a. How might a winter frost in Florida affect the lives of people in northern cities such as Minneapolis, Milwaukee, Detroit, and Cleveland?
   b. If farmers make greater use of machinery and there is less need for farmhands, where do people in the rural areas find jobs?
9. **To describe something.** Examples:
   a. What was life like for an immigrant family from Eastern Europe living in Chicago at the turn of the century?
   b. Your book tells how the people felt when they arrived at their destination after traveling for several weeks in the wagon train. What were their feelings?
10. **To verify statements or conclusions.** Examples:
    a. Which paragraph tells exactly why environmental impact statements are required?
    b. That figure seems low to me. Would you mind locating the source of these figures and rechecking that second amount?
11. **To guide independent study.** Examples:
    a. What advantages does the author give for the use of checks instead of coins and currency?
    b. What reasons are given on pages 81–87 for our strong ties with Japan?
12. **To diagnose learning difficulties.** Examples:
    a. How would you find something about the cotton gin in this book?
    b. What is the main idea in the third paragraph on page 153?
13. **To summarize ideas or to draw conclusions.** Examples:
    a. Based on what we have learned thus far, what conclusions might we make about life in these early settlements?
    b. What is the relationship between the availability of a product and its price?

"When?" Replace these with questions that require elaborative, reflective responses, for example, "Why?" "How?" "How do we know?"

2. Match the type of question with the purpose it is to serve. Questions that call for yes-no responses are not appropriate to stimulate a discussion. Reflective or discussion questions should not be used for homework or independent study.

3. State questions in ways that communicate precisely what is being asked. Sometimes children cannot respond to questions not because they do not know the material but because the question is ambiguous or otherwise poorly framed. The vocabulary level must be consistent with the age and maturity of the children. Although this may seem to be a trite reminder, it does constitute a problem for adults who have not been closely associated with children. Beginning teachers should write out in advance the main questions they plan to use.

4. Provide adequate time for the children to respond. Ask the question *before* calling on a specific respondent. This requires all children to form their own response intellectually.

5. Vary the way you acknowledge responses. In addition to "uh-huh," "all right," and "O.K.," which are commonly overused by teachers, try asking another question such as a probing or clarifying question. Avoid *always* acknowledging responses with evaluative comments such as "right," "yes," or "that's good," although these should be used from time to time to encourage children to participate.

PLANNING SHORT INSTRUCTIONAL SEQUENCES

Thus far our discussion has concerned itself only with planning a unit—a parcel of work that might take several weeks to complete. To implement such a plan, teachers must extract from the unit plan ideas that can be converted into shorter instructional sequences that may last anywhere from a single day to a week or more. Sometimes these are called daily lesson plans although there is some objection to that term because it suggests—and may lead to—fragmentation, rigidity, and old-fashioned teaching procedures. Social studies learning is, or ought to be, continuous from one day to the next. Children simply pick up where they left off in their study the day before. Lesson plans should be consistent with this continuous flow of learning. Short-range plans are a teaching trip map that the teacher has in hand and uses at the time the teaching is done. Because the teacher relies on these plans to implement the instruction, they must be complete in every detail, correctly sequenced, contingencies anticipated and accounted for, with as little as possible left to chance. As the teacher prepares such plans, it is helpful to rehearse mentally how the lesson is expected to proceed, step-by-step. This will help reduce the possibility of encountering surprises while the lesson is in progress.

⋯⋯⋯⋯⋯⋯⋯ ELLIS ISLAND

Between 1892 and 1954, Ellis Island served as the processing center for more than 17 million immigrants. Nearly half of all Americans today can trace their ancestry to someone who entered this nation through Ellis Island. These people came from all over the world, but the vast majority came from the countries of eastern and southern Europe. Many were uneducated and unable to speak English, and many were of peasant stock. For these millions of people, Ellis Island was the first stop in this promised land where freedom and economic opportunity beckoned.

Ellis Island itself was originally a three-acre mudflat in New York harbor that was owned by Samuel Ellis. New York State came into possession of it in 1808, and in the same year the federal government purchased it for $10,000. In 1965, President Lyndon B. Johnson added Ellis Island to the Statue of Liberty National Monument, thus placing it under the jurisdiction of the National Park Service.

During the heavy immigration between 1896 and 1915, 60 percent of the arrivals came from three countries—Austria, Italy, and Russia. Because the U.S. Immigration Service did not record the nationality of immigrants prior to 1899, arrivals from Austria might have been Germans, Czechs, Poles, Croatians, Moravians, Austrians, Hungarians, Slovenes, or other national groups residing within the dual monarchy of Austria-Hungary. At first the influx of these people was welcomed because they supplied needed labor for the growing industrial economy of the United States. But in a few years, deep-seated feelings of resentment against these people emerged. This resulted in the restrictive Immigration Act of 1924.

QUESTIONS REQUIRING COMPREHENSION OF LITERAL MEANING

1. During what years did Ellis Island serve as a processing center for immigrants?

2. From whom did the United States purchase Ellis Island?
3. Why do we not have good records on the nationality of immigrants prior to 1899?
4. What three countries provided most of the immigrant people?

5. How large was the original Ellis Island?
6. What governmental agency is responsible for the administration and upkeep of Ellis Island?

QUESTIONS REQUIRING INTERPRETATION OF IDEAS

1. What risks did those persons encounter who decided to pull up their roots and move to America during the period discussed?
2. Why is this place called "Ellis" Island?
3. How were the immigrants described in this article different from those who come to this country today?
4. Was Ellis Island a good location for a port of entry during the period that it served as a processing center? Why or why not?
5. What were some of the effects of the Immigration Act of 1924?
6. Why do you suppose resentment developed toward these particular immigrant people? Are there parallels in the attitudes of some toward present-day immigrants?

7. In what year was the restrictive Immigration Act passed?

8. Why were these immigrants welcomed to the United States in the early years?

7. Were the new arrivals discussed in the essay an asset or a liability to the United States?

8. How well were these immigrant people able to assimilate into the mainstream culture of the United States?

There are four essential components of plans of this type. These are (1) the purpose or objective that identifies what children will *learn;* (2) lesson development to include (a) the readiness or interest-building procedures that indicate how the sequence is to *begin* and (b) work-study activities that indicate what children will *do* to help them learn; (3) summary and evaluation that indicate how the sequence will *close;* and (4) a list of the instructional materials and resources needed to teach the sequence. The examples on pages 114–115 show how these plans can be constructed.

JUDGING THE ADEQUACY OF A LESSON PLAN

A teacher is never as well prepared as he or she *might* have been, given more time and more resources. Lesson planning is an open-ended process that can go on endlessly. Many teachers can recall, as student teachers, staying up half the night preparing a half-hour lesson to be taught the next day. Although such effort is commendable, it cannot be sustained for any length of time. At some point, the teacher must decide that the lesson is well enough planned and then be able to turn to other matters with a clear conscience.

It is not always easy, especially for the beginning teacher, to know when one has reached the point of diminishing returns in lesson planning. The checklist that follows can be useful in deciding whether all important aspects of the lesson have been given appropriate attention in the planning process.

LESSON PLAN CHECKLIST

1. Do the lesson objectives state clearly what it is that the children are expected to *learn?*
2. Do the learner activities for the lesson relate in a direct way to the stated objectives? That is, will the children learn what they are supposed to learn by doing the things they are asked to do?
3. Do you know how the lesson is to begin? What is the very first thing you will do? Say? What next? What third?
4. Have you written down the questions you plan to ask? Do you have them in the order you plan to ask them?

Lesson Plan 3

Topic:	Group membership
Grade:	Two
Time:	Two class periods
Objectives:	Children will learn to identify human groups and will become aware of reasons why people are grouped together.
Interest Building:	Display five pictures of groups. Underneath each write what type of group is represented. (Ideas: soccer team, birthday party, family, class, scout troop)
Lesson Development:	Ask class to think of one word that describes all the pictures. Elicit the word *group*.
	Generate a simple definition of a human group.
	Have children think of the names of several more groups.
	Suggest that they include groups to which they belong. Write these on chalkboard.
	Focus the class discussion on the reason people are grouped together, and place ideas on a chart as follows:

HUMAN GROUPS

What are some groups that we know about?	*Why are these people grouped together?*
family	love, help each other
team	to play games
class	to learn
birthday party	for fun
scout troop	camping, making things, helping others

	Discuss ways that groups can be identified. Look at the five original pictures for clues. Some clues might be: clothing/uniforms, symbols/mascots, official names, special songs, distinguishing looks or languages.
Summary:	Bring the concept of group into the children's immediate experience by asking the following questions: Is this class a group? How do you know? Why are we grouped together? What are *your* reasons for being a member of this group?
	Have old magazines available, and ask children to cut out a picture of a group. Have each child tell something about what the group is doing. As they make their presentation, have them finish this sentence: "I think that these people make a group because. . . ." Use the pictures to make a collage on the bulletin board.
Followup:	Have children bring in personal photos of groups to which they belong and share them with the class.
	If possible, take a photo of the class group, and have a print made for each child.
Needed Materials:	Five pictures of different groups for display purposes. White butcher paper and felt pen to make chart.
	Old magazines or newspapers that have pictures of groups.
	Option: Personal camera

Lesson Plan 4

Topic:	Futuring
Grade:	Six
Time:	Three class periods
Objective:	Learners will be able to identify present trends and to project the consequence of a specific trend.
Interest Building:	Suggest that the class has gathered together in the year 2025 for a reunion. Have them speculate on what their lives will be like then. Define *trends,* and have the students list current trends such as more mechanization in our daily lives or the increased use of computers.
Lesson Development:	With the students working in groups of three, have them choose one of the current trends and brainstorm all of the consequences of that trend, such as more leisure time in the case of the mechanization trend, which leads to more recreation needs, which means an increase in the use of state parks and the like. Ask the students to organize their ideas for sharing with their classmates.
Summary:	In the next class period have each group identify consequences that seem to be negative. Ask them to develop an ideal plan that could make this consequence beneficial to people in the future.
Materials:	None necessary, but outside sources have commercial materials on this topic. Two possible references are these: The Center for Curriculum Design 823 Foster Street Evanston, Illinois 60204 Science Fiction Research Association Box 3186 The College of Wooster Wooster, Ohio 44691

5. Do you have all the needed instructional material? Equipment? If you are planning to use a machine, have you arranged to get it? Do you know where the electrical outlets are in the room? Will you need an extension cord? Screen?

6. Are there specific directions you are planning to give the children regarding what they are to do? If so, do you know what they are?

7. If you are going to group the children, do you have productive work planned for *all* the groups, *all* the time?

8. Do you know how much time will be needed for each component of your lesson?

9. Have you provided for differences in rate and level of learning among children? Do you have productive work-study activities planned for those who complete their assignments quickly? Have you provided

additional help for the slower learners? Do you have appropriate learning activities planned for any children with handicapping conditions?

10. Have you considered whether the lesson will require changes in the
    room environment, movement of furniture, and so forth?
11. Do you know exactly how the lesson is to close—that is: What you will
    do? What you will say? What you expect the children to do?
12. Have you planned for any followup activity?
13. Have you taken into account how learning is to be evaluated?
14. Should the lesson be completed more quickly than you had planned,
    do you have some "backup" activities ready that can be used?

DISCUSSION QUESTIONS AND SUGGESTED ACTIVITIES

1. Select a unit topic that would be appropriate for a grade of your choice,
   and identify six to eight main ideas that could be developed in such a
   unit. State these as declarative sentences (generalizations). Arrange
   them in the order in which they would be presented in the unit.

2. Select one of the main ideas you identified in your response to question
   1. Develop it into a teaching plan, using the format suggested by
   Figure 4-2.

3. Using the ideas you developed in your answer to question 2, prepare
   a teaching sequence (lesson plan) using the form suggested in Lesson
   Plans 3 and 4.

4. Write behavioral objectives for a unit such as the one you identified in
   responding to question 1.

5. Suggest social studies learnings that lend themselves especially well to
   the use of behavioral objectives and some that do not. How would the
   teacher evaluate learner achievement of objectives that are not stated
   behaviorally?

6. Discuss teaching plans and how to prepare them with your supervising teacher or with some other in-service teacher you know. If possible,
   bring to class a sample of a social studies plan used by that teacher.
   Compare plans brought to class in terms of similarities in the items
   included.

7. Prepare a list of decisions that could be made in your classroom in
   which children could legitimately participate. Also, make a list of decisions in which they would not participate. What guidelines can you
   suggest regarding the involvement of children in classroom decision
   making?

8. Suppose as a teacher you were assigned to a school that had no social
   studies curriculum guide or any type of a planned social studies program. How would you go about planning the social studies program
   for your class?

9. Identify a few events, decisions, or actions that occurred at the national level that have had an impact on social studies education at the local level.

10. Prepare a lesson plan just as you would teach it to a grade of your choice. Apply the checklist given at the end of the chapter to test for its completeness. Have the plan critiqued by a practicing teacher.

11. In the assignment of questions for independent study or homework, why is it important that the child be able to get the answers from the available books and resources?

12. Do you think the kinds of questions a teacher asks reflect the major objectives the teacher has in mind for the lesson? *Should* they? Explain your response.

SELECTED REFERENCES

BARON, JOAN B., AND ROBERT J. STERNBERG. *Teaching Thinking Skills: Theory and Practice.* New York: W. H. Freeman, 1987.

BEYER, BARRY K. *Practical Strategies for the Teaching of Thinking.* Boston: Allyn and Bacon, 1987.

GALL, MEREDITH. "Synthesis of Research on Teachers' Questioning." *Educational Leadership* 42 (November 1984): 40–47.

GRONLUND, NORMAN E. *How to Write and Use Instructional Objectives.* 4th ed. New York: Macmillan, 1991.

HOLBROOK, H. T. "Writing to Learn in the Social Studies." *The Reading Teacher* 41 (November 1987): 216–19.

HUNKINS, FRANCIS P. *Teaching Thinking Through Effective Questioning.* Boston: Christopher-Gordon, 1989.

JAROLIMEK, JOHN, AND CLIFFORD D. FOSTER, SR. *Teaching and Learning in the Elementary School.* 5th ed. New York: Macmillan, 1993. Chapters 6, 7, 8, and 9.

KELLOUGH, RICHARD D., AND PATRICIA L. ROBERTS. *A Resource Guide for Elementary School Teaching: Planning for Competence.* New York: Macmillan, 1991.

McKENZIE, GARY R. "Learning and Instruction." In *Elementary School Social Studies: Research as a Guide to Practice,* Edited by Virginia A. Atwood. NCSS Bulletin No. 79. Washington, DC: National Council for the Social Studies, 1986. Chapter 8.

RESNICK, LAUREN B. *Education and Learning to Think.* Washington, DC: National Academy Press, 1987.

SCHRAG, FRANCIS. *Thinking in School and Society.* New York: Routledge, 1988.

SHAHEEN, JOANN C. "Participatory Citizenship in the Elementary Grades." *Social Education* 53 (October 1989): 361–63.

STEINBRINK, JOHN E. "The Social Studies Learner as Questioner." *The Social Studies* 76 (January/February 1985): 38–40.

WOOLEVER, ROBERTA M. "A New Framework for Developing Classroom Questions." *Social Education* 51 (October 1987): 405–10.

II

SOCIAL STUDIES CONTENT AND CONTENT-RELATED SKILLS

5 | History and Geography in the Social Studies

T he subject matter banquet table of the social studies curriculum is loaded with a myriad of offerings, each more tempting than the next. An entire curriculum could be built around history or any one of the social sciences. Or, an exciting curriculum could result from a focus on issues and problems that people try to resolve in ordinary living. A good social studies curriculum could be designed around the study of current affairs. And each of these approaches—and still others like them— could result in excellent programs. Nonetheless, history and geography remain the backbone, or central core, around which most schools organize their social studies programs. History and geography are the integrating disciplines that serve as the basic framework for the social studies curriculum, especially in the third grade and beyond. In this and the succeeding four chapters, we will examine how the several sources of subject matter contribute to the elementary school social studies curriculum.

HISTORY AND THE SOCIAL STUDIES

Throughout this century, the subject of history has been the jewel in the crown of the social studies curriculum. Indeed, even today to many teachers and parents alike, social studies means history. In spite of the heavy loading of history in the curriculum, the available objective evidence suggests that citizens' knowledge of events that have been significant to this nation's history is so meager as to constitute a national embarrassment.[1] To

---

[1] Arthur N. Applebee, Judith A. Langer, Ina V. S. Mullis, *Literature and U.S. History: The Instructional Experience and Factual Knowledge of High School Juniors.* The Nation's Report Card, Report No. 17-HL-01. Princeton, NJ: Educational Test Service, 1987; Lynne V. Cheney, *American Memory: A Report on the Humanities in the Nation's Public Schools* (Washington, DC: National Endowment for the Humanities, 1987); Report of the Bradley Commission on History in Schools, Educational Excellence Network, 1112 Sixteenth Street N.W., Suite 500, Washington, DC 20036, 1988.

121

produce citizens with a better grasp of history, schools need to give more thought to the way the subject is taught and how its importance is being perceived by students. It is a genuine thrill for students at any age to encounter a teacher who can make history come alive and seem to be more important than anything else one could want to study. But this is an experience that few learners have the good fortune of having. For untold numbers of learners, history has a reputation of being a somewhat less than engaging subject, to say the least.

In recent years there has been a revival of interest in history as a school subject because many lay persons as well as educators believe that history can and should contribute directly to attaining the broad goals of citizenship education. Most states have legislative requirements calling for the teaching of state and national history. A knowledge of history supported by actual experiences in the practice of responsible citizenship in the school and classroom unquestionably contributes to a strengthening of loyalties and helps children identify with their historical background. Persons develop love of country, loyalty, and fidelity through a knowledge, appreci-

Who says history can't be fun? Here we see students trying on clothes of their eighteenth-century forbears. This excellent instructional activity, offered by the Wythe South Office at Colonial Williamsburg, is obviously being enjoyed by these students. Colonial Williamsburg is a rich treasure of the life and culture of the people of this early settlement in Virginia.
(Photo courtesy of the Colonial Williamsburg Foundation.)

ation, and understanding of the struggles of the people who contributed to the building of this great and powerful nation. Hazel W. Hertzberg reminded us that "The improvement of history teaching in the schools is not just desirable: it is a national necessity."[2]

History teaching is valuable when it provides opportunities for the child to identify with the past. The historical experiences of the nation then become part of the heritage of individual children and, thus, a part of the common culture. This is amply demonstrated by the interest expressed by children when they dramatize events from our nation's history, events that may have occurred long before their own ancestors came to these shores. Because students can reflect on the known consequences of specific decisions that were made and can speculate on what outcomes may have occurred had other decisions been made, the subject matter of history provides many opportunities to teach critical thinking.

Knowledge of history does not lend itself to the practical solution of everyday problems *in the same way* as does a knowledge of spelling words or skills in reading or mathematics. Because little direct relationship between a knowledge of history and daily problems of living exists, it cannot and should not be thought of as an entirely practical subject. In this sense, history resembles literature, art, and music in that its contribution may lie along cultural lines rather than along strictly practical ones. Although children will not apply their knowledge of history directly to the solution of the many complex problems of the twentieth century, it will give them an insight, appreciation, and understanding of those problems.

The History Curriculum

The teaching of history in the elementary and middle schools occurs within the context of the social studies curriculum, and history contributes substantially to the program. The emphasis is on understanding the past, the people who lived during those times, their problems and ways of living, and their struggles to meet basic needs. History taught in this way helps the child develop a better understanding and appreciation of human growth through the years—not only along political lines but in all ways—that contribute to a richer and more abundant life. This would include a study of the growth of the arts, sciences, literature, humanitarian movements, and other cultural aspects of human development.

What are the central themes that should guide the study of history in the schools? The Bradley Commission on History in Schools in 1988 defined six "themes and narratives" that the commission believed need to be stressed

---

[2]Hazel W. Hertzberg, "Students, Methods and Materials of Instruction," in *History in the Schools*, Matthew T. Downey, ed., National Council for the Social Studies Bulletin 74 (Washington, DC: National Council for the Social Studies, 1985), 40.

to "comprehend the forces for change and continuity that have shaped—and will continue to shape—human life. . . ."[3] These six themes and narratives are as follows:

Civilization, Cultural Diffusion, and Innovation.   The evolution of human skills and the means of exerting power over nature and people. The rise, interaction, and decline of successive centers of such skills and power. The cultural flowering of major civilizations in the arts, literature, and thought. The role of social, religious, and political patronage of the arts and learning. The importance of the city in different eras and places.

Human Interaction with the Environment.   The relationships among geography, technology, and culture, and their effects on economic, social, and political developments. The choices made possible by climate, resources, and location, and the effect of culture and human values on such choices. The gains and losses of technological change. The central role of agriculture. The effect of disease, and disease-fighting, on plants, animals, and human beings.

Values, Beliefs, Political Ideas, and Institutions.   The origins and spread of influential religions and ideologies. The evolution of political and social institutions, at various stages of industrial and commercial development. The interplay among ideas, material conditions, moral values, and leadership, especially in the evolution of democratic societies. The tensions between the aspirations for freedom and security, for liberty and equality, for distinction and commonality, in human affairs.

Conflict and Cooperation.   The many and various causes of war, and of approaches to peacemaking and war prevention. Relations between domestic affairs and ways of dealing with the outside world. Contrasts between international conflict and cooperation, between isolation and interdependence. The consequences of war and peace for societies and their cultures.

Comparative History of Major Developments.   The characteristics of revolutionary, reactionary, and reform periods across time and place. Imperialism, ancient and modern. Comparative instances of slavery and emancipation, feudalism and centralization, human successes and failures, of wisdom and folly. Comparative elites and aristocracies; the role of family, wealth, and merit.

Patterns of Social and Political Interaction.   The changing patterns of class, ethnic, racial, and gender structures and relations. Immigration, mi-

---

[3]Bradley Commission on History in Schools, *Building a History Curriculum: Guidelines for Teaching History in Schools* (Washington, DC: Educational Excellence Network, 1988), 10. The Bradley Commission first met in 1987 and was responsible for a number of initiatives designed to enhance the teaching of history in the schools. In 1990 the National Council for History Education, Inc. was formed, and that organization has taken over many of the projects begun by the Bradley Commission.

gration, and social mobility. The effects of schooling. The new prominence of women, minorities, and the common people in the study of history, and their relation to political power and influential elites. The characteristics of multicultural societies; forces for unity and disunity.[4]

The Bradley Commission guidelines document provides examples of how these themes can be integrated into the subject matter of American history, the history of Western civilization, and world history. It also discusses how history can be incorporated in the social studies curriculum of *all* grades.

The concepts embedded in the foregoing themes can, for curriculum purposes, be organized around key ideas or major generalizations. The following represent *samples* of major generalizations from the field of history that have been used as organizing ideas in developing programs in historical study:

1. The history of a country has a definite bearing on the culture, traditions, beliefs, attitudes, and ways of living of its people.
2. People are influenced by values, ideals, and inherited institutions as well as by their environment.
3. Several civilizations have risen and fallen in the history of human societies; many have contributed to existing civilizations.
4. Human societies have undergone and are undergoing continual, although perhaps gradual, changes in response to various forces, but not all change is progress.
5. Guidelines for understanding thought and action in contemporary affairs can be derived from the historical backgrounds of society.

Teaching Suggestions

A good social studies program will help the child build psychological bridges or links with the past through a series of planned experiences. The following are examples of activities that may be helpful for this purpose.

Opportunity to Examine Objects of Historical Significance. Children are usually interested in objects of historical significance, particularly if they can examine them closely and handle them. Items from the past that will be helpful in teaching are such things as Indian arrowheads, artifacts from past wars, a facsimile of a slave contract, a family Bible, deeds, photographs, church membership rolls, school records, a hymnal, and branding irons. Children may bring items of this type to school to share with their classmates. Such objects may have some monetary value and must be handled accordingly. If a particular item is highly valued, it is best for the adult owner to bring it to the school to show the children and tell them of its significance.

---

[4]Bradley Commission, *Building a History Curriculum*, 10–11.

These students are learning firsthand about one important part of pioneer technology—printing. Experiences of this type can help learners build an appreciation for the skills and resourcefulness of those who lived in bygone days. Old Sturbridge Village is a recreated early nineteenth-century rural New England community and is a marvelous resource for enriching social studies learning.
(Photo by Henry E. Peach, Old Sturbridge Village.)

In addition to historical *realia*, that is, real things or artifacts that can be brought to the classroom, or to those that may be in a school museum, the teacher should look into the permanent museum resources of the community. Most larger communities maintain exhibits of historical materials significant to the local community and state. School groups are usually encouraged to make visits to local museums and are frequently taken on guided tours through the exhibits. Some museums change their displays from time to time and will on request furnish schools with information about their current exhibits. These resources present valuable opportunities for teaching history and need to be used extensively.

The best use of the museum can be made by children after they have had an opportunity to develop a familiarity with the subject matter related to the material on display. This means that visits will be made after the children have been able to explore ideas and concepts in the classroom through reading, study, and discussion rather than at the beginning of a unit. They will then be ready to clarify ideas: They can ask intelligent questions and can enrich their understanding through the museum visit. In taking children to a museum, teachers will want to ready the class beforehand by identifying a few relevant questions concerning the items to be observed.

Many museums in the country have assembled artifacts, pictures, and other items of interest into kits that are available to schools on a rental basis. Study kits ordinarily have a teacher's guide that provides background information as well as practical suggestions concerning the use of the material.

Opportunity to Talk with Older People of the Community.   Children are fascinated when old-timers talk of their exciting experiences in the early community. They are surprised and electrified by the thought that the person now speaking to them served with General Eisenhower or shook President Kennedy's hand. These experiences make real people out of historical figures and remove them from the realm of myth and unreality. Interviewing persons who have had firsthand experience with an event under study is a technique often used by historians.

Almost every community has one or more persons who has devoted a substantial amount of time to the study of local history as a hobby. These individuals are excellent resources for the teacher, not only in their personally speaking to the class but also in directing the teacher's attention to other resources that might otherwise be overlooked. This provides an excellent opportunity to study the social history of the local community. To catch some of the enthusiasm and interest such persons ordinarily have for history is, in itself, a valuable experience for both the teacher and the children.

Social History.   An increasing number of teachers are discovering the exciting potentials offered by *social history*. Social history explores how ordinary people met the day-to-day challenges, pleasures, disappointments, and routines of everyday life in the period in which they lived. Children are fascinated in learning how people much like themselves made a living; engaged in leisure-time activities; raised their families; celebrated important holidays; punished criminals; educated their children; and observed such important milestones in life as birth, marriage, and the death of loved ones. In social history, the common persons—as opposed to those who have achieved prominence—become the central focus of study.

Oral History.   The structured interviews or informal conversations with persons of historical significance in the local community can be preserved as oral history by using cassette tape recorders. This procedure has the added instructional value of involving children themselves on a firsthand basis in gathering historical data. The taped interviews should be structured to the extent that children have identified the questions to be asked and the sequence in which they are to be presented. Children should, however, be encouraged to include followup questions that emerge as the interview progresses. Often the interaction between the interviewer and the subject becomes stilted because the child asks only the questions that are prepared in advance. It helps if children simulate the interview or a portion of it in advance, with a classmate serving as the subject of the interview. The cassette recorder should be used for the simulation, too, just as it will be used in the real interview. A good-quality taped interview will result only if the interviewer has good interaction skills and if the substantive aspects of the subject matter and the technical elements of the recording are well planned and implemented.

If good classroom preparation precedes the interview, children may obtain taped interviews of a quality that can become a part of a central collection of local history materials. It is necessary to obtain a signed release from the person being interviewed if the material is to be used beyond the work of the class. Where it is possible to do so, children may also want to secure a photograph of the person being interviewed.

On the basis of several years of experience in helping teachers conduct oral history as an instructional activity, Professor John F. Ahern of the University of Toledo offers the following suggestions:

1. Conduct two interviews with the same person at least a day apart.
2. After the first interview, have children respond to the stem, "I wish I had said . . ." in preparing questions for the second interview.
3. Make use of the counter on the cassette to find the exact spot where something was asked or said.
4. Role play the interview in advance.
5. Brainstorm questions with students.
6. Be aware of noise in the environment that might affect the quality of the recording.
7. Test the batteries in the cassette before the interview.
8. Provide questions before the interview.
9. Get out a photo album, if there is one.
10. Interview one person at a time. (Important because one often wants to answer for or correct [modify] the response of the other!)
11. Ask ahead of time if it is o.k. to inquire about age.
12. Make sure names are spelled correctly.
13. Begin with easy questions, such as "Where were you born?" "Where did your family come from?" "Why did your family settle here?" Women like to talk about their last daughter's wedding; men like to talk about their first job.
14. Use techniques such as the following to elicit responses:
    "Tell me more about . . ."
    "Why do you think . . ."
    "Give me an example . . ."[5]

Reading Materials.   There is a plentiful supply of well-written, exciting books dealing with history that have great value in helping children identify with the past. Children do this when they become "lost in a book." In the vivid accounts of the adventures of early explorers, the child relives the perils, dangers, and excitement of Lewis and Clark; the disappointments

[5]Professor John F. Ahern, in a presentation entitled "Making History More Meaningful," Hamilton County Shared Inservice, Cincinnati, Ohio, October 2, 1987.

··················· A STUDY OF LOCAL HISTORY

A combination fifth–sixth grade class used the publication of a magazine as the integrating activity for the study of their local community. Each student in the class selected a long-time resident in the community as one source of information. The students interviewed the resident and tape recorded the conversation using oral history procedures. Each student was then requested to prepare an article for the class magazine based on the information secured in the interview. In addition to the interviews, students used other local information sources, such as printed material and photographs from local libraries or personal collections. Also, numerous resource persons were asked to make presentations to the class on such topics as local history, interviewing procedures, journal writing, and procedures associated with the production of a publication.

and trials of Abe Lincoln; the hazards of a trip across the western plains; or the rugged winters of Wisconsin. We are referring here specifically to "trade books"—books about Indians, airplanes, urban life, space travel, national parks, biographies of famous Americans, life in other lands, communities at work, and similar topics. Many contemporary children's books are not only informative but represent good children's literature. They have exceptional artwork and maintain high standards of literary quality.

Literary works useful for social studies instruction may be classified as (1) *informative accounts*—works that simply convey specific information in literary form on topics studied, such as books about trucks, trains, countries, printing, communication, homes around the world; (2) *informative fiction*—reconstruction of historical events that are built around a fictionalized plot or story; (3) *biographies*; (4) *nonfiction history*; (5) *poems*; and (6) *locally produced materials*—consisting possibly of works falling in any of the preceding five categories.

Literature and literary materials should play an important part in social studies instruction because they convey so well the affective dimension of human experience. The realism that is achieved through vivid portrayals in works of literature stirs the imagination of the young reader and helps develop a feeling for and identification with the topic being studied. The relationship between literature and some of the subjects included in the social studies—particularly history—has been noted by numerous writers. Some great works of literature are also considered important historical documents, and the reverse is also true.

One reason that literary materials are so important is that they provide rich detail that is impossible to get in even a well-designed text or an encyclopedia. A textbook, for example, may simply mention women who spearheaded the movement to gain equal rights, such as Susan B. Anthony, Elizabeth Cady Stanton, Lucretia C. Mott, and Julia Ward Howe. However, the child can learn much about these courageous and determined Americans by reading children's biographies of their lives. Here the child can get a vivid word picture of the times in which these women lived. Such supporting details add richness and meaning to an understanding of the historical period studied.

The Joint Committee of the National Council for the Social Studies and the Children's Book Council has a Book Review Subcommittee that selects and evaluates trade books useful for teaching social studies in the elementary and middle schools. An annotated list of their selections is published each April or May in *Social Education* under the title "Notable Children's Trade Books in the Field of Social Studies." The books selected for these bibliographies "(1) are written for children in grades K–8; (2) emphasize human relations; (3) present an original theme or a fresh slant on a traditional topic; (4) are highly readable; and, when appropriate, (5) include maps and illustrations." The annotations include a synopsis of content, publisher, price, and reading level. These lists are highly recommended to teachers and librarians.[6]

Films, Videotapes, and Filmstrips.   Films and videotapes have much to contribute to teaching history and geography. In a film or videotape, the children can traverse great distances and move through centuries of time, having before them a picture of places, persons, and processes that would be impossible to obtain in other ways. In many respects, the film has advantages over field trips because it singles out the most important aspects of a situation and eliminates the nonessentials. It is more selective in what it allows the viewer to see than is the human eye. It is a demanding medium and holds the attention of the viewer to a greater extent than do most other learning aids. A film can telescope great lengths of time into minutes, making it possible to observe a timeless process in a single class period. Its greatest asset, of course, is that it depicts motion, and the best use can be made of films showing situations involving motion. If motion is not a factor, a good photograph, a slide, or a filmstrip may be equally effective.

Filmstrips offer advantages over motion pictures in terms of cost, availability, and use. Because of the relatively low cost, schools ordinarily maintain their own filmstrip collection, and they are immediately available, therefore, when needed. A good instructional feature of the filmstrip is that it is possible to discuss its content as it is being shown. If it becomes necessary to refer to a picture previously shown, the filmstrip can be turned back to the frame in question. Filmstrips are easy to catalog and store and are simple to show. In this respect, they have many advantages over slides.

Filmstrips may be used to achieve a number of purposes in the social studies unit. A filmstrip on the New England States, for example, gives a clear picture of the physical features of this area and thereby assists in

---

[6]"Notable 1990 Children's Trade Books in the Field of Social Studies," *Social Education* 55 (April/May 1991): 253–60.

understanding map symbols and provides a good readiness for map reading. It may serve to introduce children to other countries of the world, showing how people in other lands live, work, and play. Filmstrips are useful in presenting material that follows a definite sequence—how a letter gets from sender to receiver; the steps in the production of milk; the history, growth and development of an area; the course of soil erosion; or the steps to be followed in the event of some emergency such as a fire, drowning, an accident, or a hurricane.

Interesting Study Projects.   In addition to the learning activities planned specifically to help the child build psychological bridges with the past, the teaching of history in the elementary school can be enlivened and made more meaningful through the use of a variety of other activities. The following are examples of only a few that have been used successfully by elementary and middle school teachers:

1. *Collect and exhibit* old photographs that show the history of the community.
2. *Collect and try* pioneer recipes; learn folk dances; investigate local cultural contributions of various nationality groups.
3. *Write items* of local history for the school paper or for the local newspaper.
4. *Write biographical sketches* of early settlers in the community.
5. *Investigate the history* of some important old buildings in the community.
6. *Trace the history* of some local industry such as mining, manufacturing, or lumbering.
7. *Make models* or sketches of oxcarts, prairie schooners, canoes, spinning wheels, or other pioneer equipment.
8. *Paint a mural* of some aspect of the history of the local community or state.
9. *Write and present* a pageant telling the story of some aspect of local, state, or national history.
10. *Collect songs* of various periods of history, and present a costumed recital of them.
11. *Make a model* of the town as it looked fifty, seventy-five, or one hundred years ago, or a diorama of life in the town at an earlier time.
12. *Make a topographical or relief map* of the local area, indicating points of historical significance.
13. *Use historical settings* for creative dramatics activities.
14. *Make pictorial time lines* tracing periods of national, state, or local history.
15. *Prepare bulletin boards* and other exhibits having a historical theme.
16. *Write, plan, and prepare* short plays or presentations in connection with holiday observances.
17. *Organize a junior historians club* in the classroom, and establish contact with the local and state historical societies.

18. *Have your class participate in the National History Day competition* (grades 6–12). Each state has a National History Day coordinator from whom information may be obtained. National History Day projects need to be started early in the school year. Local competition is usually held in March and April; state competition, in May; and national finals, in or near Washington, DC, in June.

19. *Involve students in the Civic Achievement Award Program* (grades 5–8). See "Interesting Study Projects" in Chapter 7 for information about the program.

Holiday Observances

Some of the most satisfying and long-remembered experiences children have in the elementary school are those associated with the observance of holidays. Many schools and states require observance of holidays such as Presidents' Day, Thanksgiving Day, Veterans' Day, Martin Luther King Day, and other days of import to the local community and to the state. Although school programs related to the observance of such historical holidays are often guided more by fancy than by historical fact, these

Children learn through participation that in colonial and pioneer days quilting parties, or quilting "bees," had social values as well producing necessary items for everyday life. Teachers are fortunate when they have museum resources and programs such as that of the Southern Oregon Historical Society available to enrich their social studies programs.
(Photo courtesy of the Southern Oregon Historical Society.)

occasions, nonetheless, present excellent opportunities to teach effectively history associated with the day.

The chief contribution that holiday observances can make to the education of young children is to acquaint them with their rich cultural heritage and help them grow in their appreciation of it. With this in mind, the teacher can plan a short unit related to the holiday, keeping the content simple but truthful. Commonly, such short units have as their culminating activity a dramatization that is shared with another class.

If the teacher does not plan to devote more than a class period or two to such an observance, reading an appropriate story or poem, followed by discussion, can be a profitable experience. After the reading, the children can participate in a suitable followup activity such as drawing, painting, singing a related song, writing an original poem or story, or listening to a recording; or they can use the story for creative dramatics. This is also an appropriate time to view a film dealing with some aspect of history related to the holiday or to listen to a recorded dramatization of a historical event. In this same connection, the teacher may discuss with the class the significance of a classroom picture or a symbol such as the flag, the Declaration of Independence, the Constitution, or the national anthem. The amount of time spent on activities of this type ought always to be weighed against their value as educational experiences.

GEOGRAPHY AND THE SOCIAL STUDIES

Geography has traditionally occupied and continues to occupy a position of central importance in the social studies curriculum. Events in modern times have underscored the need to study geography from a global perspective at all levels. Social studies topics have a place in space, and geography is concerned with the character of those places. The qualities that distinguish an area and the way it relates to other areas are both of great significance in understanding human occupance and use of the earth.

The Geography Curriculum

The teaching of geography has suffered somewhat because of the persistence of traditional and often stereotyped ideas about the nature of geography. School geography has too frequently meant memorizing and naming various features of the physical environment: locating rivers; naming mountains; learning places, products, capes, and bays. Such teaching allows little, if any, opportunity to do critical thinking in the study of geography. Modern geography stresses the method of geographic inquiry as a major educational outcome. It is important to know place location, of course, but one must also have the intellectual tools to grasp the significance of such information and relate it to a broader cultural and environmental context. Teaching children to think geographically must accompany the teaching of specific geographical information and facts.

Geography is a science that is concerned with the study and description of the earth. Traditionally, this has meant physical geography, with studies focusing on the unequal distribution of such phenomena as water, minerals, climate, productive land, vegetation, land forms, and so on. Undoubtedly, the intense interest that people have in the world in which they live and their desire to find out what lies beyond the immediate surroundings gave rise to the development of the science of geography. As early people began to move from one place to another on the earth, they noticed that one place differed from another and made observations of these differences. In time, these observations were systematically recorded and were gradually brought together into the discipline of geography. Geographic knowledge became extremely useful and, indeed, essential for travelers, explorers, military leaders, and those engaged in trade and commerce.

As people found their way into all parts of the world, knowledge of the physical geography of the earth greatly increased. All parts of the world were explored in a general way and were to some extent described and mapped. Then the emphasis in geography began to shift from simply describing phenomena to explaining the differences that were found from one place to another. In addition, the relationships between the physiographic and biotic elements within those areas were beginning to be explored. The study of the uniqueness of a particular area—the study of the factors that make an area different from any other area of the earth—is embodied in the concept of *areal differentiation*. Also, relationships between areas were explored, that is, the links and bonds, either natural or human made, that develop between places. Such studies concern themselves with the concept of *spatial interaction*. These two concepts—areal differentiation and spatial interaction—are central to the understanding of the concerns and approaches of modern geography.

The National Council for Geographic Education and the Association of American Geographers have prepared a guidelines document that identifies five central themes on which the K–12 program in geography should focus. These are reproduced here:

1. **Location: Position on the Earth's Surface.**   Absolute and relative location are two ways of describing the positions of people and places on the earth's surface.

2. **Place: Physical and Human Characteristics.**   All places on the earth have distinctive tangible and intangible characteristics that give them meaning and character and distinguish them from other places. Geographers generally describe places by their physical or human characteristics.

3. **Relationships Within Places: Humans and Environments.**   All places on the earth have advantages and disadvantages for human settlement.

High population densities have developed on flood plains, for example, where people could take advantage of fertile soils, water resources, and opportunities for river transportation. By comparison, population densities are usually low in deserts. Yet flood plains are periodically subjected to severe damage, and some desert areas, such as Israel, have been modified to support large population concentrations.

4. Movement: Humans Interacting on the Earth.   Human beings occupy places unevenly across the face of the earth. Some live on farms or in the country; others live in towns, villages or cities. Yet these people interact with each other: that is, they travel from one place to another, they communicate with each other or they rely upon products, information, and ideas that come from beyond their immediate environment.

The most visible evidences of global interdependence and the interaction of places are the transportation and communication lines that link every part of the world. These demonstrate that most people interact with other places almost every day of their lives. This may involve nothing more than a Georgian eating apples grown in the state of Washington and shipped to Atlanta by rail or truck. On a larger scale, international trade demonstrates that no country is self-sufficient.

5. Regions: How They Form and Change.   The basic unit of geographic study is the region, an area that displays unity in terms of selected criteria.

We are all familiar with regions showing the extent of political power such as nations, provinces, countries, or cities, yet there are almost countless ways to define meaningful regions depending on the problems being considered. Some regions are defined by one characteristic such as a governmental unit, a language group, or a landform type, and others by the interplay of many complex features. For example, Indiana as a state is a governmental region, Latin America as an area where Spanish and Portuguese are major languages can be a linguistic region, and the Rocky Mountains as a mountain range is a landform region. A geographer may delineate a neighborhood in Minneapolis by correlating the income and educational levels of residents with the assessed valuation or property and tax rate, or distinguish others by prominent boundaries such as a freeway, park, or business district. On another scale we may identify the complex of ethnic, religious, linguistic, and environmental features that delineate the Arab World from the Middle East or North Africa.[7]

The guidelines document also identifies learning outcomes for various grade levels and a suggested sequence of geographic learnings for grades K–12.

---

[7]*Guidelines for Geographic Education, Elementary and Secondary Schools,* published jointly by the Association of American Geographers, 1710 16th Street, N.W., Washington, DC 20009, and the National Council for Geographic Education, Western Illinois University, Macomb, IL 61455, 1984.

Teaching Suggestions

A thoughtful reading of the themes provided by the guidelines document will suggest many teaching possibilities. The following examples illustrate ideas that teachers have used successfully.

Geography in the Primary Grades

The primary-grade teacher will have no difficulty finding ways to include geography in social studies units. Much of the early geography teaching centers on the landscape of the local community. The primary-grade child may experience and observe firsthand in the local community various land and water forms—lakes, creeks, islands, gullies, slopes. The teacher should encourage children to explore the various forms of native plant and animal life and observe the characteristic changes of these with changing seasons of the year. With some help from the teacher, the children can build their understanding of ideas such as the following:

1. People adapt themselves to conditions in the environment.
2. Transportation plays an important part in the distribution of food.
3. Nature changes the character of the earth.
4. The same land can be used for many different purposes.
5. Every day we use things that have come from all over the world.

Local Geographical Exploration.   The opportunities for children to explore geographically in and around the school site should not be overlooked. A primary-grade class may visit a nearby basement excavation for a new home. The children observe the various layers of soil, and the teacher calls their attention to the many roots found in the fertile topsoil. The class is able to obtain samples of the various strata of soil to take back to their classroom for an experiment in seeing how well plants grow in the various layers—an early beginning in the appreciation and understanding of the value of soil conservation. The presence of earth-moving equipment suggests that human beings do things to modify the environment. Children learn that sometimes these modifications are helpful, but other times they are destructive and harmful. The imaginative teacher can plan similar experiences in purposeful exploration in connection with soil, water, water bodies, minerals, rocks, local vegetation, and surface features. Experiences of this kind provide an opportunity to learn and apply an important method of study used by geographers: careful observation of phenomena.

Weather and Climate.   Weather and climate present another area of exploration. Children have viewed weather forecasts on television. The frequency of reference to weather in adult conversations indicates the degree to which weather and climatic conditions have an effect on the lives of people. In primary-grade classrooms, children will want to have their own charts on which they can record various weather data observed each day. The teacher reads the daily temperature, or the children report the official daily temperature that they have heard over an early morning radio broadcast. These temperatures can be shown graphically, thereby applying knowledge of numbers and graphs. Over a period of several weeks or months the graph will show the changes occurring in temperatures and seasons of the year. Children can also record data dealing with wind velocities, cloud formations, precipitation, and similar subjects. They can also make their own predictions based on the data they have collected. Sensitivity to weather changes will again call attention to the changes in native plant and animal life as well as to the adaptations people make to changing seasons. Here the teacher can apply another technique of the geographer: recording data and using simple charts.

Geography in Reading and Language Arts.   A number of opportunities for teaching geography may grow out of the reading and language program of the class. In the basic reading series one will find many stories and selections with a geographical setting. The children read about the family that took a weekend trip to the lake or spent a summer in the mountains. They read about the antics of the monkeys in the zoo and wonder about their natural habitat. Brief explanations and discussions of accompanying geographic phenomena are helpful in gaining a better understanding of the meaning of the story. Primary-grade teachers often read to children, and many of these stories present opportunities for teaching geography. The selections children read in their classroom news periodical and the current affairs that they report also provide opportunities to develop geographic concepts and skills.

Geography in the Middle and Upper Grades

Children in the middle and upper grades can delve more deeply into the relationships between the earth and the activities of human beings than they could in the primary grades. They learn that people the world over attempt to satisfy their basic needs in ways that are influenced by their environment, their past experiences, and present resources. Even though the methods various people use to meet these needs in specific regions of the world may seem strange to us, they are not unusual for those who inhabit that region. Although children should *not* be taught that geographic conditions *determine* how people live, they should learn that geography sets certain limits on the choices available to them. (For example, people in the Arctic are probably not going to find it cost effective to grow oranges and bananas there even though present technology would make that possible.) In this connection, children learn that historical and cultural components of a society as well as natural features are significant to the development of geographic relationships. A few examples of some of the key geographical ideas that should be stressed in the middle and upper grades are

1. Places on the earth have a distinctiveness about them that differentiates them from all other places.

2. Physical and human changes in one part of the world affect people's lives in other parts of the world.
3. The relationship between agricultural resources and human life is less direct in highly urbanized societies than it is in other regions.
4. Areas of the earth develop bonds, interconnections, and relations with other areas.
5. The wasteful exploitation and pollution of natural and human resources pose serious problems for the welfare of the earth's rapidly growing population of human beings.

In the study of various areas of the world, the middle-grade child will follow somewhat the same pattern of exploration and problem solving as in the primary grades. When studying a specific place, such factors as these will be included, although not necessarily in this sequence: (1) the surface features, (2) the plant and animal life found there, and (3) the relationship of this life to the climatic and weather conditions that affect the occupations and way of life of the people who live there. From this systematic study of communities in various natural regions of the world, the children can discover some relationships between various geographic conditions and the activities of human groups. For example, they might discover that in places where one finds similar physical geographic conditions, people may live quite differently. The reverse could also be true. How people use natural surroundings depends mainly on cultural factors.

Studying Regions.   The study of specific communities and regions (e.g. desert people, mountain people, polar regions, and so on) presents difficult instructional problems no matter what system is used in selecting them. Too often they are treated in a superficial or romantic way. It becomes easy to make unwarranted value judgments about the people studied, to arrive at hasty and inaccurate generalizations, and to develop stereotyped ideas of people. The tendency has been to stress traditional or legendary aspects of a people's culture rather than coming to grips with their way of life in modern times. The need for accurate information and a proper instructional emphasis is essential if children are to develop valid understandings.

The geographic regions selected for study should be sufficiently different from one another to help the child learn the characteristic adjustments people make under varying conditions. These then may be compared with life in the local community, stressing the similarities in the basic requirements of life that people everywhere have to meet. Such a study should include historical and cultural elements as a natural part of geographic study.

Intensive studies of entire continents, with the exception of Australia, are usually not well suited for elementary school grades because the natural, cultural, and historical backgrounds of various regions are generally so diverse that it is difficult to select a unifying set of concepts for the study.

Consequently, children often learn a number of facts about geographic features but fail to relate these to the people who inhabit the area. It is ordinarily better to select specific communities in representative regions of the world and study those intensively.

At the beginning of the study of a community or a region, it is helpful, however, to make an overview of the continent on which the region is located. This places the area properly in its larger geographical setting. At the beginning of such units, the teacher often will use a globe and a series of wall maps. Beginning with the globe, attention should be focused on the continent on which the place to be studied is located and relate its location to other known places on the earth. Then a wall map of the continent can be used to point out the particular area to be studied. This can be followed with a brief study of the geographical features of the entire continent in terms of their relationship to the particular area. Such a spot location of places will make it easier for the child to visualize the interrelationships and associations that are possible for a given place.

Avoiding Geographic Stereotypes.   Some teachers cling to the concept of environmental determinism although geographers rejected it years ago as an explanation of differing ways of living. Geographic conditions should be taught as factors that relate to, or affect, ways of living but do not *cause* them. If geographic conditions caused people to live the way they do, everyone in a given area of the world would live the same way; and, of course, this is not the case. For example, some of the people of the world who inhabit the deserts live in tents, tend sheep, and live nomadic lives; others who live in desert areas have air-conditioned ranch-style homes, work in comfortable office buildings, and drive expensive automobiles.

The teaching of the earth's climatic zones also persists even though this concept, too, has been discarded by geographers. Traditionally, children were taught that the earth had climatic belts known as the Frigid, Temperate, and Torrid zones that encircled the earth at certain latitudes. The implication was that all places in these zones have the same climatic conditions. This conclusion is in error because there are places in the so-called Torrid Zone that have snow the year around; places in the so-called Temperate Zone that have winter temperatures as low as forty degrees below zero; and places in the Frigid Zone that record fairly mild temperatures even in the winter months. These zonal designations based on climate should *not* be taught. The terms *low latitudes, middle latitudes,* and *high latitudes* are acceptable in referring to these parts of the world because they do not imply that a specific climatic condition prevails throughout the area so designated. Climate should not be explained entirely in terms of latitude.

In the study of ways of living around the world, usually at the fourth-grade level, many programs focus on nonindustrialized societies because these people relate so directly to their surroundings in meeting their basic needs of food, clothing, and shelter. They make their homes and clothing from materials close at hand, and these necessities are usually entirely functional. All food is grown, gathered, or hunted. When there is trade or other contact with the outside world, children can see that the ways of living begin to change. Much of value can come from studies of this type, but the teacher needs to be careful not to develop the idea that just because these people meet their basic needs in simple ways, their social organization is easy to understand. Often the customs, mores, and taboos of these cultures are exceedingly complex. When studies of preliterate or preindustrial societies are undertaken, the units should be used to demonstrate specific points: People can live under a variety of geographical conditions; these people have less need for the great variety of resources required by industrial societies; certain human qualities are apparent in all people no matter how they live; people do not need great material wealth in order to be happy; some people spend a disproportionate amount of time meeting basic needs; ways of living change when people meet others from another culture; and so on.

Expanding Geographic Understanding.   In the fourth grade, one finds the study of home states to be fairly common. Many of the states are sufficiently diverse in geography to allow parallels to be drawn with similar places around the world. If the state has plains, for example, children might find out where else in the world one finds plains and how the people there make use of them. Or the state might have mountains or deserts or good harbors—any of these can be used to teach geographic concepts and relate such concepts to a broad, global context.

The same principles hold true in the fifth-grade social studies curriculum, which in many schools calls for the study of communities or sections of the United States, its history, and the movement of people from one section to another within it. In studying historical developments, life in early America, or contemporary life in various communities of the United States, the teacher should relate geographical factors to the topic. What did the geography of the region have to do with the way people lived and how they made their living? Why did large cities grow where they did? Why did the people moving west follow certain routes? How were people able to make use of the resources they found? All these questions relate to geography, and geographical understanding should be used to help explain them.

In the upper grades, many social studies units provide the opportunity to relate human activities to the environment. Children should learn how such social functions as making a living, producing goods, building homes, making clothing, transporting goods, and communicating ideas relate to the specific region in which people live. They should also develop skill in the use of the tools of geography—charts, graphs, sourcebooks, and, most particularly, maps and globes.

In the middle and upper grades, some attention should be given to the historical dimension of geography. For example, in studying the location of cities, teachers frequently have children explain why the particular place is

One could hardly select a more appropriate activity to illustrate the importance of cooperation and interdependence than a "bucket brigade"! What other social studies outcomes could be achieved through the use of this activity with middle-grade students?

(Photos courtesy of the Southern Oregon Historical Society.)

.... **Lesson Plan 5**

Topic:	Place Names: Where did they come from?
Grade:	Four
Time:	One class period and followup
Objective:	To explore the origin of names within a specific geographical area.
Interest Building:	Brainstorm a list of names of places with which you are familiar within a geographical area. After brainstorming, compile an additional list from maps that have been distributed (example: a map of the home state or local county). Perhaps a total of fifty or sixty names would be a good stopping point.
Lesson Development:	Categorize the names as to their origin: Indian names, names of explorers, famous people, early settlers, ethnic names, and so forth. 　Have the children decide on the fairest way of distributing the names so that each has two or three place names to research. 　Each child will then research the names, using resource books, interviews, and letters to various city or community information sources to determine the origin of the name. This is done over an extended period of time.
Summary:	As each child obtains the information, display it on a bulletin board, attaching it with yarn to the particular geographical location on a map. Relate this information to the history and settlement pattern of the area.
Materials:	Maps of the area under study.

a good location for a city. What is often overlooked in such an exercise is that the choice was made a hundred or two hundred or even more years ago. *At that time* in terms of the technology of the period, the site may have been a good one, but in terms of present-day technology it may be a bad site. If the choice of a place for a city were made today, perhaps it would be located somewhere else. Ghost towns are good examples of poor site selection for permanent settlement. The same applies to many other features of the environment that bear the imprint of human presence. Roads today were formerly cow paths and horse trails or old logging roads. Industrial centers grew up in places that were easily accessible to employees who walked to work or who rode trolleys. Downtown shopping centers were established before automobile parking became a problem. Instructive and interesting studies can be made of areas as they were in early days: Land division and use, the pattern of transportation, the location of processing and manufacturing facilities, the location and distribution of markets, and interactions with surrounding areas can be noted. The study then shifts to an examination and analysis of these factors in the same area as they are today; the children thereby gain an understanding and appreciation of the problems related to area growth and change.

In this connection, too, geographic thinking can be stimulated through the consideration of hypothetical propositions. For example, a fifth-grade class might consider the following proposition: Suppose instead of being located in northern Minnesota, the large iron deposits of the Mesabi had been discovered in southern Missouri. What effect might this have had on the location of northern cities? Would the major transportation systems and routes of the area be the same as they are today? Would major industrial and manufacturing centers be located where they are today? Teachers can easily devise problems of this type from time to time by selecting a situation and shifting a critical variable. Learners cannot arrive at final answers to such problems, but they can speculate on possible alternatives and can demonstrate their ability to apply their geographic knowledge. Hypothetical propositions, if well selected, provide good ways for a teacher to evaluate children's understanding of important concepts and their ability to transfer such knowledge to other situations.

One teacher used the place-names lesson (Lesson Plan 5) to alert children to the origins of place names in the local area, which led the class to the development of the geographic concept of successive occupance.

SPECIALIZED INFORMATION SOURCES FOR HISTORY AND GEOGRAPHY

Encyclopedias and Special References

In the middle and upper grades, all classrooms should have at least one and preferably two sets of encyclopedias suitable for children. Even in the primary grades, encyclopedias can be used to good advantage from time to time; and many schools are placing them in first, second, and third grades.

The value of an encyclopedia lies in the easy, quick way factual material can be obtained on a multitude of topics. It is an important source of information and one that will be referred to many times in the course of social studies units. When encyclopedias are available in the primary grades, the teacher will find the pictures and illustrations helpful in social studies instruction. Selected short portions of content may be read to the children from time to time, and some children at these early levels will be able to read portions of the encyclopedia independently. Perhaps the chief value of an encyclopedia in the primary grades is the contribution it can make to building positive attitudes toward the use of reference materials. Children learn fairly early that in the encyclopedia one can find answers to many questions on most topics. In this sense, early contact with this reference serves as a readiness for its more organized use at the upper levels. In the middle and upper grades, the encyclopedia is a constant source of factual information. Articles in an encyclopedia are highly condensed presentations, however, and this suggests the need for additional references—ones that may give interesting elaboration not ordinarily included in encyclopedia coverage.

The teacher should guard against the misuse of the encyclopedia. Children need to learn that the encyclopedia is only one source and, in some cases, may not even be the best source, of information. A children's biography, for instance, of Babe Didrikson Zaharias or Amelia Earhart might be more informative and more engaging for a 12-year-old than a factual, encyclopedia account of these women's lives. Children can become too dependent on the encyclopedia at the expense of not learning the value of other resources available to them. Thus, they may copy written reports verbatim from the encyclopedia or make oral reports based on encyclopedia accounts that are memorized but not understood. The difficulty, of course, lies not with the encyclopedia but with the way it is used. The teacher needs to make a conscious effort to discourage such misuse of this instructional resource.

For factual information there is also need for atlases, *The World Almanac,* and the state legislative manuals. Many local communities and cities also publish brochures, handbooks, and pamphlets. Local and state historical societies, museums, and art galleries may make available publications that are valuable for classroom work. These sources provide a storehouse of information, but children of elementary school age need a considerable amount of guidance and help from the teacher in their use.

Free and Inexpensive Materials

Free and inexpensive materials have become valuable resources in teaching history, geography, and social studies generally. There is a wealth of material in the form of posters, charts, bulletins, folders, booklets, films, filmstrips, and travel folders available free on request. In addition to the free material, an abundance of similar resources can be obtained at small cost. Much of the material available today is well prepared and useful for classroom work, but it does need to be examined carefully to ascertain whether or not it is suitable. Just because the material is available and free is no assurance that it is of value. Questions such as these should be considered in evaluating free and inexpensive material:

1. Is the material produced by a socially responsible organization?
2. Does the presence of advertising make the material unsuitable for use? A piece may or may not be rejected on this point, but it should, in any case, be considered.
3. Is the subject matter honestly and objectively presented? Is it consistent with democratic values and ideals? Is it free of racial and gender bias?
4. Is the material suitable in terms of readability, maturity of the children, technical qualities, and the topic under study?
5. Is the material up to date?
6. Are the sources of information given?
7. Does use of the materials carry any obligations with it?
8. In whose interest was the material prepared? Who benefits from its use in the classroom?

The teacher should not overlook the diplomatic offices of foreign countries based in the United States as a source of free material. In most cases, the best place to direct inquiries concerning the availability of such material is the embassy of the country in Washington, DC. Some countries (for example, Japan) have excellent instructional packets available for school use.

Because the demand for free and inexpensive material is great and the quantity usually limited, the teacher is advised to use an up-to-date list of sources. Professional journals carry lists in almost every issue. In addition, there are compilations of sources of free and inexpensive material that can be purchased. The most comprehensive guides (catalogs) of free instructional material are those published by Educator's Progress Service, Inc., 214 Center Street, Randolph, Wisconsin 53956. Teachers can write for a list of available guides and the cost of each.

Computer Applications

Computer programs in the form of tutorials, drill and practice, database software, and simulations are available for teaching history and geography in the elementary and middle schools social studies programs. There are several comprehensive software directories and lists that provide titles, annotations, suppliers' names and addresses, and cost.[8] *Technology in the Curriculum Resource Material* produced by the California State Department of Education in connection with the state history/social science framework is especially useful because it recommends software programs that were evaluated by a team of fifty teachers.[9]

Community Resources

It is in the local community that the teacher should sow the seeds of a lifetime study of human society. Here the social processes that function a thousand times over in communities around the world may be observed firsthand. In the local community, the child is introduced to geographical concepts, to the problems of group living, to government in operation, to the production and distribution of goods and services, and to the rich historical heritage of the nation. In most American communities, the child can see evidence that it is possible for persons of varied backgrounds, nationalities, religious faiths, and races to live and work together harmoniously.

The teacher may make use of the local community in two basic ways. One is to bring some portion of the community to the classroom; the other is to take the class out of the school to some place or person of importance in the community. As a matter of principle, it is advisable to take elementary schoolchildren into the community only for the experiences that can-

---

[8]See James O. Hodges, "Resources for Teaching with Computers," *Social Education* 51 (January 1987): 54–59; Gene E. Rooze and Terry Northup, *Using Computers to Teach Social Studies* (Littleton, Colorado: Libraries Unlimited, 1986), chapter 6.

[9]Available from California State Department of Education, Publication Sales, P.O. Box 271, Sacramento, CA 95802, $95.00.

not be duplicated in the classroom. For example, it is usually better to arrange to have a person bring photographs of early life in the community to the school and speak to the children there than it is to take a class of thirty children to a home. On the other hand, the process involved in canning tuna fish or cranberries cannot be observed in the classroom; the children must be taken to the cannery if this process is to be observed firsthand. Teachers make use of community resources when children bring materials from home for the bulletin boards, or for their construction projects; when parents are asked to assist in any way; when books are obtained from the public library; when the local newspaper is used; or when children bring items from home to share with others in "show and tell." The personal experiences children have in the community and share with the class are likewise a common use of community resources.

The teacher must always select with care the persons who are invited to spend time with the class for instructional purposes. Some people should not be asked to speak to children because they are not able to make themselves understood, they lack an understanding of children, they freely hold and express attitudes or beliefs that may be offensive to members of the group, or they fail to grasp the significance of their visit to the class. The teacher should plan to spend some time with the visitor sufficiently far enough in advance to brief the guest on the activities of the class, the purpose of the visit, and the points to be discussed and stressed. Likewise, the children must be prepared for the visitor, listing questions they should like to ask, and general courtesies extended to classroom guests. Handled in this way, persons from the community can make a significant contribution to the instructional program in the social studies. Those who might be used either for the purposes of interview or as classroom resource visitors might include

Persons with special skills: weavers, potters, jewelry makers

Armed forces personnel

Exchange students

Persons with interesting hobbies

Community helpers

Members of the local historical society

Newspaper reporters

Members of service organizations

County agent

County commissioner

Representatives of environmental and conservation groups

4-H Club leaders

Early inhabitants of the community

Professional persons: ministers, doctors, lawyers

Judges

Legislators

Members of the local business community: bankers, salespersons, shop owners

Local officials

Representatives of local industries

Travelers

Recent immigrants or other newcomers to the community

Authors

Commercial pilots

Whenever children are taken off the school site, the teacher must attend to several exceedingly important details. Adequate planning will help the teacher anticipate some of the problems that may arise in connection with the field trip and will help make the trip educationally worthwhile. Poorly planned field trips are worse than none at all, for they lack purpose, may jeopardize the safety of the children, may cause poor public relations between the school and community, and can break down learnings the teacher should have been trying to build in the classroom. Although the field trip should be pleasant for everyone including the teacher, it is first of all an educational experience, and its primary objective is not that everyone have a joyous outing. Good planning will ensure that the trip will be both a pleasant as well as an educational experience. The following suggestions will be helpful in achieving that goal.

FIELD TRIPS

Preparing for the Trip

1. Clearly establish the purposes of the trip, and make certain that the children understand the purposes, too. The excursion should provide opportunities for learning that are not possible in the classroom.
2. Obtain administrative permission for the field trip, and make arrangements for transportation. As a matter of policy, it is better to use a public conveyance or a school bus than it is to use private automobiles. In using private cars, the teacher is never sure if the driver is properly insured, is competent behind the wheel, or even if the driver has a valid operator's license.
3. Make all necessary preliminary arrangements at the place of the visit. This should include the time for the group to arrive, where the children are to go, who will guide them, and so forth. It is recommended that the teacher make the excursion prior to the time the children are taken. This will alert the teacher to circumstances and situations that should be discussed with the children before leaving the classroom. Make sure that the field trip guide is aware of the purposes of the field trip.

4. Study the literature on the subject. No teacher should approach a field trip unprepared. This knowledge will later be valuable in helping prepare children for the field trip and in initiating followup and study activities.

5. Obtain written permission from each parent for the child to go on the trip, and do not take children who cannot or do not return signed permission slips. Although this action does not in itself absolve the teacher of responsibility or liability in the event of an accident, it indicates to the teacher that the parent knows of the field trip and approves of the child's going. Most schools have forms for this purpose that are filled out by the teacher and sent home with each child for the parent's signature.

6. Prepare the class for the field trip. "What is it that we wish to find out? What things in particular do we want to look for? What questions do we want to ask the guide?" Through careful planning and preparation the teacher helps children to be more observant and makes a genuine research activity out of the field trip. The children probably will be taken to places to which many of them have been before. Most of them have seen trains, many have been to the airport, some have been to the harbor, and all have been to a filling station. Why, then, should the school take children to such places on field trips? The answer is that different purposes exist for the field trip than for incidental visits. The children are prepared to look for things they would not otherwise see. Discuss with the children how they will record the information obtained on their trip. If they are to take notes, teach the needed notetaking skills.

    The class should set up standards of conduct for the trip before leaving the school. Children are quick to accept the challenge that the responsibility for a good trip rests personally with each member of the group. Time spent on this part of the preparation for the excursion will pay dividends when the trip is underway. Nothing is more embarrassing for the teacher, more damaging to school–community relations, or more devastating to the educational purposes of the field trip than a group of rude and unruly children. This often happens when the children have been inadequately prepared for the trip.

7. If the trip is to be long, make arrangements for lunchroom and restroom facilities. Take along a first-aid kit.

8. Have an alternate plan in case the weather turns bad or something interferes with your plans.

Conducting the Trip

9. Take roll before leaving the school grounds, and "count noses" frequently during the trip to make sure that some of the children have not become lost or left in some restroom along the way. With young children it is a good idea to place them in pairs because a child will know and report immediately the absence of a partner. To assist with supervision of the children and to help ensure a safe trip, the teacher should arrange for other adults to accompany the group. Teachers can usually count on parents to assist in this way but should plan to meet with them prior to the trip and explain the purposes, standards of behavior, the route to be followed, and other important details. The adults accompanying the children must be prepared for the excursion also.

10. Arrive at the designated place on time, and have children ready for the guide. Be sure to introduce the guide to the class. Supervise children closely during the tour to prevent accidents or injury. Before leaving, check again to make sure all children are with the group.

11. Make sure that time is allowed for answering children's questions.

12. Make sure that each child can see and hear adequately. Be sure to summarize the experience before the trip is concluded.

Evaluating the Trip

13. Engage the class in appropriate followup activities. This should include writing a thank-you note to the firm and to the adults who accompanied the class. In the primary grades, the children should dictate such a letter to the teacher who writes it on the chalkboard or chart. Individual children then copy the letter, and one may be selected to be sent, or, in some cases, they may all be sent. The teacher and children will also want to evaluate carefully the extent to which the purposes of the trip have been achieved. "Did we accomplish what we set out to do? Did we get the answers to our questions? What did we learn that we didn't know before? What are some other things we will want to find out?" Finally, the teacher and children will want to evaluate the conduct of the class in terms of the standards set up before the trip was made. This evaluation should always include some favorable reactions as well as ways in which the group might improve on subsequent trips. A list might be made of these suggestions for improvement to be saved for review just before the next trip is undertaken.

14. Discuss enrichment projects in which children may engage for further study, such as construction activities, original stories, reports, dramatic plays, and diaries. Survey other resources available in the community for study.

15. Use opportunities to draw on information and experiences from the field trip in other subjects taught in the classroom.

Every community has places that can be visited by classes and thereby can contribute to the enrichment of history, geography, and all of social studies. These will differ from place to place, but any of the following could be used:

State historical society displays	Aquarium
Historical sites, monuments	Library
Flood plain, eroded areas, dam sites	Refinery
Razing of a building	Fish hatchery
Hospitals	Museum
Weather bureau	Public health department
Warehouses	Local stores
Airports	Legislative bodies in session
Railway station	Art galleries
Assembly plants	Fire station
Post office	Newspaper printing facilities
Broadcasting or telecasting station	Bakery
Courthouse	Observatory
Factories	Canal locks
Farms	The harbor
Urban planning commission	Police station
Docks	Zoo
	Parks
	Shopping centers

DISCUSSION QUESTIONS AND SUGGESTED ACTIVITIES

1. What are some ways that geography is important to the study of history? Is the reverse also true? Discuss these relationships in terms of the need for an integrated social studies program at the elementary and middle school levels.

2. Study your local community and suggest five community resources that could be used in teaching history and geography to a grade of your choice.

3. What specific out-of-school experiences of children enhance their ability to understand geography and history? Suggest television programs that would be useful in teaching history and geography.

4. Examine a social studies textbook and its accompanying teacher's manual. How are history and geography included in the book? Would the teacher and the child user clearly recognize the subject matter as history and geography? Is that important? Discuss.

5. What holidays are observed in the schools of your state? Develop a calendar of such days for the school year.

6. School librarians or media specialists or both frequently organize exhibits around selected themes during the year. For example, "Black History Month" in February provides an opportunity for librarians to draw attention to their black studies material. Visit an elementary school library. Ask the librarian or resource person about other special weeks or events during the year. How might these be tied to the social studies program?

7. What reasons can you give for the apparent revival of interest in the study of history in recent years? Are there potential negative as well as positive outcomes associated with this emphasis? Discuss.

8. Find out something about the methods of inquiry used by historians and geographers in studying their disciplines. Explain how—or if—any of these might be adapted for use with elementary and middle school students. Provide examples of such applications.

9. Secure a photograph of people at work in a culture outside the United States. By studying the photograph, answer these questions: (1) What features of the land appear to be most important to the people who live in this area? (2) What occupations seem to be most important? (3) What principal tools and machines do these people use? (4) What do the answers to these three questions tell you about the way of life of the people who live there? Can an activity of this type be used with elementary and middle grade students? Is this geography? Discuss.

10. History and geography are important in terms of their subject matter, but how can they be used to develop intellectual skills such as critical thinking and problem solving? Provide an example for a grade of your choice to illustrate your points.

SELECTED REFERENCES

ASSOCIATION OF AMERICAN GEOGRAPHERS AND NATIONAL COUNCIL FOR GEOGRAPHIC EDUCATION. *Guidelines for Geographic Education, Elementary and Secondary Schools.* Washington, DC: authors, 1984.

BECK, ISABEL L., AND MARGARET G. McKEOWN. "Toward Meaningful Accounts in History Texts for Young Learners." *Educational Researcher* 17 (August/September 1988): 31–39.

BOYTE, HARRY C. *Commonwealth: A Return to Citizen Politics.* New York: Free Press, 1989.

BRADLEY COMMISSION ON HISTORY IN SCHOOLS. *Building a History Curriculum: Guidelines for Teaching History in Schools.* Washington, DC: Education Excellence Network, 1988.

CRABTREE, CHARLOTTE. "Improving History in the Schools." *Educational Leadership* 47 (November 1989): 25–28.

DOWNEY, MATTHEW T., AND LINDA S. LEVSTIK. "Teaching and Learning History." In *Handbook of Research on Social Studies Teaching and Learning,* edited by James P. Shaver, 400–410. New York: Macmillan, 1991.

FREEMAN, EVELYN B., AND LINDA S. LEVSTIK. "Recreating the Past: Historical Fiction in the Social Studies Curriculum." *The Elementary School Journal* 88 (March 1988): 329–37.

GAGNON, PAUL, ed. *Historical Literacy: The Case for History in American Education.* New York: Macmillan, 1989.

GIFFORD, BERNARD R. *History in the Schools: What Shall We Teach?* New York: Macmillan, 1988.

MEHAFFY, GEORGE L. "Oral History in Elementary Classrooms." *Social Education* 48 (September/October 1984): 470–72.

MUESSIG, RAYMOND H. "An Analysis of Developments in Geographic Education." *The Elementary School Journal* 87 (May 1987): 518–30.

NATIONAL COMMISSION ON SOCIAL STUDIES IN THE SCHOOLS. *Charting a Course: Social Studies for the 21st Century.* Washington, DC: author, 1989.

NELSON, JACK L. "Charting a Course Backwards: A Response to the National Commission's Nineteenth Century Social Studies Program." *Social Education* 54 (November/December 1990): 434–37.

RAVITCH, DIANE. "The Plight of History in American Schools." In *Historical Literacy: The Case for History in American Education,* edited by Paul Gagnon, 50–68. New York: Macmillan, 1989.

STOLTMAN, JOSEPH P. "Research on Geography Teaching." In *Handbook of Research on Social Studies Teaching and Learning,* edited by James P. Shaver, 437–47. New York: Macmillan, 1991.

SUNAL, CYNTHIA S., AND BARBARA ANN HATCHER. "Studying History through Art." How To Do It series 5, no. 2. Washington, DC: National Council for the Social Studies, 1986.

6 Space and Time Dimensions of Social Studies: Maps, Globes, and Graphics

S uppose someone came into a roomful of people and announced, "There has been a disastrous earthquake!" What would be said by the others present? Most likely the next things to be said would be,

"Where did it happen?"
"When did it happen?"

Only after these questions were answered would there be an interest in whether anyone was injured and the extent of the damage. Events hold little meaning for us unless we know the *place* and the *time* of their occurrence. Consequently, in social studies we find ourselves constantly making references to *where* something happened and *when* it happened. Such references to time and place may be specific, such as Lexington, Massachusetts, April 18, 1775; or they may be general, such as "a long time ago, in the area where three continents meet." These definite and indefinite references to time and space also involve *quantitative* concepts:

SPACE	TIME
A great distance	Soon thereafter
Forty miles	A long journey
1,500 acres	Three decades
Largest continent	Four centuries earlier
55,000 square miles	A fortnight later
23 ½° north latitude	A four-hour interval

Definite and indefinite references to time and space can be bothersome for children. For example, if children read that Columbus's ship, the *Santa Maria*, was 98 feet long, such a reference to distance probably will mean something different to every child in the class. It might be conceptualized as a distance ranging from one not greater than the length of the classroom to one of several city blocks. When there is such confusion over a relatively

153

simple and definite reference to distance, one can only speculate on the misunderstandings that must abound when we use such references as the following:

> A township was to be a square, 6 miles long on each side. Each township was to be divided into 36 sections. A section, therefore, was 1 mile square and had 640 acres in it.

The research that has been conducted on time, space, and quantitative concepts in social studies confirms that children often misunderstand them. The tendency is to overestimate the ability of children to handle such concepts. As a result, maps often are used that are more complex than they should be in view of the maturity of the children using them. Also children may make and use time lines that they really do not comprehend. Because children so easily verbalize quantitative concepts such as decade, century, thousands, hundreds, several miles, many years, and 10 percent, the assumption is that they are understood. Research on this subject indicates that such assumptions are often in error.

When the abstractness of these concepts is reduced, they are made meaningful to children. We try, therefore, to provide children with a concrete reference to space and time, preferably one that is a part of their experiences. This is why current news events provide such a good vehicle for teaching some concepts and skills. The children read about current happenings in the classroom periodical or hear and see them reported on radio and television news. Thus, finding places on a map is a natural extension of everyday experiences.

The social studies curriculum operates within a matrix that might be represented very simply as follows:

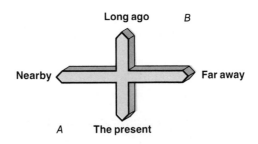

Experiences that could be charted at point *A* would be the least abstract and would usually be found in the early grades. Experiences at point *B* would be most difficult to make concrete for children because they are remote not only in space but also in time. Because many children today have firsthand experiences that acquaint them with places beyond their immediate environment, it is not as necessary to confine the social studies program to the local area as it once was. There can be more movement from the near at hand to the far away even at early grade levels. This is more difficult to do with the time dimension, however. The reality of events of the past needs to be tied to the present, again calling attention to the importance of using current news events.

There are many instructional aids that can help one teach and learn these complex concepts. For example, globes and maps are indispensable tools for working with space and spatial relationships. Time lines and charts can make time and chronology meaningful. Graphs and tables can make some types of quantitative relationships easier to comprehend. It is imperative, therefore, that the social studies program teach children how to use these tools.

MAP AND GLOBE SKILLS ESSENTIAL TO THE SOCIAL STUDIES CURRICULUM

Maps and globes are vehicles for representing space symbolically. The essential features of all maps and globes are a grid, color, scale, symbols, and a legend that explains the symbol system used. The ability to read and interpret maps and globes, like conventional reading, is a summarizing skill in that it represents a composite of several subskills. These subskills can be inferred by making an analysis of the behavior of someone reading a map who is skillful at it. Fortunately, this will not be necessary because it has been done by specialists several times and always with somewhat the same results. One list that is available to school districts throughout the nation is published by the National Council for the Social Studies. According to this source, the essential map-reading skills include the ability to

1. orient a map and note directions,
2. locate places on map and globe,
3. use scale and compute distances,
4. interpret map symbols and visualize what they mean,
5. compare maps and make inferences, and
6. express relative location.[1]

Directional Orientation

To deal with directional relationships on maps and globes, the child must first understand them in reality. The easiest directions to use are those that express relative location, such as close to, near, over here, and over there. These can be learned in the primary grades. The *cardinal directions* are also learned in the primary grades by having them pointed out and by referring to places that are known to children as being north of, east of, south of, and so on. Placing direction labels on the various walls of the classroom helps remind children of cardinal directions. They can associate east and west

---

[1]National Council for the Social Studies, *Social Studies Curriculum Planning Resources* (Dubuque, IA: Kendall/Hunt, 1991), 36.

with the rising and setting of the sun. They can learn how a compass is used to find direction. While on field trips, children should be given practice in noting directions, observing especially the directions of streets and roads. Gradually, they learn the purpose of the poles, the meridians of longitude, and the parallels of latitude in orienting a map and noting directions. When maps with unfamiliar projections are introduced, children should be taught how to establish correct directional relationships on them.

Using Map Scales

In making a map, the cartographer tries to reproduce as accurately as possible that portion of the earth being represented. Because globes are models of the earth, they can represent the earth more correctly than can maps. No map can altogether faithfully represent the earth simply because the earth is round and maps are flat. The flattening process inevitably results in some distortion.

Scaling is the process of reducing everything in the same amount. When one works with children in the primary grades, scaling should be done in the relative sense. Some things are larger or smaller than other things, and the maps should show their *relative size* as accurately as possible. For example, a fifty-foot-high tree in the schoolyard should be about five times larger than the ten-foot-tall playground set. On conventional maps, three types of scales are used:

1. The graphic scale

2. The inches-to-miles scale

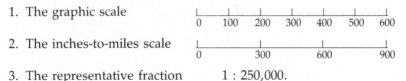

3. The representative fraction   1 : 250,000.

Of these, the graphic scale is the easiest to use and can be taught at about fourth grade. The inches-to-miles scale is more complex, but it can also be taught in the middle grades. The representative fraction is usually considered beyond the scope of the elementary school program.

As children become more global in their experiences, they will encounter map scales in metric measures. If metric measurement is used, the distance on a graphic scale would be recorded in kilometers. Likewise, rather than as inches to miles, the scale would show the relationship as centimeters to kilometers. The following graphic scale illustrates the same distance expressed in miles and in kilometers:

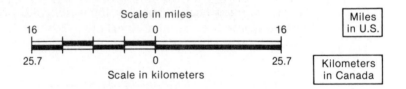

Locating Places

The ability to locate places on maps and globes comes with a familiarity with these devices cultivated over a period of several years. Children first learn to locate places that are known to them on simple maps and layouts that they make in the classroom. In the early grades, too, children can learn the names and shapes of some of the major geographic features, such as continents, oceans, the equator, and the poles. The commercially prepared maps and globes designed for the lower grades are quite plain, having only a few features shown. Gradually, children increase their repertoire of known places they can find on the map and globe because of frequent references to the location of important cities, countries, rivers, mountains, and other physical features.

In the middle grades, children are taught to use coordinates to locate places. Local highway maps are well suited for use in teaching this skill because they deal with an area familiar to the children. One set of lines of the grid—perhaps the north–south lines—is identified with letters; the other set of lines is numbered as is done in Figure 6-1. The teacher can have the children (this is usually done in fourth grade) find several places lo-

The use of plastic-coated desk maps allow students to place data on maps with felt-tip pens. Corrections can be made easily on such surfaces, and they can be cleaned and used over and over again.
(Photo by Carla Anderson, Northshore School District.)

FIGURE 6-1

Middle-grade children can learn to use a grid in locating places by using road maps that have coordinates of the type shown on this map. Test your own memory of place locations by responding to these questions:

1. What major city is located in square C2?
2. What major city lies near the intersection of the squares D1, D2, E1, and E2?
3. Describe the location of Savannah by using the coordinates provided on this map.

Check your answers by consulting a map of Georgia that shows cities.

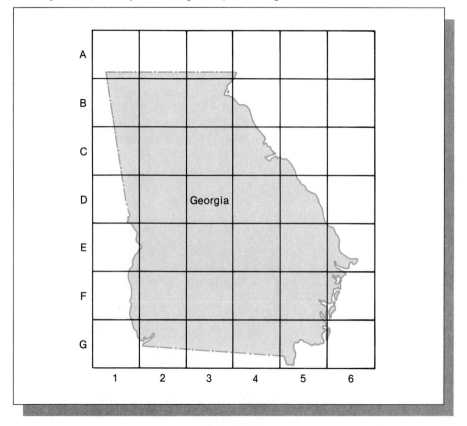

cated on or very near to a north–south line, say D. Then several places can be found on an east–west line, say 7. If the teacher is clever enough to pick two coordinates that intersect on a major point of interest, the children will discover that some city or other important feature is located at the point where D and 7 intersect. Figure 6-1 is an example of an exercise of this kind. This experience provides readiness for the use of meridians of longitude and parallels of latitude in locating places on wall maps and the globe. At this stage, children are mature enough to understand why reference points such as poles, the equator, and the prime meridian are essential in locating places on a sphere.

Reading Map Symbols

Maps use symbols to represent real things: Dots of varying sizes stand for cities of different populations; color is used to represent elevation; hash marks stand for escarpments; and lines are used to show boundaries, coastlines, and rivers. Naturally, the reader will not comprehend the messages of maps unless he or she knows what these symbols represent. Children begin to learn their meanings early in the elementary school social studies program. The development of this subskill closely parallels that of locating places on maps.

Map and globe symbols vary in their abstractness. Indeed, some simple maps for children in the primary grades use symbols that are pictorial or semipictorial. These symbols either look like the object being represented or provide a strong clue as to its identity, as shown in Figures 6-2 and 6-3. It would not take much imagination, for example, to differentiate water areas from land areas on a globe simply on the basis of their color.

The instructional sequence to be followed in teaching the symbol system of maps is to move gradually from pictorial and semipictorial symbols on maps made by children to the abstract symbols used on conventional wall maps, globes, and maps that are included in the textbooks of the middle and upper grades. It is essential that children learn to consult the map legend or key to confirm which symbols are being used. In most cases, children in the middle and upper grades will be dealing with maps that use conventional map symbols; but special-purpose maps such as those showing vegetation, rainfall, population density, and so on, often use symbols that are unique to the particular map.

It is always a good idea to make generous use of photographs of the areas shown on a map in order to help the children associate the map symbol with what the place actually looks like. Similarly, when children go on field trips, they should be encouraged to observe carefully the appearance of landscapes and other features that are shown on maps. In time they will be able to visualize the reality that the abstract map symbols represent.

Understanding Relative Location

Understanding relative location is an interpretive skill that requires information beyond that provided by the map itself. It has to do with thinking about how places relate to each other in terms of political, cultural, religious, commercial, or historical perspectives. It has nothing to do with how close or how far away places may be in the absolute sense. For example, the non-Asian people—and even many Asians—of the British Crown Colony of Hong Kong feel closer to Great Britain (10,000 miles away) than they do to the People's Republic of China (less than twenty miles away) because of political, economic, and cultural ties.

Relative location may also be thought of in terms of the amount of time required to get to a place using the kind of transportation available. This is commonly expressed nowadays in ordinary conversation and small talk as

FIGURE 6-2
Children can be introduced to the concept of symbols through pictorial representations that they encounter in real life, such as the ones shown here.

people say, "It takes me thirty minutes to get to work," or "I'm about two hours from Washington." Distances that now take two hours to traverse would have taken two days a hundred years ago and two weeks or even more at the time of the founding of the Republic. Increasingly, we reckon distances in terms of time. Consequently, places may be thought of as being remote or near in terms of how difficult it is to get to them. Air crash survivors stranded in the High Sierras in the dead of winter, no more than fifty miles from Fresno, California, might be as far away from civilization in the relative sense as they would be if they were in Antarctica.

FIGURE 6-3

Examples of standard symbols used on maps.

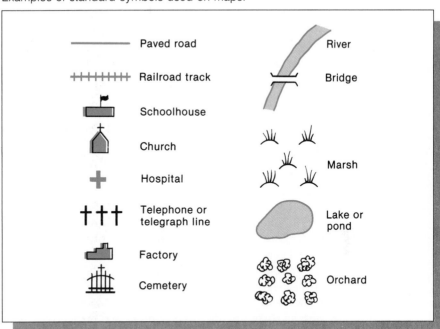

Comparing Maps and Making Inferences

Comparing maps and making inferences are also inferential skills because to some extent the reader has to project what he or she already knows on the map data. In this process the map reader discovers relationships among the sets of data presented by different maps. In the middle elementary grades, teachers often have children compare vegetation maps with rainfall maps. They also have them compare maps showing the location of important resources, such as iron and coal, with maps showing the location of industrial centers, population densities, and so on. It is quite common to find special-purpose maps of the same region in the children's textbooks, making comparisons easy. These provide excellent settings for critical thinking as the children can study the data presented on two or more maps, make predictions or hypotheses about these data, and then go on to the next step of verifying or rejecting their speculations.

Children in the late middle and upper elementary grades should study maps based on different projections and compare the shapes and sizes of known areas with those same areas as shown on the globe. This will familiarize them with the concept of distortion, which, in greater or lesser amounts, is present in all flat maps. Children should learn why distortion occurs and what cartographers have done to minimize its effect.

INSTRUCTIONAL EXPERIENCES WITH THE GLOBE

Every social studies classroom should have and use a globe. In grades one, two, and three a simplified twelve-inch globe is generally recommended because small children find this size easier to handle than the larger sixteen-inch one. For primary grades, the globe selected should have a minimum amount of information on it. It should not use more than three colors to represent land elevation or more than two colors to represent water depth. Only the largest cities, rivers, and water bodies should be shown. In the middle and upper grades, a sixteen-inch globe is recommended because of its easy scale of one inch to five hundred miles. Moreover, its larger size allows more detail to be shown without the globe's becoming a confused collection of facts. Globes for middle- and upper-grade children will ordinarily use seven colors to represent land elevations and three colors to represent water depths.

The chief value of the globe in grades one, two, and three is to familiarize the children with the basic roundness of the earth and to begin to develop a global perspective. The primary-grade child does not necessarily need formal lessons on the use of the globe. If the globe is in the classroom, it will provoke curiosity and a desire to know more about it and how to use it. Parents speak of places in the news, and the children wonder where those places are. They hear of earth satellites and wonder about their orbits. Perhaps a girl has just joined the class; her family has recently moved to this country from another part of the world, and she wants to show the class the location of her former home. The teacher will use situations such as these—and hundreds more like them—to acquaint the young child with the globe.

The teacher should help children discover other things about the globe—differences between water and land areas and that these are represented by different colors; the line that separates the water and the land is called the seacoast. Children may be shown pictures to help them visualize different kinds of coastlines. Similarly, the teacher extends their understanding of other concepts—oceans, cities, rivers, mountains. Children learn that most of the brown areas that represent land are on the half of the earth that has the North Pole and that it is here that the majority of the people of the world live.

In addition to the incidental references made to the globe, the teacher should make frequent use of the globe when teaching social studies and other subjects. For instance, in a reading lesson, children might find where their book friends "live." Thus, the globe can be used in a great variety of ways to lay a good foundation for more formal aspects of the teaching of these skills later on.

The following are examples of the *types* of learnings and experiences that can be planned with the globe for children in the lower grades:

1. Stress that the globe is a very small model of the earth. Good models look exactly like the real thing but are smaller. The globe is a good model of the earth.

2. Show the children how land areas and water bodies are represented on the globe. Have them find land areas and water bodies. Names of these need not be taught at this level, but children might already know the large water bodies such as the Pacific and Atlantic oceans. Similarly, they might be familiar with North and South America, Africa or the Antarctic, and these can be pointed out. Explain that all water bodies and land areas have names.

3. Have children discover that there is considerably more water than land shown on the globe. Ask children to find the half of the globe that has most of the land. Explain that this is the half on which we live and is the part of the earth where most of the world's people make their homes.

4. Show children the location of the North Pole. Explain that most of the land of the world is on the same half of the world as the North Pole. We call this the northern half.

5. Show children the location of the South Pole. Explain that most of the water areas of the world are on the same half of the world as the South Pole. We call this the southern half.

6. Explain that our earth is a planet.

7. Show children how they can find their country, their continent, their state, and possibly their city on the globe.

8. Use the globe to find places that are familiar to the children—places they have visited on vacations, places in the news, homes of book friends and visitors from other countries, or places in the world from which some circus or zoo animals are brought.

9. Encourage children to handle the globe and to find places on it themselves.

10. Answer questions the children ask concerning the globe in simple, nontechnical language.

Lesson Plan 6 is an example of a plan used by one teacher to familiarize primary-grade children with geographic concepts and skills using the globe.

As children move into the middle and upper grades, instruction in the use of the globe should take two forms. First, the teacher should take time from regularly scheduled unit activities to teach skills needed in reading and interpreting the globe. Second, in unit work and other classroom activities, there should be frequent reference to the globe and maps. Both of these aspects of instruction are important, and one should supplement the other. To hope that children will become skillful in the use of a globe or maps simply by making incidental references to them when the occasion presents itself is wishful thinking. At the same time, formal lessons in the use of these devices without application of the newly acquired skills in purposeful situations is equally ineffective. The best arrangement is to provide for systematic instruction in the use of map- and globe-reading skills as a part of unit activities, reinforcing this with direct teaching of these skills as the need arises.

Lesson Plan 6

Topic:	Using the globe to learn about the earth
Grade:	One or two
Time:	One class period
Objective:	To develop a familiarity with concepts relating to the globe.
Interest Building:	Give the children free time to manipulate a globe and explore it on their own.
Lesson Development:	The teacher directs the following questions to the children:
	What shape is a globe?
	Can you find the North Pole? Place your finger on it.
	Where is north on a globe?
	Where is south on a globe?
	Is south the opposite direction of north?
	What divides the north from the south?
	Have any of you been to the equator?
	Is the equator really a line?
	How much of the globe is north?
	How much of the globe is south?
	What is half of a sphere?
	Does anyone know what we call the northern half of the globe?
	Does anyone know what we call the southern half of the globe?
	How can we tell water from land on the globe?
	Does anyone know what we call these large pieces of land?
	Can you find a continent in the Northern Hemisphere?
	Can you find a continent in the Southern Hemisphere?
	Are there any continents that are in both hemispheres?
Summary:	How is the globe divided?
	Can you name the parts of the globe we talked about?
	Can you point to the Northern Hemisphere?
	Can you point to the Southern Hemisphere?
	Can you point to a continent?
Materials:	As many globes as are available in order that each child can easily explore and manipulate the globe.

Maps may be used to find distances between points only under certain conditions, but the globe represents distances accurately and true to scale at all points on the surface of the earth. It is easy to place a flexible ruler on the globe and measure directly the distance between two points in question, then refer to the scale and determine the actual distance between the two places. The air routes of the world use great circles because these are the shortest distances from place to place on the earth's surface. If nothing but flat maps are used, it is difficult to understand the concept of great circle routes, and, therefore, of airplane routes. The globe can help clarify this concept (see Figure 6-4). In this connection, the slated globe (sometimes called the project globe) is useful because it is possible to write on the surface of it with a piece of chalk.

Globes are helpful, too, in establishing concepts of direction. It is not difficult to think of north as being in the direction of the North Pole when using a globe. On the other hand, this may be confusing if only a flat map is used. Furthermore, the relative direction of various parts of the earth can be better understood through the use of a globe. Many Americans are

FIGURE 6-4
Notice how differently the map and globe portray global relationships. In the space age we need to think of the world more as it is shown by the globe than the map.

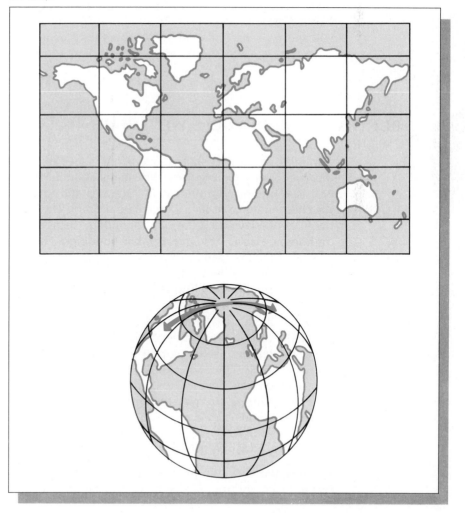

surprised, for example, when they learn that Great Britain lies in a more northerly latitude than do any of the forty-eight mid-continent states of our country; that Boston has nearly the same latitude as Rome; that our most westerly state is not Hawaii but Alaska; that our most southerly state is not Florida but Hawaii; that Moscow and Glasgow have approximately the same latitude, both being farther south than any city of Norway or Finland. These facts illustrate that one perceives the earth differently on a globe than on a flat map.

A definite advantage that globes have over maps is that they show the size and shapes of areas exactly as they appear on the earth's surface whereas maps cannot. The classical examples of distortions in the size and shapes of land areas are Greenland on the Mercator projection and Australia on the polar projection. On the Mercator projection, Greenland appears as a very large area—larger than South America. On a polar projection, Australia appears to have a greater east–west distance and a shorter north–south distance than is actually the case. Notice the different shapes North America takes on various maps as illustrated in Figure 6-5. A globe will show all these map shapes and sizes to be inaccurately represented. Therefore, a globe should be used with maps to prevent wrong conceptions.

INSTRUCTIONAL EXPERIENCES WITH MAPS

A number of complex skills are involved in map reading and interpretation; therefore, early experiences with maps should be kept simple. This can best be done through the use of diagrams and maps that the teacher and the children make of their immediate vicinity. These experiences may take the form of a layout on the classroom floor, using blocks and other objects for houses, streets, trees, and public buildings. The layout can be done on a table, or the map can be drawn on a large piece of wrapping paper on the classroom floor. When the floor surface will permit, masking tape can be placed on the floor itself to represent boundaries, streets, or roads.

Opportunities to teach and apply these skills often arise in the everyday life of the classroom. For instance, children in one class learned about map direction when a new student joined the group. Soon after the child arrived, the teacher used a map to show the class the location of the child's previous home. They determined the direction the child's family traveled to reach their new home. The teacher then used a map of the local area and had the children discover the direction they travel in going from their homes to school each day.

Teaching Map Symbols

A fundamental skill in map reading is to learn that a symbol represents a real and actual thing. The symbol may be arbitrarily chosen and bear no

FIGURE 6-5

A land area such as North America may take a variety of shapes on maps, depending on the projection that is used. Professional cartographers continually search for more exact ways to show the earth's surface on flat maps. In 1988, its centennial year, the National Geographic Society selected a new map projection that more accurately represents the earth than did earlier projections. The new projection was developed by Arthur H. Robinson, Professor Emeritus of Cartography and Geography at the University of Wisconsin-Madison. The Robinson projection replaces the Van der Grinten projection that had been used by the Society for its world maps for more than five decades.

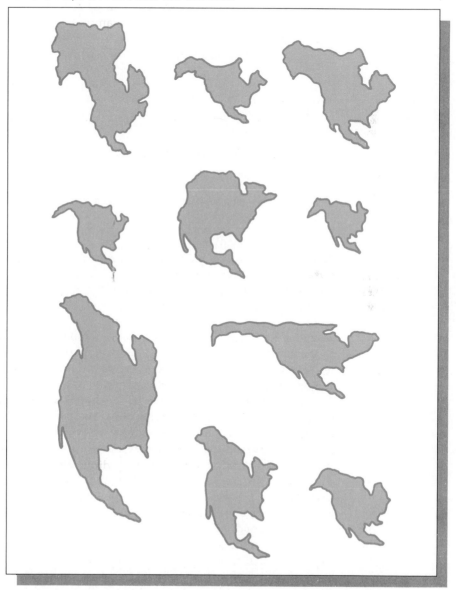

··················· DO-IT-YOURSELF MAP

This exercise can be used in the middle and upper grades for teaching, diagnosing, or evaluating map skills. The teacher can have everyone in class do the exercise as the directions are read, one step at a time. Directions can also be displayed with an overhead projector. When the maps are completed, the exercise should be discussed. Children can be invited to walk around the room to see maps drawn by their classmates. Maps can also be displayed on the bulletin boards.

Directions:

1. On a clean sheet of paper, draw an outline map of an imaginary continent. You may make it any shape you wish, but you must include at least one peninsula and one bay.
2. Show a scale of miles in your legend for the map.
3. Draw east–west and north–south lines on your map.
4. Draw a mountain range running east and west across your continent, but include at least one mountain pass. Place the symbol you use for your mountain range in your legend.
5. Show a city in the northern half of your continent and one in the southern half. Make each one a seaport.
6. Show a railway joining the two cities.
7. Show three rivers on your continent; show a lake and a swamp. Place all the symbols you use for cities, rivers, lakes, and swamps in the legend.
8. Place a third city somewhere on your map where you think a city should be. On the bottom of your map tell why you think a city should be where you have placed it.
9. Show boundary lines that divide your continent into three large countries and one small country.

resemblance to the object represented, or it may be one that would suggest to the reader what is intended. A school might be represented by a small circle or by a small square with a flag placed on top. It is easier to associate the flag and square with a school than to associate the circle with it. The flag and square are, therefore, less abstract. With young children, it is better to use pictorial or semipictorial symbols of this sort than to use completely abstract ones. In teaching map-reading skills, one must remember that both reading and interpretive skills are involved, and the interpretive skills depend heavily on maturity and background knowledge. Primary-grade children will do less with interpreting maps than they will with reading them.

The idea of objects representing other objects, people, or things is not new to the children; they have substituted symbols for the actual things many times in the imaginative play of childhood. The teacher can begin by explaining that they are going to draw a map of the schoolroom, schoolyard, or some segment of the immediate vicinity. It is best if this can be done on the classroom floor, so the layout can be oriented exactly as it appears in relationship to the classroom; this sidesteps the matter of orientation to directions at this early stage. Trees, doors, playground equipment, parking areas, and other objects appear in relation to other objects, and only the major ones should be included. The purpose of this experience is simply to show that it is possible to represent space symbolically and that symbols stand for real things. Their maps should have a title and a key to tell what the symbols stand for. This is the first experience in the development of skill in comprehending the significance of symbols, and it will be continued and extended as long as maps are used.

As the children become ready for more abstract symbols, such symbols will be introduced, taught, and used, as will more conventional map symbols. As a part of this instruction in the middle and upper grades, it is important to make generous use of pictures and other visual aids that will help children visualize the area represented. It is helpful, too, to take children to some high point in the community where they can look down on an area and see what it actually looks like from above. In most localities it is possible to purchase inexpensive aerial photographs of the local community, and these can be used in studying map symbols and in making maps of the local area. Some map companies have prepared wall charts designed to help children visualize things represented by map symbols; these are excellent devices for teaching this skill to middle- and upper-grade children. The teacher also should take advantage of the many fine photographs in social studies textbooks to acquaint children with the appearance of various areas, landscapes, surface features, land and water forms, and people-made things that are represented symbolically on maps.

Teaching Map Directions

For reasons of simplicity, orientation to direction may be avoided in the children's first attempts at making diagrams or maps. But the need to orient a map properly for direction will become apparent to them if their classroom map is rotated. Being able to note and read directions is a prerequisite to serious map study, and this skill should be introduced fairly early, perhaps in the second grade. Children can learn the cardinal directions by having the directions pointed out to them. They learn which wall of the room is north, south, east, and west because the teacher may have placed labels on the walls. They learn that if one knows the direction of north, the other directions can be determined; for if one faces north, the direction of south will be to one's back, east to the right, and west to the left. To extend their ability to orient themselves, children should be taken outdoors and the directions pointed out to them. If this is done at noon on a sunny day, the children's shadows will point in an approximate northerly direction. After the children have this basic orientation to direction, subsequent mapwork should include reference to direction and should become increasingly more complex as the children mature.

Finding directions on conventional wall maps can be facilitated with the aid of a globe and perhaps should not be taught much below the fourth grade. When this concept is introduced, it should be done through reference to north–south and east–west grid lines. Children are taught that north is in the direction of the North Pole and that south is in the direction of the South Pole. The poles can be easily found by following the meridians of longitude. The east–west directions can be found by following the parallels of latitude. Generalizations such as "north is at the top of the map" and "south is at the bottom of the map" should *not* be taught because they are not correct and because they may be confusing when one uses a variety of different map projections. Similarly, references to north as "up" and south as "down" should not be taught in connection with either maps or globes. When we speak of the earth, the term *down* means toward the center of the earth and *up* means away from the center of the earth, and both terms should be taught only in that way. The matter of associating *up* with north introduces many instructional problems as children learn more of the geography of the earth. For example, if north is up, how can so many of the world's rivers flow north? The children will invariably ask why we say "way down South" or "the Land Down Under"; these can be explained as being colorful expressions and figures of speech similar to "way out West" or "out at sea" that have crept into our language but have nothing at all to do with direction itself. (See Figure 6-6.)

There is merit in taking time to have children point out and discuss directions on the map. In the middle and upper grades, the teacher should duplicate maps on various grids and have the children place directional data on them. When this is done, the need to use east–west and north–south lines should be emphasized. This will give the children experiences noting directions on various map grids as well as keeping the teacher up to date on the progress that the children are making in learning this skill.

Teaching Map Scale

Children can be helped to understand the need for map scales by indicating to them that maps must be small enough to bring into the classroom or carry around. We cannot make maps as big as the area we wish to show because that would make the maps so large they could not be used. A map must, therefore, be made smaller, and everything on the map must be made smaller in the same amount. Just as a photograph of the family shows everyone smaller in the same amount, so must the map; otherwise, it would not give a true picture. Children should learn that maps are precise and accurate instruments. In primary grades, the scaling is not done in the mathematical sense, but the reductions are correctly made in the relative sense. That is, lakes would be larger than houses; streets, longer than driveways; cars, smaller than business buildings; and so on. In middle grades, when children have had sufficient background in mathematics, they can deal with graphic reductions more precisely. They learn that wall maps have the scale printed on them and are taught how to read the various ways by which scale can be indicated. The experiences children

FIGURE 6-6
This map illustrates why generalizations such as "north is at the top of the map" are incorrect. East–west lines or parallels of latitude have been omitted in order to draw attention to north–south directions. What questions might you pose to students studying this map?

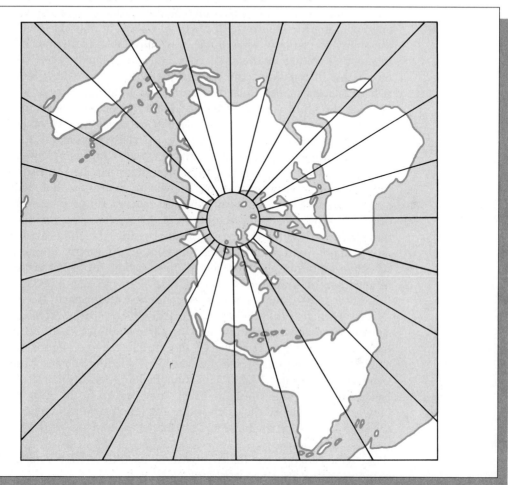

have using map scales provide a good context in which to call their attention to distances between various places. Children can be helped to visualize these distances through an appreciation of the amount of time needed to traverse the distances in question by air travel. These times may be obtained from commercial airlines.

Teaching Map Interpretation

When children have learned the meaning of map symbols, are skillful in orienting a map to direction, and can recognize and use map scales, they are well on their way toward an understanding of the language of maps. This does not mean, however, that they find maps especially useful or that they regard them as a valuable source of information. The development of skills that deal largely with map language must be accompanied by associated interpretive skills. Proficiency in interpreting maps will vary considerably among the children. One who is skillful in map use has developed the ability to visualize what an area actually looks like when it is seen on the map. Looking at the map color, one in a sense "sees" the rugged mountains of our West, the waving grainfields of western Montana, the rich farmlands of the Midwest, and the rolling countryside of Virginia. Because the child cannot visualize places not actually seen except in an imaginative way, the *generous use of additional visual material along with maps is suggested.* Good-quality pictures are especially important, and the class should see several pictures of an area to avoid fixing a single impression of the area in their minds. Filmstrips and slides can be used for the same purpose, and motion pictures and television are also excellent aids. As was previously noted, in the early stages of map reading, an excellent procedure is to have an aerial photograph of the local area as well as a conventional map. When these are placed side by side, the child can see how the area actually looks and how it is represented on a map. Stories and other narrative accounts also are helpful in assisting the child visualize areas represented on maps.

In the 1970s, the National Aeronautics and Space Administration (NASA) launched the satellite system called "Landsat," which uses remote sensing to obtain color images of the earth's surface. Landsat imagery is then used to construct maps of the earth's surface. Landsat maps are available for school use (NASA Code 130.3, Goddard Space Flight Center, Greenbelt, Maryland 20771, Attn. Elva Bailey). Because Landsat maps are based on actual images of the earth, they are useful in bridging the gap between the reality of the earth and the abstractness of conventional maps. One can *see* the actual shape and surface characteristics of the area shown on a Landsat map.

Activities such as the following can be used to relate the abstractions of maps to the reality they represent:

1. Observing local landscapes and geographical features, preferably from a high point.
2. Using pictorial and semipictorial symbols, especially at the lower grade levels.
3. Using three-dimensional models of the areas mapped; using blocks and models to represent buildings.
4. Making maps of the local area with which children are familiar.
5. Making generous use of pictures, films, and filmstrips of the areas shown on maps.
6. Relating aerial photographs (angle shots rather than perpendicular ones) to maps of the same area.

The teacher offers a suggestion to these middle graders regarding a relief map they are constructing. Contrast the advantages and limitations in the use of student-made relief maps with those prepared commercially. What would you identify as the most important value of using student-made maps?
(Photo by Carla Anderson, Northshore School District.)

7. Comparing areas shown on the wall map with the same area shown in a picture.
8. Developing descriptive words (adjectives) that apply to a particular area shown on a map.
9. Making use of current events that relate to the area shown on a map.
10. Visiting places shown on the map, such as the airport, harbor, park, and downtown area.

Through years of experience with maps, children will develop skill in locating places and will become familiar with the shape and size of better-known areas. Places should be located precisely. In pointing to Chicago, for example, children should locate it exactly—not by sweeping a hand across the general location of Chicago, thereby including parts of Iowa, Illinois, Wisconsin, Michigan, and Indiana. But the location exercises must go beyond simply pointing to places and objects that appear on the map. It is these situations that provide ready-made opportunities to teach thinking skills in geography. For example, the teacher might pursue questions such as the following: What information can be obtained from the map that might account for the large settlement of people in the Chicago area? What features tend to encourage or discourage settlers? Such factors as natural transportation routes, waterways, waterfalls, mouths of rivers, coastlines, temperature, gaps in mountains, and outlets for products of the surrounding areas will become apparent as being important in population density and settlement. Why do certain areas of the Red River Valley in Minnesota and North Dakota experience frequent spring flood problems? The facts that the Red River is north-flowing and its headwaters thaw while the sections farther north are still frozen help explain this recurring problem. What is the relationship of the grazing lands of the West to the farmlands of Iowa to the meat-processing plants of Omaha, Chicago, and Kansas City? Map study, along with some knowledge of the geography of these areas, will help answer questions of this type. Children gain insights into geographical relationships by having a helpful teacher who can assist them in seeing possibilities for interpreting and making inferences from facts gained through map study.

The types of information that can be read directly or inferred from map study can be classified as follows:

Land and water forms—continents, oceans, bays, peninsulas, islands, straits.

Relief features—plains, mountains, rivers, deserts, plateaus, swamps, valleys.

Direction and distance—cardinal directions, distance in miles or kilometers and relative distance, scale.

Social data—population density, size of communities, location of major cities, relationship of social data to other factors.

Economic information—industrial and agricultural production, soil fertility, trade factors, location of industries.

Political information—political divisions, boundaries, capitals, territorial possessions, types of government, political parties.

Scientific information—location of discoveries, ocean currents, location of mineral and ore deposits, geological formations, air movements.

Human factors—cities, canals, railroads, highways, coaxial and fiber optic cables, telephone lines, bridges, dams, nuclear power plants.

Teaching Map Color

The use of color has caused confusion for children trying to visualize elevations. Children seem to believe that all areas represented by one color are precisely the same elevation, not recognizing that there are variations in elevations that occur within the limits of the interval used by the color representation. (See Figure 6-7.) Moreover, children develop the mistaken idea that elevations occur abruptly where colors change. Conventional color symbols give no impression of gradual elevations or depressions and

·················· MAKING A TRIP MAP

The teacher showed children color photographs of several states and discussed the many interesting things that can be seen and done in the various states. Children shared some of their own travel experiences. The teacher provided the class with road maps of several different states and asked them to find places that might be of interest to someone visiting those states. These places of interest were discussed briefly. Children were then asked to think about and select a state they would enjoy visiting. Choices were to be made by the next day.

The following day the children made their selections of states they wanted to "visit." Using a road map of that state provided by the teacher and using references available in and outside the classroom, they were to plan a route of travel through the state of their choice, making at least five stops at places that would be interesting to a visitor. These places were to be marked with a large dot. A short narrative description was to be written to accompany the map telling about the travel route, state or national parks, natural areas of interest, historical landmarks, or other items of interest. If the children preferred, they could prepare a verbal rather than a written narrative by using the cassette recorder in the classroom.

The children responded to the teacher's encouragement to be creative in describing their imaginary trips, and several prepared travel brochures and recorded travelogs. They began a classroom exhibit of their trip maps and narratives, and in a week the room resembled a travel agency office. This generated a considerable amount of discussion and sharing of ideas and, of course, numerous opportunities to learn about maps. Also, through this activity the children acquired a great deal of information about their country, applied important skills (reading, research, writing, discussion, speaking), and developed an appreciation for the diversity and variety of their own country.

create the illusion that changes are abrupt. The use of a relief map is helpful in showing that changes in elevation occur gradually. Comparing colors of a wall map with elevations on a relief map helps children gain a better understanding of map color as used to represent elevations. It is important to remember, however, that relief maps use two scales—one for vertical distances and another for horizontal distances. If the horizontal scale were used for vertical distances, the elevations would be imperceptible on a relief map of the size usually found in elementary school classrooms. Some maps combine shaded relief with altitude colors; this adds a third-dimensional effect to the mountains and valleys. Oblique shading and blending of color from one elevation to the other gives a graduated effect to land elevations that more accurately portray the surface of the earth. Children must also be taught that color may be used to designate political divisions such as states, nations, and territories and that the color chosen is an arbitrary one having nothing to do with the way the area actually looks. Pictures of state boundaries, for example, will illustrate that if it were not for the boundary marker, one would not be able to tell where one state ends and the other begins.

Landform maps are often used in middle- and upper-grade social studies textbooks. The usual landforms shown are *plains, plateaus, hills,* and

FIGURE 6-7

This diagram shows two methods of illustrating keys to colors used to express elevations on classroom maps. Some teachers find it helpful to construct a three-dimensional papier-mâché model of the key to help students associate elevation with the color code.

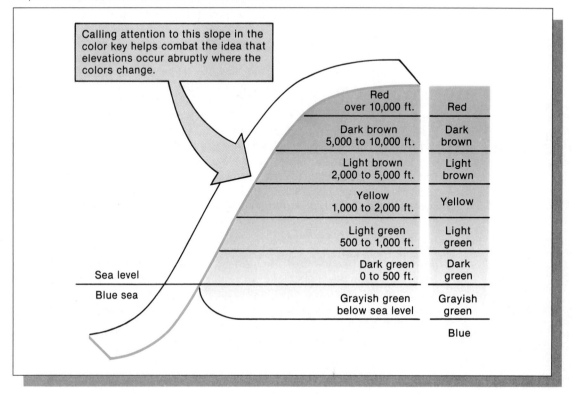

mountains; each is represented by a different color. Difficulty in using these maps arises when the child mistakenly thinks of the colors as representing elevations in absolute amounts. For example, there are high mountains and low mountains, yet on a landform map they may appear in the same color. Some high plateaus are actually higher in absolute elevation than some low mountains. Some hills may be lower in elevation than plateaus and plains. Children need to learn that landform maps show only where the plains, plateaus, hills, and mountains are located, not how high they are above sea level.

Applying Map and Globe Skills

Map- and globe-reading skills are learned through direct teaching and by application in situations in which the skill is normally used. In many instances, these processes can be combined. Let us say, for example, that children in a fifth-grade class read that "Permafrost is a condition found only in high latitudes." The teacher can use this encounter with *high lati-*

tudes to teach map reading in connection with that concept. That is, class time can be taken to teach the meaning of *high, low,* and *middle latitudes* on maps and globes, and the teaching would occur in what we refer to as a functional setting. Teachers are encouraged to teach as many map and globe skills as possible in this way rather than to isolate the skills from their relevant subject matter. After direct teaching there must be a generous application and use of the skills if proficiency is to be developed and maintained.

Because these skills are *developmental,* one cannot expect to teach them once and assume that they have been learned. Most skills are introduced early in the grades and then are retaught, reviewed, or expanded later on. We expect that children will show increased proficiency and maturity in their use of these skills each year that they are in school. Such development comes through continued teaching and use, not automatically through the natural process of maturation.

What follows is a list of map and globe activities that will provide the teacher with a few examples of the kinds of activities that can be used to stimulate interest and at the same time teach important concepts and thinking skills related to map and globe reading.

1. After an on-the-spot observation of the school grounds or the immediate vicinity, construct a three-dimensional floor map of the area.
2. Locate the place where stories about children in other lands take place or where news events are occurring.
3. Find pictures in magazines that illustrate various landforms: plains, plateaus, hills, and mountains.
4. Make maps of the same area, such as the local county, using different scales for each map.
5. Trace great circle air routes on maps and on globes, and compare the two.
6. Compare the shapes of known areas on different map projections.
7. Develop a classroom exhibit of maps found in current newspapers and periodicals, and compare them with conventional maps and globes.
8. Develop an illustrated glossary of concepts and terms associated with map reading.
9. Secure an outdated political map of the world (1950–1960 vintage), and have the class compare it with a current political map of the world.
10. Illustrate *mis*conceptions about maps such as "north is at the top of the map" or "the climate is temperate in the Temperate Zone."
11. Make use of computer programs designed to build or reinforce map and globe skills, such as *Maps and Globes* (Society for Visual Education) or *Exploring America* (Eye Gate Media).

Teaching map and globe skills does require some amount of special resources and equipment. Every classroom should have a globe along with wall maps appropriate to the curriculum content of the grade. In fourth grade and above, all classrooms should have a wall map of the world. Outline maps are needed in the middle and upper grades. It helps to have available a three-dimensional relief map of the United States and of the home state. Additional equipment might include charts showing conventional map symbols; slated maps and globe; and special-purpose maps showing vegetation, historical development, and natural resources. When children engage in map making, they will need to have available essential construction materials: boxes, blocks, butcher paper, black tape, tracing paper, colored pencils, pens or crayons, paints and brushes, papier-mâché, plaster, salt and flour, or other modeling material.

Regular social studies unit work and the current events program provide natural settings for teaching map and globe skills. Children can use maps to record their data or observations as they study unit topics. They can think through the significance of the relationships they detect in maps. They can use maps as a means of communicating ideas and findings to their classmates. It has been said that maps are the constant companions of geographers, and the same might be said about children as they engage in the social studies.

Children develop skill in map and globe reading in settings where teachers know which variations of the skills are to be taught at each level and where there is some method of accountability for such teaching. Regrettably, this does not occur as often as it should, and, as a result, the systematic teaching of these important skills becomes vulnerable to neglect. If we depend only on incidental references to maps and globes as a way of having children learn these skills, it will only be a fortunate accident if children become proficient in their use.

As a first step in developing a program of instruction in maps and globes, therefore, the teacher must determine which variations of the essential skills will be taught during the year. Naturally, it is helpful if the school district provides this information in a curriculum document. If such a document is not provided, the teacher should develop his or her own list of skills to be taught, looking for guidance to such sources as the textbook teacher's guide, the skills section of the NCSS document, *Social Studies Curriculum Planning Resources,* cited in chapter 1, curriculum documents from other districts, or college methods books in social studies. The summary that follows is an example of material that could be used for this purpose.

A SUMMARY OF MAP AND GLOBE SKILLS

Elementary- and middle-school children should develop map and globe skills associated with the following concepts and generalizations:

1. Primary grades.

    • A map is a drawing or other representation of all or part of the earth.
    • On maps and globes, symbols are used to stand for real things.

- The earth is a huge sphere.
- A globe is a small model of the earth and is the most accurate representation of the earth.
- Half of the earth is called a hemisphere.
- The earth can be divided into several hemispheres. The most common ones are the Eastern, Western, Northern, and Southern Hemispheres; land hemisphere and water hemisphere; and day hemisphere and night hemisphere.
- Any part of the globe can be shown on a map.
- Large bodies of land are called continents.
- Large bodies of water are called oceans.
- Terms such as *left, right, near, far, above, below, up,* and *down* can be useful in expressing relative location.
- A legend or key on a map tells the meaning of colors and symbols used on the map.
- Directions on a map are determined by the poles; to go north means to go in the direction of the North Pole, to go south means to go in the direction of the South Pole.
- North may be shown any place on a map; north is *not* always at the top of a map.
- The North Pole is the point farthest north on the earth; the South Pole is the point farthest south.
- The scale on a map or globe makes it possible to determine distances between places.
- Maps are drawn to different scales; scale ensures that all objects are made smaller in the same amount.
- Maps and globes use legends, or keys, that tell the meaning of the symbols used on the map.
- The cardinal directions are north, south, east, and west; intermediate directions are northeast, northwest, southeast, and southwest.
- All places on the earth can be located on maps and globes. Different maps provide different information about the earth.

2. Intermediate and upper grades.

- The larger the scale used, the larger each feature appears on the map.
- The same symbol may mean different things from one map to another; the legend tells what the symbols stand for.
- The elevation of land is measured from sea level; some maps provide information about elevation.
- Physical maps can be used to determine land elevations, slopes of land, and directions of rivers.
- Parallels of latitude can be used to establish east–west direction and are also used to measure distances in degrees north and south of the equator.
- All places on the same east–west line (parallel of latitude) are directly east or west of one another and are the same distance north or south of the equator.

- All places north of the equator are in north latitudes; all places south of the equator are in south latitudes.
- The Tropic of Cancer and the Tropic of Capricorn are imaginary lines of latitude lying north and south of the equator. The part of the earth between them is known as the tropics.
- The Arctic and Antarctic Circles are imaginary lines that define the polar regions.
- The low latitudes lie on either side of the equator; the high latitudes surround the poles; and the middle latitudes lie between the low and high latitudes.
- Parallels of latitude, parallel to the equator, get shorter as they progress from the equator to the poles.
- Knowing the latitude of a place makes it possible to locate its north–south position on the earth.
- Meridians of longitude can be used to determine north–south direction and are also used to measure distances in degrees east and west of the prime meridian.
- The zero or *prime* meridian passes through Greenwich, a suburb of London.
- Meridians of longitude are imaginary north–south lines that converge on both poles.
- Meridians of longitude are *great circles* because they divide the earth into two hemispheres.
- The shortest distance between any two places on the earth follows a great circle.
- West longitude is measured to the west of the prime meridian from zero to 180°; east longitude is measured to the east of the prime meridian from zero to 180°.
- All places on the same north–south line (meridian of longitude) are directly north or south of each other and are the same distance in degrees east or west of the prime meridian.
- The latitude and longitude of any place determine its exact location on a globe or map.
- Longitude is used in determining the time of day at places around the world. The earth rotates through 15° of longitude every hour; the earth is divided into twenty-four time zones.
- Globes give such information as distance, direction, relative and exact location, and sizes and shapes of areas more accurately than flat maps can.
- Maps and globes often use abbreviations to identify places and things.
- An imaginary line through the center of the earth, running from pole to pole, is called the earth's axis; the earth rotates on its axis from west to east.
- Night and day are the result of the rotation of the earth.
- Maps and globes provide data about the nature of areas by using color contour, visual relief, and contour lines.

- All flat maps contain some distortion because they represent a round object on a flat surface.
- Different map projections provide different perspectives on the sizes and shapes of areas shown.

DEVELOPING A SENSE OF TIME AND CHRONOLOGY

There is much in the modern, urban, industrialized world to remind one of the importance of time. Airlines, trains, and buses operate on time schedules, as do places of business, factories, churches, public institutions, sports events, and television programs, to name just a few. Benjamin Franklin said, "Remember that time is money," this being one of several such proverbs that equate time with economic gain. When we speak of persons making "wise use" of their time, we usually mean that they are busy at something perceived to be "productive." Because time is such an important commodity in the lives of most of us, we have little tolerance for those we perceive to be time wasters and loafers.

In spite of the substantial amount of research that has been conducted on the ability of human beings to deal with time concepts and chronology, much about this phenomenon remains shrouded in mystery. There can be no question that one's perception of time grows out of cultural conditioning. There are few cultures in which people are as compulsive about punctuality as are Americans. To some extent, one's time orientation relates to one's social-class membership, but research suggests that human beings vary greatly in their ability to understand time concepts. Circumstances also condition one's perception of time so that in some cases we say that "time flies" whereas in other settings time seems to drag on endlessly.

Children, of course, learn much about time relationships through ordinary living outside of school. Undoubtedly most children would learn how to tell time, would learn the days of the week and months of the year, and would become familiar with terms ordinarily used in referring to units of time, such as noon, midnight, afternoon, and morning, even if these were not taught in school. The school program can ensure that these skills are correctly and are adequately learned, however, and can provide children the opportunity to practice using them. A few lessons with a simulated clock, supported by practical application in noting when things happen in the schedule of activities during the day, will be adequate to teach most children how to deal with clock time. It is rare to find a mentally competent grown person who cannot tell the time of day. In any case, the increased use of digital clocks should eliminate entirely any problems in reading clock time.

The main thrust of the school program should be, therefore, on those aspects of time and chronology that are not likely to be learned outside of school. This includes (1) the more technical language of time and chronology, such as century, decade, fortnight, fiscal year, calendar year, generation, score, millennium, A.M., P.M., B.C., and A.D.; (2) placing events in chronological order; (3) developing an understanding of the time spans that separate historical events. References to *indefinite* units of time—such as many years ago, soon thereafter, several years had passed, and in a few years—need special attention because they are apt to mean almost any amount of time to young children. Definite references to time can more easily be made meaningful by associating them with units of time that are known to the children: their own ages, the length of time they have been in school, when their parents or grandparents were children of their ages, and so on. The teaching of these relationships can and should take place within the context of social studies units, especially those that focus on history, and in connection with current news stories.

Time lines are often used to show how related events are arranged in chronological order and to show the relative amount of time that separates them. Though widely used, experts are not in agreement as to the value of time lines in clarifying time and chronology for young children. Research on this problem seems to indicate that below the sixth grade the use of time lines is questionable. Nonetheless, teachers report success in helping children arrange events in proper sequence by using time lines. Using only a limited number of events that are clearly and saliently a part of the subject matter studied seems to enhance understanding.

Children can develop the concept of representing time on a continuum by first charting events that they experience firsthand. This helps them arrange the events in the correct sequence. They can make time lines that show things that happened to them yesterday, today, or are being planned for tomorrow. The amount of time included on the line can gradually be expanded to cover several months and then years. Time lines are more interesting to children if events are shown pictorially rather than simply as dots and dates. With middle- and upper-grade children, frequent use can be made of time lines in connection with historical studies of their home state and their nation. Such time lines need not stop with the present date but may be projected into the future, thus illustrating that time is continuous and that the present stands between the past and the future.

The understanding of time in the historical sense represents a fairly mature level of dealing with time and, therefore, should not be expected of young children. The development of time concepts should begin with time situations that are within their realm of experience. Children should be given help in learning to read clock time and in understanding references to the parts of the day, days of the week, months, seasons, and the year. Even though primary-grade children make statements about things that happened "a hundred years ago," they have little comprehension of the real meaning of the expression and simply use it as a vague reference to something that happened in what seems to them a long time ago.

In the teaching of history, references to the past are often made through the use of indefinite expressions such as "a long time ago," "many years ago," and "several years later." These expressions are not well understood even by adults, and for young children they are often devoid of any specific meaning. To a child, "a long time ago" could very well be no more than a decade ago. Teachers need to build meaning into these abstract quantitative time concepts by discussing their meaning within the context of events of the period studied and by relating the time interval to things that are familiar to the children, such as the length of the school year, when their parents or grandparents were children, or the amount of time that has passed since they were born, and so on. (See also pages 302–303 in chapter 10.)

TEACHING CHILDREN THE USE OF GRAPHS AND CHARTS

Because of the widespread use of graphs and charts in social studies and in printed material outside of school, it is imperative that children develop the skills needed to read and interpret them. Just leafing through a daily newspaper or weekly news magazine reminds one of how commonly these graphics are used and how powerfully their messages are conveyed. Citizens today are "digest" oriented. They do not have the time or the inclination to wade through a mountain of narrative that explains social events or conditions. They want to see these ideas in summary form and in stark relief. Besides, the complexity of social data, much of which is in statistical form, lends itself well to a graphic format.

Graphs

Graphs are used to illustrate relationships among quantities. These relationships may be spread over a period of time, thus showing trends. The most commonly used graphs are some variation of the *bar graph,* the *pie* or *circle graph,* and the *line graph.* Any of these graphs may include pictorial representations, thereby making them more interesting to young children and making the content less abstract. For instance, with primary-grade children, stick figures can be used to represent children in a bar graph showing the number absent from class each day. It is easy to visualize the relationships of the parts to the whole in a circle graph, but to construct one accurately requires the ability to compute percentages, usually not possible in the elementary school grades. Modern elementary school textbooks make liberal use of graphs in presenting data, but children need to be instructed in how to read and interpret them. Because graphs can be designed to present distorted pictures of data, children in the middle and upper grades should be taught how bias is introduced in a graph. (See Figures 6-9, 6-10, and 6-11.)

Children can learn much about graphs and how to read them by constructing their own graphs. Such learner-made graphs can be used in making oral or written reports and for bulletin board displays. In the making of graphs, accuracy in the presentation should be emphasized rather than artistic perfection (see Figure 6-8).

FIGURE 6-8

Examples of graphs and data suitable for use with elementary schoolchildren.

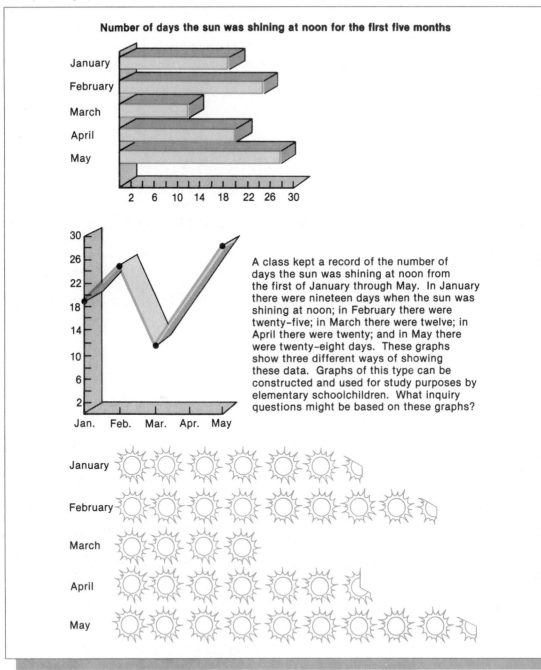

Number of days the sun was shining at noon for the first five months

A class kept a record of the number of days the sun was shining at noon from the first of January through May. In January there were nineteen days when the sun was shining at noon; in February there were twenty-five; in March there were twelve; in April there were twenty; and in May there were twenty-eight days. These graphs show three different ways of showing these data. Graphs of this type can be constructed and used for study purposes by elementary schoolchildren. What inquiry questions might be based on these graphs?

FIGURE 6-9

The drawing illustrates how the popular "pie" graph is sometimes used to create an incorrect impression. Because the sketch is shown in perspective, the sizes of the sections are distorted. Thus, sections that seem to be farthest from the viewer appear smaller than those in the foreground, although arithmetically they represent equal amounts.

FIGURE 6-10

It is important for children to learn that graphs can create false impressions. In these line graphs, the same data were used on three different grids, resulting in varying steepness in the slopes of the lines. Consequently, although the facts are the same, the rate of change appears markedly different.

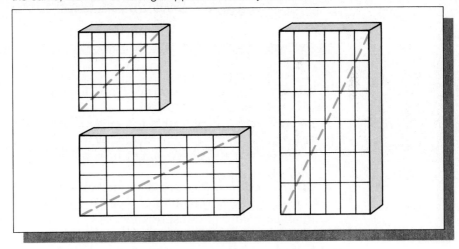

Formal Charts

Like graphs, charts are widely used to present ideas in a vivid and forceful way. Formal charts are often designated as follows:

1. *Narrative chart:* Tells a story; shows events in sequence. (Example: how plywood is made, stages of the development of civilization, how to use a computer, or the construction of homes.)

FIGURE 6-11
How much larger were profits in 1990 than in 1992? The chances are that you
have said "about twice as large." This graph illustrates how wrong impressions
are conveyed when pictorial graphs are improperly constructed. Careful examination of this graph will show that the 1992 profits are not even twice those of 1989.
The basic error in this graph is that it does not show the first $500,000 of profit. A
more accurate perception of the growth in profits can be made if the correct position of the baseline is established. Can you locate the place where the baseline
should be?

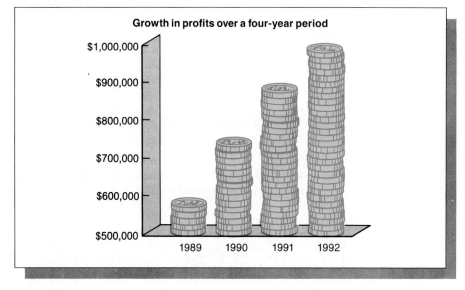

2. *Tabulation chart:* Lists data in table form to facilitate making comparisons.
   (Example: data placed in tabular form to show infant mortality rates,
   illiteracy rates, or per capita income among nations of the world.)
3. *Pedigree chart:* Shows events stemming from a common origin. (Example:
   a family tree, the development of a political party, or the history of
   language.)
4. *Classification chart:* Groups data into various categories. (Example: the
   various types of restaurants, types of personal services available, or
   different modes of transportation.)
5. *Organization chart:* Shows the structure of an organization. (Example: the
   three branches of government, the structure of a corporation, or the
   organization of a city government or a school district.)
6. *Flow chart:* Shows a process involving change at certain points. (Example: how raw materials are transformed into finished products, the
   break of bulk in shipping as at a harbor facility, or how scrap iron is
   converted into a usable raw material.)

The frequent use of formal charts in children's books provides a good basis
for inquiry learning. In the process children not only learn how to read and

interpret the chart, but also broaden their substantive knowledge and build their understanding of associated concepts.

Informal Charts

Informal charts are charts that are developed and constructed by the teacher or by the children. They are commonly placed on wrapping paper, oak tagboard, newsprint, "butcher" paper, chart paper, or the chalkboard. They may contain diagrams, sketches, pictures, or other illustrative material or simply may be written accounts of experiences or activities related to the unit under study.

When charts are constructed for use with primary-grade children, it is essential that the mechanics and makeup of the charts conform exactly to the patterns that are taught in the basic language arts program. For example, the style of lettering used should be exactly the same as that used by the children in manuscript writing, capital letters and punctuation marks should be used only where they are used in ordinary writing, and the reading vocabulary should follow as closely as possible the vocabulary being developed in the basic reading program. Careful attention should be given to the format to facilitate ease of reading: uniform margins; well-spaced letters, words, and lines; natural phrases of appropriate length; and sharp, clear lettering. Phrases should not be broken at the end of a line such as:

**Cross the street at
the crosswalk.**

But rather:

**Cross the street
at the crosswalk.**

Middle- and upper-grade children can be encouraged to make and use charts in connection with their reports, committee work, and displays. As was true with graphs, the children need be less concerned with the artistic perfection of the chart than with the manner in which it conveys ideas. Simplicity, vividness, concreteness, and accuracy of the idea presented are more important considerations than artistic finish.

Data-Retrieval Charts

The *data-retrieval chart* consists of a set of questions related to the topic under study and an indication of the groups or situations from which data are to be secured. It provides a convenient way for children to record information they gather in the process of study. It also has the advantage of displaying the data in a form that can be used or "retrieved" for study and analysis at a later time. The data-retrieval chart is useful in making comparisons and contrasts because comparable data can be secured from two or more samples. (See Figure 6-12 and pages 38–40.)

FIGURE 6-12
DATA-RETRIEVAL CHART

Our Next-Door Neighbors		
Analytical Concepts	**Canada**	**Mexico**
Geographical features		
Size		
Climate		
Physical features		
Natural resources		
History		
Native people		
Foreign influences		
Relations with U.S.		
Type of government today		
Economic development		
Main occupations		
Average per capita income		
Exports		
Population		
Ethnic groups		
Density		
Major cities		
Levels of education		
Religious groups		
Languages		

It is in the processing and presenting of data that the computer can be put to good use. Computers are excellent tools for making electronic spreadsheets of graphs, data-retrieval charts, data displays, or other visuals. Commercial programs are available that help students transform raw data to visual forms on the microcomputer. Today a child with a microcomputer can produce graphics that just a few years ago would have required the talents of a skilled artist to create.

TEACHING CHILDREN THE USE OF CARTOONS

Cartoons are an accepted form of social commentary. Through a dramatic visual format, the reader projects meaning into the visual by virtue of his or her own experience. Cartoons are often humorous because they exaggerate, subjects are presented in caricature, and the cartoons are designed to show all the vices or virtues associated with a particular character in our

FIGURE 6-13
This cartoon is a good illustration of how much the reader must bring to such visuals if they are to have meaning. Ordinarily, we do not get new information from editorial cartoons. The artist relies on what we already know and provides a visual that places that information in a setting that conveys a powerful social, economic, and/or political message. (Reprinted with special permission of NAS, Inc.)

culture. Cartoons are especially effective in calling attention to the ironies that surround our lives. They use an amusing way to make a serious point.

Editorial cartoons are not necessarily humorous. Indeed, they are often biting in their comment on social issues. The techniques of symbolism, the use of familiar situations, exaggerations, satire, and caricature are used to present forcefully a single point of view. Political cartoons usually deal more with irony, hypocrisy, and cynicism than they do with humor. The cartoon does not allow the reader or the person portrayed in it an opportunity for rebuttal. Recognition of the fact that only one point of view is represented in cartoons is important in their interpretation. Older children need to be taught the general makeup of cartoons that deal with social and political problems and need the experience of evaluating their message critically. It is well for the children to present an opposite point of view from the one depicted in the cartoon.

The symbolism used in cartoons causes much confusion in the minds of some children. When the characters are portrayed as animals, the children tend to associate those animals with various national groups. Cartoons use stereotypes of people that add little to the type of international understanding we are attempting to foster and encourage in the social studies program. A figurative term such as *sitting on the fence* may be shown as a caricature of a political figure literally sitting on a fence, thus leaving the child with a misleading impression. Cartoons usually demand a high level of understanding of the issues involved if they are to tell their story accurately; thus, the child needs to be instructed and helped in developing the skill of interpreting cartoons. (See Figure 6-13.)

DISCUSSION QUESTIONS AND SUGGESTED ACTIVITIES

1. Select a topic for a grade of your choice, and plan specific map- and globe-reading activities that could be incorporated in a study of it.

2. Prepare a series of posters showing map symbols, and accompany each symbol with a photograph of the object being represented.

3. Make a list of words or phrases related to the understanding of maps and globes that are misleading (for example, *up, down*). For each entry, suggest an alternate word or phrase that would be more accurate.

4. What misunderstandings might develop when characters in charts and cartoons appear in caricature? What might be done to prevent such misunderstandings from occurring?

5. Develop an inquiry-oriented learning experience based on a map, chart, or cartoon. Arrange to teach it to your peers.

6. How might a data-retrieval chart constructed by the children be useful to them in unit study? Suggest a specific topic and variables that could be used in constructing such a chart.

7. Select a map-reading skill, and show by examples of learning activities how it is sequenced through the elementary grades on a simple to complex continuum.

8. Select a social studies textbook, and examine it in terms of its treatment of the skills discussed in this chapter.

9. If you are teaching or if you have access to a class, try these three activities:
   a. Have children find indefinite references to time and space in their social studies texts or in a newspaper (expressions such as "many years ago," "shortly after," "several acres," "a large area"). Discuss the meaning of these terms with the children. How accurate are their understanding of these terms? Report your findings to your classmates.

b. Have the class discuss situations in which they think "time flies" and others in which they think time "moves at a snail's pace." Encourage them to identify reasons for this difference. Are the situations the same for all children?

c. Have the class think of as many popular expressions or proverbs as they can that have to do with time. Conduct this activity for a period of days, and as expressions or proverbs are suggested, place them on the bulletin board. Have children make drawings to illustrate them. Discuss this in terms of the importance of time in our lives.

SELECTED REFERENCES

ATKINS, CAMMIE L. "Introducing Basic Map and Globe Skills to Young Children." *Journal of Geography* 83 (March 1984): 228–33.

BENNETT, CLIFFORD T., DONNA BLISS, MARCIA S. DEFREN, WILLIAM RAY HEITZMANN, BRENDA HOLUB, AND JOHN E. STEINBRINK. These authors contribute six articles to a special section on using political cartoons in the classroom. *The Social Studies* 79 (September/October 1988): 205–27.

CAREY, HELEN H. *How to Use Maps and Globes.* New York: Franklin Watts, 1983. (A children's book.)

FRAZEE, BRUCE M. "Foundations for An Elementary Map Skills Program." *The Social Studies* 75 (March/April 1984): 79–82.

HATCHER, BARBARA. "Putting Young Cartographers 'On the Map.'" *Childhood Education* 59 (May/June 1983): 311–15.

MILLER, JACK W. "Teaching Map Skills: Theory, Research, Practice." *Social Education* 49 (January 1985): 30–33.

MONAHAN, DAVID P. "How to Stimulate Student Writing with Political Cartoons." *Social Education* 47 (January 1983): 62–64.

MUESSIG, RAYMOND H., ED., AND JACK W. MILLER, LINDA S. LEVSTIK, AND VAL ARNSDORF. "Building Map Skills to Advance Geographic Understanding." *Social Education* 49 (January 1985): 28–46.

MUIR, SHARON PRAY. "Understanding and Improving Students' Map Reading Skills." *The Elementary School Journal* 86 (November 1985): 207–16.

RICE, GWENDA H. "Teaching Students to Become Discriminating Map Users." *Social Education* 54 (October 1990): 393–97.

RUSHDOONY, HAIG A. *The Language of Maps.* Belmont, CA: Pitman, 1983. (A book of map skill exercises for grades 4–8.)

SALTER, CHRISTOPHER L. AND CATHY RIGGS-SALTER. "Five Themes in Geography and the Primary-Grade Learner." *Social Studies and the Young Learner* 1 (November/December 1988): 10–13.

VAN CLEAF, DAVID W. "The Environment as a Data Source: Map Activities for Young Children." *Social Education* 49 (February 1985): 145–46.

WINSTON, BARBARA J. *Map and Globe Skills: K–8 Teaching Guide.* Western Illinois University: National Council for Geographic Education, 1984.

7 | Contributions of the Social Sciences

The four social sciences—economics, political science, sociology, and anthropology—make essential contributions to the social studies curriculum of the elementary and middle schools. It would be a mistake, however, to place their importance on a par with history and geography as contributors of subject matter. For the most part, these disciplines do not have a secure anchor in the curriculum as do history and geography. Therefore, they must find their way into the program by infusion or by the integration of their important concepts and skills into the mainstream social studies units and topics.

We deal with four of the social sciences in this chapter—economics, political science, sociology, and anthropology. Some programs add psychology, philosophy, and religion to this list. These latter three are not included here because psychology makes its contribution through the *process* of teaching and learning rather than by providing substantive content. Concepts and subject matter from philosophy and religion are such that they can be conveniently subsumed under history or anthropology for purposes of the elementary and middle school curriculum.

ECONOMICS AND THE SOCIAL STUDIES

Of the newer social sciences that are gaining a place in the social studies program, none has received more attention or been promoted with more enthusiasm than has economics. In one form or another, economic education has been a part of the American school curriculum for many years. The Joint Council on Economic Education, representing business, labor, education, agriculture, and other groups, was organized in 1948. Along with its affiliated local and state councils, it has actively promoted economic education in the schools. The Foundation for Teaching Economics, a

California-based organization, has also worked for the improved teaching of economics in the schools.

Economics is the study of the production, distribution, exchange, and consumption of goods and services that people need or want. In a modern industrialized society such as ours, wants and needs are great because individuals have an expectation of a high standard of living. Moreover, the processes involved in the production, distribution, exchange, and consumption form an interrelated web of relationships. So directly are individuals enmeshed in it that almost everything they do is, in one way or another, related to our economic system. Economic education concerns itself with helping children achieve an understanding of some of the basic relationships between our economic system and our way of life, thereby enabling them to make informed decisions on economic matters. Another major purpose of economic education is to teach students a way of thinking about economics and economic issues based on orderliness and reasoning.

These samples represent major generalizations from economics that have been used as organizing ideas in developing programs in economic education:

1. The wants of people are unlimited whereas resources needed to fulfill wants are scarce; hence, societies and individuals have to make choices as to which needs are to be met and which are to be sacrificed.
2. The interdependence of peoples of the world makes exchange and trade a necessity in the modern world.
3. Economic systems are usually mixed with both public and private ownership and with decisions made both by the government and by individual members of society.
4. Increased specialization in production has led to interdependence among individuals, communities, states, and nations.
5. In the complex, modern industrialized society of today, government plays an important role in the economic life of society.

Teaching Suggestions

The elementary and middle school program of instruction should be built around basic economic concepts (such as scarcity, production, distribution, exchange, and consumption) that are related to one or more generalizations of the type listed earlier. Each of these economic concepts can be developed in many of the topics included in the social studies curriculum. There may be times, however, when particular topics are selected because they have special usefulness in developing specific economic concepts. Units on The Market in the primary grades are of this type and ordinarily focus on the distribution of needed goods.

Learning resources and teaching materials for economic education in elementary and middle schools are available in increasing quantities. The best sources of such instructional materials are the Joint Council on Economic Education, 2 West 46 Street, New York City 10036, the Foundation

Basic economic knowledge and skills are being taught to these middle school students through *demonstration* and *application*. In addition to the technical aspects of check writing, what else should students learn about checking as a system of money exchange?
(Photos by Carla Anderson, Northshore School District.)

for Teaching Economics, 260 Russell Blvd., Suite B, Davis, CA 95616, and the home state council for economic education. From these sources the teacher can secure sample units, scope and sequence charts, background information, and other teaching materials, as well as information concerning other sources of aids for teaching economic concepts.

Learning activities such as the following can be used in developing economic concepts:

1. *Examine ways that people depend on each other* in their families, neighborhoods, and communities. Relate this to the need for many different kinds of jobs.
2. *Compare work roles* of today with those in colonial times to discover differences between cottage-industry procedures with assembly-line production.
3. *Study different types of advertising* to learn how producers create consumer needs and wants.
4. *Compare wages* paid to workers in terms of such things as the *(a)* level of education required for the job; *(b)* extent to which the job requires highly developed skills; *(c)* length of the preparation or training program for the job; *(d)* amount of risk to the worker.
5. *Role play negotiations* between buyers and sellers; employers and employees in a salary dispute; a consumer with a complaint about a product and a retailer; a customer who has been overcharged and the person who did the repair work.
6. *Use newspapers* to compare prices of items among various retailers. Relate this to factors that affect pricing policies.
7. *Study the concept of seasonal employment* as it relates to employment patterns in different parts of the country.
8. *Study government regulation* of business operations in terms of consumer protection, quality control, and ethical business practices.
9. *Familiarize children with local businesses* through the use of field trips and resource persons.
10. *Study personal and family budgeting procedures* to illustrate the relationship between income and expenditures, the difference between wants and needs, and the necessity of choice making.
11. *Participate in simulation games* designed to teach economic concepts (see chapter 14 for an example).
12. *Use computer programs,* such as *The Market Place* series (by MECC), *Economics* (by SVE), or *Stock Markets* (by Learning Arts), to build economic concepts and relationships.
13. *In grades seven and eight, involve your class in ECONOMICS TODAY,* an eight-lesson program that provides students with an introduction to the economy using news stories found in *USA Today.* Developed by the Foundation for Teaching Economics and *USA Today.* For information write to: Foundation for Teaching Economics, 260 Russell Blvd., Suite B, Davis, CA 95616.

The World of Work

The world of work is a subset of economic education, and elementary and middle schools have for many years included it in their social studies programs. Units on family life, neighborhood relationships, workers in the community, transportation and communication, food, clothing and shelter, and ways of living in societies past and present are familiar subjects in elementary school social studies. Even though many changes have been made in the social studies program in recent years, these topics are still in the curriculum of most schools. These units and others like them stress work roles, jobs, the importance of work to the community and to the individual, interdependence, and simplified producer and consumer economics. In this context the social studies program is a natural vehicle to teach important ideas and attitudes relating to the world of work.

In the early 1970s, influential persons in this country argued persuasively that preparation for work, including the attitudes and skills needed to perform work, should be the primary emphasis of the school curriculum.[1] No less a figure than the U.S. commissioner of education challenged school leadership of America to attend to what he called "career education" of its children and youth.[2] By this he meant that the school experience should equip all children and youth with salable skills that would be useful to them in relating to the world of work. The term *career education* was and is used to describe the schools' effort to help children and youth relate to the world of work. Federal funds were made available to schools and colleges to encourage and promote career education. Presently, career education as an educational movement lacks the high priority it had a decade earlier, but concern for preparing individuals for the world of work remains an important component of the economic education of students.

In teaching about the work world, as is the case with energy and environmental education, safety, law-related education, and other such topics, a systematic, integrated approach is probably more effective than special units spaced throughout the grades. This, of course, does not preclude the possibility of having special units with a world of work focus, but simply suggests that such an approach is not in itself adequate. Teaching is strengthened when concepts from the work world are built into many of the existing units of the social studies program. Most who have been involved in curriculum work in this field suggest that *awareness building* should be a major goal of a program relating to the world of work in the elementary school. The major components of such a program are these:

---

[1]Larry J. Bailey and Ronald W. Stadt, *Career Education: New Approaches to Human Development* (Bloomington, IL: McKnight, 1973).

[2]Sidney P. Marland, Jr., "Educating for the Real World," *Business Education Forum* 26 (November 1971): 3–5.

Information About the World of Work. Persons are often uninformed about choices available to them when they decide on a vocation. They simply select from those few occupations they have learned about firsthand from a close relative or from a friend. This explains why some occupations seem to "run in families." Children should *not* be encouraged to make occupational choices when they are in the elementary school. But they can begin to build a background of knowledge about a broad spectrum of occupations that will one day help them make an intelligent career choice.

Opportunity to Explore Work Values. Children need to see the connection between values that are stressed in school, such as responsibility, dependability, punctuality, cooperation, trustworthiness, and others, and the world of work. They need to develop a sense of appreciation for a job that is well done. They need to learn what it means to take pride in one's work.

Personal Choice Making. Part of the awareness building of the world of work should include the opportunity to make decisions and to exercise choices. Decisions surrounding career choices will one day be an extension of decision-making skills the child has exercised throughout life.

Society and the World of Work. Children need to learn about the relationship of the individual to society *through* the world of work. What one does for a living does not simply have to be a job that has no purpose other than as a way of earning enough money to pay bills and stay alive. Work contributes to the life and health of the larger society. Society's need to have jobs performed and performed well can be learned by the youngest children. All of us depend on others to help us meet our basic needs. Social studies units that deal with so-called community helpers provide opportunities for learning outcomes of this type. Work is so important to society that individuals are often identified by others in accordance with what they do for a living: "He is a data analysis specialist," "He is a commercial airlines pilot," "She is a doctor in town," "She is the city manager at Augusta," and so on.

Many of the outcomes sought in career education are affective, dealing with attitudes, appreciations, and feelings. This means that children will need a broad exposure to the world of work and opportunities to respond to it in a variety of ways. Such experiences have feeling as well as knowledge dimensions. For example, children may want to express their own feelings about certain occupations, and the strength of those feelings should be explored. Children should be encouraged to find out the attitudes of their parents toward the jobs they hold. Why do they like them or dislike them?

Some attention should also be given to related economic concepts such as producer, consumer, goods, services, division of labor, and interdependence. Children must understand the importance of work both to the individual and to society. Instruction should stress society's need for a wide range of talents and abilities in order that the many jobs that need doing will get done. Society has a need for a constant flow of competent persons to operate the complex systems that go into making up our way of life. The study of basic economic concepts can help the child develop a sense of appreciation of our absolute dependence on others for the things we need in ordinary everyday living.

Education about the work world clearly must be sensitive to sex-role and ethnic stereotyping. Traditionally, women have been stereotyped along the lines of domestic roles, and a certain limited number of occupational roles—elementary school teaching, nursing, secretarial services, food services, and so on. School programs have often reinforced these stereotypes, with the result that women have a much more restricted set of occupational choices than do men. Boys and girls need to learn that the traditional ideas about what is "woman's work" and what is "man's work" no longer apply and that people now have greater opportunities to do the things *they* want to do to lead self-fulfilling, productive lives. Much the same can be said in connection with ethnic stereotyping. Although a great deal has been done in recent years to eliminate such stereotyping in learning resources, the teacher still must be careful not to associate certain occupations with specific national, ethnic, or racial groups.

Activities for Studying the World of Work.   *Conduct interviews* to find out how adults in the community earn money. Have the children compile a list of categories for their questionnaire such as these:

People Who Produce Things

People Who Fix Things

People Who Create

People Who Work with Ideas

Analyze these data in terms of different subpopulations in the questionnaire compilation, such as women, minorities, and so forth.

Brainstorm a list of reasons why people might have selected particular occupations. This list should include such things as "It provides me with a chance to be my own boss" or "I earn a good salary." Have this list refined and duplicated, and then use it in a survey with working adults in your community. Have the adults choose three reasons from the list, and ask them to rank them in order of most important to least important.

Administer an interest inventory on possible career opportunities. Then invite adults from the community to come to talk to your class in the areas in which the most interest was expressed.

Identify four or five careers that interest them (upper grades). Have them arrange to visit at least one of the work settings so they can see what the career is actually like. Create a checklist with such topics as Working

Conditions and Job Requirements to use as a guideline for the children's investigations.

Brainstorm a list of occupations—say twenty-five to fifty. In groups have the children organize the data into four categories, using any system they wish to devise. Have each group explain its system. Discuss the standard career area classifications.

To sensitize children to sex-role stereotyping, *have them generate lists of occupations* that are associated with males, those associated with females, and those that are neutral. Discuss these in terms of equality of job opportunity and whether or not a person's sex has anything to do with performance of the jobs listed in the male and female categories.

Analyze television commercials and newspaper and magazine advertisements to detect evidence of sex-role and racial stereotyping in certain occupations.

Use "classified ad" sections of local newspapers to discover the types of jobs that are most available. Relate this to a study of changing needs of the work world over a period of time; for example, what jobs are available now that were not available ten, twenty, fifty, or one hundred years ago?

Study the relationship between the number of producers and consumers and the growing demand for increased social services. Relate this to taxing policies and the increasing need for persons employed by various levels of government; that is, local, state, and federal.

Lesson Plan 7 illustrates how a primary-grade teacher developed the concept *division of labor* with a class.

POLITICAL SCIENCE AND THE SOCIAL STUDIES

For purposes of the elementary and middle school social studies curriculum, political science can be defined as a discipline concerned with the study of government, political processes, and political decision making.[3] Some of this is handled through content in courses that are nominally history. In the upper grades, many schools have had courses called *civics*, comprised of instruction in the role, function, and organization of government with some attention to political processes, political institutions, and political decision making as these apply to citizenship behavior.

Three ideas are basic to the understanding of the organization of human societies. One is that all societies have developed ways of establishing and maintaining social order; the second is that the central order-maintaining instrument has great power over the lives of individuals subjected to it; the

---

[3]Political science concepts and content are closely related to law-related education discussed in the next chapter, and it is reasonable to assume that the two would be combined in the social studies curriculum of the elementary and middle schools.

·················· **Lesson Plan 7**

Topic:	Division of labor
Grade:	Two or three
Time:	Two class periods
Objective:	Children will be able to give an example of division of labor.
Interest Building:	Have children discuss jobs they know about in their family or neighborhood by responding to these questions:

Do *you* have a job at home? What do you do?
What is the difference between your job and the jobs of grownups?
Explain that during the next few days they are going to learn about different kinds of jobs in the community.

Lesson Development: Have the children make a chart with the following headings:

NAME OF JOB	REASONS FOR THE JOB
1. _____	_____
2. _____	_____
3. _____	_____

Instruct the children to take the chart home with them and complete it with the help of their parents, naming three different jobs in the community.

On the following day have the children compare and discuss their lists with each other.

Compile a list of as many different jobs as possible on the chalkboard. Children should pick one from their individual lists until everyone has had a turn to name one. Keep going as long as *different* jobs are named.

Have children discuss the need for a variety of jobs by responding to these questions:

Why is it that we have so many different jobs in our community?

Why couldn't each family do all these jobs itself?

Why do you suppose people in a community divide the work the way they do?

Do you mean that people who have these jobs have special skills? What do you mean?

Do you think people can do their jobs better when each person has a special job? Why do you think so?

Tell the children that when people divide work so that each one does something special, we call that *division of labor*. Write this term on the chalkboard. Discuss this term by having the class respond to these questions:

Does anyone know another word for *labor*? (Children suggest *work* as a synonym for labor. This is discussed and examples are provided.)

Can anyone tell us in his or her own words what division of labor means? (Children respond that "division of labor means dividing the work.") This is discussed and examples are provided.

(continued)

Conclusion:	Have children tell in their own words how they see the division of labor in these places
	in their school at the shopping center in their families in a hospital in the supermarket at the airport at the post office anywhere else they may have visited
Materials:	No special materials are needed.

third is that all such systems demand and expect a loyalty to them when they are threatened by hostile opposing forces. It is apparent that if individuals are to function in a society, they must conduct themselves in politically appropriate ways. Not to do so might result in disastrous consequences. Therefore, societies provide ways of inducting the young into the political life of the society. Through this process, children internalize a set of values, beliefs, and attitudes that are consistent with the political system of the society. They learn how the system functions and eventually they contribute to its perpetuation. This process of learning has come to be called *political socialization.*

All this is relevant to the elementary and middle school teacher of social studies. Recent research suggests that the values and attitudes undergirding political socialization are formed fairly early in life. Children are able to add to their fund of information and knowledge, to be sure, but basic political orientation is well established during the early years. When children are in the elementary, middle, and junior high schools, they are still relatively flexible in their political outlook, making these years extremely important from the standpoint of their political socialization.

As is the case in all the other disciplines contributing to the social studies curriculum, certain organizing ideas from political science are used to provide a focus for studies. The following represent samples of major generalizations from political science that have been used as organizing ideas in planning units of study:

1. Every known society has some kind of authority structure that can be called its government; such a government is granted coercive power.
2. A stable government facilitates the social and economic development of a nation.
3. All societies have made policies or laws about how groups of people should live together.
4. The decisions, policies, and laws that have been made for a given society reflect and are based on the values, beliefs, and traditions of that society.
5. Throughout history human societies have experimented with many different systems of government.

Civitas

A major new set of teaching guidelines related mainly to the discipline of political science was published in 1991. Called *Civitas*, it recommends extensive instruction, even in the lower elementary grades, on two of the most basic themes of political science: *Civic Participation* and *The Nature of the State*.[4] *Civitas* is a cooperative, bipartisan coalition of political scientists, educators, national associations, and civic leaders who share love for democracy and alarm at the increasing apathy of average citizens in the United States.

Civitas's sponsors and authors believe that nonparticipation is a central threat to a society that is endeavoring to be democratic. They are referring not only to the well-known failure to vote, but what over the long term may be even more serious: the failure of large numbers of citizens to make the time to engage in informed discussion of social problems and to monitor elected officials.

An excessive retreat from public life to private life—to family, relationships, entertainment, job, and consumption—may be understandable in a totalitarian society where people try their best to avoid government, but it can be fatal to social stability in a political system that is supposed to be run by the people themselves. In a society such as ours that has a broad range of social problems, *Civitas* contends, citizen complacency becomes all the more inappropriate. History has been clear about the consequences:

> It is a general truth that societies that neither understand nor practice their own principles are liable to find their institutions in decay or overthrown. This could be said of the ancient Roman Republic, of royal absolutism, including the *ancien regime* in France, and of communist states in the late twentieth century. The decline of institutions that follows the widespread disbelief or cynicism regarding the principles that underlie them is the political expression of the biblical proverb, "where there is no vision, the people perish."[5]

Political science, we see, is not an abstract discipline filled with theories that are irrelevant to school children. Quite the opposite, it is the study of how we live and how we want to live. It is the study of what we each have to give up in order to live together well. Clearly, it deals with *the* essential questions of social life and social responsibility. Figure 7–1 reproduces a portion of *Civitas* objectives for the primary grades.[6]

Teaching Suggestions

The school program needs to begin early in helping children develop a political orientation. They need school experiences that familiarize them with the techniques of democratic procedures and that help develop a

---

[4]*Civitas: A Framework for Civic Education* (Calabasas, CA: Center for Civic Education, and Washington, DC: National Council for the Social Studies, 1991).

[5]*Civitas*, 5.

[6]*Civitas*, 45, 161.

FIGURE 7–1
CIVITAS Objectives, K–3

Governing and managing groups. Students should be able to:
1. acquire and use information about the governance of the groups to which they belong
2. explain how the rules and persons in authority of the groups to which they belong affect their lives
3. take part in creating rules and selecting persons to serve in positions of authority in the groups to which they belong

Monitoring public policy. Students should be able to:

1. acquire information regarding public policy
2. identify current issues of public policy that are of interest to them

Influencing public policy. Students should be able to:

1. develop an effective plan for influencing public policy
2. carry out a plan to influence the public policy

Civic knowledge. Students should be able to:

1. explain some of the most important purposes served by government in the United States
2. describe the essential characteristics of American constitutional democracy, i.e.,
   a. the people are the ultimate source of the government's authority
   b. all citizens have the right to vote and influence government in other ways
   c. the government is run by the people either directly or through representatives selected by them
   d. all people have certain basic rights guaranteed to them by the Constitution.

sense of appreciation for the liberties enjoyed by citizens of this nation. Such appreciations and skills must be built in part on a foundation of knowledge. Accompanying the development of these understandings, children should be given practice in using their knowledge and skills in the regular work of the class and the school.

The Primary Grades.   Perhaps the best way to teach concepts drawn from political science at the early levels is to select those that can become a part of the immediate life of the child. For example, primary-grade children can learn that when people live together they must establish and observe rules. When people have rules, they know what they can and what they cannot do. Rules are made so that everyone is treated fairly. Children can understand this because they have rules in their classroom, in their school, and in their homes. They can learn that grownups have rules, too. These are written down and are called laws. When people break the rules, or laws, they are usually punished in some way. If some people keep on breaking the law or do things that are harmful to other people, they are not allowed to live with other people in the community. In this way, children learn not only that laws limit what one can do but also that laws have a protective function. As a result of instruction and firsthand experiences in group life, children's concepts of rules and laws, as needed for orderly living, develop. Naturally, such concepts are given increasingly greater depth as children progress through the grades. For example, later in the grades, they will learn that rules and laws are not exactly alike; laws are more binding than are rules.

The program for building civic competence begins with the introduction of the most elementary concepts relating to people living and working together under a system of order that preserves individual freedom. Great stress is placed on applying learnings as they are presented. Theoretical and complex explanations of the structure of government are inappropriate at this level. The main goals are to get children to handle themselves in responsible ways, to see the need for order in living, to govern their actions with consideration for the rights of others, and to realize that the whole realm of human activity is based on a system of rules and laws. Although children at this level are too immature to comprehend the meaning of freedom as an abstract concept, they can, nevertheless, understand it in terms of activities in which they can choose their own leaders or help to establish their classroom rules.

As children advance to the middle grades, more can be done in direct teaching of the ways our system of government functions. At this level, they also have greater opportunity to participate in school activities that promote civic learnings. For example, they can take a more active part in the school council if there is one, they can serve as members of the safety patrol or as playground monitors, and they can assume greater responsibilities for duties within their own classroom.

The Middle Grades.   The exact concepts and learnings to be included in each of the three middle grades will depend on the content of the school curriculum. In the fourth grade, units on the home state are filled with good possibilities for civic learnings. Children can study the early beginnings of their state and learn how its government developed. The teacher will need to be careful not to make the concepts relating to state government too difficult for children of this age. Even the matter of differentiating between a city, a state, and a county, for example, may be quite difficult for some fourth-graders. Should the curriculum call for a study of communities around the world, a part of the study should stress that all of them have some type of government. Children should learn that governments are not all like ours, and the teacher will have to guard against having them make unwarranted value judgments about other governments. The essential points to be learned are that all people have some type of government; and although we would not choose their systems for ourselves, their governments may serve the people of those particular countries very well.

There may be other cases, of course, where the teacher will want to call attention to actions of governments that clearly violate international human rights.

Grade-five units dealing with the development of the United States emphasize ways of living during the periods of exploration, colonization, and the westward movement. However, this does not mean that early beginnings in representative government should be ignored. Youngsters at this level can achieve substantial understanding of some of the foundations of the government of this country. They are particularly interested in and ready to learn of the lives of some of the great champions of American freedom. Children can learn the differences in the way Spain, France, Portugal, and England ruled their colonies in the New World and relate these colonial attitudes to the kinds of governments that developed in the colonies ruled by these countries. They can learn how local representative government developed in the English colonies and can grasp simple concepts relating to the development of our own national government. It is easy to make such studies too technical and difficult for fifth-graders; ideas will have to be dealt with at a level of complexity suitable for ten-year-olds.

The sixth-grade program affords opportunities to learn something of the governments of other nations because, at this level, units often deal with countries in various parts of the world. Some schools include a study of early civilizations on the Mediterranean, and this affords an opportunity to show the origins of the democratic concept of government and law and how this idea found its way into our own system of government. If countries of Western Europe are studied, children can learn of the growth of freedom and that modern-day monarchies are based on democratic principles of government. They can also learn that in many nations of the world, individual citizens have little or nothing to say about the way they are governed. Units on Africa are popular in this grade, which makes it possible to show the problems of the governments of new nations.

A unit on the United Nations may be included in the sixth grade, in which case the need for lawful international relations can be developed. This will provide an opportunity to learn how and why national governments join together for the fulfillment of mutual self-interests. The concept of alliances and their purpose can be studied as it applies to the United States.

The Upper Grades.   The program of the seventh grade depends on the sixth–seventh grade sequence followed in the school. If nations of the Western Hemisphere are studied in the sixth grade, the Eastern Hemisphere nations are usually studied in the seventh grade; or the order can be reversed. Some schools also include home-state studies in the seventh grade. Whatever pattern is followed, there will be many opportunities to include learnings related to government in connection either with other nations or with the home state.

In most schools, grade eight deals with the development of the United States, and there is ordinarily a heavy emphasis on the growth of the government of this nation. Attention is directed to the early Colonial governments, events that led to the American Revolution, and the formation of the new government. Children study the significance of such documents as the Declaration of Independence, the Articles of Confederation, and the Constitution. They learn about our political system and how it functions. They learn how the government of the United States grew in power and how it relates to the private lives of citizens. When students complete the eight grades, they should have a functional, citizen's knowledge of government and civic responsibility. They also should have had a great many experiences that will have given them the opportunity to learn, practice, and use democratic citizenship skills. This does not mean that they need not or cannot learn more; it means simply that they have completed the basic, introductory work in civic education that serves as the common foundation for all citizens of the United States.

In grades five through eight, the teacher may want to involve students in the Civic Achievement Award Program (CAAP) established under Public Law 100-158 in honor of the Office of the Speaker of the House of Representatives. It can be used as a supplementary segment to the regular social studies program in the classroom. The program consists of three parts: (1) The Learning Project; (2) The Research Project; and (3) The Civics Project. The program focuses on the development of a common body of civic knowledge and related skills. The research project and civic project components stress participation as an important aspect of civic competence. The CAAP is administered by the Close Up Foundation, and the Foundation will provide the materials needed to conduct the program. Information about participating in CAAP can be obtained by writing to Civic Achievement Award Program, Close Up Foundation, 44 Canal Center Plaza, Alexandria, VA 22314.

SOCIOLOGY AND THE SOCIAL STUDIES

Sociology is a broad social science that deals with the study of the structure of society, its groups, institutions, and culture. Sociological studies often focus on the diverse societal and cultural phenomena that influence the behavior of individuals and groups. Sociology is especially concerned with social organization and the way people organize themselves into groups, subgroups, social classes, and institutions. It is difficult to draw a sharp line between the content of sociology and some of the other social sciences because their areas of concern overlap.

Social psychology and sociology concern themselves with somewhat the same social phenomena. Whereas sociology focuses on groups, social psychology studies the individual in a social situation. Social psychology is particularly concerned with the effects of group life on the behavior of individuals. Studies in social psychology deal with the problems of the individual's role in groups; the development of the self-concept; the effects of group pressure on individual behavior, attitudes, and how they are formed; leadership; followership; and the effects of social-class structure.

The following are representative samples of major generalizations from sociology that have been used as organizing ideas in developing social studies units with a sociological emphasis:

1. The family is the basic social unit in most cultures and is the source of some of the most fundamental and necessary learnings in a culture.
2. Social classes have always existed in every society although the bases of class distinction and the degree of rigidity of the class structure have varied.
3. Every society develops a system of roles, norms, values, and sanctions to guide the behavior of individuals and groups within the society.
4. All societies develop systems of social control; conflicts often arise between individual liberty and social control in societies where both values are sought.
5. The social environment in which a person is reared and lives has a profound effect on the personal growth and development of that individual.

Teaching Suggestions

A considerable amount of content of the elementary school social studies is drawn from sociology. This is particularly true in the primary grades. One of the units studied in first grade is "The Family." Children learn about the structure of this basic group in our society, some of its functions, and the roles of various members. This is usually followed in the primary grades by units dealing with the neighborhood, community workers, community living, and community institutions. As children study the diversification of work that is done in a modern community, they begin to see how various groups are formed and learn of the purposes of these groups. Later, in the higher grades, students will learn that the interests of such community groups are often in conflict and that this sometimes results in disorganization and community problems.

Studies of various cultures should focus on basic social processes rather than on the quaint ways used by the group to achieve them; that is, all groups have systems of communication, worship, education, and government. Much of value can be learned by showing what factors tend to disrupt conventional ways of living and cause people to change to other ways. Students in the middle and upper grades can also learn the consequences that befall cultures that do not make necessary changes in their way of living as external conditions change.

In units on the growth of the United States in grades five and eight, as well as in home-state units in the fourth grade, children should study the cultural, religious, and racial backgrounds of the people who live there. Such a study will show that the United States is pluralistic in its cultural legacy and has benefited from the contributions of a great many cultures of the world. Often it is possible for children to see concrete evidences of contributions of other cultures in the life about them in things such as the names of towns, cities, bodies of water, festivals, customs, language, and famous men and women in our history. A knowledge of, and appreciation for, the contributions of other cultures to our own can be a strong force in combating harmful aspects of ethnocentrism. Such studies provide a setting in which to deal realistically with pluralism and with the distinctive multiethnic and multicultural composition of the United States.

Certainly, a problem that will be receiving increasing attention in the social studies is that of population distribution. In its simplest form, the study of population might call for the examination of the location of settlements and population centers. Which areas are densely populated? Which are more sparsely settled and why? In the upper grades, students can study more intensively some of the problems that develop in areas of high population density. They can trace the movements of peoples and discover why they move when and where they do. They can study population trends, birth and death rates in countries, and examine problems faced by countries with rapidly increasing numbers of people.

ANTHROPOLOGY AND THE SOCIAL STUDIES

Anthropology, with its several divisions, is often thought of as a unifying social science because it is by definition the study of human beings in their totality, their culture, and their growth toward civilization. Anthropology is concerned with the development of language, social institutions, religion, arts and crafts, physical and mental traits, and similarities and differences of cultures. Much of the research that has been done on the characteristics of various racial groups has been done by anthropologists. Anthropological concepts become a part of the social studies in the culture studies that are made of human societies.

Anthropological studies are often comparative. Such comparative, cross-cultural studies show the wide range of capabilities of human beings: modern medical practice and the tribal medicine man; affluence and poverty; humanitarian behavior and cruelty and war; urban living and rural life; life in extremely cold areas and life in hot, desert regions. People are, therefore, contradictory creatures, highly adaptive in their behavior, capable of remarkable achievements, rational yet often acting in irrational ways. They can, within limits, control and shape their environment and build a culture. They rely on their ability to think, imagine, and innovate to solve problems of living. This characteristic results in great diversity among the people of the world in how they live, what they believe, and how they conduct their affairs. Nonetheless, people are all part of the human family; all are a part of what is called humankind, and all have many common physical and social needs.

A considerable amount of interest has developed in the exciting possibilities for social studies programs with an anthropological orientation. This may be, in part, a result of the increased importance of the non-Western world in international affairs and the traditional interest of the anthropologists in non-Western cultures. The increased interest in anthropology may also stem from the concern of the discipline with concepts that are so closely related to the shaping of the human personality, human institutions, and the evolution of human societies.

The following are representative generalizations from anthropology that have been used as organizing ideas in developing social studies units:

1. Every society has formed its own system of beliefs, knowledge, values, traditions, and skills that can be called its culture.
2. Culture is socially learned and serves as a potential guide for human behavior in any given society.
3. Although people everywhere are confronted with the same psychological and physiological needs, the ways in which they meet these needs differ according to their culture.
4. The art, music, architecture, food, clothing, sports, and customs of a people help to produce a national identity.
5. Nearly all human beings, regardless of their racial or ethnic background, are capable of participating in and contributing to any culture.

Teaching Suggestions

Anthropological studies deal with the concept of culture from many different perspectives—cultural determinism, cultural relativity, cultural diffusion, cultural borrowing, and cultural change. Other concepts included in anthropological studies are environment, languages, tools, adaptation, technology, human variation, values, authority, institutions, socialization, and of course, many others. These concepts cut across several of the social science disciplines. Thus, social studies units often contain a substantial amount of information that could be defined as anthropological even though it may not be made explicit in the curriculum. The point is that there is already much in the social studies curriculum of most schools that is anthropological in content. Indeed, the unified concept of social studies has a closer kinship to anthropology, in terms of its attempt to deal with the totality of social phenomena, than it does to any of the other social sciences.

Activities such as the following have been used by elementary school teachers in studies having an anthropological emphasis:

1. *Trace the development and use of certain tools;* associate ways of living with the use of tools.
2. *Follow the development of language and communication* systems from early signs and symbols to modern information dissemination devices.

Field trips provide students with learning experiences they could not possibly duplicate in the classroom. Here we see students actually participating in an archeological dig and sifting through the diggings in search of authentic artifacts.
(Photos courtesy of the Southern Oregon Historical Society.)

Topic:	Cultural borrowing
Grade:	Six
Time:	Two class periods
Objective:	To learn how contact with another culture changes ways of living.
Interest Building:	Begin the presentation by discussing with the class changes in ways of living with which they are familiar. This should lead to the idea that the ways of living of people all over the world are changing.
	Display a photograph of the tundra region showing a sled being drawn by a snowmobile with sled dogs and a tent in the background.
	Ask students whether they think the photograph is one that was taken a long time ago or in recent years and why they think as they do. This should lead to a discussion of the presence of the snowmobile, which means that the group has had contact with the industrial world.
Lesson Development:	Divide the class into groups of three, and using the resources available have students make an inquiry into the specific changes that have taken place in Eskimo life as a result of contact with the outside world and the impact of those changes on traditional Eskimo life. Their findings should be recorded on a chart as follows:

CHANGE	RESULT
Motorboats	
Snowmobiles	
Guns and steel traps	
Canvas tents	
Sewing machines	
Schools	
Others (specify)	

	Provide sufficient time for the groups to do their research, then reassemble as a whole group. Summarize the findings of all groups on a master chart on the chalkboard. Discuss the findings along these lines: How have these changes been helpful to Eskimo life? How have these changes been harmful to Eskimo life? Is it important to keep Eskimo traditions and skills alive? How might this be done?
	Lead the discussion toward the more general problem of what happens when people of one culture have contact with another culture. This deals with the concept of cultural borrowing, although the term need not be introduced to the children at this time.
Summary/ Followup:	Have the children, again in groups of three, find other examples of cultural borrowing in back issues of *National Geographic* magazines you have provided. Have them explain how their examples illustrate cultural borrowing.
Materials:	Large photos of traditional Eskimo life.
	Texts, supplementary books, and references on Eskimo culture.
	Several back copies of *National Geographic* magazine.

3. *Identify ways that inventions have changed civilizations.*
4. *Have children serve as participant observers* in groups of which they are a part, such as their families.
5. *Prepare data-retrieval charts* to compare the use of resources, tools, technology, or other variables by different groups.
6. *Use role playing, simulations, and creative dramatics* for cross-cultural comparisons of human behavior.
7. *Use music and art* to gain insight into the culture of a people.
8. In the upper grades *participate in a simulated archaeological dig.*
9. *Provide experiences in the exchange of goods and services,* as for example, a simulation game involving medium of exchange.
10. *Study artifacts from the local area* that provide traces of the early history of the community.

Lesson Plan 8 illustrates how one teacher used a concept from anthropology in a social studies unit entitled "Changing Ways of Living."

SOCIAL STUDIES: AN INTEGRATED FIELD

As we will see in chapter 8, social problems do not appear, nor are they solved, within the confines of one discipline or another. Consider the worldwide problem of industrial pollution, for example. Concepts, generalizations, and methods of study drawn from economics, sociology, history, and geography all will be crucial if progress is to be made and the environment prevented from ruin. Furthermore, no era of American or world history, no region of the United States, and no society on the planet can be understood fully without exploring the multiple dimensions of social life: government, power, location, culture, social class, labor, the distribution of goods and service, roles and rites of passage, religion, and so on. Imagine trying to understand the early civilizations of Africa and China without peering through the lenses of history, geography, and all the social sciences. The very term *social studies* was coined to emphasize the need to draw on the various social sciences and history and geography.

We close this chapter, then, with two basic plans that should help the teacher prepare interdisciplinary units of study. The first plan uses problem-centered instruction; the second event-centered instruction. An extended discussion of interdisciplinary education will be found in chapter 11.

Plan 1: Problem-Centered Units

Problem-centered, also known as issue-centered, education has long been one of the most popular approaches to social studies education among the very best teachers.[7] The central focus of a problem-centered unit is a real

---

[7]For more information on this approach, see the special section in *The Social Studies* 80 (October 1989), Ronald Evans, ed.

public problem. It should be a problem that has challenged people throughout history and in many cultures, for example:

1. Who is responsible for the poor?
2. How much environmental degradation should be allowed for the sake of economic productivity or, simply, How much pollution should be permitted for the sake of providing jobs?
3. How should society punish lawbreakers? Are there better forms of punishment than "an eye for an eye?"
4. Is the public ever justified to use violence to achieve its objectives?

Note that the problems are stated as questions, and that the questions are mighty. They apply to many times and cultures. They are *recurring* issues: People have grappled with them for years but never answered them once and for all. And, one of the responsibilities of being a member of "the public" is to tackle such problems. They are, of course, the sort of questions on which reasonable people will disagree; they lend themselves above all, therefore, to discussion.

With such a question as the unit's centerpiece, the teacher plans learning activities that inform the children's discussion and writing. This, then, is the instructional goal: to have children discuss and write and read on the problem, and to *inform* these activities through study. Discussion without study, while not worthless (at least it activates prior knowledge), has none of the power and depth of discussions to which participants bring information, judgment, competing viewpoints they have read elsewhere, and the like. Consequently, the problem-centered unit moves through iterations of discussion, study, and writing. In this way, not only are the social sciences and history integrated, so are reading and writing instruction.

Let us consider an example using the focus question, Who is responsible for the poor? Figure 7-2 shows that the children will endeavor to gather information from the various disciplines to inform their decisions on this matter. The suggested procedure on page 215 can be altered considerably to suit a teacher's knowledge of the problem and related curriculum materials. Its focus can be shifted, for example, from U.S. to world history. Its essence, however, is discussion. There should be plenty of discussion. There also needs to be ample opportunity for students to reflect on the quality of their discussions.

Plan 2: Event-Centered Units

Event-centered units feature a remarkable happening drawn from the historical record. There are far more examples than pages in this book, but consider just a few: Columbus's voyage of 1492, the Salem witchcraft trials, Gandhi's nonviolent revolution in India, the collapse of the Soviet Union, the volcanic eruption that buried Pompeii, the development of the U.S. Constitution, the invention of the telegraph, the surrender of Chief Joseph.

In an event-centered unit, children study the selected event as journalists would. This means that keeping notes, writing drafts, and revising are

WHO IS RESPONSIBLE FOR THE POOR?
(a problem-centered unit)

1. *Initial discussion* of the unit question followed by writing on the question in a "discussion journal" or "learning log."
2. *Instruction* on the characteristics of good discussion (see chapter 13).
3. *Historical study:* Using a time line that has been drawn on the board, the teacher describes for children several historical eras in which poverty was a problem and who did what about it.

   a. poor African slaves living on plantations
   b. poor immigrants
   c. poor unemployed during the Great Depression
   d. a current, local example (rural or inner-city poverty; homelessness)

4. *Additional data gathering:* The class is divided into four committees. Each is assigned to one of the four examples. The committee's job is to find out more about its example and, to give children a sense of the era, interesting facts about society at that time. (See chapter 13, Cooperative Learning).

   Option. If the children are too young to conduct small-group research, the teacher can provide the additional information on each example using the same material the small groups would—films, stories, guest speakers, the textbook, primary documents, and references.
5. *Second discussion* of the question, now informed by historical information. Discussion followed by reflection on the quality of the discussion.
6. *Second writing in journals* on the unit question. Revise and share with peers.
7. *Additional data gathering.* Again using a small-group research format (option: teacher provides the data), the children divide among group members the four social sciences: economics, sociology, anthropology, and political science. Each is given study questions and works with others from the other groups assigned to the same topic.[8] Study questions should be designed with the capabilities of students and available curriculum materials in mind. For example:

ECONOMICS: For two or three of the examples, describe (a) who else in society was poor, and (b) who was rich?

SOCIOLOGY: For two or three of the examples, find out (a) what conflicts occurred? (b) how were families affected by poverty?

POLITICAL SCIENCE: For two or three of the examples, find out (a) did government help the poor? if so, how? (b) who else helped?

ANTHROPOLOGY: For two or three of the examples, describe (a) how the life style of the poor people—their culture—was different from the nonpoor; (b) find an example of poverty in another nation and describe it.

8. *Third discussion* of the unit question, informed by the additional data.
9. *Third writing in journals* on the unit question. Share, revise, and publish.

---

[8]This technique, called "Jigsaw," is explained fully in chapter 13.

FIGURE 7-2

Problem-Centered Units

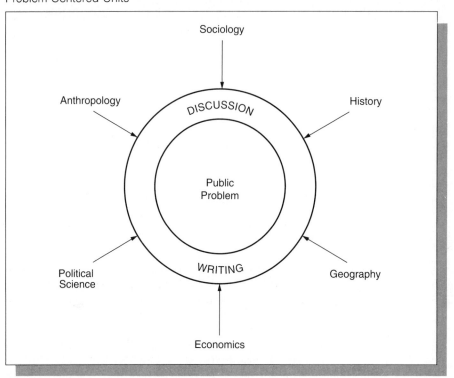

paramount activities. Children are taught to use the journalist's five key questions, which are displayed prominently about the room: *Who, what, where, why,* and *how?* Figure 7-3 shows that, as in problem-centered units, children use the lenses of the various disciplines better to see, and eventually to understand, the event.

On page 218 is a suggested procedure for a unit centered on the Columbus voyage of 1492. This event, the 500th anniversary of which was commemorated in 1992, lends itself particularly well to interdisciplinary study since this voyage and the expeditions that followed quite literally changed the world—*both* worlds. Both the American and European worlds were in 1492 "old worlds" with long histories. At the same time, each was a "new world" from the perspective of the other. Much new curriculum material is available on this event, thanks mainly to the Smithsonian Institution's project, *Seeds of Change.*[9]

---

[9]For example, see Sharryl Davis Hawke and James E. Davis, *Seeds of Change: The Story of Cultural Exchange after 1492* (Reading, MA: Addison-Wesley, 1992). (Prepared for middle grades.) Also, *Smithsonian* magazine features good background articles on this subject in 1991 and 1992 issues. Tracking them down in the library would be a good task for a student committee.

FIGURE 7-3

Event-Centered Units

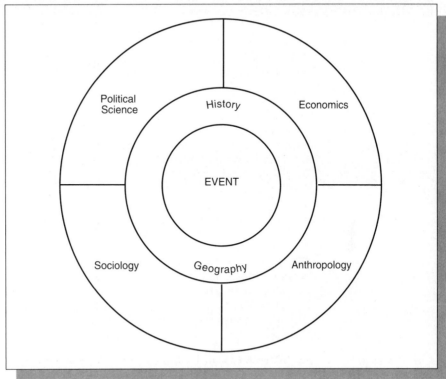

Both plans are widely applicable in all the elementary and middle school grades. Younger and older children alike are fascinated by the events of history, particularly when events are studied in sufficient detail to bring them fully to life in a child's mind. As for social problems, those to which kindergartners can become engaged will generally be close to classroom and school life: rules of fair play at recess, sharing classroom resources, and dividing the labor equitably for classroom cleanup, for example. Older children typically have somewhat more information and experience with community, national, and international problems, and they can study these problems with greater interest and comprehension. But good teachers take care not to let these generalizations become stereotypes that limit their students' opportunities to learn. Young children watch the world news on television, too, and are concerned about homeless people they see on the street. Older children, meanwhile, are just as interested in fair rules for classroom and playground interaction.

A wealth of information, concepts, generalizations, and methods of study can be drawn from the social sciences to enrich social studies units.

1492 CULTURAL EXCHANGE BETWEEN TWO WORLDS (an event-centered unit)

1. *Initial discussion* on the question: Who knows what about 1492? Students prepare initial semantic maps (see chapter 10).
2. *Biographical study.* Working in cooperative groups, students produce an illustrated biography of Columbus, using available expository and narrative material, but especially his diary. (Chapter 11 has details on biography writing in cooperative groups.)
3. *Multiple perspectives.* In the same groups, students produce a second book, this time a "Question and Answer" book about the Arawak Indians. (This was the Caribbean society that greeted Columbus in 1492, later to be destroyed.) Children are directed to write at least one "chapter" of questions and answers about Arawak food and shelter, history, and their encounter with Columbus and subsequent demise.
4. *Second discussion,* now on the question, "How has your knowledge of the Columbus voyages grown?" Students revise their semantic maps.
5. *Newspaper report, first draft.* Students write newspaper reports on the theme, "The Meeting of Two Worlds," using what they have learned so far. These are shared, revised, and set aside.
6. *Additional data gathering: Cultural Exchange.* Using material drawn from the *Seeds of Change* project of the Smithsonian Institution, students study five exchanges between Europe and America. Cooperative groups may be used, as in Plan 1.

HORSE. Columbus introduced the horse to the Americas changing, for example, the way North American natives hunted buffalo.

CORN. Hungry for gold, the conquistadors found mainly corn, a staple of the American diet. They took it back to Spain and in Europe it flourished.

DISEASE. Measles, mumps, and smallpox were the deadly allies of Europeans against Americans, killing millions soon after 1492.

POTATO. Like corn, the conquistadors carried this Peruvian vegetable to Europe where it fed a growing population. Ironically, 350 years later, the potato famine in Ireland produced a wave of immigrants back to America.

SUGAR. Columbus brought this crop to the Caribbean. Soon, Africans were captured by the thousands for forced labor on sugar plantations.

7. *Third discussion,* same question as in second discussion. Students revise again the semantic maps. In this way, students can concretely see their knowledge grow.
8. *Newspaper reports.* The class now prepares a special issue of their class newsletter focused on the voyage that changed the world.

Even the youngest child should be given the opportunity to begin exploring these disciplines. By assembling a broad foundation of knowledge
early, a child is better prepared for the advanced studies to come.

DISCUSSION QUESTIONS AND SUGGESTED ACTIVITIES

1. Select one of the disciplines discussed in this chapter, and find out
   what particular methods of inquiry are used by scholars in that discipline. Explain how—or if—any of these might be adapted for use with
   elementary and middle school children.

2. Examine a social studies textbook and its accompanying teacher's manual. Which of the social sciences are included? Are any not included?
   Does the text or the manual explain how the content of the book relates
   to the social sciences?

3. Visit your curriculum library on campus, and examine two or three
   curriculum guides to see how the social sciences are incorporated in
   the program.

4. How can the study of the various disciplines discussed in this chapter
   help children learn social roles such as *family member, consumer, friend,
   worker, member of social groups, citizen,* and *self-identity?*

5. Much of the subject matter from the disciplines discussed in this chapter are brought into the program by *infusion* into existing units. What
   are the advantages and limitations of infusion procedures?

6. Why is it that the disciplines discussed in this chapter have not been
   institutionalized into the social studies curriculum as have history and
   geography?

7. Do you think it is a good practice for state legislatures to require that
   aspects of economics and political science be included in the public
   school curriculum? Why or why not?

8. A year-long program entitled MAN: A COURSE OF STUDY (MACOS)
   was an anthropology-based program developed during the 1960s for
   the fifth grade. It was widely acclaimed by scholars as a fine effort to
   build social science concepts into the social studies curriculum. Yet,
   this program was thoroughly rejected by many parents and religious
   groups as being secular humanist in its philosophy, that it promoted
   relativism in teaching values, and that it taught children to question
   the authority of their parents and church leaders. Disregarding the
   specific issues of this particular program, discuss what you believe
   should be the appropriate role of parents in deciding the subject matter
   and procedures used in teaching social studies at the elementary and
   middle school levels. Do you have the same view regarding their role
   at the high school level? Why or why not?

9. Develop a unit using either the problem-centered plan or the event-centered plan given in this chapter.

10. Brainstorm with classmates additional types of unit plans for integrating the social science disciplines. For example, a Then and Now plan, an Ecology-Centered plan, a Biography-Centered plan.

SELECTED REFERENCES

General

BROWN, LESTER R. *State of the World: 1991.* New York: W. W. Norton, 1991.

HAWKE, SHARRYL DAVIS, AND JAMES E. DAVIS. *Seeds of Change: The Story of Cultural Exchange after 1492.* Reading, MA: Addison-Wesley, 1992.

WRONSKI, STANLEY P. AND DONALD H. BRAGAW, eds. *Social Studies and Social Sciences: A Fifty-Year Perspective,* NCSS Bulletin No. 78. Washington, DC: National Council for the Social Studies, 1986.

Anthropology

BARNES, BUCKLEY R. "Using Children's Literature in the Early Anthropology Curriculum." *Social Education* 55 (January 1991): 17–18.

BATESON, MARY CATHERINE. *With a Daughter's Eye: A Memoir of Margaret Mead and Gregory Bateson.* New York: Pocket Books, 1984.

COLE, JOHNNETTA, ed. *Anthropology for the Nineties: Introductory Readings.* New York: Free Press, 1988.

LITTLE SOLDIER, LEE. "Making Anthropology a Part of the Elementary Social Studies Curriculum." *Social Education* 54 (January 1990): 18–19.

Sociology

BELLAH, ROBERT N., RICHARD MADSEN, WILLIAM M. SULLIVAN, ANN SWIDLER, AND STEVEN M. TIPTON. *The Good Society.* New York: Knopf, 1991.

BOULDING, ELISE. *Building a Global Civic Culture: Education for an Interdependent World.* New York: Teachers College Press, 1988.

COHEN, ELIZABETH G. *Designing Groupwork: Strategies for the Heterogeneous Classroom.* New York: Teachers College Press, 1986.

Political Science

CENTER FOR CIVIC EDUCATION. *Civitas: A Framework for Civic Education.* Calabasas, CA: Center for Civic Education, and Washington, DC: National Council for the Social Studies, 1991.

FARBER, DANIEL A., AND SUZANNA SHERRY. *A History of the American Constitution.* Saint Paul, MN: West, 1990.

NIELSEN, LYNN E., AND JUDITH M. FINKELSTEIN. "Citizenship Education: Looking at Government." *Social Studies and the Young Learner* 1 (September/October 1988): 10–13.

PALONSKY, STUART B. "Political Socialization in Elementary Schools." *The Elementary School Journal* 87 (May 1987): 493–505.

Economics

HEILBRONER, ROBERT L. *The Worldly Philosophers: The Lives, Times and Ideas of the Great Economic Thinkers.* 6th ed. New York: Touchstone, 1987.

JOINT COUNCIL ON ECONOMIC EDUCATION. *Economics: What and When: Scope and Sequence Guidelines, K–12.* (A master curriculum guide in economics.) New York: author, 1988.

KOURILSKY, MARILYN L. "Children's Learning of Economics: The Imperatives and the Hurdles." *Theory Into Practice* 36 (Summer 1987): 198–205.

SCHUG, MARK C. "Children's Understanding of Economics." *The Elementary School Journal* 87 (May 1987): 507–18.

8

Social Concerns as Priorities for Social Studies Education

S ocial issues and contemporary challenges that confront society do not always fit neatly within the subject matter boundaries of a social science discipline. Indeed, the effects of many of the problems of modern social life are so far reaching that they must be studied from an interdisciplinary perspective that goes quite beyond any or all the social sciences. Moreover, these problems and issues cannot be studied at one grade level and presumed to have been learned adequately. If they are to be understood, the child must return to them time and time again at various grades, each time at an increased level of complexity. Often schools handle these topics as recurring themes that spiral at increased levels of complexity throughout the curriculums of the elementary and secondary schools. Also, most of these topics can and *should* be taught within the context of the regular subject matter of social studies units. This chapter deals with several such vital topics that are thought by many to be priorities for society and, therefore, for social studies education.

GLOBAL PERSPECTIVES EDUCATION

Barring some global catastrophe, it is likely that international relationships will continue to grow among the people of this planet. This has many implications for social studies instruction. Today, international concerns are dominating the attention of our national political, economic, and cultural leaders. It could hardly be otherwise given the realities of the modern world. Consequently, social studies programs are being planned to equip the young citizen to deal thoughtfully and intelligently with problems of international import.[1]

---

[1]See National Council for the Social Studies, "Position Statement on Global Education," *Social Education* 46 (January 1982): 36–38.

We live in a world fraught with danger, which is likely to increase as modern instruments of destruction become available to more and more nations. Even a minor power, if armed with modern weapons, constitutes a threat to the entire world. To ignore the real danger that exists or to minimize it could result in disastrous consequences for the entire human population. The recent efforts to reduce the potential for armed conflict between the United States and the former Soviet Union provide hope that more sensible approaches to international relations will eventually prevail. Perhaps through educational programs directed toward the understanding of others and toward a search for world peace, a more satisfactory method of resolving international disputes can be found than the oldest and least effective method, war. Many believe that a global perspective that engenders worldmindedness, therefore, is essential if humankind is to survive.

Although teachers should help children develop a sense of hope for the future, instruction for international understanding should not be allowed to become based on sentimentalism and naive optimism. The harsh realities of the world are ever present and must be faced. Teachers will want to help students develop feelings of goodwill, mutual trust, and understanding of others, but at the same time, it must be understood that these feelings cannot be one-sided in their application. No matter how strongly men and women of goodwill of *any* nation long for peace, it cannot be a realizable goal so long as huge sections of the world's people are taught to hate and distrust others. As has been said many times, we deal with the world the way it is, not as we wish it to be. Global perspectives education in American schools is crucial, therefore, when viewed in this context. American schoolchildren must be alerted to these realities, for it is they who will be representing the United States to the rest of the world in the years to come and who will be the decision makers of the future.

When education for a global perspective is regarded as one of the broad goals of education, it becomes apparent that the addition of a new subject to the curriculum is not necessary. Rather, it should represent an *extension and broader interpretation of what is already taught in most schools.* Teaching for a global perspective can occur through experiences the child has in music, art, science, literature, reading—in fact, in almost any of the various curricular areas.

To broaden instruction as described in the preceding paragraph, teachers will need to be imaginative in exploring and discovering new avenues to a worldview. For example, when children in the primary grades are studying homes and home life, that is the time to begin developing the understanding that people all over the world need homes and that they build them in a variety of ways. Or when the food market is studied, time might be spent on an examination of food markets around the world. Units on transportation and communication can, likewise, be expanded to familiarize the child with these functions on a broader basis than the local community. Almost any topic has within it such possibilities for teaching global relationships.

If a school accepts global perspectives education as one of its primary purposes, it will concern itself with ideas such as these:

1. The interdependence of peoples.
2. The need for peaceful relations among nations.
3. Basic similarities and differences in peoples because of geographical, cultural, and historical considerations, including an elementary understanding of the ways of living in the modern world.
4. The philosophy and practice of respect for the dignity of the individual irrespective of race or other factors over which he or she has no control.
5. The need to develop a sensitivity to and respect for the cultures of other people.

International Networks and Global Education

Social studies units that deal with international relationships ordinarily focus on specific nations. Children learn certain geographic, economic, and political information about a nation. They learn what the country produces and what it contributes to the world markets. They may even learn how our own country—or perhaps their specific community—interacts with specific nations through trade, through "sister city" programs, or through

"Consideration for others" is a human value that can be promoted in various ways through social studies activities. Here we see children from the Maywood Hills Elementary School in Bothell, Washington, loading learning and recreational resources they have gathered to be shipped to their "Sister School" in Uganda.
(Photo by Carla Anderson, Northshore School District.)

cultural exchanges. They learn how specific nations align themselves with other nations in forming power blocs and how our own nation fits into such international arrangements.

What is described in the foregoing paragraph is a more or less conventional approach to building global awareness, and much of value can come from such learning experiences. The realities of the world today, however, are such that another dimension must be added to the study of the contemporary world and its people. In modern times international networks have been developed that are superimposed on the world of nation states, and these networks affect the lives of people almost everywhere in the world. Moreover, these effects are felt differentially even within a single country. For example, in our own nation, those who live and work in oil-producing and processing areas of the country may benefit when the price of oil goes up. Those who live in the northern tier of states and who heat their homes with oil are affected adversely by such a price hike. Furthermore, the price change may have been made by an international group of officials representing not only the Arab countries but oil-producing nations from several places in the world, including some in this hemisphere.

Because the things that people everywhere value and want are differentially distributed in the world and because increasing numbers of people want and value the same things, some systems for sharing those values and wants have to be devised. The result is a complicated set of systems and subsystems that are worldwide and extend into virtually every community and household in America.[2] Modern systems of production and distribution have little regard for national boundaries.

Some of these concepts can be illustrated with a familiar product, *blue jeans*. Here we have a fashion fad that began in this country during the 1960s and suddenly spread worldwide. Everyone wanted blue jeans, even the young people in the Soviet Union and other Communist bloc countries wanted good-quality blue jeans. Thus, there arose an unexpected international market for this product. Responding to this market, factories to produce blue jeans were established in several parts of the world—the United States, South Korea, Mexico, the Philippines, Hong Kong, Great Britain, and others. Clearly those responsible for marketing this product—bankers, shippers, distributors, and retailers—also represented the international community. Global perspectives education will need to focus on such international linkages that are a part of the everyday life of most of us.

The international networks are not limited to economic linkages. People of the world are linked through political systems and alliances, through international church affiliations, through their common ethnic heritages, and through the arts and humanities. When one hears a modern-day re-

---

[2]Robert B. Woyach, "Using the Local Community to Teach About the Global Community," in *Community Study: Applications and Opportunities,* ed. by Mark C. Schug and R. Beery (NCSS Bulletin No. 73, Washington, DC: National Council for the Social Studies, 1984), chap. 2.

cording of Dvorak's "Slavonic Dances" or any other symphonic work, it may not be possible even for an expert to tell whether the performing group is the Cleveland Orchestra or the Prague Symphony Orchestra. Americans who return to the homeland of their forebears expecting to hear traditional folk music will find, instead, the same popular and rock music played on instruments with electronically enhanced sound that they heard back home!

Experiences to Help Build a Global Orientation

Use Experiences from the Everyday Lives of Children to Initiate Study Projects. The everyday experiences of children might include the return of a parent from an overseas assignment, the presence of a foreign visitor, a curio from another country, a story or television program about children in other lands, or a news item familiar to the children. Successful activities that grow out of ordinary life experiences usually begin in class discussions under the guidance of an alert teacher who can identify experiences of children that lend themselves to such a study. The local community and its ties with the rest of the world are logical springboards for building a global perspective.

Be Sure Information about Other People Is Accurate and Authentic. Misguided teaching resulting in erroneous concepts of other people, the development of stereotypes, or overemphasis on those aspects of the lives of others that are drastically different from our own leads to distorted ideas about other cultures and should be avoided. In order to get up-to-date information about the society being studied, the teacher might consult the local library or local travel bureaus, write to the appropriate embassy in Washington, DC, or the nation's consulate, or request information about the country through the United Nations. Other sources of information are persons who were or are citizens of a foreign country—exchange students, recent immigrants to the United States, or foreign nationals visiting here.

Keep Instruction and Experiences for Primary-Grade Children Simple, Child-Oriented. Difficult concepts relating to international understanding, geography, and intercultural relations should be avoided in teaching young children. One of the major purposes of these studies at the primary-grade level is to develop the concept of friendliness and neighborliness among the people of the world. Learning activities should be simple ones, dealing with ideas and things that are consistent with the experience and maturity of the young child. Specifically, this means learning about the ways children in other lands live, play, dress, and eat. The primary-grade child can understand that everyone needs a home, a family, and friends; must go to school; and feels sad, happy, or angry at times.

Make Direct Contact with the Life of the Group Studied. One of the best learning experiences for young children in making a study of people in other lands is to have direct contact with a person from the country, especially with a child their own age, who can answer questions about the clothes they wear, their schools, games, celebrations, homes, foods, stories, and similar ways of living. Other types of contacts include material things that have come from other countries. These are especially interesting to children if the items are similar to something they use in their own lives each day. A doll, an article of clothing, recorded music, a book, and a toy are examples of items that help children understand that there are differences in the ways of doing things but that children everywhere do many of the same things. With help from the teacher and their parents, even primary-grade children can carry on correspondence with children abroad, which invariably leads to the exchange of photographs and other objects. Teachers who wish to have their classes or individual members of their classes correspond with children in other lands may obtain information and addresses from the following sources:

Student Letter Exchange
630 Third Avenue
New York, NY 10017

($5.00 for 1–3 names)

League of Friendship, Inc.
P.O. Box 509
Mount Vernon, OH 43050-0509

(Ages 12 and older; a charge of $1.50 for each name; include a stamped, self-addressed envelope)

Use Story and Literature Resources Related to Other Lands.   The amount of fictional reading material dealing with children's lives in other lands has been increasing substantially in recent years. Typically, these little books are illustrated vividly, and primary-grade children get as much from the pictures as from the story as the teacher reads it to them. As children advance to the second and third grades, some of them can read the stories themselves.

In addition to the principles discussed in connection with the primary-grade program, the following suggestions apply to the middle and upper grades.

Explore More Deeply Some of the Reasons for the Differences in Ways of Living.   People everywhere are products of their backgrounds— historical, geographical, sociological, psychological, and religious factors help explain how and why people live the way they do. Children in the middle and upper grades can begin to sense these relationships. They can learn, for example, how the presence of natural barriers such as mountains has tended to isolate people and that these barriers usually stabilize borders between nations; they can see the cultural impact of missionaries, explorers, and colonists; they learn that modes of dress or types of homes people select are related to climatic conditions of the region; they can understand why island people turn to the sea for their livelihood and why desert people move toward water and food. In studying other cultures, children need experiences that will help them perceive the world through the eyes of the people of that culture insofar as that is possible. They need to imagine how the world would look to them if they were a member of the culture studied. When children begin to see even partially how others view themselves and the world, they come to understand some of the reasons for differences in ways of living, and the differences tend not to seem unusual to them. Rather, they come to the conclusion that people the world over are resourceful, logical, and show considerable ingenuity in dealing with environmental factors and forces.

Teach about the United Nations and Its Specialized Agencies.   Children everywhere need to learn about the United Nations and its work because it is the world's only organization with the potential to develop and implement global strategies to deal with pervasive human problems. Having had their people brutalized by two world wars in the first half of the twentieth century, the leaders of the Allied Powers of World War II decided to establish a world organization that would serve as a deterrent to war and that would encourage peaceful relationships among nations. Out of this concern was generated the idea of a United Nations organization, loosely modeled on the earlier League of Nations. Since its founding, it has grown in size and stature and has played a significant role in international affairs in the second half of the century. Fifty-one nations were members of the United Nations when its charter was signed in 1945; there were one hundred sixty-six member nations in December 1991.

In addition to its efforts to promote international peace and security, the United Nations has been instrumental in the development of international law and in pursuing economic, social, and cultural cooperation among nations. It has provided humanitarian service to many peoples, assisting with economic development and with the repatriation of displaced persons and the relocation of refugees, providing technical assistance to developing nations, and supplying emergency food and medicine following natural or human disasters. The United Nations has been a powerful force in promoting the concept of human rights as the birthright of human beings everywhere. Much of the work of the United Nations is carried on through its specialized agencies, the best known of which are the Educational, Scientific, and Cultural Organization (UNESCO), the Food and Agricultural Organization (FAO), the World Bank, the United Nations International Children's Emergency Fund (UNICEF), and the World Health Organization (WHO).

In the early years of the United Nations, certain individuals and groups in the United States feared that our membership in the United Nations would compromise the sovereignty of the United States. Some perceived the United Nations as an arm of international communism that would eventually be used against the United States in the Cold War. These feelings were so strongly held in certain parts of the country that schools in those places were forbidden to teach about the United Nations.

Today that has changed. The United Nations has a proven track record as a peacekeeping organization and as an influential voice in human affairs. Now that the Cold War is over, the Berlin Wall gone, and communism no longer a threat to the free world, the United Nations continues to provide avenues for communication and problem solving for all the world's people.

Activities for Global Perspectives Education

Compile an international cookbook, a game book, a book of holidays, or a book of national sports.

Invite foreign-born local residents to the classroom to display traditional national costumes or skills.

Set aside one bulletin board for current events in other countries around the world. Associate such new stories with their map and globe location.

Write to embassies, consulates, airlines, or travel bureaus for material on the countries being studied.

Develop simulated situations and instructional games to teach about other countries. This can be combined with role playing for additional insights. Topics such as city life, education, agricultural problems, and government would be appropriate for this activity.

Teach folk songs, national anthems, poems, dances, and games of other countries.

Study the origin, growth, and change of languages. Examine the derivation of specific words.

Develop dramatic activities based on legends, myths, or stories of other peoples around the world.

Study contributions to American culture that have been made by immigrants.

Prepare a travel brochure on a country, continent, or region; role play the part of a tourist representative from that country telling about a fifteen-day tour of the country.

Enter into correspondence with a class in another country.

Organize an International Club as a means of sponsoring all-school activities with an international emphasis.

Develop a tape exchange with children of another country.

Exchange artwork with a school in a foreign country or with children from a sister city if one exists.

Contact a local agency for foreign student placement, and arrange to have a foreign student spend a day with your class.

ENERGY AND ENVIRONMENTAL EDUCATION
· ·

One of the essential characteristics that distinguishes a modern nation such as the United States from a less well-developed nation is its use of and dependence on various forms of energy. Modern nations have taken burdens off the backs of human beings and animals and have substituted inanimate sources of power and energy. The dependence on various forms of such energy—and in huge and escalating amounts—is absolute in modernized nations. Their economic systems cannot survive without it. They could not sustain their present standards of living if their energy sources were curtailed. The United States consumes more energy on a per capita basis simply to provide food for its people than developing nations such as the People's Republic of China use for the entire operation of the country. Perhaps no topic is related more directly to the day-to-day lives of citizens than is energy.

Energy is, of course, related to the environment. The relationship occurs at all stages of the energy production–delivery–consumption sequence. Extracting energy sources such as coal, gas, and oil from the earth either scars or pollutes the environment. Processing the raw materials of energy into usable forms and delivering the finished products also do violence to the environment. Similarly, the consumption of energy in most instances has some environmental impact. Thus, one of the major profound social issues of our time is that of providing for the vast energy needs of our modern industrial society while at the same time preserving an environment that can sustain human and other forms of life at an acceptable level of quality.

When European settlers first came to North America, the incredible vastness and abundance of resources they found produced no concern in their minds for the environment. There was fresh water aplenty. Forests and trees were in such abundance that they were perceived as obstacles to land use. There was no shortage of places to dispose of solid wastes. There were no internal combustion engines or other devices creating large quantities of harmful hydrocarbons to pollute the air. The forests and streams were well stocked with wildlife and fish. What happened in the three hundred years that followed provides us with a shocking case study of unbelievable exploitation and waste and an almost total lack of concern for the consequences of this behavior. All this is now too familiar history.

Serious efforts to reverse this trend got underway about three decades ago. National and state leadership, combined with publicity in the popular press and, most importantly, concerned citizen groups, raised the consciousness of the general public to the violence being perpetrated on the ecosystem. More than that, these forces were successful in securing state, national, and local legislation that mandated a halt to environmental abuse. Scientific data relating to the use of certain energy-producing fuels raised the frightening possibility that the planet could experience something in the way of an "eco-catastrophe" in the foreseeable future. The most significant danger signals seemed to be those associated with (1) the use of pesticides, (2) the disposal of solid wastes, (3) air pollution, (4) water pollution, (5) radiation and radioactive substances, and (6) overpopulation.

The present concern for energy use and the related problems of environmental contamination are extensions of earlier efforts in the general area of conservation. The concept of conservation—meaning prudent use—has a reasonably long history in this country. Even during the colonial period some of the thoughtful men of the time (among them Washington and Jefferson) were concerned with conservation in the broad sense. During the middle of the nineteenth century, conservation efforts were institutionalized, largely as a result of rapidly diminishing forest resources. The U.S. Department of Agriculture established a Division of Forestry in 1880. Federal legislation during the latter half of the nineteenth century and extending into this century encouraged conservation and conservation education. The amount of federal, state, and local legislation dealing with environmental control has grown at a phenomenal rate in recent years.

It is clear that the turning point in the battle against pollution has now been reached and that people—in this country at least—will henceforth not be allowed to contaminate their surroundings with the same abandon as they have been able to do in the past. Almost everywhere in this nation local and state laws, following the lead of the federal authorities, are becoming much more strict in their control of human behavior that further contributes to environmental problems. More is being done to encourage citizens to be sensitive to the needless use and waste of energy. Similarly, educational programs are being implemented to help citizens use their surroundings more wisely. Recognition of the need for major remedial efforts to alleviate environmental pollution is growing.

Unfortunately, the burden—both financial and personal—of environmental preservation is not equally shared among citizens. When old-growth forests are protected as spotted owl habitats, thousands of citizens who make their livelihood in the lumber industry are adversely affected. When companies are forced to modify their manufacturing procedures to comply with environmental impact requirements, their operations may no longer be cost effective. This may result in their shutting down or relocating, perhaps even to an overseas site. Such moves have had a devastating effect on many American communities. Examples of the type discussed here could be drawn from any section of the country. In teaching about environmental preservation, it is important to stress the issue of fairness. Students need to learn that there must be some sense of balance between the legitimate concern for maintaining a quality environment for all living things, and the necessity for people to earn a living and support their families. It is also important to stress that where dislocations occur as a result of environmental rehabilitation, that the burden of such social policies must be shared equitably by all our citizens, not just by those who are directly affected.

Energy and environmental studies are, of course, not the sole province of the social studies. The subject is such a comprehensive one that it can be studied from many perspectives. It can be approached from the standpoint of science education, for, clearly, much of our polluted environment is a direct consequence of science and technology. Likewise, the subject is appropriate for health education because research has established relationships between air pollution and respiratory ailments such as asthma, emphysema, lung cancer, and bronchitis. Certainly, energy and environmental studies have geographical, esthetic, sociological, economic, and even political dimensions. Thus, the broad topic is highly appropriate for social studies programs because of its implications for human societies and human life. It is an ideal subject for interdisciplinary studies.

A program of energy and environmental studies should concern itself with three types of broad goals:

1. **Knowledge.** It should provide children with an opportunity to develop a basic understanding of the dimensions of problems surrounding energy and the environment, the causes and consequences of ecological disaster, the remedial measures now underway, the need for additional corrective legislation and action, *and* similar inputs of information that bear on these important topics.

2. **Concern.** It should help children develop an attitude of responsible concern for energy use and the quality of the environment. It should leave them with the feeling that they have a personal investment in their natural surroundings—that energy and environment truly are everybody's business.

3. **Action.** It should provide children with the opportunity to do something themselves about improving the environment. That is, if goals 1 and 2 are concerned with knowledge, thinking, and valuing, this goal constitutes the action dimension of the program.

Studies of energy and the environment as broadly defined here should be included in the social studies curriculum in at least two ways. First, every unit studied should include attention to energy and related environmental problems throughout the entire curriculum when the topic under study lends itself to such an emphasis. This will include most topics, as can be seen by examining the typical unit titles in chapter 1. Second, every grade should include one unit of study each year devoted entirely to the systematic treatment of energy and the environment. This problem should be planned on a K–12 basis in order to develop important learnings cumulatively as children progress through the grades.

Key Ideas in Energy and Environmental Education

The program of instruction in energy and environmental education should focus on a limited number of key ideas. These ideas can be defined along a continuum of complexity and be included in the curriculum at several points. Such a basic idea as the need for food by all living creatures can be dealt with in a simple way in the primary grades in the context of the units on family living, the local community, changing seasons, or meeting basic needs. In the middle school grades, this idea can be expanded and made more complex by getting into such dimensions of it as food chains and webs of life. The planned curriculum should provide ideas, identify emphases, suggest activities, and list learning resources, but, at the same time, should allow for and encourage inspired teaching and learning in this field.

What gives environmental studies vitality and freshness is a spontaneity and originality that are not often found when teaching conventional unit topics. Children can easily relate to energy and environment because these topics are so much a part of their day-to-day lives. Much of what they hear discussed by the adults around them, what they see on television, and what they hear and read in the news has to do with subject matter related to energy and the environment. Teachers can capitalize on this readiness in planning interesting and engaging studies on these topics.

The following key ideas can provide a focus for studies dealing with energy and the environment. They are not the only ones that could be used; indeed, they are probably not even the best ones for all parts of the country. They are, rather, a *sample* of ideas that can be, and have been, used as central organizing ideas for energy and environmental studies:

ENVIRONMENT

1. People are now facing critical environmental problems of their own doing.
2. One of the crucial problems facing people of the world is food shortage.
3. The problem of food shortage is presently differentially distributed around the world but could ultimately affect all people.
4. Some rehabilitation of the environment and greater restraint of its use are needed in order to maintain an acceptable quality of life.
5. Most of what human beings do has a detrimental effect on natural balances because it interferes with natural communities.
6. The earth is a self-contained, self-sustaining life-support system, consisting of an infinite number of ecosystems.
7. All living organisms fit into a complex environmental interrelationship known as a *food chain*.
8. The food supply for all living organisms depends ultimately on sunlight, soil, air, and water; consequently, anything that destroys these essential resources disturbs the quality of life.
9. All living organisms in some way affect and are affected by their environment.
10. Living things must have minimum space requirements for optimum development.

11. The quality of human life depends ultimately on the natural environment.
12. Increase in human population, if continued at the present rate, will, in the long run, have disastrous consequences for human societies.
13. Waste disposal potentially is at least as severe a problem as is the fulfillment of basic food needs.
14. The effects of the presence of people on the environment has esthetic as well as survival dimensions.

ENERGY

1. All life depends on energy, the most basic being energy supplied by the sun.
2. Food provides energy for the bodies of human beings.
3. Energy is the ability to do work.
4. The amount of energy is constant; it cannot be created or destroyed; it simply changes form.
5. Energy can be changed from one form to another: mechanical to electrical, electrical to heat, chemical to electrical, and so on.
6. Through the years human beings have discovered new sources of energy.
7. Most of the serious environmental problems that we face are the result of economic growth that greatly depends on energy consumption.
8. The standard of living of a society is related to productivity; productivity is related to energy use.
9. Energy resources and their use are related to the level of cultural and technological development; industrial societies place heavy demands on the earth's resources.
10. Economic development is highly dependent on industrialization, which in turn demands a high level of energy consumption.
11. The introduction and use of new energy sources often result in significant social changes.
12. Energy resources are unevenly distributed around the world; thus, as more nations become developed, interdependence among them is imperative if energy is to be shared.

These ideas are suggested as providing a focus for planning instruction. The specific subject matter should and probably will, in most cases, be selected from topics relating to the local region. Quite naturally, there will be a considerable overlap because many problems are common throughout the country. But case studies and examples should be drawn from the local area.

What follows is a series of specific types of energy-related environmental problems around which studies have been planned, along with a few examples of activities that teachers have used successfully with elementary school children. The activities are provided simply as examples of things

················· POPULATION

Activities to Build Awareness of Rapid Growth

1. Using *The World Almanac* or a copy of the U.S. Census, compare the population of the twenty leading American cities in 1950, 1960, 1970, 1980, and 1990. Are they still ranked in their original order? Which one has increased the most? Why?
2. Make a chart comparing the present-day population of a selected area with its population twenty years ago, one hundred years ago, two hundred years ago.
3. Make a chart comparing the present birth and death rates of a particular area with the birth and death rates of 1900.
4. Use the telephone directories of 1950, 1960, 1970, 1980, and 1990 to discover growth in such things as (a) schools, (b) hotels and motels, and (c) service stations.

Activities to Discover Population Distribution

1. Using a map and reference books, compare the populations of various parts of the United States. Why do people live where they do? What areas have the fewest people? Could people be moved to those areas? Why or why not?
2. Construct a map showing areas of heavy population in the city, state, nation, or world. Identify sparsely populated areas. Have children give reasons for both conditions.
3. Make a chart of the most rapidly growing areas of population in the state, nation, or world. Discuss the reasons for the rapid increase in these areas.

Activities to Understand the Meaning of Rapid Growth

1. Use a checkerboard or other similar squares and kernels of corn, and try doubling the number of kernels in each square, starting with one. How many kernels can be used before there is no longer room to double again? Discuss how this relates to population growth and its implications.
2. Encourage children to suggest problems that would be caused by an increase of twice as many persons in their environment.
3. Find pictures of the local area that were taken ten, fifteen, and twenty or more years ago. Have children compare those with the appearance of the same area today, noting especially reasons for changes and the effects of changes on the environment.

···

that children can do. They are not meaningful unless they are placed within the context of a larger study. Just to do the activity would hardly be sound teaching and would probably not lead to good learning.

Not all schools in the country have instructional resource centers that provide the teacher with the tools needed for teaching. But in the case of energy and environmental education, every school does have an instructional resource center immediately at hand. All that is required is an imaginative

LAND AND WATER USE

Activities to Build Awareness of Need for Concern

1. Creative dramatics: A public meeting is held to protest closing of a lake to fishing. A biologist explains why it was closed. Have children discover what he or she should say. Conduct the drama, and include the discussion that followed the biologist's presentation.
2. Compare status reports of your state from the 1850s with those of the present day on some animal, fish, or bird. Identify the reasons for the change.
3. Collect pictures from newspapers and magazines showing misuse of land. Suggest remedial measures for improved use or what might have been done by foresighted planners to have prevented the misuse from occurring.
4. Obtain data on acres of land under cultivation in 1950, 1960, 1970, 1980, and 1990 in the local area. Find out why changes occurred.
5. List ways that productive farmland is used for other purposes, for example, for urban sprawl, for freeway construction, as land flooded or submerged behind dams. Consider other problems that might have resulted if urban growth had been stopped and no freeways had been built.

TRANSPORTATION

Activities to Understand Problems of Congestion

1. Construct a chart to compare the amount of space on a highway required to transport forty persons in forty cars as compared with that required to transport forty persons in a bus. Suggest differences in residential patterns and concentrations of workplaces that would result if everyone were required to ride a bus to work.
2. On a local map, identify points of congestion and hours of highest congestion. Study traffic flows, and suggest alternative routes.
3. Prepare a map of the local area showing existing transportation routes. Prepare another map showing an improved arrangement.
4. Show by illustration how air, water, and noise pollution are related to transportation.
5. Carry out a roadside improvement project. This could be a cleanup campaign or the planting of trees, shrubs, or flowers.

teacher who will open the door of the classroom and step outside. What better instructional center is there for energy and environmental education than the local natural surroundings? Happily, it makes no difference if the school is located in the most congested section of our largest cities or in a remote rural area. Wherever one is, there is an environment that can profitably be studied, and we are all surrounded by energy resources.

················ **NOISE POLLUTION**

Activities to Build Awareness of the Problem

1. Make a tape of various sources of noise pollution. Use this to build awareness of sounds in the environment.
2. Demonstrate instruments that measure the level of sound. Measure the level of sound in and around school at various times of the day.
3. Demonstrate familiar sounds of noise pollution such as that of jet planes, stereo rock music, motors, machines, horns, and construction.
4. Take a field trip into the local area to build an awareness of sound. Identify points of especially high noise pollution.
5. Make a map of the local area, and label the places with most noises.
6. Prepare guidelines to reduce noise at home and at school. Develop a program of action to reduce noise. Suggest costs of these measures. Where would money come from? What would have to be sacrificed?

················ **AIR POLLUTION**

Activities to Understand Dimensions of the Problem

1. Construct a map of the local region showing places of highest pollution. Explain why these areas have a high level of pollution.
2. Discover the major sources of air pollution. Present these on charts.
3. Have the class attend a meeting of the local Air Pollution Control Board. Discuss issues considered by the board.
4. Show by illustration why air pollution cannot be only a local problem.
5. Relate air pollutants to problems of health.
6. Discover effects of air pollution on vegetation.
7. Have class gather data associating smoking with lung cancer and other respiratory ailments.

Activities for Conservation Education

Some schools may choose to focus on conservation education rather than on the broader topics of energy and environment. Although it is not possible to suggest a great number of learning activities and resources for soil, water, wildlife, mineral, and forest conservation education because of space limitations, the teacher may find the following suggestions helpful. They are intended to serve as *samples* of activities that have been used with success with elementary and middle school-age children.

Use the many good films now available on the topic of conservation. They are thoughtfully prepared, use modern photographic techniques and color to present forcefully the problem of waste and the need for better conservation practices.

WATER POLLUTION

Activities to Understand the Relationship of Polluted Waters to Recreation

1. Discover major sources of water pollution in the local area. Prepare a chart showing those sources. Discuss. Present the chart to local government officials.
2. Make a map of a specified area through which a large river flows. Find out if or to what extent the river becomes polluted as it flows.
3. On a map of the United States, identify water bodies that once were contaminated but that have been rehabilitated.
4. Select a water body in the local area that is not available for recreation because of contamination. Plan a strategy to have it rehabilitated. Present the plan to local officials. Begin a movement to mobilize public opinion in support of such an action.

ENERGY USE

Activities to Build Awareness of Energy Dependence

1. Through discussion, establish the relationship between increasing wants and needs and increased energy consumption. Find pictures from magazines to illustrate points.
2. Develop a class project to encourage energy conservation in the children's homes (turning off lights, turning down thermostats, shutting off TV and appliances not in use, and so on).
3. Prepare a bulletin board display of energy-related news stories. Through discussion, establish the importance of energy to the everyday lives of everyone.
4. Make a survey of their homes to identify energy uses that would not have been in homes fifty years ago, one hundred years ago. Discuss in terms of new demands on energy resources.
5. Secure data on sources of energy on which we depend, and construct maps, graphs, and other visuals based on the data.
6. Identify values that emphasize increased energy use and values that emphasize energy conservation.
7. Relate energy use to the production of goods and services and to standard of living.
8. Identify recreational activities that contribute to increased energy consumption and those that do not. Children can prepare displays to illustrate points.
9. Familiarize students with state and federal agencies that are concerned with energy matters.
10. Determine the relationship between energy cost and energy use. For example, what impact have higher gasoline prices had on gasoline consumption?

Take field trips to local conservation or ranger stations, fish hatcheries, farms, and local parks.

Invite speakers to class such as an environmentalist, the county agent, a ranger, an agriculture teacher from the local high school, or a member of an outdoor or recreation club.

Relate soil fertility in various ways to plant food elements and community prosperity.

Develop and exchange correspondence with children from different parts of the country, asking for firsthand information about their local conservation problems and what is being done to correct them.

Illustrate in various ways the time needed to recover resources and the impossibility of recovering some resources lost through waste.

Familiarize children with the interest and action of government (local, county, state, and national) in conservation.

Integrate conservation education of such groups as Boy and Girl Scouts, 4-H Club, Future Farmers of America, Camp Fire Boys and Girls, and other youth groups with the school program.

Place instructional emphasis on new developments in conservation through the application of scientific knowledge—new uses of resources, more productive farmland, new flood-control techniques, and new energy sources.

Conduct experiments dealing with conservation:

1. Collect runoff water and determine what it carries.
2. Discover how and why grass protects soil.
3. Demonstrate the effect of rapidly falling water on soil.
4. Test the productivity of various types of soil.

Contact various agencies that have an interest in, or dedication to, the cause of conservation for suggestions, teaching materials, or help. Such a list can be obtained from your local county agent; the Department of Natural Resources of your home state, or the U.S. Department of Agriculture Forest Service.

LAW-RELATED EDUCATION

The escalating rate of crime and youth gangs, the negative attitudes of young people and adults toward the legal system, the widespread and illegal drug traffic, and the evidence of widespread ignorance of the justice system among citizens are a few of the reasons why there is an interest in, and concern for, what has come to be called "law-related education." Law-related education seeks to help children develop an understanding of the legal and justice systems and to provide them with a functional knowledge of the operation of legal institutions. It stresses law as an essential component of social life, not as a set of abstract and theoretical concepts relating to the organization and structure of the legal system and government. Support for law-related education has come not only from educators and educational groups but from prominent jurists, the legal profession through the American Bar Association and local bar associations, political leaders, parents, and virtually every segment of responsible leadership in society.

This narrative may remind the reader of boring lessons on law and government endured in ninth-grade civics class. If so, the reader should have a sense of appreciation of the urgency for doing a more effective job on law-related education with the present generation of schoolchildren. Traditional approaches to teaching about the legal and justice systems were tied to courses in civics, history, and government. Often the learners would find little in these courses that would provide them with any practical sense of how the legal system actually operates. Learners might study the functions of the three branches of government, memorize the Preamble to the Constitution and the Bill of Rights, define a few legal terms, and know the difference between petty larceny and grand larceny, and yet be unable to relate such learning to their day-to-day living. School programs dealing with the law are often criticized because substantive content is either inappropriate or lacking altogether and because teaching methods are such that they engender no student interest in the subject. Recent thrusts in the law-related education field have attempted to correct both of these deficiencies.

The object of the school program of law-related education is not to make lawyers out of children. Nonetheless, a knowledge of the legal system and the skills associated with legal education and the practice of law are not beyond the grasp of ordinary citizens. These skills and this knowledge can no longer be reserved for those who have had legal training, namely, lawyers. When we live in a time in which aspects of the law touch our lives daily from our birth to our death, we cannot remain ignorant of its pervasive influence and uphold our responsibilities as free citizens. Accordingly, a program of law-related education should concern itself with broad goals such as the following:

1. Develop an understanding of concepts that are basic to the legal system, such as liberty, justice, fairness, toleration, power, honesty, property, equality, and responsibility.
2. Develop an understanding and appreciation of the constitutional basis of the American legal system.
3. Develop a functional knowledge of how the institutions of the legal and justice systems operate.
4. Develop an understanding of and respect for the need for a system of law and justice as prerequisite for orderly and harmonious living.

A vast number of national, regional, and local projects and centers have dealt with law-related education in recent years. Perhaps the best known are those projects conducted by the following groups:

National Street Law Institute
605 G Street, N.W.
Washington, DC 20001

Center for Civic Education
(formerly Law in a Free Society Project)
5115 Douglas Fir Drive, Suite 1
Calabasas, CA 91302

Constitutional Rights Foundation
601 South Kingsley Drive
Los Angeles, CA 90005

Special Committee on Youth for Citizenship
American Bar Association
1155 East 60th Street
Chicago, IL 60637

Key Concepts in Law-Related Education

There is no agreement on the exact list of concepts to be included in a
law-related program, but the overlap of concepts identified by various
projects is considerable. The Law in a Free Society Project (now the Center
for Civic Education) developed its program around eight basic concepts:
authority, justice, privacy, responsibility, participation, diversity, property,
freedom. These are typical and are included in most programs. Such concepts as equality, power, honesty, fairness, and others could reasonably be
subsumed in the eight listed by the Law in a Free Society Project. Instructional resources, student materials, teacher training materials, study guides,
and other related instructional materials that develop these concepts are
available through the projects and through commercial publishers.

Activities for Law-Related Education

Invite a local police officer to talk to the class about law enforcement, drug
   traffic, youth gangs, or some other real or potential problems in the
   community.

Bring in news clippings describing acts of vandalism; discuss the effects and
   costs of such behavior.

Discuss rights versus responsibilities along lines familiar to children such as
   "Can we go to the movies and talk out loud even if we disturb others?"

Research the latest legislation on drugs (upper grades). Find out if the legal
   penalties for drug abuse are the same for adults as for juveniles.

Take a field trip to a court, the state legislature, or a city council meeting.

Find out how a jury is selected. Invite someone who has recently served on a
   jury to speak to the class about the responsibilities and duties of jurors.

Relate rules and laws to personal safety. For primary grades this could include moving to and from school, bicycle safety, and safety in the neighborhood. For older children this could be extended to laws relating to trespass, vehicle use, drug and alcohol use, assault, and other activities that are at the edge of experience of preadolescents.

Find examples of advertisements from magazines, newspapers, radio, and television that could be interpreted as being deceptive. Relate this to consumer protection laws. Find out about agencies that deal with consumer protection.

Make use of whatever services are provided the school by local law enforcement agencies and the local bar association.

With the help of a local attorney, *have students discuss the accuracy* of a law-related television program (upper grades).

Develop classroom rules of conduct, and discuss the need for rules (laws) in group life.

Conduct a mock trial in the upper grades.

Discuss citizens' rights and responsibilities in terms of specific cases that appear in the news.

List legal needs of their community at the beginning of the twentieth century. List legal needs of their community today. Discuss differences, and have children explain why legal needs have changed.

Study the structure and functions of local community government, and relate them to the daily lives of the people who live there.

Develop appropriate activities in connection with "Law Day USA," observed each year on May 1. Write to Law Day USA, American Bar Association, 8th Floor, 750 North Lake Shore Drive, Chicago, IL 60611, or telephone (312) 988-6140 to receive information about Law Day USA.

MULTICULTURAL EDUCATION AND ETHNIC HERITAGE STUDIES

In chapter 1, we discussed at some length the changing demographic composition of this nation and some implications of this change for social studies education. The question of what constitutes an appropriate emphasis on multicultural education is a matter of present controversy. Attention usually focuses on extreme positions resulting in what James Banks describes as strident voices that "rarely engage in reflective dialog. Rather, scholars on each side of the debate marshall data to support their briefs and ignore facts, interpretations, and perspectives that are inconsistent with their positions and visions of the present and future."[3] If one were to take

---

[3]James A. Banks, "Multicultural Education: For Freedom's Sake," *Educational Leadership* 49 (December 1991/January 1992): 32.

seriously the rhetoric of some, one would conclude that the most important defining attribute of American citizens is their ethnic origin. For others, only the study of Western civilization seems relevant to citizenship education. In contrast to these extreme positions, the statement of Governor Mario M. Cuomo of New York is one that many teachers and parents would accept as a sensible approach to multicultural education:

> For all of our differences over ideology, politics, and ethnicity, most Americans are not as far apart on the dry substance of multicultural education as many in the current debate imply. Between the extreme of using our educational system to foster an "ethnicity first" identity and the opposite extreme of denying any diversity, is a wide area of generally accepted common ground and common sense. Most Americans can understand both the need to recognize and encourage an enriched diversity as well as the need to ensure that such a broadened multicultural perspective leads to unity and an enriched sense of what being an American is, and not to destructive factionalism that would tear us apart.[4]

There can be no question that regardless of one's ethnic origins, when and how one came to this country, or one's racial identity, the American experience has had a powerful influence on each one of us as individual human beings. Although we no longer embrace a melting pot ideology, there is, nonetheless, something in the interaction between and among the land, the people, the democratic political system, the market-driven economic system, and the freedom of the individual to make choices that has fashioned this unique human being we call an American. The imprint is so indelible and so noticeable that, regardless of ethnic origin or racial identity, an American is easily identified anywhere in the world and is clearly distinguishable even from his or her closest non-American genetic relatives.

Multicultural education and ethnic heritage studies should be directed toward the ultimate goal of improving the quality of human relations in this country. This purpose has become increasingly important since we have shifted our conception of American society from the traditional melting pot ideology to one of pluralism. Many implications may be found in this shift for all of education and most especially for the social studies. Race and racism remain serious problems for this society, and many believe that multicultural education and ethnic heritage studies will help combat some of the evils that flow from racism and racist practices. Ethnic heritage studies are also intended to acquaint young people with the multiethnic composition of this society to help them become more fully aware of who they are as individuals and as a nation.

The society of the United States is multicultural, multisocial class, multiracial, and multiethnic. Consequently, considerable confusion over ter-

---

[4]Governor Mario M. Cuomo, statement issued July 10, 1991, following release of the report of the New York State Social Studies Review and Development Committee on multicultural education. Cited in *Education Week*, September 25, 1991, p. 26.

minology and meanings occurs when discussing issues relating to the pluralistic character of this society. Social class groups have to do with grouping individuals on the basis of income, occupation, lifestyles, and, in the case of the upper classes, family background. These are status groups and represent a hierarchical arrangement from high to low on some basis of preference. Racial groups result from genetically transmitted physical characteristics that are innate and immutable. They are often visibly different from other groups on the basis of physical qualities. Ethnic groups, on the other hand, are formed on the basis of common cultural variables such as language, customs, religion, nationality, traditions, and history that give some groups a sense of "peoplehood." It should be clear that socioeconomic level or social class membership has nothing whatever to do with one's ethnic identity. All ethnic groups have individuals who are wealthy and those who are poor; all have individuals in upper social classes and those in lower social classes.

Race and ethnicity are often confused because in some cases they overlap. For example, the Japanese have physical characteristics that identify them as an Asian racial group. At the same time, the Japanese people have a language, tradition, common heritage, and history that give them an ethnic identity. A blond European baby boy who, at the moment of birth, was adopted and raised by a Japanese family would as an adult be ethnically Japanese in spite of his physical (racial) characteristics that he inherited from his European ancestors. Perhaps it would be difficult for such an individual to be fully assimilated by the Japanese society because of clearly differing physical characteristics. This is because negative social values are being associated with physical characteristics. This is an obvious illustration of *racism*, which is the practice of attaching nonphysical characteristics to physical qualities of human beings. It should also be obvious that this practice has been and continues to be quite common in the United States. *Race and racism are problems not because of the reality of physical differences between human beings but because there are social values attached to those differences.*

This country is exceptional among the nations of the world because it is composed of representatives or their descendants of almost all the world's many cultures. In terms of ethnic heritage, we are among the most diverse people on earth. But Americans vary greatly in the extent to which they retain their ethnic identity. Many have no knowledge or even interest in their forebears. Others lack a clear ethnic identity because of intermarriage, name changes, and migrations. Others may be nominally members of an identified ethnic group but do little more than attend a once-a-year picnic of such groups as Sons of Norway. Still others are more active in retaining their ethnicity by maintaining a fluency in the language of their ancestors, observing traditional holidays associated with their ethnic group, continuing traditional church affiliations, and so on. A small group remains totally immersed in its ethnic culture, as for example the Navajo people. Thus, the level of enthusiasm for ethnic heritage studies can vary greatly from one individual to another, and attempts to impose interest in such studies are not likely to be productive or even desirable.

The major purposes of multicultural education and ethnic heritage studies ought to be along the lines of the following:

1. To present truthful accounts of the multiethnic composition of this society.
2. To develop a sense of pride in the multiethnic and multicultural heritages of this nation.
3. To develop a respect for the contributions of all groups to the life and culture of this nation.
4. To develop harmonious social relations resulting from the use of acceptable methods of resolving social conflicts.
5. To develop a reasoned pride in one's own ethnic heritage.
6. To understand that much of the strength of this nation derives from the diversity of its ethnic heritages and cultural origins.
7. To develop an understanding of and an appreciation for the imprint that the American experience has had on *all* citizens regardless of cultural, racial, or ethnic origins.

Multicultural education and ethnic heritage studies should be firmly rooted in the local community but should not be limited to the study of ethnic groups of the local area. A broad spectrum of ethnic groups should be represented in the program so as to present social reality as accurately as possible. Much of the content of ethnic studies is affectively toned, and thus it can be expected that providing knowledge alone is not likely to be very powerful in achieving the goals of ethnic education. Activities need to be planned that will engender positive feelings toward others.

Ethnic studies can be interesting and enriching and can do much to build social cohesiveness by helping all children gain a better understanding of the diverse people we really are. There is much of which we, as a nation, can be proud that comes as a direct consequence of our multicultural backgrounds. However, there is a potential danger that such studies may contribute to social disunity and the development of ethnocentric attitudes. If ethnic studies are allowed to become rallying grounds for the advocacy of political and social goals of specific ethnic groups, if groups become polarized over issues that are ethnically based, or if these studies become politicized, they can do little to enhance human relations. It must be emphasized that there are common values that we embrace as a nation that are shared by all individuals and groups regardless of their cultural or ethnic identity. The concept of "one Nation under God, indivisible, with liberty and justice for all" must be made a reality if the nation is to escape internal conflict and strife of untold proportions.

Instructional resources for teaching multicultural education and ethnic heritage studies are available in generous amounts from many suppliers. The Council on Interracial Books for Children (1841 Broadway, New York, NY 10023) produces many materials useful to teachers, as does the National Council for the Social Studies (3501 Newark Street, N.W., Washington, DC 20016), and the Anti-Defamation League of B'nai B'rith (345 East 46 Street, New York, NY 10017).

Activities for Multicultural Education and Ethnic Heritage Studies

Research contemporary groups that have been organized because of particular ethnic identities. Discover their purpose and identify their leaders, if possible.

Make a scrapbook of outstanding individuals in an ethnic group. Include their accomplishments and what they have contributed to the whole society, to their ethnic group, and to the individual.

Read a fiction book in which the main character is a member of a minority ethnic group. Have a discussion about the main character with another person who has read the book or with the teacher. How was the life of the main character affected by his or her ethnic background?

Create puppets and act out a folktale or legend from a particular ethnic culture.

Write a newspaper article advocating the position of an ethnic group in a conflict situation, such as an Indian tribe in its land or fishing disputes.

Find out about class's own ethnic origins. Show on a world map where their ancestors came from. Discuss this in terms of the areas of the world represented in the class. Study settlement patterns in the United States of various immigrant groups. (Note: *Activities such as this one or studies of family genealogy ought always to be optional. Some parents and children do not wish to divulge personal family information, and their wishes must be respected.*)

Learn folk songs and folk dances of various ethnic groups.

Prepare a bulletin board or other displays that show the contributions of various ethnic groups to American life and culture. Have children bring newspaper clippings and photographs of various ethnic groups in the news.

Use the local telephone directory to find names that can be identified with a particular ethnic group, for example, French, Irish, German, Chinese, Slavic, Scandinavian. Try to detect a pattern in terms of the dominance of any group. Check also the yellow pages to find out which ethnic restaurants are found locally. If possible, compare data found in the local telephone directory with that found in a directory of a city in some other part of the country.

Invite representatives of various ethnic groups in the community to your class. Ask them about their cultural roots. Have them discuss their language and customs. Inquire about their connections, if any, with the homeland of their forebears.

Encourage children to view television programs or listen to radio broadcasts of ethnic groups in the local area.

Visit museums that display exhibits, artifacts, and collections of materials from ethnic groups of the community and state.

Learn about holidays and festivals of ethnic groups in the community.

Conduct a survey of the school or the local area to find out the number of different languages spoken and identify each.

Survey the community to find places of business or service groups (food stores, funeral homes, specialty shops, churches) that cater to particular ethnic groups.

Study local community history to discover what ethnic groups first settled there, what groups came later, and what traces of their occupance are imprinted on the community.[5]

STUDIES IN SEXUAL EQUITY

In August 1920 the Nineteenth Amendment to the Constitution became the law of the land, and thereby women were given the right to vote, a right enjoyed by most white free men since the founding of the Republic. The discrimination against women, however, did not end with the Nineteenth Amendment. The evidence is clear that women have not achieved full status with men in the business and professional worlds, in education, in political affairs, or in any field that has been traditionally dominated by men. For a variety of reasons, the traditional roles of men and women in society have undergone great changes in the second half of the twentieth century, resulting in the emancipation of women. The independence of women, which without question is one of the most significant social developments of our time, has many implications for social studies education in the elementary and middle schools.

Many believe that school programs of the past actually contributed to discrimination against women because they reinforced conventional sex roles that emphasized male superiority. Where this can be studied with a degree of objectivity, as, for example, in analyzing school textbooks, the evidence is overwhelming that males had a clear advantage. They have been consistently represented in positions of greater prestige and as being more courageous, more clever, more witty, and more skillful than women. Women tended to be represented in subservient positions and most generally in social-service roles or in roles that require serving men, as, for example, secretarial service and nursing. Thus, discrimination against women became institutionalized in that both boys *and* girls came to believe in the superiority of the male. Much of such blatant sexist portrayal does

---

[5]For a more complete treatment of multicultural education, see James A. Banks, *Teaching Strategies for Ethnic Studies*, 5th ed. (Boston: Allyn & Bacon, 1991); and Donna M. Gollnick and Philip C. Chinn, *Multicultural Education in a Pluralistic Society*, 3d ed. (Columbus, OH: Merrill, 1990).

not now appear in recently published textbooks and other instructional material.

Discrimination on the basis of sex is explicitly forbidden by several pieces of federal legislation, the best known being Titles VI and VII of the Civil Rights Act of 1964, and Title IX of the Education Amendments of 1972. Title IX deals with discrimination in education, and the intent of the law is made clear by its opening statement:

> No person in the United States shall on the basis of sex be excluded from participation in, be denied the benefits of, or be subjected to discrimination under any education program or activity receiving Federal financial assistance . . .

Because nearly all schools receive federal financial assistance in some form, the law is for all practical purposes universal. In addition to these federal laws, many state laws and constitutions prohibit discrimination.

There is much greater awareness of sex-role stereotyping now than there was even a decade ago, and many of the practices that contribute to this attitude are being eliminated. The contributions of women to the life, culture, and development of this nation are becoming more visible in the curriculum and in learning resources. Women are seen in prestigious occupations as being coequal with men. Men and women are shown sharing responsibilities associated with maintaining a household, caring for children, and providing family income. Other forms of invidious distinctions between men and women are being eradicated from the printed and visual material used by children in school.

These changes obviously represent great gains for women in broadening the potential for their self-fulfillment. What is often overlooked is that it does the same for men. Both sexes will have greater opportunity for choice if neither male nor female role is stereotyped. This applies not only to career choices but to leisure-time activities, hobbies, reading interests, school activities, sports, and, indeed, all other aspects of life except those specifically limited by biological differences between the sexes.

Major Goals of Sexual Equity Education

A major overall goal of the socialization of American children is that of engendering values and attitudes based on principles of equality among human beings. Many groups and institutions in the community contribute to the achievement of this goal, including the family, religious institutions, and the school. Regrettably, children may receive mixed signals regarding sexual equity from these socializing agencies. Be that as it may, sexism and sex-role stereotyping are forms of discrimination because they are the result of arbitrary judgments based on the sex (or more correctly, the *gender*) of the individual. Social studies programs have a responsibility to combat the formation of such values and attitudes because they are contrary to the goals and purposes of the school curriculum and are contrary to the ideals and laws of the nation. Instruction in sexual equity should be directed toward the attainment of goals along such lines as these:

1. To develop a sensitivity in children to the stereotyping of males and females along the lines of occupations, home life, lifestyles, community life, recreation, and other life choices.
2. To learn about the contributions of both men and women to American life and culture, especially in areas that have traditionally been closed to one or the other of the sexes.
3. To have children become aware of the nature and impact of sex bias in all walks of life and have them become familiar with some of the more obvious examples of sex bias and inequities based on sex.
4. To stress the importance of providing both sexes with the right of *choice* in directing the affairs of their lives and in considering career options.
5. To gain an understanding of sex roles in terms of physiological and biological differences between males and females on the one hand and in terms of gender distinctions influenced by cultural beliefs on the other.

Activities for Sexual Equity Education

Compare and contrast roles of men, women, boys, and girls in an earlier historical period, such as in Colonial times, with those same roles today. Similarly, compare and contrast those roles in other cultures with those in the United States. Discuss reasons for such differences. Have children provide reasons why roles change.

List as many different behaviors associated with males and females that are based on customs and traditions (e.g., ladies first, women wear dresses and men do not, and so on). Have children speculate on how these customs may have originated. Discuss items on the list in terms of changes that may be taking place in them.

Generate a list of different tasks members of the family do at home. Have children identify the person best able to do each task. Discuss whether the task could be performed by other members of the family.

Ask children to bring to school pictures from magazines or newspapers of men and women engaging in various occupations. Post these on the bulletin board in terms of those almost always performed by men and those almost always performed by women, and those performed by either. Discuss reasons why some occupations attract men, others attract women, and others are attractive to both men and women.

In a brainstorming session have children name as many important people in American history—living or dead—as they can think of in a ten-minute period. Write the names on the chalkboard. Then have the class group the individuals on some self-determined criteria (occupation, ethnic or racial minority, living or dead, men or women, and so on). Note discrepancy between the number of men and the number of women. Speculate on why this is so. Conduct an inquiry to test their hypotheses.

In the middle and upper grades, *have learners investigate* the daily lives of ordinary women one hundred to two hundred years ago; what they did;

their roles in family life; and their contributions to their home, family, and communities.

Read children's biographies of prominent women who have championed the cause of sexual equity.

Invite men and women who have made nontraditional career choices (e.g., male nurses, female airline pilots) to speak to the class about their experiences in pursuing their career goals.

CHILD ABUSE, AIDS, DRUG ABUSE, AND YOUTH GANGS

Child abuse, AIDS, drug abuse, and youth gangs are the great social tragedies of our time. Schools share in the responsibility with the rest of society for turning the tide against these scourges that are destroying the lives of so many of our nation's people. Because these problems have severe social consequences, it can be expected that the social studies curriculum will give some serious attention to them. These topics are so intensely sensitive that the way they are handled in schools has to be guided by policies generated and approved at the local and state levels.

It is a mistake to think of educating children about child abuse, AIDS, drug abuse, and youth gangs as the sole responsibility of any single area of the curriculum, such as health, science, or social studies. The entire school program needs to be infused with concepts and information regarding these social problems as appropriate for each of the various curriculum areas. In addition to such infusion, schools will need to provide some systematic instruction specifically targeted on these topics each year the child is in school, K–12. It can be presumed that some of these instructional units would be incorporated in the social studies program. The teacher is advised to seek assistance at the local level regarding policies and programs dealing with these problems.

DISCUSSION QUESTIONS AND SUGGESTED ACTIVITIES

1. What is *your* view of the role of global education in the schools, and how does it compare with that expressed in this chapter? If you were making a case for it to the school board, what would be the main points in your rationale?

2. Visit the curriculum library on your campus, and examine some of the newer materials related to the topics included in this chapter.

3. How are *racism* and *ethnocentrism* alike, and how are they different? What danger does each present in terms of desirable human relations?

4. How do you define *ethnicity?* Are all ethnic groups also minority groups?

5. What resource persons in the local community might be of help in teaching the topics included in this chapter?

6. Provide specific examples of how social studies topics in a grade in which you have a special interest can be studied from a global perspective.

7. Select one of the key ideas listed on pages 234–235, and show by a short example how it could be taught meaningfully to children in each grade of the elementary or middle school.

8. Locate a photograph relating to an environmental problem. Prepare six interpretation and analysis questions (see chapter 4) based on the photograph.

9. The inclusion of energy and environmental education, the world of work, law-related education, and multicultural education in the social studies curriculum is being challenged by a parent at a public meeting. If you were asked to respond to such a concern, what points would you make?

10. Explain how topics discussed in this chapter relate to the goals for social studies education listed in chapter 1.

11. Some parents, for religious or other reasons, object to the teaching of sexual equity. How do you define your boundaries of responsibility in dealing with this topic while at the same time respecting the right of parents to believe as they do?

12. In your view, what can social studies programs contribute to the education of children about AIDS that is different from that provided in science or health classes? At what age do you think such education should begin, and how explicit should the instruction be? Acquaint yourself with local and state policies in your community regarding these issues. Also, familiarize yourself with local and state regulations regarding the teacher's responsibility in cases of suspected child abuse and suspected drug use by schoolchildren.

SUGGESTED REFERENCES

BANKS, JAMES A. *Teaching Strategies for Ethnic Studies.* 5th ed. Boston: Allyn & Bacon, 1991.

Educational Leadership 49 (December 1991/January 1992). Entire issue focuses on multicultural education.

ENGLE, SHIRLEY H., AND ANNA S. OCHOA. *Education for Democratic Citizenship.* New York: Teachers College Press, 1988.

EVANS, CHARLES S. "Teaching a Global Perspective in Elementary Classrooms." *The Elementary School Journal* 87 (May 1987): 545–55.

GOLLNICK, DONNA M., AND PHILIP C. CHINN. *Multicultural Education in a Pluralistic Society.* 3d ed. Columbus, OH: Merrill, 1990.

HAHN, CAROLE L. "Controversial Issues in Social Studies." In *Handbook of Research on Social Studies Teaching and Learning*, edited by James P. Shaver, 470–80. New York: Macmillan, 1991.

KING, EDITH W. *Teaching Ethnic and Gender Awareness*. Dubuque, IA: Kendall/Hunt, 1990.

LYNCH, JAMES. *Multicultural Education in a Gobal Society*. London: Falmer, 1989.

NATIONAL WOMEN'S HISTORY PROJECT. *Catalog*. For a free copy, write to the project at 7738 Bell Road, Windsor, CA 95492-8518.

NICKELL, PAT, AND MIKE KENNEDY. "Global Perspectives Through Children's Games." How To Do It series 5, no. 3. Washington, DC: National Council for the Social Studies, 1987.

MERRYFIELD, MERRY. *Teaching About the World: Teacher Education Programs with a Global Perspective*. Columbus, OH: Mershon Center, 1990.

RAVITCH, DIANE. "A Culture in Common." *Educational Leadership* 49 (December 1991/January 1992): 8–11.

TYE, KENNETH A., ed. *Global Education: From Thought to Action*. 1991 ASCD Yearbook. Alexandria, VA: Association for Supervision and Curriculum Development, 1991.

VOCKE, DAVID E. "Those Varying Perspectives on Global Education." *The Social Studies* 79 (January/February 1988): 18–20.

WOYACH, ROBERT B., AND RICHARD C. REMY. *Approaches to World Studies*. Boston: Allyn & Bacon, 1989.

ZARNOWSKI, MYRA. "Learning about Contemporary Women: Sharing Biographies with Children." *The Social Studies* 79 (March/April 1988): 61–63.

9 | Using Current Events in the Social Studies

> "But they can't *do* that! It's against the Constitution!"
>
> "What Constitution?"
>
> "The *United States* Constitution!"
>
> "What does the United States Constitution have to do with it?"
>
> "I don't know; but it just doesn't seem right. If a person has some land with some trees on it, he shouldn't have to get permission from the Ecology Department to cut them. They're *his*."

This lively exchange took place between a boy and a girl in a fifth-grade class as a result of a story in the local newspaper under the headline shown in Figure 9–1.

The teacher brought this article to class because it dealt with an issue of local interest that had been in the news for several weeks and because it illustrated so well the conflict between individual rights and community values, something the class had been dealing with in social studies. The example also illustrates how the use of current events can add vitality and meaning to what might otherwise seem to be abstract and remote concepts. Although these children may not have the facts of the case straight, it is obvious that they have strong feelings about the issue. This discussion has motivated them to get additional information, and their teacher can help them and their classmates get the facts they need.

The point of view to be developed in this chapter is that the program of current events is a matter of importance in the school program and, as such, requires careful planning and teaching. Children cannot be subjected to several years of boring experiences with current events in school and leave convinced that they have any responsibility to keep themselves informed on the affairs of the world. It is not easy to persuade children of the importance of current events if during news sharing the teacher takes roll, collects lunch money, completes plans for another lesson, or does other things about the room that draw full attention from the news reports. The

FIGURE 9–1

COURT STOPS FURTHER TREE REMOVAL
Orders Environmental Impact Statement

Opponents to the clearing of land on the Richards's property succeeded in getting a court order to stop the tree removal until a study is done to determine the environmental impact of such cutting.

The owner, Charles Richards has insisted that he has a legal right to harvest the timber on his property. The local . . .

teacher could not successfully teach mathematics, reading, or spelling in this way, and there is no reason to believe that current events can be taught with success that way either.

If the nation expects its adults to have an abiding interest in news and current developments and have a desire to keep informed, the groundwork for these attitudes, interests, and skills must be laid in the elementary school. The first major purpose of current events teaching at the elementary school level is, therefore, *to promote interest in current events and news developments.*

Intelligent analysis of current events requires the use of a variety of skills and abilities: (1) to read news materials, (2) to discriminate between important and less significant news items, (3) to take a position on issues based on a knowledge and a critical evaluation of the facts, and (4) to predict likely consequences in terms of present developments. *Promoting the growth of these skills and abilities represents the second major purpose of current events instruction at the elementary school level.* These skills evolve over several years through the study of current events under the direction and guidance of capable teachers. It is unrealistic to hope for an adult population that can exercise critical judgment regarding social problems and issues unless individuals have at their command the fundamental skills and abilities such action demands.

The third major purpose of current events teaching is *to help the child relate school learning to life outside school.* The constant reference to current events is good insurance against the separation of school activities from the nonacademic life of the child. Good teachers recognize that printed material begins to become obsolete shortly after it is written, and there is always a gap between the information contained in books and changing developments in the world. A generous use of current events materials helps to close this gap. Some encyclopedia publishers recognize the need for timely information and issue annual supplements that include changes that have occurred during the preceding year. Because textbooks and supplementary books usually are not revised each year, teachers must depend on such sources as newspapers and magazines for the latest information on some topics.

THE PROGRAM OF CURRENT EVENTS INSTRUCTION

The three most common methods of including current events in the elementary school program are (1) teaching current events in addition to social studies, (2) using current events to supplement or reinforce the regular social studies program, and (3) using current events as the basis for social studies units. A discussion of each of these methods follows.

Teaching Current Events in Addition to Social Studies

Ms. Hansen, who teachs fourth grade, plans to spend a few minutes each morning during the sharing period for the discussion of important news stories. She encourages children to bring news clippings from daily newspapers or from weekly magazines for the class bulletin board. Children are encouraged to bring news stories related to classroom work, and Ms. Hansen helps interpret these stories for the children by her comments and leading questions, such as

"How do you suppose the new highway will help our town?"

"What are the explorers looking for on these expeditions?"

"Why do you suppose the animals died when they were brought here?"

"Can you show the class on the map the exact location of the new airport?"

Ms. Hansen uses a classroom periodical and plans to spend a half hour on it with the children each week. This consists of reading the material or portions of it, with a discussion following. She varies the procedure from week to week and uses the suggestions provided in the teacher's edition that accompanies the classroom periodical.

This method has the advantage of providing a regularly scheduled time for news each day. Such periods can be useful in building interest in current events and in teaching skills of reading and interpreting news stories. It has the clear disadvantage of isolating current affairs from the remainder of the school program, most especially from the social studies. If current events teaching is handled as is done by Ms. Hansen in the example, time should be taken to relate news content to topics and units in social studies. This can be done by (1) interpreting news stories within the context of topics that have been studied or are under study; (2) extending the meaning of concepts developed in social studies; (3) applying social studies skills, such as map, graph, or chart reading to the news stories; or (4) comparing and contrasting events in the news with events encountered in social studies units.

Using Current Events to Supplement or Reinforce the Regular Social Studies Program

Mr. Ray schedules his social studies period immediately following morning opening activities for his fifth-grade class. As a part of the beginning activities, he provides time for reporting of news and encourages children to report news items related to social studies. He and his class maintain a news bulletin board as well as a small table on which are placed news articles, magazines, current maps, or similar materials of a timely nature related to the social studies unit. He uses current events materials in this way to augment other instructional resources and as a means of reminding his class of the need for up-to-date information.

Mr. Ray often suggests parallels between events that happened long ago and events that are occurring today, thereby illustrating recurrent problems in the conduct of human affairs. For example, in the study of the struggle for freedom and independence in America, he used examples from present-day affairs to show that some people of the world are still struggling for the right to govern themselves. When the class studied early explorers, Mr. Ray related this study to present-day exploration. In the unit on the Westward Movement, he called the attention of the class to current population movements and trends in the United States.

The difference between this method and the one used by Ms. Hansen is that Mr. Ray is more explicit in making the connection between current events and social studies. He is concerned mainly with those news stories that can be related to his social studies program. He builds an awareness of the relationship between what is currently happening in the world and what the class is studying in social studies. He is using the affairs of the world as reported in the news media as a current information source for social studies. This method has the advantage of keeping the information base for social studies up-to-date. It has the disadvantage of restricting the range of news stories that are appropriate. Therefore, if this approach is used, the teacher should provide some opportunity to examine news items that are significant and timely, yet may not be directly related to the social studies unit under study at the time.

Using Current Events as the Basis for Social Studies Units

Ms. Diaz likes to develop social studies units with her sixth-grade class around topics that are currently in the news. She schedules these between the regular units she is required to teach. During her years as a teacher, she has found that units of this type must be carefully selected because it is not always possible to find a sufficient amount of instructional material suitable for children that deals with topics in the news. Units that she has taught with success in this way in the past have dealt with alliances, such as NATO; meeting our needs for oil; migration of the world's people as a result of news of newcomers to the United States; twentieth-century explorers; progress in science, medicine, and industry; and elections. When Ms. Diaz selects the unit topics carefully, she finds it possible to include much of the subject matter ordinarily included in her social studies curriculum under other unit titles. She believes that the use of current news happenings as a starting point for units does much to stimulate interest and discussion in her class.

This method has the advantage of being highly motivating because it deals with subject matter that is of immediate interest. It also bridges school learning with life outside of school. It has the disadvantage of being difficult to plan because news events may not relate directly to the social studies curriculum. Also, news stories may not provide a continuing or sustaining source of information on topics, and, therefore, other sources would need to be available. This method works best for short, minitype units as described in the example rather than as a structure for the entire social studies program.

TEACHING CURRENT EVENTS SUCCESSFULLY

Any of the three current events programs described here can be used successfully. In good programs there will be time during the school day devoted to the study and discussion of current affairs that may be entirely unrelated to topics under study in the social studies units, and perhaps unrelated to any other curricular area as well. At the same time, in guiding unit work, the teacher will not ignore current events relating to the topic being studied but will, in fact, seek with enthusiasm the current events materials that will add strength to the unit. From time to time, too, the teacher and children can plan an entire social studies unit from current news developments. Units dealing with the topics of energy, environment, safety, intercultural relations, law and justice, housing, food, elections, discoveries in science, and items of local news may, and frequently do, grow out of current events. When the social studies program includes these three methods, the teacher and class will use any or all of the procedures described in the following sections.

Daily Discussion of News

Children enjoy discussing the news and should be given the opportunity to do so within the school program. It is a fairly common procedure for classes to have a morning meeting or sharing period at the beginning of each school day, during which time the children can report news items. Children in the primary grades frequently report only news that affects them directly: Daddy took a business trip, the family has a new baby, the pet cat had kittens, or other similar items of "news." As children mature, they move away from news items that are of concern only to them personally to news of more general interest.

In reporting, discussing, and analyzing daily news occurrences, elementary schoolchildren frequently report the sensational headline news that may or may not be particularly significant. Without guidance, children are likely to report murders or robberies or hold postmortems on the previous night's television programs. The teacher should help children evaluate the importance of news stories and teach them to discriminate between significant news and the sensational.

In general, the practice of reporting news should be encouraged by the teacher rather than be required. Some teachers require children to bring a news clipping on specified days. This usually means a hurried breakfast for the child while Mother peruses the morning or evening paper hoping to find a suitable item that she can explain to the child before the child leaves for school. A better procedure is to build the children's interest in news to the extent that they voluntarily bring news clippings that they believe are important enough to bring to school. Similarly, in the reporting of news items, on some days there will be many items and much discussion; other days there may be none. The teacher must bear in mind that the purpose of this procedure is to *develop the children's interest* in current events and that this is usually not done by requiring children to spend specified amounts of time on news whether the content justifies the time or not.

As children approach the middle and upper grades, they will not only report news events but will also begin to include issues on which there are conflicting points of view. This should be encouraged, and eventually the emphasis can be placed almost entirely on problems and issues rather than on simple events. The movement from the consideration of simple events to simple issues to complex issues is a gradual one for the child.

There can be no doubt that the social studies teacher has a responsibility to include controversial issues in the current events–social studies curriculum. In so doing, the teacher has a strong ally in the National Council for the Social Studies. An NCSS policy statement on the subject reads in part as follows:

> It is the prime responsibility of the schools to help students assume the responsibilities of democratic citizenship. To do this, education must impart the skills needed for intelligent study and orderly resolution of the problems inherent in a democratic society. Students need to study issues upon which there is disagreement and to practice analyzing problems, gathering and organizing facts, discriminating between facts and opinions, discussing differing viewpoints, and drawing tentative conclusions. It is the clear obligation of schools to promote full and free contemplation of controversial issues and to foster appreciation of the role of controversy as an instrument of progress in a democracy.[1]

In teaching controversial issues, the teacher has a special responsibility to help children develop habits of critical judgment and open-mindedness, to evaluate sources of information, and to appraise the soundness of facts. Young children are impressionable, and the habit of insisting on getting multiple sides of a question before taking a stand can be taught to youngsters by the teacher's example. There has been some discussion of the necessity of keeping the teacher's stand on issues unknown to the children. This is not possible or entirely desirable. To be sure, the teacher does not begin the discussion of an issue by stating his or her own bias to the class. It is the teacher's responsibility to see that all sides of the issue being discussed are presented fairly and impartially and that the reasons underlying points of view are thoroughly aired. If the class requests the teacher's own views on an issue, it is clearly the teacher's right to express them and to state the reasons for the position taken. The professional obligation remains, however, not to attempt to impose a personal point of view on the children on issues that are unsettled and on which there may be honest differences of opinion among well-informed persons. In such cases, the teacher should encourage children to discuss the matter with other adults whom they respect whose views may be different. The child thus learns that there may be honest differences of opinion among intelligent, well-educated persons who consider problems in good faith. The children will respect the teacher who is willing to take a stand on issues, who gives reasons for the position taken, and who accepts and honors the differences in points of view of others.

---

[1]"Academic Freedom and the Social Studies Teacher" (a policy statement of the National Council for the Social Studies), published in C. Benjamin Cox, *The Censorship Game and How to Play It*, Bulletin No. 50 (Washington, DC: National Council for the Social Studies, 1977), 42.

Teaching Suggestions for Controversial Issues

The news story shown in Figure 9–1 is a good example of the types of controversial issues that can be found in nearly all communities, large or small. Here are a few other examples:

Whether to

- Allow an area to be rezoned for a shopping center.
- Permit freeway construction through a residential or farming area.
- Close an elementary school.
- Build an athletic stadium.
- Allow a golf course to be built.
- Pass a dog leash ordinance.
- Allow animals to be used for medical research.
- Allow certain forms of gambling.
- Restrict trash burning.
- Construct a new hospital.

These issues present good opportunities for teaching how to deal with controversy. A teacher might proceed as follows:

1. Have the children identify the facts of the case. In an examination of the airport news story (Figure 9–2), some of the facts are these:

   a. Jet aircraft produce objectionable noise.
   b. A sizable number of homeowners are disturbed over the noise level.
   c. The homeowners are insisting that the Airport Commission do something about the problem.
   d. The homeowners have engaged an attorney to represent them.
   e. The noise problem reduces the possibility of sale of the homes in the affected area.
   f. Money for the purchase of the homes by the Airport Commission is not now available.
   g. Modern urban areas must have conveniently located jet plane air service.

   In identifying facts, it is important not to confuse them with opinions or with issues. For example, one would need further documentation that the noise "is endangering the health of residents" as is claimed in the story. Also, it is *not* a fact that the only solution to the problem is the purchase of the homes by the commission.

2. Have students identify the *issues* in the case. In looking for issues, one is seeking to find out why there is a problem. Usually, this involves conflicts of values. In the airport case, for example, the following are some of the issues:

   a. Is it possible to locate metropolitan airports completely away from residential areas?
   b. Have the dollar values of these homes been reduced because of the airport location?

FIGURE 9–2

HOMEOWNERS PROTEST AIRCRAFT NOISE

More than two hundred irate homeowners jammed the chambers of the Metropolitan Airport Commission last evening to protest noise from jets at the International Airport. Property owners are demanding that the commission secure funds to purchase homes immediately adjacent to the airport. They insist that the noise has reached a level that is intolerable and that it is endangering the health of residents.

"When a plane flies over our home, all conversation must stop," claimed one resident. Similar complaints were made by other homeowners. "It is impossible for us to conduct instruction when planes fly overhead," said Brian Sorokin, a teacher at Stevens School, located near the airport.

Marvin Sherwin, attorney for the homeowners, said his group would resort to legal action if appropriate measures are not taken immediately by the Airport Commission. He could foresee no satisfactory solution to the problem short of clearing the area of homes. "These families bought their homes without knowing that an international airport was to be placed next door to them," he said. "They cannot sell their homes and they cannot live with the present noise level. The commission must deal with this problem," he added.

Members of the Airport Commission refused comment except to say that the problem is a serious one and that funds were not presently available for the mass evacuation being proposed by the residents. Robert Randall, chairman of the commission, said he did not know whether federal monies are available for such removals, but that "all possibilities would be explored."

---

   c. Should the homes of those residents who moved into the area *after* the airport was in operation be purchased?

   d. How can the residents insist on the commission's purchasing their homes when there is no money available?

   e. Who should bear the cost of the purchase of the homes? The local taxpayers? Travelers who use the airport? The airline companies whose planes make the noise? The federal government?

   f. Does a public facility that results in a nuisance to nearby residents require that the homeowners be paid for damages?

   g. How severe must the nuisance be before a claim can be justified?

3. Have students identify alternative solutions to the problem and list the consequences of each alternative. In this type of analysis it is not necessary to come to consensus as to the best solution. In the airport case, these alternatives might be proposed:

PROPOSALS	CONSEQUENCES
a. Reduce jet noise by reducing landing and takeoff speeds.	a. May not be safe; would not solve the problem completely.
b. Develop less noisy jet engines.	b. Would take too long to develop quieter engines. May not be possible to develop such engines.
c. Relocate the airport.	c. Would be very costly. Would simply move the problem somewhere else.
d. Purchase homes and relocate only those residents who owned their property before the airport location was established.	d. Does not solve the problem for the remaining residents. It is unfair and probably not legal.
e. Purchase all homes in the affected area.	e. Would require huge sums of money not now available. Would establish a precedent for other cases of a public facility creating a nuisance.
f. Do nothing.	f. Commission would be subject to legal action and would eventually have to do what the court directs rather than making the decision themselves. Would generate additional public ill will.

Cases such as this lend themselves well to role playing and simulation. For example, some children could play the parts of the commission members, the homeowners, the attorney, the teacher, and others. The information could be secured by the students from the point of view of the role they are playing. If a local issue is the focus of the study, children can get information from the community by interviewing individuals, researching background information on the problem, and through local news stories. If the airport case were used, the teacher would need to provide data for the various roles. For example, each player or group of players would receive information prepared by the teacher such as:

Homeowner. You have owned your home ten years. The airport planning began three years after you made the purchase. You and your wife have three children, ages eight, six, and two. You are worried that your children's hearing will be damaged by the noise. You have had your home for sale for a year. Three buyers looked at it, but decided not to buy when they found out about the jet noise problem.

Similar instructions would need to be prepared for all other players in the simulation. Directions for developing simulation games along with an example are provided in chapter 14.

Situations such as this also can be used to have students speculate about the future. For example, how might we deal with the problem of jet aircraft noise (or any of several other issues) in a futuristic setting? Here the children do not need to be constrained by what is practicable and feasible—or even possible. They simply let their creative minds imagine what might possibly become alternatives at some future time.

Use of a News Bulletin Board

The teacher should prepare a display of interesting news pictures and stories to which the child can turn for information concerning current events. Because items on the news bulletin board should be changed frequently, it should be in a place in the room where children pass regularly. A point near the doorway is a good location.

It is good procedure to discuss the significance of the news articles in class before they are posted on the bulletin board. The display should contain items of national and international import as well as items of local interest, sports stories, developments in science, people in the news, and perhaps oddities and jokes for variety and spice. It is helpful to have various sections of the bulletin board specifically designated for such groupings as local news, science in the news, news of our country, and global happenings. This serves as a means of meaningfully organizing the display.

The following suggestions are offered as a way of making bulletin boards more effective as an instructional tool:

1. Use captivating captions of one type and color. Letters for captions might be made from dark construction paper, corrugated paper, cardboard, yarn, aluminum foil, or material that has a related design such as discarded book jackets, newspaper, or woodgrain.

2. Use sound principles of design, balance, order, and color. Too much material carelessly displayed gives a cluttered effect. Adapt the display to the physical makeup of the room. Take into consideration door and window heights, other displays, lighting, and the location of the display in terms of its basic purpose. Secure an organized effect by developing continuity in the display. Anchor material squarely and securely on all four corners.

3. Change the displays frequently, and use variety in the material posted. There should be a purpose for posting any material, and after it has served its purpose, it should be removed.

4. Take time to discuss the material on the bulletin boards; call attention to new material posted; teach directly from the bulletin board from time to time.

5. Encourage children to bring or prepare material suitable for bulletin board display. As soon as the children are sufficiently mature, involve them in the planning and preparation of some of the displays.

Use of a News Map

In the middle and upper grades, the news map can be used to teach current events. A world map is displayed in the center of a bulletin board allowing sufficient space around the map for the posting of current news clippings or pictures. Colored string can be used to connect the news story with the location of the spot where the event occurred. This has the value of combining the study of current events with map-reading skills. Children should have a major responsibility for keeping the news map up to date and for handling the mechanics of its preparation. It is also possible to subscribe to a commercially prepared news map published weekly during the school year.[2]

Use of a Classroom Newspaper

Many teachers consider the classroom newspaper or periodical an indispensable tool in the teaching of current events. These materials have a number of definite strengths as well as some limitations that are frequently overlooked. The limitations of classroom current events periodicals lie not so much in their makeup but in the way they are used. The papers themselves are generally well prepared. Companies producing these materials have editorial advisory staffs composed of nationally recognized educators in the field of elementary education, and their editorial staffs consist of carefully selected and highly qualified personnel. Two of the better-known sources of classroom periodicals are:

Scholastic Inc.
P.O. Box 3710
Jefferson City, MO 65102
Pilot Edition, grade 1
Ranger Edition, grade 2
Trails Edition, grade 3
Explorer Edition, grade 4
Citizen Edition, grade 5
Junior Scholastic, grades 6–8

Weekly Reader   Phone: 1-800-456-8220
4343 Equity Drive
P.O. Box 16626
Columbus, OH 43216

---

[2]WORLD NEWSMAP OF THE WEEK, Weekly Reader Corporation, 245 Long Hill Road, Middletown CT 06457.

Weekly Reader, kindergarten through grade 6
Current Events, grades 6 and up

The chief strengths of the classroom newspaper are (1) its careful attention to reading difficulty, (2) its selection of current materials that are significant yet within the comprehension of children, (3) its unbiased presentation, and (4) the common background of information it presents to the class. These advantages cannot be obtained through the use of any other single source. They are designed and published for use in a classroom, and, therefore, their writing style, readability, and illustrations are suitable to children.

Classroom periodicals also have some limitations of which the teacher should be aware. Even though the readability is controlled, there is no published material that will meet the reading needs of every child in class. Some children will find the material too difficult; others will find it too simple. In a sense, the classroom periodical is the "textbook" for current events, and its use should be governed by the same pedagogical principles that apply to the use of textbooks generally.

There is a tendency for teachers to formalize the teaching of current events through the use of such a classroom periodical. One period a week is set aside for "current events" consisting of the reading of the paper followed by what is called "discussion" but amounts to the presentation of some questions by the teacher to be answered by the children. Overemphasis on the formal use of classroom periodicals crowds out the consideration of current affairs from the remainder of the curriculum.

A third limitation of classroom periodicals is that they select items of general interest either nationally or internationally and cannot deal adequately with local news. The teacher will find it necessary to turn to local sources for such news items. This is another reminder to the teacher not to depend entirely on the classroom periodical to carry the entire current events program.

Teaching Suggestions for Using Classroom Periodicals.   The service bulletins that accompany classroom periodicals often suggest ways to make good use of the papers. A procedure similar to this should be followed:

The teacher prepares and preplans—

Read the periodical and accompanying teachers' edition.

Keep up to date on current affairs by regularly reading an adult newspaper and news magazine and by listening to radio and television newscasts.

Build your own background on topics included in the classroom periodical.

Plan how to use the periodical and vary the procedure from week to week.

These children may make the local evening TV news show as they help break ground for their new school! Not all social participation gets as much public attention as this one, but any such involvement in civic affairs can make a valuable contribution to the citizenship education of children.
(Photo by Edna Kellman, Seattle Public Schools.)

The teacher prepares the classroom —

Post related pictures, maps, and diagrams on the bulletin board.

Have additional references available.

Place new words and terms on the chalkboard.

The teacher prepares the children —

Present the periodical to the class by calling attention to a picture, a map, or a particular story.

Discuss reasons why certain topics are in the news.

Develop meanings of new words and terms.

Use maps and the globe to orient children.

Develop purposes for reading.

Differentiate requirements to provide for individual differences.

Use the bulletin board, pictures, or other visual aids to motivate the class and to develop concepts.

Plan any special activities relating to the news stories, such as reports, dramatic presentations, and panels.

The children read the periodical—

Vary the reading assignments according to reading ability.

Have specific purposes for the reading.

Be available to assist with difficult vocabulary.

Direct the study of slower readers.

Have additional references on topics for more advanced learners.

The teacher and children conduct discussion and followup—

Discuss the periodical in terms of the purposes established.

Relate news stories to other classroom work.

Have children present any special activities that were planned.

Make generous use of maps and the globe.

Synthesize and summarize ideas and conclusions reached.

Plan further research or other creative followup activities.

Use of Daily Newspapers

Some teachers in the middle and upper grades find a daily newspaper helpful in promoting the goals of current events instruction. In units dealing with aspects of communication, the newspaper is an important learning resource. Students will profit from classroom instruction on the use of the newspaper that focuses on items such as these:

1. The organization of newspapers, purposes of various sections, where to look for certain kinds of information.
2. The nature of news stories, why some appear on the front page and others elsewhere.
3. The purpose and use of headlines.
4. Newspaper illustrations: wire photos, maps, charts, graphs, cartoons.
5. The editorial page and its function.
6. Detecting bias in news stories.
7. How to read a newspaper.

From time to time the teacher can devise practice exercises such as the following ones to help students develop their skills in using a daily newspaper:

Many teachers have found the Newspaper in Education (NIE) program sponsored by the American Newspaper Publishers Association (ANPA) Foundation to be a useful resource in teaching current events and, more specifically, in using the newspaper. For information about the NIE program and the several materials available through it, contact your local newspaper, or write to the ANPA Foundation, 11600 Sunrise Valley Dr., Reston, VA 22091, or call 703-648-1000. The NIE program provides many

----

················· **WHERE WOULD YOU FIND IT?**

Features in Today's *Tribune*

Bridge	B-2	Horoscope	B-2
Business	B-3–6	Landers	D-6
Classified	C-7–15	Lifestyle	D-1–6
Comics	D-7	Marine	B-6
Crosswords	B-2	Obituaries	B-10
Dr. Feelgood	B-2	Sports	C-1–6
Editorial	A-14, 15	Television	B-9
Films/Arts	B-6–B-8	Travel	D-8, 9
Graham	B-2	Word Sleuth	B-2

In what section of the newspaper would you look if you wanted to know

the results of a major league baseball game?

what movies were showing at local theaters?

if your mother's "For Sale" ad was carried in the newspaper?

something about a person who had died?

the newspaper's position (or opinion) on some current issue?

OR
In what section of the newspaper might you find expressions such as these?

"the series of double plays along with the bases-loaded homer in the ninth . . ."

"nominated for five Oscars . . ."

"For Sale. Three-year-old duplex . . ."

"Dear Ann . . ."

"some influence from Gemini . . ."

"She died in a local hospital after a long illness."

"The market was sharply up today . . ."

----

teaching and learning resources; two that are especially recommended are (1) *The Newspaper as an Effective Teaching Tool*, and (2) *Bibliography: Newspaper in Education Publications*.

Use of Television and Videotapes

Research on the television-viewing habits of children during out-of-school hours indicates that television viewing is a well-established pastime of nearly all American schoolchildren.[3] Studies consistently have shown that

---

[3]Based on data collected during 1983–84, the National Assessment of Educational Progress found that more than 40 percent of fourth graders, 25 percent of eighth graders, and 12 percent

NEWS MEDIA LINGO

Persons who report the news often use expressions that are peculiar to their profession. Here are a few common ones. Can you tell what they mean?

"A usually reliable source . . ."

"The information was leaked to reporters . . ."

"The story was scooped by the *Post* . . ."

"The senator tried to extricate his foot from his mouth . . ."

"In a news release from the White House . . ."

"There is a touch of irony in the president's statement . . ."

"This is a live broadcast . . ."

"Both Moscow and Beijing said last night . . ."

"In its lead story this morning . . ."

"The story was first carried by syndicated columnist . . ."

"An informed source, who asked to remain anonymous, said that . . ."

children view television from two to four or more hours each day during the week with some increase in this amount on weekends. The child in school, therefore, is well acquainted with this medium and is accustomed to viewing professionally produced programs even if the substance of such programs is not always of high quality.

There is an inclination to use instructional television in the same way a "live" teacher is used. This practice works to the disadvantage of television because the unique characteristics of the television medium are lost in the process. If television has instructional value, it is because it can do something more effectively than other media or because it can do some things that other media cannot do at all. Educational television can be of tremendous assistance to the elementary schoolteacher in enriching and vitalizing social studies providing it is used to achieve purposes the teacher cannot accomplish at least as well through the use of books and other conventional learning resources.

One valuable contribution television can make to social studies instruction is to motivate children. The television program has the total resources of the world outside the classroom to use in constructing programs that are highly interesting and motivating. Television can span both time and space in bringing relevant events into the classroom in capsule form. Television can visually transport children to the areas they are studying. It can also show them details they would probably miss if they were actually there. The most eminent authorities and world leaders can be their teachers

of eleventh graders watch five hours or more of television daily. Reported in *Education Week,* May 15, 1985, p. 6.

Topic:	Bias in news articles
Grade:	6–8
Time:	One class period
Objective:	To learn to detect bias in news accounts.
Interest Building:	Secure two accounts of the same news story, such as those in the following example. Make copies and distribute one of each to members of the class.

OPPOSITION TO GUN CONTROL REMAINS STRONG

Legislation pending in Congress would ban possession of the kind of handgun used in the attempted assassination of President Reagan in Washington, DC, in March, 1981. But opposition remains strong, especially in the House.

The present law banning imports of manufactured cheap handguns was passed in 1968 after the killings of Senator Robert F. Kennedy and Rev. Dr. Martin Luther King, civil rights leader. The law permits importing parts that can be assembled and sold in the United States.

A much tougher bill was approved by the Senate in 1972 after the shooting of Governor George C. Wallace, but the House never acted on it. Senate sources said that the members have shown a willingness to pass tough gun control laws but are waiting for some sign that the House is ready to do so, too.

Meanwhile, the lobbyists opposing gun control continue their efforts to stop such legislation. They remain consistent in their view that there is not necessarily a correlation between gun control and the actions of fanatics.

LITTLE HOPE SEEN FOR GUN CONTROL LEGISLATION

Long overdue legislation pending in the foot-dragging Congress would ban possession of the kind of vicious handgun used in the nearly successful assassination attempt on President Reagan in Washington, DC, in March 1981. But the carefully coordinated opposition to tough gun control remains strong, especially in the politically sensitive House.

The present mild law banning imports of manufactured cheap handguns was reluctantly passed in 1968 after the ruthless murders of the popular and respected Senator Robert F. Kennedy and Rev. Dr. Martin Luther King, Nobel prize-winning civil rights leader. The so-called gun control law permits importing parts that can be easily assembled and freely sold to fanatics in the crime-ridden United States.

A much tougher bill was approved by the Senate in 1972 after the brutal shooting of Governor George C. Wallace, but, as usual, the conservative House never acted on it. Senate sources said that enlightened members have shown a willingness to pass much-needed tough gun-control laws but are waiting patiently for some hopeful sign that the House is ready to do so, too, however belatedly.

Meanwhile, the lobbyists opposing reasonable gun controls continue their clandestine efforts to sabotage such legislation. They remain consistent in their warped view that there is no correlation between gun control and the actions of fanatics.

(*continued*)

Lesson Development:	Have the children underline the *facts* in each story.
	Using a chart, analyze the stories separately according to FACTS and NON-FACTS. Compare the facts in each account to determine if there are any discrepancies.
	Analyze the two accounts sentence by sentence by having students identify all nouns and the words that describe them (adjectives). List these on the chalkboard or a chart as follows:

Account No. 1		Account No. 2	
Nouns	Adjectives	Nouns	Adjectives
opposition	strong	opposition	carefully coordinated strong
		gun control	tough
House		House	politically sensitive

Conclusion:	Have children search newspapers and listen to news programs on television and radio on their own and bring to class examples of stories that contain elements of bias in the way they were reported.
	Discuss with the class the conditions under which it is appropriate for news media to express opinions on issues.

through television. The dramatic capabilities of good television production can be used in making a subject alive and exciting for children.

A second contribution television can make is to provide information not available through other sources. Some of these possibilities were suggested in the previous paragraph. No other medium can make it possible for a child to witness the inauguration of the president taking place a thousand miles away. A young man from Africa cannot visit all fourth-grade classrooms in a large city and tell the children interesting things about his homeland. But he can share his ideas with them via television. A major strength of television is that it can assemble and distribute information widely and quickly.

A third contribution of television to social studies is to clarify, elaborate, interpret, and enrich information that may be available through other sources. For example, a museum curator may be able to explain the religious significance of certain artifacts of early Indians who lived in the region. An authority or a traveler might be able to provide interesting details to help children understand why people of another culture do some particular thing the way they do. Television is an excellent medium for vitalizing knowledge because it can provide intimate, personal details that are not readily available through other sources.

Increasing numbers of schools have video cassette recorders available, and this has increased the flexibility of this medium. No longer is it necessary to view the program at the precise time it is telecast. In addition to television programs that have been recorded for classroom use, there is a growing amount of educational video available for social studies instruction.[4]

Use of a Variety of Activities

Many learning activities can be used profitably to study current affairs:

Conducting round-table discussions—dividing the class into five or six discussion groups, each to discuss a question related to some item in the news. Each group would be responsible to present to the entire class a short four- or five-sentence summary of its major ideas.

Having panel discussions—selecting five children to prepare a twenty-minute presentation to the class on some topic currently in the news. These five children would be given a few days or a week to prepare the presentation and would be the class "experts" on the topic discussed. After the presentation, the remainder of the class could ask questions, clarify points, or add to what the panel has said.

Making charts, maps, graphs—showing increases in school population, steps in an event that led to a crisis, decline or increase in employment, the number of highway accidents over a holiday weekend, the route of a recent air flight of importance, and so on.

Constructing posters, murals—to emphasize safe living, progress in preventive medicine, changes in air travel, progress in space, and other topics.

Keeping scrapbooks of news stories or pictures—clipping and keeping the headlines from the evening paper for several weeks. This helps children to distinguish between news stories that are of continuing interest and those that are transitory in nature. Collections of news clippings can be a valuable resource if the topic selected is one that is likely to be in the news for a period of several weeks or months. Careful selection of articles in the scrapbook will allow the class to follow the development of the news story.

Drawing cartoons to illustrate news—can be used effectively with older children. Care must be taken to avoid having children draw cartoons that might be offensive to individuals or groups. Cartoons dealing with a community fund drive, a sports story, safety or health habits, conservation practices, good citizenship, and other topics can be used.

Giving reports—is a widely used technique for handling current affairs by having individuals report news items to the class.

Conducting television news programs—can be used from time to time to dramatize news stories. Children can take turns as reporters; variety can be

---

[4]Amy Grotevant, "Social Education Resource List," *Social Education* 52 (September 1988): 370–71. An annotated list of selected distributors and developers of educational and instructional video.

obtained by using a tape recorder and playing the recorded "broadcast" for the class.

Dramatizing news events—when they lend themselves to dramatization. Not all do, but items dealing with festivals, meetings, conferences, and negotiations can be used.

Viewing telecasts of special events—reporting inaugurations, visits of foreign dignitaries, dedications, and other newsworthy programs can be used for in-school viewing in the elementary school. Children can also be encouraged to view news programs out of school and report on these to their classmates.

OTHER POSSIBILITIES FOR TEACHING SOCIAL STUDIES THROUGH NEWS STORIES

This chapter concludes with a created news story (Figure 9–3) that is a typical example of the type of controversial issue that can be useful in teaching social studies concepts and skills. As you read this story, based on an actual incident in the Puget Sound area, think of (1) the issues it presents and (2) what possibilities it holds as a teaching vehicle in the middle and upper grades. What follows now are a few teaching suggestions based on the story.

How can a news story of this type be used for social studies instruction? Here are a few suggestions:

1. Use the procedure discussed on pages 262–264 in making an analysis of this situation—that is (a) have students identify the *facts* of the case; (b) have students identify the *issues* in the case; and (c) have students identify *alternative solutions* to the problem and list the consequences of each alternative.
2. Use this story as a springboard for an in-depth study of endangered species. More than *five hundred* kinds of animals are listed as rare or in danger of extinction, including blue whales, Indian and Siberian tigers, Asiatic lions, snow leopards, eagles, condors, grizzly bears, alligators, and whooping cranes. Students should get into the values question of whether or not an animal has to be "useful" in order to be protected.
3. Have children study the roles of federal, state, local, and volunteer groups in decision making regarding issues of the type presented in this story. This should get them into local and state regulations concerning the conservation of natural resources and environmental contamination. It should also confront the matter of what individual citizens or groups of citizens can do when they see something happening that they believe to be unconscionable, even if legal.
4. This story provides an excellent setting for the study of the issue of capture of wild animals for use in circuses and zoos. Should zoos be allowed at all? Do animals benefit from zoos?

FIGURE 9–3
A Sample Controversial Issue

WHALE CAPTURE CREATES WAIL

Six killer whales are being held inside the Aqua Life, Inc. nets at Cook Inlet while Bill Holberg decides which ones, if any, will be kept for aquarium exhibits. Hundreds of people watched the capture from boats and shore yesterday afternoon.

The huge mammals swam slowly round and round inside two purse seine nets today, surfacing to "blow" for only moments. They stayed under for five minutes at a time. A large bull whale and a small calf that escaped the capture were nowhere to be found.

Governor Reconsidering

Meanwhile, a political storm was gathering over the capture operation. The governor today interrupted his skiing vacation long enough to say that he was "reconsidering" the state's position on making the inlet a sanctuary for killer whales. The state's senior senator in Washington said that a declaration of support for the governor for a whale sanctuary would clear the way for protection of the sea animals. Earlier efforts to get support from state officials for the idea were unsuccessful. The senator also said, "Apparently this man [Holberg] had a valid permit. But there aren't going to be any more. This is the end!"

Depth Charges Used

An assistant to the State Game and Fisheries director, Jack Binns, watched the capture from about fifty feet away. Binns said Aqua Life, Inc. boats used "sonar, radar, and 'depth' charges" to drive the whales into smaller and smaller coves and finally into the nets. He said he watched three men in power boats racing across the water atop the whale school, "dropping 'depth charges' as fast as they could light them. I've never seen anything so disgusting in all my life," he said today. "This ought to be stopped right now."

A federal enforcement officer who supervised yesterday's operation said, "there is nothing in the permit that prohibits the use of such explosives."

Use of Charges Denied

Many citizens complained about the capture operation. An automobile dealer from South Harbor said he saw an airplane dropping "tomato can"-size cannisters that apparently exploded as the plane herded the whales. Bill Moss, veterinarian for Aqua Life, Inc. said no such charges were used. He said the whale chasers used "firecracker"-type explosives thrown from boats to herd the whales. Holberg himself was aboard the Aqua Life, Inc. boat, *KANDU*, and was unavailable for comment.

Court Action Threatened

Environmentalists and others bitterly opposed the capture of the whales. Fred Russell, president of the state's largest environmental protection group, PROTEX, demanded that the whales be released. He said his group was prepared to take the matter to court if necessary to prevent Aqua Life, Inc. from keeping the creatures. "This is an outrage," he said," and we are not going to sit by and let it happen."

Russell cited a Canadian biologist who found that only about sixty-five killer whales remain in the Straits of Georgia and Juan de Fuca and in Puget Sound. Earlier data had placed the number of whales at about three hundred.

Overlapping Jurisdiction

The power to create a whale sanctuary rests with the federal government, but federal law says the governor of a state that contains the sanctuary may veto its creation. This overlapping of jurisdiction sometimes creates confusion or results in no action being taken.

Until today, federal officials thought the governor opposed creation of a killer whale sanctuary in this area. The governor's staff said that no record could be found of the governor's ever having opposed such a proposal.

The senior senator renewed his call for a sanctuary, something he has advocated since 1974. There is no reason to believe that the governor will oppose the creation of the killer whale sanctuary.

5. This story can provide the basis for the study of the web of life food chains—that is, how changes in the population of one animal change the number of another animal on which it feeds. This can be coupled with a study of wildlife management, hunting and fishing regulations, and the concept of *open season.*

6. Study the lives of individuals who have dedicated themselves to the preservation of wildlife and other natural resources: John Muir, Jack Miner, Rachel Carson, Gifford Pinchot, and local environmentalists.

7. Develop this news story into a role-playing activity in which the issues are highlighted and satisfactory resolutions played out.

8. Have children in committees develop "position statements" to represent the point of view of the various principals in this controversy: the whale hunter, the governor, the president of the environmentalist group, an irate citizen, the director of Aqua Life, Inc., who would receive the captured whales, and so on.

9. Use the story to build interest in developing a social-action project dealing with ecology or conservation. A second-grade teacher in Wisconsin reports the following activities that were developed in such a project:

   a. The children helped others become aware of the problems faced by endangered wildlife by sharing their research findings with their family, friends, schoolmates, clergy, and neighbors.

   b. They wrote letters to state and federal officials to urge their support of legislation designed to protect wildlife.

   c. They presented programs that dealt with the potential threats to wildlife by land developers, trappers, poachers, snowmobilers, hunters, pesticide programs, campers, and so on.

   d. They compiled a list of guidelines and distributed them to each child in the school, explaining ways individuals can help. These are some of the guidelines:

      (1) Refuse to shoot birds and other wild creatures "just for the fun of it."

      (2) Refuse to participate in cruel and senseless "chases" of wild animals on snowmobiles, in cars, on bikes, on foot, or in boats or planes.

      (3) Refuse to destroy animal homes.

      (4) Refuse to disturb baby birds and animal babies in their nests.[5]

10. Find out about the purposes and activities of organizations concerned about protecting the environment such as the Sierra Club, the National Wildlife Federation, Nature Conservancy, and Greenpeace.

These suggestions provide interesting extensions of a news story. Of course, no one class would engage in all of them; indeed, it is unlikely that

---

[5]Marsha Gravitz, "You and Me in the Classroom," *Instructor* 82:8 (April 1973): 43.

more than one would be used. Perhaps the teacher could create others even more suitable than those provided here. The point of this list is simply to illustrate the wide range of possibilities that inhere in well-selected current news stories. They provide the excitement of controversy, they are relevant to the current stream of human events, they deal with public policy issues, and they lend themselves exceedingly well to social participation projects.

DISCUSSION QUESTIONS AND SUGGESTED ACTIVITIES

1. How can map and globe reading be related to the study of current events? What possibilities do you see for relating social science concepts to current events and vice versa?

2. What would be the strengths and weaknesses of a social studies program built entirely around current events?

3. Examine copies of a children's periodical such as those published by Scholastic Inc. What can a teacher do to ensure imaginative use of such material?

4. Develop appropriate exercises of the types given in this chapter based on a newspaper story.

5. In what ways can current events topics be used for inquiry and valuing experiences for children?

6. Select a news story, and explain how it could be used as a springboard for a role-playing or simulation exercise.

7. Find a local news item that would be appropriate for teaching the skills needed to deal with controversial issues.

8. In dealing with controversial topics, what issues relating to the teacher's academic freedom are involved?

9. How can the understanding of important social studies concepts and generalizations be expanded by the study of current events?

SELECTED REFERENCES

FOLEY, ROBERT. "The Community's Role in Dealing with Censorship." *Educational Leadership* 40 (January 1983): 51–54.

FONTANA, LYNN A. "Television and the Social Studies." *Social Education* 52 (September 1988): 348–50. One of seven articles in a special section on television and social studies.

JUNIOR SCHOLASTIC, TEACHER'S EDITION. Scholastic, Inc: P.O. Box 3710, Jefferson City, MO 65102. Published biweekly during the school year.

HAHN, CAROLE L. "Controversial Issues in Social Studies." In *Handbook of Research on Social Studies Teaching and Learning,* edited by James P. Shaver, 470–80. New York: Macmillan, 1991.

KIRMAN, JOSEPH M. "Using Newspapers to Study Media Bias." *Social Education* 56 (January 1992): 47–51.

MOLNAR, ALEX, LOREN E. SANCHEZ, DAVID C. KING, HERBERT J. GROVEN, JOEL J. KUPPERMAN, AND MARK C. SCHUG. *Educational Leadership* 42 (December 1984/January 1985): 60–78. Each of these authors contributes an article to the theme, "Contemporary Issues in the Curriculum."

NELSON, JACK L., AND ANNA S. OCHOA. "Academic Freedom, Censorship, and the Social Studies." *Social Education* 51 (October 1987): 424–49. Several authors contribute to this special section of the journal.

OTTO, ROBERT (CHAIRPERSON), SARA ANDERSON, HELEN CAREY, NANCY ROBERTS, ROBERT SNAVELY, PHILLIP HEATH, AND BARBARA BARCHI. "Guidelines for Teaching Science-Related Social Issues." *Social Education* 47 (April 1983): 258–61. NCSS position statement.

OTTO, ROBERT. "Teaching Science-Related Social Issues." How To Do It series 5, no. 4. Washington, DC: National Council for the Social Studies, 1987.

PARKER, WALTER C., BENJAMIN BARBER, THOMAS E. KELLY, JOANN SHAHEEN. "Participatory Citizenship: Civics in the Strong Sense." *Social Education* 53 (October 1989). These authors contribute to a special section of the journal about teaching current events in ways that endure.

WELLS, JAMES, EDWARD REICHBACH, SHARON KOSSACK, AND JOAN DUNGEY. "Newspapers Facilitate Content Area Learning: Social Studies." *Journal of Reading* 31 (December 1987): 270–72.

III

PROCESSES
AND
SKILLS

10 Reading and Writing to Learn Social Studies

C hapters 10 and 11 take up the subject of literacy education in the context of social studies education. Two principal goals of literacy education will be explored, for both are essential to social studies learning. First, children will accomplish reading and writing tasks efficiently and with care. Second, they will do so mindfully, that is, by selecting and using well the skills they have learned.[1]

In these two chapters, we suggest principles and strategies for accomplishing these goals in a way that accomplishes social studies learning at the same time. The main ideas in both chapters are, first, that reading and writing are best thought of as a common enterprise rather than as distinct endeavors. Readers make meaning when they comprehend text in much the same way that writers make meaning when they compose text.[2] Skillful teachers attend to this similarity by paying special attention to the meaning-making process itself, whether situated in reading or writing. Second, children do not make meaning in a vacuum; children read and write to accomplish goals. In social studies, for example, they read and write to investigate the disappearance of the American buffalo, to follow rivers to the sea, to grasp how the Aztecs could possibly have been conquered, and to figure out why there are homeless people and what can be done about it. They read and write, then, to build and express social studies understandings.

This view of literacy education and content learning sees each situated in the other—mutually dependent. And it sees the central work of the

---

[1]Annemarie Sullivan Palinscar and Ann L. Brown, "Instruction for Self-Regulated Reading," in *Toward the Thinking Curriculum: Current Cognitive Research,* ed. Lauren B. Resnick and Leopold E. Klopfer (Alexandria, VA: Association for Supervision and Curriculum Development, 1989), 19–39.

[2]Marjorie Y. Lipson and Karen K. Wixson, *Assessment and Instruction of Reading Disability* (New York: HarperCollins, 1991).

This student is interviewing one of the costumed residents of Old Sturbridge Village, Sturbridge, Massachusetts, a re-created early nineteenth-century New England village. The child will incorporate the interview responses into a report she is writing on life in Old Sturbridge. In this way, the learning of skills and content are joined. *(Photo by Henry E. Peach, Old Sturbridge Village.)*

skillful teacher as creating *apprenticeships* for children in which they are gradually helped to achieve expertise in both. By apprenticeship we mean a learning situation with at least three characteristics: (a) learners learn as a consequence of being coached into higher levels of capability by adults and/or more capable peers; (b) practice occurs as learners work to accomplish all or part of a worthwhile task with the guidance and support of the coach or coaches; and (c) the coaching gradually decreases as the learner's capability increases.[3]

In the conventional classroom situation, of course, the coach is the teacher. Sometimes, the teacher will orchestrate situations in which peers who are more capable on the particular task at hand will provide guidance and support to students who are less capable on that task. In a cooperative group work strategy called Jigsaw (discussed in chapter 13) learning is fashioned in such a way that every student serves as a more capable "coach" to other students and is in the same way coached by other stu-

---

[3]See the influential study of coached practice, also known as "scaffolding," by Annemarie Sullivan Palinscar and Ann L. Brown, "Reciprocal Teaching of Comprehension Fostering and Monitoring Activities," *Cognition and Instruction* 1: 2 (1984): 117–75.

dents. This should be familiar to every parent who has had the older child teach the younger one to wash dishes.

This kind of literacy learning places less emphasis on traditional "drill and practice" than has been customary in the elementary school. The reason is that drill and practice typically is conducted in isolation from the tasks in which we want children actually to *use* those skills. While not discarding drill and practice, for it surely has its place, the apprenticeship approach strives as a rule of thumb to locate skills instruction in or as close as possible to the very situations where skillful means are needed. In this respect, the apprenticeship approach is merely another method of *socialization.* As with any other object of socialization, such as learning to like pancakes rather than salad for breakfast, learning to read and write in particular ways depends on a child being immersed in a community of practitioners who teach and model these.

Literacy, properly understood, then, is a cultural practice. Three literacy practices deserve the attention of elementary school teachers, and each requires its own form of cultural practice or apprenticeship.[4] The first is the practice of reading or writing written texts in order to function in everyday life. This is *practical* literacy. Examples include reading food labels and bus schedules, following instructions for videotaping a television program or assembling a bookshelf, completing job applications, and writing letters. Most of this apprenticeship occurs within families with the guidance and modeling of parents and older siblings. The second practice is reading or writing to gather data about the world. This is *informational* literacy. Typical examples are reading newspapers and weekly news magazines, studying campaign literature, writing letters to the editor, taking notes at lectures, looking up the location of Iraq in an almanac, and reading about the Vietnam War in a history textbook or reference book. For much of this information-driven learning, we depend on the school curriculum. The third form of apprenticeship concerns reading for pleasure. *Pleasurable literacy* is the one form of literacy practice that clearly is not a means to an end. It is an end in itself: one picks up and puts down the book or article at will. This apprenticeship often occurs at home, when children are read to by parents, but also at school when literature is read aloud to children and then dramatized, or when children read engaging stories themselves and then discuss them with other children or use them as a springboard for writing an original story.[5] Figure 10-1 shows these three practices, or apprenticeships, in relation to one another.

Schools can become "sites for true literacy apprenticeships," writes Lauren Resnick,[6] but this mandates ample school activities that require students to *use* reading and writing skills in the pursuit of practical and in-

---

[4]Lauren B. Resnick, "Literacy In School and Out," *Daedalus* 119 (Spring 1990): 169–85.

[5]For wonderful examples of dramatization, see Vivian G. Paley, *Wally's Stories* (Cambridge, MA: Harvard University Press, 1981).

[6]Resnick, "Literacy In School and Out," 183.

FIGURE 10-1
Literacy Apprenticeships in Social Studies

Practical Literacy	Informational Literacy	Pleasurable Literacy
Reading the ballot Reading directions to the polls Reading the returns	Studying the candidates' positions Reading a political analysis Reading a news article about a political campaign	Enjoying a biography of Thomas Jefferson Reading an absorbing historical novel featuring famous actual persons Enjoying a nonfiction book about a past political event

formational goals, as well as for pleasure. Among other things, *this means that reading and writing skills must be taught and used and refined in the content areas*, such as social studies, science, and mathematics. This chapter is focused primarily on these skills. In chapter 11, we turn our attention to apprenticeship opportunities that may integrate skills learning with social studies learning in the pursuit of worthwhile goals.

READING SKILLS ESSENTIAL TO SOCIAL STUDIES LEARNING

Reading remains the chief avenue to information needed in learning social studies, yet children are often unable to read well enough to secure that information. Inability to read well, therefore, is a major cause of poor achievement in social studies, and, unfortunately, the problem becomes worse each year the child is in school.

The usual recommendations for attending to the wide range of reading abilities among learners are these: (1) use multiple texts, (2) rewrite the material at a simpler level, (3) use a nonreading approach to social studies, and (4) secure simpler nontext materials for slower readers. But teachers on the job find these recommendations require resources, time, or skills that they do not have. The college methods courses in reading generally focus on the "basal" program and give minimum attention to reading in the content fields. Here we will examine in detail the relationship between reading and social studies.

Most elementary schools provide time during the school day when a major effort is made to teach basic reading skills. In this developmental reading program, children acquire a basic reading vocabulary and learn to

FIGURE 10-2
Social Studies Reading Skills

In social studies, the capable reader

- Reads flexibly
- Uses chapter and section headings as aids to reading
- Uses context clues to gain meaning
- Adjusts reading speed to purpose
- Hypothesizes cause-effect relationships
- Uses reference material when necessary to understand essential terms and vocabulary
- Seeks data in maps, charts, pictures, and illustrations and interprets data found there
- Uses various sections of a book (index, table of contents, introduction, etc.) as aids to reading
- Previews the selection to become familiar with text structure and to hypothesize general meaning
- Skims to locate facts and hypothesize main ideas
- Compares one account with another
- Recognizes topic sentences
- Uses library skills to find needed material

use various word recognition techniques along with other skills and abilities that characterize the flexible, independent reader. For example, they learn to identify words, create hypotheses about the meaning of a selection, and revise their hypotheses as they read and reread. But a strong basic reading program will not be able to meet all the reading needs of children because each area of the school curriculum requires reading tasks that are somewhat unique to that special area. *Helping children develop the specific reading skills and the abilities associated with each area of the curriculum must, therefore, go hand in hand with other instruction in the special subject area.*

The special reading skills needed to make sense of social studies material may be identified by examining the sorts of reading tasks children will confront. An examination of textbooks, historical fiction, biographies, primary documents, maps, and reference books will suggest reading skills such as those given in Figure 10-2.

Reading is *thinking*, and its centerpiece is the process of making sense, of constructing meaning. The building blocks in the process are the reader, the particular selection at hand, and the situation in which the reader and text have been brought together. Reading is thus an interaction among reader, text, and context.[7] While this surely is a complex cognitive process, there is every indication that this fact has not fully been appreciated by

---

[7]Lipson and Wixson, *Assessment and Instruction*, 13.

educators in the past. Perhaps this is because to the expert reader the remarkable act of reading seems easy, even mundane.

> An expert can make a complex skill look easy. But the apparent effortlessness of a chess master or concert pianist does not deceive us. What we sometimes fail to appreciate is that skilled reading is an intellectual feat no less complex than chess playing. Readers of this book are, in many ways, as expert at reading as chess masters are expert at chess. But because of the deceptively effortless look and feel of reading, and the fact that there are relatively many "reading masters" in our society, reading skill is not given as much credit for complexity as other forms of expertise. Its complexity is also one reason why not everyone learns to read (one in five adults in the United States!), and certainly not everyone becomes an expert reader.[8]

At the core of reading's complexity is the requirement that a reader be able to make sense of the symbolic system of print—those scratch marks on the page that the accomplished reader seems almost automatically to comprehend. This requires much more than sounding them out, though it is a good beginning. Making sense of printed symbols requires that the reader bring a deep reservoir of meaning to them. This is ironic when we realize that this reservoir—this rich conceptual base—is itself to a great extent the product of reading!

This is not to say that the reading task cannot be simplified for instructional purposes by attending to vocabulary development and reducing sentence length. The problem, however, is that explanations of specialized subjects and topics in print require the use of words and concepts that are peculiar to those subjects and topics. The reader will not comprehend the passage unless the meanings of the words and concepts used are understood. For this reason, the best remedy for poor vocabulary is not more vocabulary instruction but more reading.[9]

The teacher's responsibility regarding reading instruction in the social studies is, therefore, twofold. First, those special reading skills unique to social studies must be taught simultaneously with the subject matter under study. These are the skills listed in Figure 10-2. The teacher's second responsibility is to help children learn how to use reading as a tool in gaining needed information. Of course, reading should not be the only means through which children encounter new social studies information. Throughout this text, the idea is stressed repeatedly that a multimedia approach is vital to inspired teaching of social studies. But in that broad spectrum of media and activities that is at least potentially available to children today, reading remains undoubtedly the most important and, in the long run, the most critical to their success in learning social studies.

---

[8]M. A. Just and P. A. Carpenter, *The Psychology of Reading and Language Comprehension* (Boston: Allyn & Bacon, 1987).

[9]William E. Nagy, *Teaching Vocabulary to Improve Reading Comprehension* (Urbana, IL: ERIC Clearinghouse on Reading and Communication Skills, National Council of Teachers of English, and International Reading Association, 1988).

LEARNING ABOUT THE READING LEVELS
OF CHILDREN

Elementary and middle school teachers in self-contained classrooms provide basic reading instruction to children and, therefore, should be well acquainted with their reading levels. Unfortunately, however, teachers who may be sensitive to differences in reading ability while conducting reading instruction may ignore those differences when it comes to social studies. Or they conduct social studies instruction as if those variations in reading ability did not exist. Most elementary school teachers have had adequate training in the teaching of reading, and although they are not expected to do intensive diagnostic analyses of the reading problems of learners, they should be able to make informal assessments of learner performance in reading. We are assuming here, therefore, that through daily contact with children in the basal reading program, through standardized test data, and through observation, the teacher already has some understanding of the ability of individual learners to apply word-attack skills and to comprehend what is read.

In social studies the teacher should regard diagnostic and instructional procedures as two essential components of the same process. Suppose, for example, the teacher wanted to teach a relatively simple skill such as learning to skim to locate facts. As an initial step, the teacher ought to prepare a diagnostic exercise that will indicate how well children are able to perform this skill. For example, an exercise such as the one on page 290 might be devised. If a child cannot do such an exercise, it may be that the exercise itself is too difficult to read. In that case, the reading instruction must begin with attention to more basic skills and abilities having to do with decoding and simple comprehension. However, if the child can read the questions but does not know how to locate the answers quickly through skimming, this skill can be taught and practiced. This sequence—diagnosis, instruction, and followup practice—can be applied to any of the social studies skills listed in Figure 10-2.

A few other sample diagnostic exercises are provided on page 291.

USING STUDY AIDS AND STUDY SKILLS
TO IMPROVE READING

In contrast to reading a library book simply for enjoyment, much of the reading in social studies involves a search for information. The design of a social studies textbook provides many aids to make the job of reading easier. The teacher cannot assume, however, that children will make use of such aids unless they are taught to do so. The skills associated with the use of study aids must be taught, reviewed, and retaught each year throughout

SKIMMING TO LOCATE FACTS

Directions:

1. Open your book to the correct page.
2. Find the answer as quickly as you can.
3. Write your answer in the space.
4. You will have exactly twenty minutes to do the exercise.

a. Page 117.   What does "VP" mean? _____

b. Page 121.   The goods and services a worker can get in exchange for money wages are called _____

c. Page 149.   The number of farm workers in 1870 was _____

d. Page 152.   The percent of women doctors in Russia is _____

e. Page 192.   The cause of the crisis was _____

f. Page 209.   The number of miles of inland waterways in the United States is _____

g. Page 209.   The cheapest transportation in the United States is by _____

h. Page 230.   Places in cities that have no business buildings are called __

i. Page 241.   Towns and villages outside large cities are called _____

j. Page 246.   The date San Francisco opened its Bay Area Rapid Transit System—BART—was _____

the elementary and middle school grades. Here are few teaching suggestions, each of which is discussed in turn:

1. Using various parts of a book.
2. Recognizing topic sentences.
3. Using the organization of the book.
4. Using pictures to aid comprehension.

I. Using Context Clues to Gain Meaning

Select the words that belong in the blank spaces in this paragraph from the list of words that follows the paragraph.

The work of the TVA was started by building _____. A _____ is a wall or bank built across a river to stop its flow. The _____ hold back the water so the rivers do not overflow their banks and cause floods. Lakes, or _____, are formed behind the _____. Water from the _____ is allowed to flow into the streams when the rivers are low. This makes them _____ at all times. Power plants were built at the foot of some _____. These plants _____, or make, electricity. The electricity generated in the plants supplies _____ and to factories, towns, and farms for a 200-mile area.

reservoirs	navigable	power
generate	dams	light
dam		

II. Recognizing Topic Sentences

Open your book to page 57. This page contains four paragraphs. Read each paragraph and find the sentence that best tells what the paragraph is all about. In the spaces here, write the beginning two words of the sentences you select.

Paragraph 1. _____   _____
Paragraph 2. _____   _____
Paragraph 3. _____   _____
Paragraph 4. _____   _____

III. Understanding Terms and Vocabulary

Acronyms (AK′-row-nimz) are words that are formed from the first letter of each word in the full name of something. For example, NOW is an acronym for *N*ational *O*rganization for *W*omen. Acronyms are abbreviated expressions.

Use your text to find the full title of the following acronyms:

1. MADD_____
2. OPEC_____
3. UNICEF_____
4. NASA_____
5. RADAR_____
6. AMTRAK_____
7. BART_____

Using Various Parts of a Book

The parts of a book should be taught as aids in getting information. For example, if a fifth-grade child, Sara, in her study of famous women in American history, wanted to know the name of the Native American woman who assisted Lewis and Clark, how would she find it? She might find a reference to the Lewis and Clark Expedition in the Table of Contents, but that would be less likely than finding the names of these two explorers in the Index. She looks in the Index and finds

Lee, Robert E., 410

Legislative branch, 323

Leif Ericson, 128

Leirich, Julie, 235, 533

Lewis and Clark expedition, 345–347

Lewis, Meriwether, 346–347

Lexington, Massachusetts, 281–282

Liberator, The, 393, 402[10]

She turns to page 345 and notes a boldfaced section heading near the bottom of the page that reads, "The Lewis and Clark Expedition." She skims the sentences that follow it on page 345. Nothing. She turns the page, skimming quickly, and finds it. In the second column on page 346 she reads, "The expedition spent the winter with the Mandan Indians beside the great bend of the Missouri River. There a French fur trapper and his wife, a Shoshone Indian named Sacajawea, joined the expedition. As a young girl, Sacajawea had been forced to live with the Mandan Indians. Lewis and Clark hoped she would translate for them when they reached Shoshone country."[11]

Thus, in a matter of moments, Sara is able to find precisely the information she seeks. Contrast this with the girl sitting next to her who needs the same information, but, lacking an efficient way of finding it, goes through the book page by page looking for a picture or a clue that will reveal the name of that famous Indian woman. She may never find what she is looking for.

Rather than teaching parts of a book in an expository mode, the teacher should use exercises that require children to apply these skills. Often such exercises are included in the book itself. The one on page 293 is an example.

Other more complex variations of this exercise are possible. For example, the right-hand column can be omitted, and the child can be asked to find and supply the information. Or the child can be asked to indicate the specific page on which the information appears. Once learned, many of

---

[10] *The United States and Its Neighbors* (New York: Macmillan/McGraw-Hill, 1990), 626.

[11] *The United States and Its Neighbors,* 346.

···················· LEARNING THE PARTS OF A BOOK

In the right-hand column are listed the parts of your book. In the left-hand column are listed some things you might want to find out. For each item in the left-hand column, tell what part of the book you would turn to *first* in order to get the information.

You want to know	Parts of your book
the number of chapters in the book	title page
the meaning of *treaty*	copyright page
how to say the word *bauxite*	preface
when the book was published	table of contents
the population of various states	list of maps
the date the Dutch bought Manhattan Island	list of illustrations
what a sod house looks like	glossary
the route of the first railroad to the west coast	pronunciation key
whether the book tells anything about Canada	appendix
	index

these skills can be transferred to many other situations. If the children can use an alphabetical arrangement, as in the case of an index, they should also be able to use the dictionary, the encyclopedia, and the card catalog. Also, if they develop the habit of knowing exactly what information they seek before beginning the search, information gathering will be more efficient.

Naturally, the complexity of activities of this type should be appropriate to the age and maturity of the learners. Even in the first grade, children learn that books have titles and that pages are numbered. They also learn that sections of their books and stories have titles. In the second and third grades, they can begin to make use of the table of contents to find a particular story. In the third and fourth grades they can learn simple variations of alphabetical arrangements that assist them in using an index.

Recognizing Topic Sentences

If children learn to recognize the main idea developed in a paragraph, they can organize the ideas developed by the author in some order of importance. They learn to separate the topic being discussed from the elaborative and supporting detail. Before they can deal with topic sentences, however, they have to understand that a paragraph is a group of sentences all of which deal with the same topic or idea. They learn that the *topic sentence* is the critical one in the paragraph because it tells the reader what the paragraph is about. A little practice will help them understand the singleness of purpose of paragraphs. Exercises such as the one on page 291 can be used.

An exercise of this type should be followed by practice in identifying topic sentences in paragraphs selected from the children's text. They should learn

·················· LEARNING HOW PARAGRAPHS AID COMPREHENSION

Read these selections, and decide which is easier to understand.[12]

A

As they drove on, he told them stories he'd heard about the old days on the Chathams, about the ships and the men who hunted the whales and seals, about the Morioris and how they had been almost killed out by the Maoris who came out here over a hundred years ago. "There's lots of people here with Maori blood," he said. "But there's not many with Moriori blood." The road curved round the lake, through hills, paddocks and beside smaller lakes. Ducks and swans were on all the lakes. They bumped across some paddocks and came to the airstrip. There were a lot of Landrovers and the yellow truck beside two sheds. They heard the plane before they could see it. It came low over the trees and bumped along on the grass of the airstrip. People got off, and others got on. Bags of mail and parcels of goods were carried off through the big doors, and others were put on. The fisherman was carried on.

B

As they drove on, he told them stories he'd heard about the old days on the Chathams, about the ships and men who hunted the whales and seals, about the Morioris and how they had been almost killed out by the Maoris who came out here over a hundred years ago. "There's lots of people here with Maori blood," he said. "But there's not many with Moriori blood."

The road curved round the lake, through hills, paddocks and beside smaller lakes. Ducks and swans were on all the lakes. They bumped across some paddocks and came to the airstrip. There were a lot of Landrovers and the yellow truck beside two sheds.

They heard the plane before they could see it. It came low over the trees and bumped along on the grass of the airstrip. People got off, and others got on. Bags of mail and parcels of goods were carried off through the big doors, and others were put on. The fisherman was carried on.

1. Why is one selection easier to read than the other?
2. Why did the author group the sentences the way he did in selection B?
3. Is there something about the grouping of sentences that makes them a paragraph?
4. Which sentence in each paragraph in selection B tells what the paragraph is about?
··

(1) that the topic sentence tells what the paragraph is about, (2) that other sentences in the paragraph elaborate on the topic, and (3) that the topic sentence is usually, but not always, the first sentence in a paragraph.

Using the Organization of a Book

Units, chapters, section heads, and subheads; ends of section, chapter, or unit study aids; maps, charts, or picture captions; introductory questions—

[12]From Jack Lasenby, *The Chatham Islands* (A Bulletin for Schools; Wellington, New Zealand: Department of Education, n.d.), 32.

all of these make sense to the mature reader who uses them as valuable aids in understanding the organization of a book. But left unguided, a child is not likely to make good use of them as aids to reading. Even teachers may not be familiar with the way a particular book is organized. Figure 10-3 illustrates organizational components that are commonly found in social studies textbooks. Research indicates that knowledge of text *structure* is a significant variable in children being able to recall information.[13]

Using Pictures to Aid Comprehension

The most widely used of all visual aids are pictures, photographs, and illustrations. These are used to obtain realism, to clarify ideas, to recall the real object, and, in short, to give meaning to learning. It is well known that words cannot convey meanings as accurately, vividly, or quickly as pictures. Pictures can also be helpful in promoting inquiry skills. For this reason, some textbooks now use questions for captions instead of a description of the content of the picture or illustration.

Publishers invest huge sums of money to provide instructive illustrations for social studies textbooks. Unfortunately, the full value of these aids to reading is not realized unless children are taught how to make good use of them. Illustrations are not simply cosmetic touches to make the book more appealing. They are, or should be, an integral part of the message system of the text.

Pictures and illustrations elaborate concepts presented in the narrative but usually do not repeat exactly what is said in the text. Neither do picture captions simply tell what would be obvious to the reader only by looking at the picture. Thus, captions should call attention to some element or relationship in the picture or illustration that might be missed by the casual viewer. Often this is done by using a question or series of questions. In this way pictures and illustrations can provide the reader with a wealth of information. In teaching children how to use pictures and illustrations, teachers will find questions such as these appropriate:

1. Exactly what is being shown in the picture?
2. What relationships are illustrated by the picture?
3. When was this picture taken? (recently, years ago, time of day, and so on)
4. How does the picture illustrate something we discussed in class?
5. What influences (causes or effects) can be detected in the picture?
6. What does the picture tell about the lifestyles of the people?
7. How does the picture illustrate something valued by people?
8. How does the picture show conflicts between traditional and modern ways of doing things?

---

[13]Barbara M. Taylor and S. Jay Samuels, "Children's Use of Text Structure in the Recall of Expository Material," *American Educational Research Journal* 20 (Winter 1983): 517–28.

FIGURE 10-3
Organizational Structure of Social Studies Textbooks

USING YOUR TEXTBOOK

TABLE OF CONTENTS
Lists all parts of your book and tells you where to find them

Y our textbook contains many special features that will help you learn about communities.

TRADITIONS
Lessons that help you understand the cultures of the communities you are studying

REVIEWING MAPS AND GLOBES
Reviews skills that will help you use the maps in your book

LESSON OPENER
Important vocabulary, people and places introduced in the lesson

Lesson introduction

Asks you what you know from a lesson you have already read or from your own experience

Question you should think about as you read the lesson

LESSON 1 A New Country

READ TO LEARN

■ **Key Vocabulary**
American Revolution
Declaration of Independence

■ **Key People**
Thomas Jefferson

■ **Key Places**
Lexington, Massachusetts
Philadelphia, Pennsylvania

■ **Read Aloud**
A little over 200 years ago, our country was not a country at all. Parts of it were colonies ruled by governments in Europe. By 1750 England ruled 13 colonies along the coast near the Atlantic Ocean. But as the English colonies grew, so did the fights between England's leaders and the colonists.

This handmade blanket shows what a community in the American colonies looked like.

■ **Read for Purpose**
1. WHAT YOU KNOW: Name two communities in North America that began as colonies.
2. WHAT YOU WILL LEARN: Why did the English colonies decide to break away from England?

271

FIGURE 10-3
(*continued*)

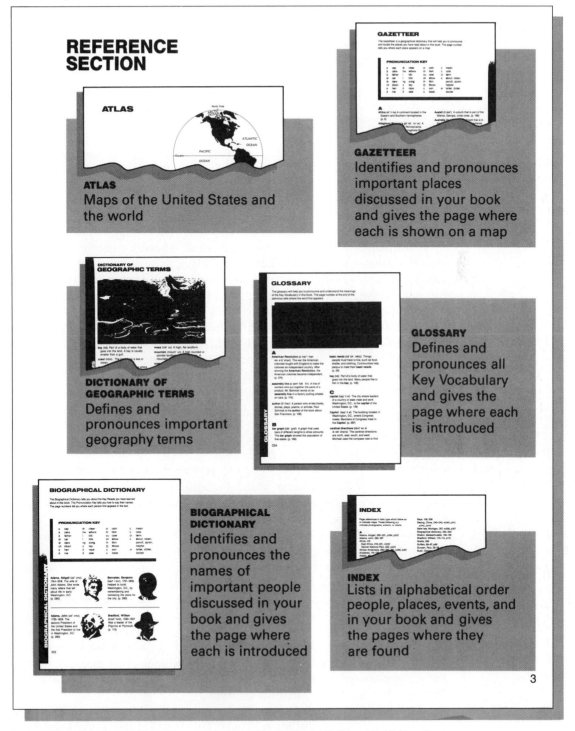

REFERENCE SECTION

ATLAS
Maps of the United States and the world

GAZETTEER
Identifies and pronounces important places discussed in your book and gives the page where each is shown on a map

DICTIONARY OF GEOGRAPHIC TERMS
Defines and pronounces important geography terms

GLOSSARY
Defines and pronounces all Key Vocabulary and gives the page where each is introduced

BIOGRAPHICAL DICTIONARY
Identifies and pronounces the names of important people discussed in your book and gives the page where each is introduced

INDEX
Lists in alphabetical order people, places, events, and in your book and gives the pages where they are found

3

Source: *The World Around Us,* 1990, pp. 2–3, Macmillan/McGraw-Hill School Publishing Company.

9. What does the picture show that illustrates the roles of men, women, and children in that society?
10. What characteristics of the culture are shown in the picture?
11. What can you say about the geography of the area shown by the picture?
12. What conversation might be going on between the persons in the picture?
13. What would you judge to be the educational level of the people who live there?
14. Would you describe this area as being technologically advanced? Why or why not?
15. Why do farmers make use of their land in this way?
16. Do you think the people use most of what they produce or sell their products outside their community? What makes you think so?

What makes a picture, photograph, or illustration suitable for instructional purposes in social studies? Certainly, the most important consideration is accuracy of the portrayal. The fundamental purpose of any learning aid is to convey accurate meaning; and if this is lacking, the picture, photograph, or illustration must be rejected unless, of course, it is being used to illustrate inaccuracy. Other factors that should be considered are that it be of sufficient size for the purpose it is to serve, appropriate to the age children with which it is to be used, of good artistic quality, impressive, of easy interpretation, and that it have a definite center of interest that is not subordinated by a great many details.

BUILDING SOCIAL STUDIES VOCABULARY

The vocabulary load of social studies reading material is one of the major causes of poor comprehension and faulty reading in social studies. Even with the more careful attention that contemporary authors give to word difficulties, the social studies vocabulary remains a stumbling block for many children. Although a degree of simplification is possible, it is true that there are limits beyond which the use of a specialized vocabulary cannot be avoided. If one is speaking or writing about social studies concepts, appropriate vocabulary must be used. This is not altogether undesirable if the teacher accepts vocabulary development as one of the goals of the total social studies program. The same situation exists in other areas of the curriculum; the child must learn the language associated with mathematics, science, art, music—all of which have their own peculiar words, terms, or phrases. Figure 10-4 shows some of the types of words and terms that are peculiar to social studies.

The teacher should anticipate likely word difficulties *before* children are asked to read a social studies selection. Two types of word problems must be expected. One is the inability to recognize the word in print; the other

FIGURE 10-4
Words and Terms Needing Special Attention in Social Studies

Technical terms—Words, terms, and expressions peculiar to social studies and usually not encountered when reading selections from other fields of knowledge. *Examples:* veto, meridian, frontier, latitude, longitude, legislature, polls, franchise, temperate, plateau, hemisphere, mountainous, wasteland, balance of power, capitalism, democracy, nationalism, civilization, century, ancient, decade, pueblo, fjord, iceberg.

Figurative terms—Expressions that are metaphorical; having a different connotation from the literal meaning usually associated with the word. *Examples:* political platform, cold war, closed shop, Iron Curtain, logrolling, pork barrel, open door, hat in the ring, domino theory, Sunbelt.

Words with multiple meanings—Words that have identical spelling but whose meaning is derived from context. *Examples:* cabinet, belt, bill, chamber, mouth, bank, revolution, fork, court, assembly, range.

Terms peculiar to a locality—Expressions peculiar to a specific part of the country that are not commonly used elsewhere. *Examples:* truck, meeting, borough, gandy, draw, coulee, right, prairie, section, run, butte, arroyo, geoduck, goobers, grits, potlatch, bayou, haul cane road.

Words easily confused with other words—Words that are closely similar in general configuration. *Examples:* peasant for pheasant, alien for allies, principal for principle, longitude for latitude, executive for execution, conversation for conservation

Acronyms—Words that are abbreviated expressions. *Examples:* NATO, NASA, OPEC, SALT, NOW, UNICEF, AIDS, MADD.

Quantitative terms—Words and terms signifying amounts of time, space, or objects. *Examples:* shortly after, century, fortnight, several years later, score, one hundred fifty tons.

is not knowing the meaning of the word once it is recognized. Therefore, new words and terms should be presented and developed in the context of a phrase or a sentence rather than in isolation.

Vocabulary development should be conducted in relatively short, highly motivated settings. Having children look up a long list of terms in the dictionary prior to reading a selection is not productive. No expert reader does this. A better strategy is to write the key terms in a sentence on the chalkboard and discuss their meanings. These should be the few terms that, in the teacher's judgment, are critical to student comprehension of the selection. Better still, the sentence in the text in which the word or term appears can be selected for directed study.

It is essential for the teacher to model a sensitivity to, and interest in, new words and terms. Curiosity about words and a genuine interest in good communication, after all, are central features of a successful apprenticeship in reading and writing. Teachers should encourage children to use the specialized social studies vocabulary in their discussions and writing. They should also, from time to time, encourage children to create new words or nicknames for old ideas. During a concept-formation lesson (see chapter 2) on *culture*, the children may be encouraged to think of a term other than culture that might more powerfully convey the meaning of the concept—"lifeway," for example. Creating new words puts children at the inventing end of language, rather than the receiving end, which can be an enlightening change of vantage point.[14]

Moreover, the teacher may want to involve them in word games. Devising riddles, providing synonyms or antonyms, making or completing crossword puzzles, or constructing variants of words are helpful in maintaining an awareness of new terms. Bulletin board displays and other classroom exhibits can feature new words encountered in social studies.

Teaching how known words can be used to construct new words can be of help in recognizing new words and understanding their meanings. Among the simplest variations are compound words or the addition of prefixes or suffixes. Some examples are these: construct, constructed, constructing, construction; consume, consumer, consumed, consuming; loyal, disloyal, loyalist; dictate, dictator, dictatorship.

One of the most useful skills in reading social studies materials is the use of context clues. A reader, for example, should have no problem gaining meaning from the following passage even though many of the words are missing.

> **At exactly 4:05 P.M. the _____ landed at the _____ . Hundreds of _____ were waiting in the _____ . It was the first time many of them had seen our nation's leader. When the _____ came down the _____ , he _____ . The crowd _____ . He made a short _____ . The crowd _____ again. In a few _____ he was on his way again, this time in a _____ . As the _____ went straight up, the_____ could see the _____ through the window of the _____ .**

Gaining meaning through context is especially appropriate to social studies because it ensures that the reading is done thoughtfully. This contrasts with defining words and terms in isolation, in which case the wrong meaning might be selected. Many social studies terms and words have multiple meanings. For example:

- He established the first *bank* in the region.
- The river overflowed its left *bank*.
- "You can *bank* on that," he said.
- Directly ahead was a big *bank* of snow.
- As he looked west, he could see a large *bank* of clouds.
- Just before crashing, the plane seemed to *bank* to the left.
- The assembly line consisted of a long *bank* of machines.

When terms that have multiple meanings are encountered in a passage, only the meaning being used in the passage should be developed at that time, and it should be developed in context.

Glossaries do not provide the meanings of words and terms in context and, therefore, have some limitations in acquainting children with the

---

[14]Walter C. Parker and Samuel A. Perez, "Beyond the Rattle of Empty Wagons," *Social Education* 51 (March 1987): 164–66.

precise meaning of new terms. For instance, a child may read the following sentence:

> Several well-known people from this city were killed in the crash of a charter flight.

Looking in the glossary of a text for the meaning of the word *charter*, the child finds

> **char'ter:** a paper giving a person or company special rights

It happens that the definition of *charter* given is only one of about five that correctly defines the word.

After anticipated word difficulties have been attended to and the purposes for doing the reading have been established, children will usually read selections silently the first time through (middle grades). The teacher should be available to assist those who encounter problems with words. Children should be encouraged to figure out the meaning of words for themselves, but if a child cannot do so in two or three tries, the teacher should explain the term, pronounce it, and have the child proceed with the reading. Reading of the entire selection should not be held up because of a problem with a few unfamiliar words or terms.

It is often helpful to keep a special social studies vocabulary list posted in the classroom. Lists can be developed by individual children, too, and made into a social studies picture dictionary. If a word is likely to be used frequently in writing, such a word might be added to an individualized spelling list. However, many social studies words are not often used by children in their writing and, therefore, do not make good selections for spelling lists. They are more likely to be a part of children's reading vocabulary than their writing vocabulary.

Most social studies texts provide extensive study aids to assist with vocabulary development, including any or all of the following:

1. Contextual definition of words and terms.
   Examples: Thousands of persons in this city earn their living by *processing* food. Processing means preparing food for marketing.
   In recent years people have become concerned about *pollution*. Pollution comes about when something harmful is placed into the water or air.
2. Use of boldface type and/or italics.
   Examples: The things from which products are made are called **raw materials.** Three *raw materials*—iron ore, coal, and limestone—are found in the Midwest.
3. End of unit, chapter, or section exercises.
   Examples: Matching exercises.
   Selecting terms for incomplete sentences.
   Finding definitions of key terms in the text.

4. Glossaries.

Examples:

Pig iron: melted iron that hardens into bars

Pilgrim: a person who travels to holy places to worship

Plantation: a large farm that specializes in one crop

Polar regions: areas in the high latitudes

5. Pronunciation guide.

Examples: **tropics** (trop′iks)

volcano (vol-ka′no)

The teacher should give special attention to the meaning of quantitative concepts because they are used with high frequency in social studies prose and because research has repeatedly shown that they are not well understood by children. If a class reads in the text that "the Empire State Building reaches a height of 1,250 feet," individual children might think of 1,250 feet as meaning anything from a distance of perhaps 50 feet to 14 miles! Quantitative concepts deal with time, space, or objects (including people) and may be definite or indefinite. Figure 10-5 provides examples of these categories.

The meanings of quantitative concepts need to be developed within the context in which they are studied and, whenever possible, related to the child's experience. For example, the area of a faraway place may be compared to that of their home state. Populations of places may be related to their own city or to a city in their state. An acre of space can be compared with their playfield or a football field. Indefinite references to quantity must be discussed in terms of the topic and period studied. For example, an hour's wait in the dentist's office would be considered "a long time,"

FIGURE 10-5
Examples of Various Quantitative Concepts

	Time	Space	Objects
Definite	10 years ago	480 square miles	Columbus had a crew of 90 sailors.
	A century passed.	the area of two football fields	2000 cars were manufactured each day.
	two decades later	Each farm was 80 acres in size.	The explorers had only three canoes.
Indefinite	a short while later	The Sahara covers a vast area.	The state produces a great amount of wheat.
	It took several weeks.	Much of the land is used for farming.	Millions of barrels of oil
	Years passed before anything happened.	The Miller family had a large spread.	Untold numbers of ships sailed into the harbor.

but a "long time" in terms of rehabilitating a polluted lake might be twenty-five years, whereas a "long time" when referring to the formation of the earth's surface would be millions of years. Through discussion, the teacher can help children gain greater meaning of these complex references to quantity.

IMPROVING READING COMPREHENSION: MAKING SENSE

Reading with comprehension means that readers are able to make sense of what they are reading, that is, to come away from the selection with mental pictures of essential facts and understandings. Through discussion with the teacher and classmates, writing, and returning to the selection perhaps numerous times, children can check the sense they made with the sense made by others, perhaps revise their interpretation and, in this trial-and-error way, come to some negotiated understanding about what the author meant to say.

It is obvious that the child who brings the most to a reading situation—whether practical, informational, or strictly for pleasure—will receive the most in return. What the child brings that will enhance social studies reading the most are intellectual aptitude, a storehouse of experience and ideas (put simply, prior knowledge), knowledge about reading, and motivation or will. There is not much a teacher can do to increase children's intellectual aptitude, but a great deal can be done about the other three: Teachers can capitalize on the knowledge and cultural experience children bring to the reading situation, they can build children's knowledge of important components of the reading process itself, and they can establish clear purposes for reading tasks. In order to help children *want* to comprehend, teachers can make connections to students' interests and goals, and they can make sure that the reading tasks they give students to accomplish are authentic—that is, they are not mere "busywork," nor are they the sort of thing that has no larger purpose. ("Drill and practice" activities often are off the mark on both counts.) Rather, tasks are related to a worthy and larger challenge. Children are not just practicing writing sentences, for example, but they are writing sentences in the biographies they are producing about people who work to protect the environment from polluters. In these ways, children can be helped to perform at or near their full potential.

Perhaps the most important general rule of thumb used by good readers is the one that seems so mundane: *read flexibly*. This means that readers should vary their speed and the skills they use depending on the selection at hand. Expert readers do this routinely; poor readers do it rarely; mediocre readers do it unevenly. Apprenticing children into the routine practice of flexible reading should be a daily goal in social studies teaching and learning. The reason is straightforward: A reader's prior knowledge will vary greatly from topic to topic. For this reason, a good reader's comprehension is high on some topics and low on others. On a topic where the reader's prior knowledge is vast, comprehension will come more easily and few special strategies will need to be employed. On a topic where prior knowledge is relatively thin, however, good readers will proceed in a much different way. Most important, they will *recognize* that their prior knowledge on this topic is weak, and will marshall needed strategies to aid comprehension.

Because reading comprehension varies according to the particular topic and selection at hand, *previewing* may be the most important single comprehension strategy. It means, essentially, looking before you leap. Good readers use it because it tells them what lies ahead, providing a general picture of the terrain. Looking ahead indicates whether familiar or strange material is at hand and, consequently, which additional strategies, such as skimming, may be required. Previewing in this way builds prior knowledge "on the spot."

The simple narrative account of an African American girl who must survive on her own during the American Revolution for example, may be relatively easy to understand for many children.[15] They can read accounts of this type without difficulty because they rely on motivating storylines, familiar story structures (e.g., problem–solution), and well-known words. On the other hand the child may encounter in the textbook an expository selection on the topic, "Democracy and Dictatorship." This is a complex idea that may be difficult for many young children. Not only is its vocabulary specialized (checks and balances; scapegoating; civil liberties, and so on), its place in children's experience will be marginal. Yet, it is easily one of the most important topics in the social studies curriculum.

What's to be done? Several strategies have been shown to be effective in improving reading comprehension:

1. Activate prior knowledge
2. Preview
3. Skim for ideas and related details
4. Establish clear purposes for reading
5. Use study and organization aids provided in textbooks
6. Teach children to vary their rate of reading
7. Relate what is read to life experiences of children
8. Check comprehension regularly and keep individual records

Activate Prior Knowledge

Just as the rich get richer, the knowledgeable get more knowledgeable. What we know before coming to a learning task influences, often greatly,

---

[15]James Lincoln Collier and Christopher Collier, *War Comes to Willy Freeman* (New York: Dell, 1983).

the kind and amount of learning we will accomplish once we get
Learners who have more background knowledge about the topic of th
selection they are about to read, all things being equal, will better com
hend that chapter than learners who know little or nothing about it. Minimally, they will comprehend it differently, making different sense of it
than their less knowledgeable counterparts. Such is the influence of prior
knowledge on comprehending text. Over the long term, therefore, schools
should do everything possible to contribute to the prior knowledge of
students. Extensive use of field trips to construction sites and factories,
study trips to museums, exposure to films of historical events and far away
places, assemblies, plays and pageants, projects, pictures, guest speakers,
displays, artifacts—all will assist the child in comprehending the ideas
encountered in reading.

But there is a problem. When the next learning task is here, staring them
in the face, learners will not necessarily use the prior knowledge they have.
Ask any teacher! The knowledge they have built up over the years, even in
last week's lesson, may lay dormant and untapped in today's lesson. How
can a teacher "activate" this prior knowledge so that students can use it to
make sense of the coming reading? We give two time-honored strategies
here.

List, Group, and Label.   We encountered this strategy in chapter 2 as one
of three used by skillful teachers to help children build and refine concepts.
Here it is a prereading activity, used to activate knowledge related to a
concept that is central to the text selection children are about to read.

Suppose a teacher had observed in previous groups of children much
difficulty comprehending a lesson in the third grade text that explained the
concept *community*. It *is* a difficult concept, let us note, even for adults. It is
used in various ways: the community in which one lives, the medical
community, and the black community, for example. It is an important
concept since not only this lesson but the entire third-grade social studies
curriculum centers on communities of the world. It is worth the trouble,
then, to implement a prereading activity that will boost comprehension.

The teacher asks students, What are some of the things you think of
when you hear the term *community?* All their responses are recorded on the
chalkboard (listing). The teacher listens, and prompts students to think in
areas they may overlook. (Do animals have communities? Can you belong
to more than one community? What kinds? What happens in communities?) Then the teacher asks students to examine their list to see if two or
more things seem to go together (grouping). Students are reminded that an
item can belong to more than one group. Once the groups are formed, the
teacher asks students to explain their groups, and then to think of names
that would be good for these groups (labeling). Students are encouraged to
come up with clever names, nicknames, names that really grasp the essence of the group, and so on.

List for Community, 3rd-Grade Class

neighborhood	teachers	new communities
Boston	animals	first communities
doctors	cooperation	Indian communities
firefighters	working	Plymouth
grocery stores	playing	Mesa Verde
New York	cleaning up	prisons
Los Angeles	eating	policemen
Disneyland	living	Palm Springs
herd of cattle	government	Miami
flock of geese	rules	towns
family	vertebrates	suburbs
relatives	schools	cities
nests	school district	mayor
living things	farms	
nonliving things	solar system	
flora	galaxy	
fauna	old communities	

We should note that all the items on the list are words—vocabulary. For this reason, this strategy usually is considered a vocabulary builder.[16] It functions to activate prior knowledge because the vocabulary on the list comes from students' present store of words. In this sense, it is the children's prior vocabulary that is being activated. Meanwhile, the strategy focuses that vocabulary on the key concept to be explored in the new text selection, in this case *community*. The focusing function of the strategy is not to be taken lightly, for research has shown that knowledge activation procedures that fail to focus student attention on the most important ideas in the text fail also to boost comprehension as much as we would hope.[17]

Semantic Maps.   Semantic mapping is a closely related knowledge activation strategy, but it provides a more graphic representation of the key text concept that the teacher has chosen. Let us leave the *community* example and consider a teacher who has chosen "Exploring North America" as the central theme for a fourth-grade social studies/language arts curriculum. Developing in-depth knowledge of each region of the United States is the content focus, and the Lewis and Clark expedition has been selected as the first unit. Before having students read a selection from the textbook on Lewis and Clark, the teacher decides to activate the whole array of ideas

---

[16]Dale D. Johnson and P. David Pearson, *Teaching Reading Vocabulary*, 2d ed. (New York: Holt, Rinehart, and Winston, 1984).

[17]Janice A. Dole, Sheila W. Valencia, Eunice Ann Greer, and James L. Wardrop, "Effects of Two Types of Prereading Instruction on the Comprehension of Narrative and Expository Text," *Reading Research Quarterly* 16: 2 (1991): 143–59.

FIGURE 10-6
A Simple Semantic Map on the Theme "Exploration."

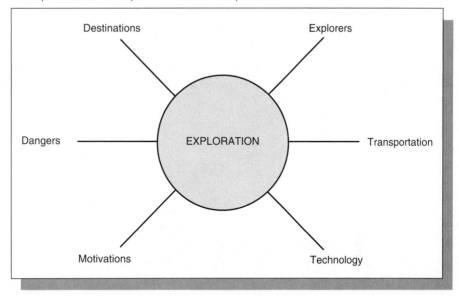

and information students associate with the concept *exploration*. The procedure follows.[18]

1. The teacher places the term *exploration* on the chalkboard and asks students to jot down individually any words they can think of related to this theme. They may think of words such as Columbus, Marco Polo, past, future, time machine, explorers, ships, astronauts, underwater exploration, and so on.

2. Next the teacher identifies or elicits from students major category labels related to the theme, prompting students to think of categories they may overlook. These are arrayed graphically around the concept term, which serves as a hub (see Figure 10–6).

3. Now the teacher asks students to generate additional ideas under each category. As well, the teacher can suggest items and ask students to decide under which category label they belong. Figure 10–7 shows two sample categorization exercises.

List, group, and label and *semantic mapping* are two closely related ways to activate the knowledge children have prior to reading. Either one should help them make sense of the material they are about to read. The teacher must be careful, however, to focus the activity on the main ideas in the text.

---

[18]Nagy, *Teaching Vocabulary*, 10–23.

FIGURE 10-7

Expanded Semantic Maps on the Themes "Exploration" and "Shelter."

EXPLORATION

destinations	explorers	transport	dangers	technology	motivations
space	Columbus	time machine	sea monsters	sextant	greed
land	Marco Polo	boat	aliens	horsehoe	gold
underwater	Sally Ride	ship	disease	solid fuel	adventure
	Capt. Kirk	horse	starvation	unleaded gas	power
		feet	mutiny	solar power	fame
		plane	pirates		glory
		space shuttle			freedom

WATER

PLAYING	OCEANS	UNDERGROUND	LAKES	SEAS	RIVERS
-diving	-Atlantic	-wells	-Great Lakes	-Baltic	-Colorado
-swimming	-Pacific	-springs	-Salt Lake	-Caspian	-Mississippi
-polo	-Indian	-streams		-Red	-Missouri
-skiing					
-boating					

HUMAN USES

-electricity
-farming
-transportation
-drinking
-manufacturing
-playing

Preview

Good readers have a general idea of what material is about before starting to read it. How do they get it? By previewing. Comprehension is significantly increased because previewing sheds some light on the subject; consequently, the reader does not have to proceed totally in the dark. It is a method for acquiring prior knowledge "on the spot."

Previewing generally will be directed by the teacher, and the teacher typically introduces this strategy to children and helps them initially learn it. But children should develop the habit of previewing material themselves; if instruction goes as planned, the teacher's coaching gradually should diminish as students begin to assume responsibility for previewing.

Indeed, this is the goal of instruction on all reading strategies. Let us say that a class is about to read *part* of a new unit entitled "The World of Carmelita and José." The teacher speaks to the class:

TEACHER: Boys and girls, for the next few days we will be reading from our social studies books. I would like to introduce you to two children we will visit in this unit whose names are Carmelita and José. Please open your books to page 86. (The children take time to find the page.) Notice that the large print says "The World of Carmelita and José." Just looking at this page, what do you think this unit is about?

FRIEDA: Mexico.

TEACHER: Why did you say Mexico, Frieda?

FRIEDA: Because Carmelita and José are Mexican names. Besides, it shows their pictures and they are dressed in Mexican clothes. . . . We learned that when we studied the community in Texas. . . .

DAVID: That doesn't mean they are from Mexico. They could be from several countries in South America and have names like that. They would dress like that, too.

TEACHER: Those are both good ideas. Perhaps if we page through this unit, we can discover the country it talks about. Turn to the map on page 88. . . .

It is established that the unit is, indeed, about Mexico, and the teacher continues:

TEACHER: As you look at these pages, what do you suppose you will be reading about in the world of Carmelita and José?

ERIC: Well, it looks like . . . uh . . . it tells like . . . you know . . . what they do every day . . . in school . . . at home, you know. . . .

LISA: It shows how they do many of the same things we do.

TEACHER: What do you mean?

LISA: Well, we have homes and families, we go to school, we go shopping, and things like that, and they do, too.

The discussion concludes after the teacher is satisfied that the children are oriented to the material to be read. Previews should do the following:

1. Help the reader get the general idea of the selection.
2. Help the reader understand how the material is organized and understand the nature of the narrative.
3. Help the reader see how the subject matter to be read relates to prior studies or experiences.
4. Help the reader understand how illustrations relate to the subject matter to be read.

Skim for Ideas and Related Details

Once children have previewed the selection of text they intend to read, it is a good idea to skim it for ideas and related details. The teacher begins:

TEACHER: Now that you have some general ideas about what you will be reading, let's take some time to become still more familiar with it. We will be using a strategy good readers use called *skimming*. What do you think skimming means?

MEI: It means taking something off the top, like skimming off the bugs at the swimming pool in the park. I see them do it because we go early in the morning.

EDDY: Yeah, and it means going really fast.

The teacher helps the children define skimming and then directs them as follows:

1. Students are given thirty seconds to thumb through the selection, noticing as best they can what is on every page.
2. The teacher asks what they noticed and takes responses.
3. The teacher directs students to read the questions under the last heading, **Review.** Students are asked if, based on those questions, they want to revise what they earlier said the selection was about. The teacher elicits revisions. For example, a student responds:

LISA: Well, it must not be only about Carmelita and José. I mean, it's also about the country because the second question asks about the climate.

4. The teacher directs students' attention to the other section headings and asks students to skim again to find out the number of sections and the topic of each.
5. Next, students are directed to quickly read the first few sentences under each section head. After just one minute or so, the teacher asks them what they found.

Establish Clear Purposes for Reading

Reading for a purpose is critical to comprehension. Children may pore over their social studies texts for endless hours without really knowing what they are looking for or why they are doing the reading. Clearly, it is the teacher's responsibility to make sure that the reading children do is purposeful. In directed study, these purposes may be given orally by the teacher:

Find the sentence near the top of page 115 that begins, "Each time this happens. . . ." Put your finger on that sentence. (The teacher sees that all children have the correct place.) Now read the next three paragraphs to find out three different ways of controlling air pollution.

If the reading is to be done independently, that is, not directed by the teacher, as in the example given, the purposes of the reading can be written on the chalkboard:

As you read the section "Dangers to Health" on pages 143–146, find the answers to these questions:
1. Why are scientists worried about air pollution?

2. Why has the government stopped the sale of some products?
3. What does the author mean on page 145 when he says, "Time is running out"?

The book itself may provide aids for setting purposes for reading. For example, the teacher says:

> For several days we have been learning about life in and around Big City. Today we will be doing some reading about how people get to work in Big City. On page 25 of your book there is a section that begins with the question "How Do People in Big City Get to Work?" Open your book to page 25. Can you find that question? Fine. As you read this part, find out as many ways as you can how people get to work in Big City. When you are finished reading, we will talk about the ways you found. See if each of you can find all the ways the author tells about.

The teacher should vary the purposes from time to time to allow children to practice a variety of skills. Purposes can relate directly to the four basic components of comprehension; namely, getting the literal meaning, getting facts and details, sensing a sequence of events or ideas, and following directions.

Use Study and Organization Aids Provided in the Book

The use of study and organization aids was discussed earlier in this chapter. Attention is called to these aids again here because their use can be enormously helpful in comprehending what is read. It should be stressed that time must be taken to explain the organization of material and to instruct children in the use of the various aids presented. In learning about the organization of the material, children are also learning skills that are associated with organizing their own ideas to gain a better understanding.

Teach Children to Vary Their Rate of Reading

As a regular part of social studies instruction, the teacher should devise reading situations that require children to vary their rate of reading for a particular purpose. This may be in the form of questions, some calling for rapid reading or skimming, others for more detailed careful reading and rereading. Commonly, the answers to names of places, persons, situations, dates, and similar factual data can be obtained through skimming, whereas answers to reflective questions will require slower, more careful reading.

Relate What Is Read to Life Experiences of Children

Relating what is read to one's experiences not only helps comprehension but is motivating as well. It tends to give the material an added dimension of meaningfulness. Here are a few examples:

THE CHILDREN READ ABOUT:	THEY RELATE THIS TO:
1. Fire hazards.	1. Danger spots in their homes.
2. Discoverers, explorers, pioneers.	2. Present-day mountain climbers, adventurers, astronauts.
3. Ecology.	3. Local environmental contamination.
4. Occupations and careers.	4. Their own career interests and ambitions.
5. The law and justice systems.	5. Their own involvement with the law (in the civil, not criminal area).
6. The interdependence of nations.	6. The energy crisis, foreign-made products they use.

Check Comprehension Regularly and Keep Individual Records

When one wants to improve, it helps to record progress. In working toward improved reading comprehension, the teacher should follow a systematic cycle of instruction, practice, evaluation, and feedback to the learner. Social studies education is or should be more than reading. But beginning at about the third grade and continuing through the middle and upper grades, indeed, through high school, reading (especially reading *comprehension*) is critical to success in social studies. Comprehension suffers when the teacher assumes that the learner has the skills developed well enough to meet the reading requirements of the social studies.

Short teacher-made tests similar to several of the examples provided in this chapter can be used to assess student comprehension. Test questions should focus on those items of information that are believed to be important to learn and to remember.[19] It is recommended that time limits be set for such evaluations and that these be kept constant from one test to the next. Providing the children with information about the improvement they have made in reading over a period of time is likely to encourage greater effort on their part to improve their reading comprehension.

LEARNING TO INTERPRET DATA

Social studies materials often require that the reader interpret data. This involves *making inferences, sensing relationships, noting cause-and-effect occurrences, detecting the emotional bias of the author, reading critically, evaluating the material, and being able to anticipate or predict likely outcomes.* It requires the

---

[19]Karen K. Wixson, "Levels of Importance of Postquestions and Children's Learning from Text," *American Educational Research Journal* 21 (September 1984): 419–33.

reader to go beyond the literal presentation of the facts and to sense the significance of them. This process is referred to as "reading between and beyond the lines." Consider the following example that might be a passage from a selection read by fifth graders:

> All day long the wagon train moved slowly westward. The travelers were tired and weary from the long, dusty journey. The wagonmaster looked at his watch. It was four o'clock, but the sun was still high in the sky. Directly ahead was the river that had to be crossed. On the other side was high ground. Near the river bank was a fine grove of trees. The wagonmaster wondered if he should have the tired travelers cross the river yet today or camp on this side of the river and cross over the first thing in the morning. He decided to make the crossing that evening.

Now answer the questions: (1) In what season of the year were the people traveling? (2) Why do you suppose the wagonmaster decided in favor of crossing that evening? Notice that the material does not give the answers to either of the questions, yet the answers can be inferred from the information given. Many passages in social studies books lend themselves to questions of this type.

Making Inferences

Research in children's thinking supports the view that reasoning and problem-solving abilities begin at about age three and develop continually with increasing age and experience. Stimulating experiences in critical thinking and problem solving during the formative years of early childhood can do much to foster the growth of such skills. The example "Ellis Island," in chapter 4 shows how two different kinds of questions can be based on the same piece of prose, each requiring different reading skills and different intellectual processes.

In a comparison of these two sets of questions, it is obvious that one set can be answered directly from the text and that the other cannot. In the latter case the readers must go beyond the information provided by the author; they have to bring prior knowledge to bear on the questions. They have to be able to speculate, to wonder, and to imagine. Moreover, there are probably no absolutely correct answers to these questions. In the case of the first set of questions, right answers can be established if one uses the authority of the narrative in determining correctness. Clearly, questions such as those in the right-hand column are best suited for discussion in class and should not be given as homework assignments.

Sensing Relationships

Social studies material often requires the reader to sense relationships among variables and to come to conclusions. Although factors may occur at the same time or follow in an established sequence, this does not mean that one *causes* the other. For example, areas of poor housing also show high incidence of law violation, but one would not conclude that crime occurs because people live in poor housing. There are, no doubt, other causal factors that relate to both housing and crime. Thus, the reader may not necessarily be searching for cause and effect but for things that seem to "go together." Or the reader may want to sort through the ideas presented to determine whether they are major ideas or supporting detail. In some instances, the reader is expected to use the information given and predict what consequences are likely to flow from the given situation. Here are examples to illustrate this type of interpretive reading:

SENSING CAUSE AND EFFECT

In each of the following situations, decide whether the price of the product is likely to (1) go *up*, (2) go *down*, or (3) stay the *same*. If unable to tell, give reasons for your answer.

A. Nearly one-third of the Florida nurseries are out of production because of citrus canker. There is no remedy for citrus canker. The only way to save the state's 761,000 acres of trees is to burn every contaminated tree, leaf, and twig. This disaster comes just as growers were beginning to recover from last year's killer freeze. How does this affect the price of oranges?

B. Scientists are not sure why the El Niño condition occurs. For unexplained reasons, the warm ocean currents of the tropics move in a northerly direction along the west coast of North America. The warmer water temperature, even though slight, is harmful to the food chain of certain marine animals. Thus, clams and crabs were nearly wiped out along parts of the west coast. Even the life cycle of the salmon was affected by El Niño. How does this affect the price of Alaskan king crab?

C. In the wake of monumental losses in car sales, General Motors announced plans to close fourteen assembly plants and to lay off thousands of workers. Plans are under way to modernize existing operations, to reduce production costs, and to restore GM's image of a builder of quality automobiles. These moves are designed to make GM products more competitive. How will this affect the price of cars?

D. The surgeon general's office announced today that there was a clear link between "the product" and cancer in laboratory animals. The surgeon general was advising against the use of "the product," particularly by young adults, until further tests could be made on human subjects. How will this affect the price of "the product"?

PREDICTING OUTCOMES

In a medium-sized city, a large company needed to hire 1,500 more workers. Would the population of the city increase by 1,500 or by more than that number? How can you tell? What problems would such a city face in taking care of this many people?

LOCATING AND USING REFERENCE MATERIALS

Children should make use of a wide variety of reference material in studying social studies topics. The value of such references depends not only on their availability but also on the ability of the children to make use of them. The teacher's responsibility in this respect is, therefore, twofold: teaching children (1) which references to use for various purposes and (2) how to use the reference efficiently once it is found. These are continuing responsibilities of the social studies program and cannot be completely taught in any one grade or any one year. A beginning will be made in the primary grades, but the child will continue to extend and refine the ability to use references throughout high school, college, and in later life. Instruction usually will begin as soon as the child develops a degree of independence in reading.

The reference materials used in the social studies may be grouped meaningfully as follows:

Books

Textbooks
Supplementary reading books
Picture books
Biographies
Historical fiction

Special References

Encyclopedias
Maps and globes
Atlases
Dictionaries
World Almanac
Charts and graphs
Yearbooks
Legislative Manuals
Who's Who in America
Junior Book of Authors
Statesman's Yearbook
Computers

Reference Aids

Card catalog
The Reader's Guide
Bibliographies
COMCATS

Miscellaneous Materials

Advertisements
Magazines and periodicals
Recipes
City and telephone directories
Labels
Guidebooks and tour books
Letters and diaries
Travel folders
Postcards
Newspapers and news clippings
Comic books
Pictures
Schedules and timetables
Pamphlets and booklets (such as those from the information services of foreign countries, superintendent of documents, conservation departments, historical societies, art galleries)
Weather reports
Manufacturers' guarantees and warranties
Money, checks, coupons for premiums, receipts
Reviews, government documents

Much of the instruction given on the use of references will have to be specific to the particular resource used. For example, one uses the *World Almanac* differently from the way one uses an atlas or a tour book. Moreover,

FIGURE 10-8.

An Example of Teacher-Prepared Task Cards.

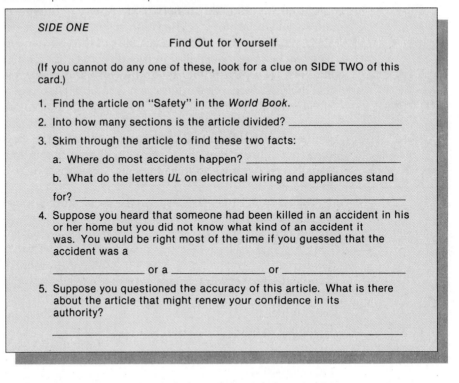

SIDE ONE

Find Out for Yourself

(If you cannot do any one of these, look for a clue on SIDE TWO of this card.)

1. Find the article on "Safety" in the *World Book*.

2. Into how many sections is the article divided? _____

3. Skim through the article to find these two facts:

   a. Where do most accidents happen? _____

   b. What do the letters *UL* on electrical wiring and appliances stand for? _____

4. Suppose you heard that someone had been killed in an accident in his or her home but you did not know what kind of an accident it was. You would be right most of the time if you guessed that the accident was a

   _____ or a _____ or _____

5. Suppose you questioned the accuracy of this article. What is there about the article that might renew your confidence in its authority?

   _____

the references may be used at varying levels of sophistication. The library may be used by primary-grade children under teacher guidance to check out books, to look at magazines, or to have stories read to them whereas upper-grade children should be able to use the library independently, making use of the card catalog and locating books themselves. The use of the various references should be taught as the need for them arises in the social studies.

Skills needed to use references can be practiced and learned on an individual basis or by children in pairs using *task cards,* as is illustrated in Figure 10-8.

If teachers regard the teaching of reading as something that is done in three small groups during the reading period and ignore the reading needs of children during the remainder of the school day, they may expect children to have many disappointing experiences reading social studies material. The feeling that children learn to read in the basic reading program and read to learn in the social studies, for example, is not an entirely correct concept of the relationship between these two processes. Actually, the two occur simultaneously; children improve their reading ability *as they read to learn.* Children can extend and improve their reading skills and abilities quite apart from the basic reading program as they use reading for a variety of purposes.

FIGURE 10-8.
(*continued*)

SIDE TWO

CLUES

1. Select volume S–Sn. Look for the article according to the alphabet.

2. See the "Outline" at the end of the article.

3. a. Look under the section "Safety/Home."
   b. Look under "Safety with Electricity."

4. What does the article say about the major causes of accidental deaths in the home?

   _____

   _____

   _____

5. What group critically reviewed the article?

   _____

   _____

   _____

   _____

Lesson Plan 10 shows how one teacher organized a research project for a sixth-grade class.

USING WRITING SKILLS IN SOCIAL STUDIES

The learning activities associated with social studies present many opportunities to teach all of the communication skills, not only reading. Children read for information and often share that newly gained knowledge through oral reports and in class discussions. In such interactions, they use speech and speaking skills, and, correspondingly, others are listening to what is being communicated. Or children may prepare written notes or reports on what they have read or heard. And as we detail in the next chapter, they may produce books. We see, therefore, that there is a constant and close relationship between and among the several language arts—reading, speaking, listening, writing—as skills that are essential to learning social studies. The reverse is also true; social studies presents excellent functional settings in which to teach such skills.

The elementary school curriculum often becomes fragmented with bits and pieces of subjects and skills that are not tied into an integrated organized framework. Moreover, subjects and skills such as writing, reading,

LEARNING TO USE REFERENCES

In the Primary Grades

1. Acquaint the children with the school library, and provide pleasurable experiences for them with this facility by having them look through books, check out books, look at magazines, and have stories read to them. Enlist the help of the librarian if there is one.
2. Provide learning centers that are well stocked with easy reading and picture books related to the topic under study.
3. Make frequent use of references in the regular work of the classroom. This may mean comparing a seashell that a child has brought with the picture of one in the book of shells; finding out whether we eat the roots, stems, or leaves of broccoli; finding out about the different kinds of boats and their uses; and hundreds of other questions that children wonder about during the course of the unit. It is helpful to have an encyclopedia handy for this purpose. Not all children will be able to use it, but its presence and use by the teacher provide an excellent means of developing positive attitudes toward reference materials.
4. Identify the children who are progressing rapidly in reading and teach and encourage them to use references such as encyclopedias, magazines, pamphlets, and other material from which they can profit but that may be too complex for the rest of the class.
5. Give children experiences in helping to locate materials—finding appropriate pictures, stories, or sections of books that relate to the social studies topic.
6. Develop prerequisite competencies for the efficient use of a dictionary: alphabetical ordering, use of guide words, antonyms, synonyms, multiple meanings of words. Primary-grade children could make a class picture dictionary of social studies words and terms they encounter.

In the Middle and Upper Grades

1. Make certain that children know how to use the various parts of a book (see pp. 292–293).
2. Take time out to teach children how to use the library, card catalog, the *Reader's Guide,* and other aids for the purpose of locating information, including COM-CATS.
3. Teach the various skills needed to use each of the special references: encyclopedia, *World Almanac,* atlas. Provide for practice as well as application in purposeful settings.
4. Plan social studies activities that require the use of a wide variety of references.
5. Have children browse through the library and other sources to locate material that is appropriate for the unit under study.
6. Teach children how to identify key words in using reference material. Children may know how to use the references but not know what to look for with regard to the information they are seeking.
7. Teach children how to use titles of books as guides to their content, and select books that are appropriate for the purpose.

Topic:	China today
Grade:	Six or seven
Time:	Ten class periods
Objectives:	Students will learn basic information about the People's Republic of China. Students will refine research and small-group skills.
Interest Building:	For several days as the class is reading the text's overview of China, invite students to bring to school other recently published materials about China (books, magazines, travel brochures). Display these in a learning center.
Lesson Development:	Preview the resources.
	Using the text and resources for inspiration, brainstorm a list of topics that would be suitable for small-group information gathering projects.
	Have a member of the class list the topics on a chart in the learning center (see Sample Chart).
	Divide the class into study groups of five children each.
	Study group assignment: Elect a leader. Meet, discuss, and agree on and sign up for a topic.
	Decide on subtopics to study.
	Use outline format for taking notes.
	Organize report into an introduction, main body, and conclusion.
	Prepare visuals. Some ideas include charts, graphs, time lines, and illustrations from resources.
	Practice giving the oral report.
	Assign report dates.
	Give students a copy of each evaluation form. Discuss expectations (see Sample Evaluation Forms).
Summary:	Groups give their oral reports with each member contributing to the presentation. They field questions and comments from their audience.

Sample Chart: China Today Reports

Topics	Names of Group Members	Report Date
Family life and education Geography and natural resources Economy: Agriculture and industry Political system: Leaders and history Holidays and festivals Cities Tourism and transportation Arts and athletics Science and technology		

(continued)

China Today Report: Sample Teacher Evaluation	Yes	No	Comments
Was an introduction used? Were the main ideas presented? Were supporting details given? Was there a clear conclusion? Were visuals used? Was teamwork evident? Group Grade:_____			

China Today Report: Sample Group Evaluation

Topic:_____

_____

What did you do well?
How could you have improved your report?
List the resources that you used.

Evaluation: Complete the evaluation forms. Base the group's grade on a consideration of both evaluations.
Collect each student's notes. Evaluate these on an individual basis.

Resources: Text: *World Regions*, Macmillan/McGraw-Hill
Recommended trade books:
China, Here We Come! Tang Yungmei
Two Chinese Families, Catherine Edwards Sadler
Red Star & Green Dragon: Looking at New China, Lila Perl
The People's Republic of China: Red Star of the East, Jane Werner Watson
Dragonwings, Lawrence Yep

spelling, and listening often become make-believe exercises when they are taught in isolation, outside of a subject matter context. These skills become much more meaningful for a learner when they are taught in purposeful settings. The child is then reading to find out something of importance to the subject under study. Or the child is writing something that will be shared with others as a contribution to knowledge about a topic. With greater attention to the inclusion of important communication skills in the units planned for social studies, the teaching of social studies *and* the language arts would be improved. We have discussed this subject as related to one component of the language arts, namely, reading; now let us direct our attention to writing skills.

Whereas reading has to do with the use of coded symbols to build ideas and feelings, writing reverses the process. Nonetheless, there is a reciprocal relationship between the two skills. One always reads what has already been written. Indeed, one reads one's own writing. One writes something with the expectation that either oneself or someone else will read what has been written. Writers often say that it is not until they have read what they wrote that they know what they think!

In addition to the skills associated with the mechanics of writing, such as capitalization, spelling, punctuation, and handwriting, Figure 10-9 lists writing skills that can and should be taught within the context of social studies.

Writing skill is developed when the individual engages in a considerable amount of writing and is provided instructive and supportive feedback on what is written. In short, writing requires practice with the intent to improve. Therefore, if the only writing children do in the social studies consists of filling in single words or short phrases in workbooks or worksheets, one cannot expect much progress in any of the important writing skills identified in the foregoing paragraph. Accordingly, the teacher must involve children in social studies-related writing assignments as a regular part of the work of the class. Such writing tasks need to be appropriate to the developmental level of the children.

Simply providing the *opportunity* for children to write is not in itself enough to develop writing habits and skills. They also need instruction, and they need to be motivated. Writing is often drudgery because the individual does not know how to go about doing it or has no inclination to want to do it or both. Consequently, school writing assignments frequently stifle writing abilities rather than encourage them. Teachers who have taught writing successfully create an environment or climate that places high value on writing and makes it seem an exciting adventure for young learners. Techniques that have been used successfully by teachers follow.

FIGURE 10-9
Writing Abilities and Skills Related to Social Studies

- Mechanical skills (spelling, punctuation, capitalization, etc.).
- Notetaking.
- Letter writing.
- Organizing and outlining.
- Preparing written reports.
- Recordkeeping.
- Writing letters to elected representatives.
- Composing biographies of great citizens.
- Summarizing ideas.
- Writing creative material, for example, poems, historical fiction, plays.
- Describing events, such as a field trip.
- Explaining causes, such as for the Civil War.
- Preparing public notices, announcements, advertisements.
- Preparing written analyses of school and community problems, and proposals for solving them.

Ten Techniques That Make Writing Easier

1. Have students write to identifiable audiences such as other students, readers of the class newsletter, guest speakers, the mayor, and parents.

2. List and post difficult technical terms that students might find useful in their writing, such as *due process* and *interdependence.*

3. Use imaginative springboards to encourage creative writing. For example (1) write a story about a pioneer girl, a pony, and a snowstorm; (2) keep a one-month diary of a newly arrived African child in the year 1750; (3) describe how you ordered breakfast in a restaurant in a country where no one knew how to speak your language; (4) write what happened to you when you were lost in a large city.

4. Remind children to use what knowledge about writing they have already learned (indenting paragraphs, using exclamation marks, using quotation marks to indicate conversations, edit work at least once before asking someone to read it, and so on).

5. Regularly provide opportunities for children to share their written work with others *and then to revise it.*

6. Display children's work, for example, on the bulletin board, in the class newsletter, in the town newspaper, and at "parent night."

7. Use word games to develop more elaborate vocabulary—rhyming words, synonyms, antonyms, "happy" words, "sad" words, night sounds, city noises, and so on.

These children are improving their writing skills by editing and revising books they have written. Discussing possible revisions with classmates and the teacher helps to clarify ideas central to the topic being written about. According to an old saying, we learn what we think by reading what we have written.
(Photo by Carla Anderson, Northshore School District.)

8. Have children respond to questions that ask for an out-of-the ordinary answer. For example, after examining a portrait, ask, "What mineral do the eyes remind you of?" Or "Does the mouth tell you anything about this person?" In studying situations or photographs, such questions as these could be asked: "What colors do you think of when you see this (or smells, sounds, and so on)?" Or "Write a story about the Pilgrims from the point of view of the Indians." Or "Describe Columbus's place in history if there had been no North or South America."

9. Encourage children to evaluate their writing using checklists and in this way to monitor their progress as writers.

10. Have writers of all sorts visit the class and describe their writing *process* and its benefits.

Writing Activities for Social Studies

The best writing activities for social studies are those that children do within the context of what they are studying. Writing assignments take on a sense of importance and purpose when they are needed as a part of the process of achieving other objectives. A letter written to obtain information, for example, is likely to be more meaningful than is a make-believe letter written to a fictitious person. Thus, insofar as possible, writing activities in social studies should be functionally related to the class work. This gives writing practice authenticity: Children are writing in real ways for real purposes.[20]

The activities on the following list have been used by elementary and middle school teachers who have successfully related the teaching of writing skills to social studies:

1. Write endings to reaction stories or situations in which the outcome is in doubt.
2. Prepare a classroom newsletter or newspaper.
3. Prepare an original script for dramatization.
4. Maintain a class or personal diary ("Today I learned how to jump rope." "Today I lost a tooth." "Today we had a visitor from China.")
5. Prepare outlines or notes for an oral report.
6. Prepare captions for pictures, illustrations, exhibits, cartoons.
7. Write explanations of events or exhibits or after a field trip.
8. Make holiday greeting cards, and write appropriate messages.
9. Write letters requesting information or material or both, letters inviting visitors to the classroom, thank-you letters, and get-well messages to classmates and teachers.
10. Create "news" stories about historical events; create descriptive headlines for historical events.

---

[20]John Seely Brown, Alan Collins, and Paul Duguid, "Situated Cognition and the Culture of Learning," *Educational Researcher* 18 (January/February 1989): 32–42.

LESSON PLAN 11

Topic:	Members of our community
Grade:	Three or four
Time:	Two class periods
Objectives:	To reinforce the value of consideration for others. To learn how to write thank-you letters.
Interest Building:	The class was invited to and visited a senior center for the purpose of seeing a display of crafts prepared by the members. The experience was a positive one for the children, and the teacher has suggested that they prepare and send thank-you letters.
Lesson Development:	Ask children to brainstorm what they *liked* about their visit and what they *learned* from their experience. List these, in separate columns, on the chalkboard and save.
	Explain that thank-you letters are an appropriate way to express gratitude for visits, hospitality, and so on, and that is how each member of the class will thank the senior citizens.
	Review letter format.
	Distribute the assignment sheet in the form of a letter for the class to use as a reference.
	(The body of *your* letter could be the following: "Your assignment is to write a thank-you letter to our friends at the Forest Park Center. Remember to include one thing you liked about the visit and one thing you learned. Your paragraph should be at least five sentences long. Please hand in your rough draft by Friday.")
	Review your letter directions with them. Children write first draft of individual letters. Make corrections as needed. Children write final drafts of letters. Send letters.

11. Keep minutes of meetings.
12. Write directions for doing something, such as making soap, reading a chart, or operating a machine.
13. Take notes from several different sources for use in a discussion.
14. Take notes while listening to a speaker.
15. Organize material, and prepare a written report for others to read.
16. Write narrative descriptions of a class project.
17. Write a position statement in preparation for a class discussion or schoolwide meeting.
18. Label items on maps.
19. Write answers to questions.
20. Summarize ideas into topic sentences to be developed into paragraphs.

21. Prepare short annotations of trade books used in social studies.
22. Write a script for a tape-recorded program.
23. Write a short history of the school and the community.
24. List words that describe particularly well some event or period.
25. Write a poem to express feelings about a topic or period studied.
26. Write entries in a diary that might have been kept by an explorer or a pioneer.
27. Prepare maps of various types, and write accompanying explanations.
28. Write book reviews.
29. Write a short story based on subject matter studied in social studies.
30. Write a letter home as it might have been written by a member of the Lewis and Clark Expedition.

DISCUSSION QUESTIONS AND SUGGESTED ACTIVITIES

1. If social studies textbooks are written for the average reader, why is it that all good social studies textbooks tend to be difficult for the average reader?
2. Select a children's social studies text, and examine it to find examples of the reading skills listed in Figure 10-2.
3. Select a children's textbook, and provide sample exercises based on the points made in the section entitled "Using Study Aids and Study Skills to Improve Reading."
4. Using the text you selected in your answer to question 3, find examples of the social studies words and terms listed in Figure 10-4.
5. Select a passage from a children's social studies textbook, and develop comprehension questions (see chapter 4). Develop an equal number of interpretive-type questions.
6. What reference books do you believe are the most useful to children? Why do you think so?
7. Pick a social studies topic for a grade of your choice. Make a list of poems, stories, biographies, and other reading sources that develop a strong mental set or mood appropriate to the topic. Read selected passages to your classmates.
8. Choose one of the references listed on page 315. What prerequisite skills must the child have in order to use that reference effectively and efficiently?
9. Prepare a lesson plan for social studies that incorporates the teaching of a related writing skill.
10. How might the teaching of writing be linked to a lesson designed to teach improved reading comprehension? Provide an example of such a lesson.

11.   Outline a full-year plan to apprentice children into the three literacy
practices discussed at the beginning of the chapter.

SELECTED REFERENCES

CAMPERELL, KAY, AND RICHARD S. KNIGHT. "Reading Research and Social Studies." In
Handbook of Research on Social Studies Teaching and Learning, edited by James P.
Shaver, 567–77. New York: Macmillan, 1991.

GILSTRAP, ROBERT L. "Writing for the Social Studies." In *Handbook of Research on Social
Studies Teaching and Learning,* edited by James P. Shaver, 578–88. New York:
Macmillan, 1991.

GOODMAN, KENNETH. *What's Whole in Whole Language?* Richmond Hill, Ontario: Scholastic, 1986.

JOHNSON, DALE D., AND P. DAVID PEARSON. *Teaching Reading Vocabulary.* 2d ed. New
York: Holt, Rinehart, and Winston, 1984.

LIPSON, MARJORIE Y., AND KAREN K. WIXSON. *Assessment and Instruction of Reading Disability.* New York: HarperCollins, 1991.

NAGY, WILLIAM E. *Teaching Vocabulary to Improve Reading Comprehension.* Urbana, IL:
ERIC Clearinghouse on Reading and Communication Skills, the National Council of Teachers of English, and the International Reading Association, 1988.

PAPPAS, CHRISTINE C., BARBARA Z. KIEFER, AND LINDA S. LEVSTIK. *An Integrated Language
Perspective in the Elementary School.* White Plains, NY: Longman, 1990.

RESNICK, LAUREN B., "Literacy In School and Out." *Daedalus* 119: 2 (Spring 1990):
169–85.

TCHUDI, STEPHEN. *Planning and Assessing the Curriculum in English Language Arts.* Alexandria, VA: Association for Supervision and Curriculum Development, 1991.

WINTEROWD, W. ROSS. *The Culture and Politics of Literacy.* New York: Oxford University
Press, 1989.

11 Social Studies as the Integrating Core: Literacy, Literature, and Culture

I magine that five third-grade teachers at a nearby elementary school decide to plan two interdisciplinary units together over the course of the year, one in the winter and one in the spring. They are making a commitment not only to meet regularly in the fall for planning, but also to gear their planning toward units that would bring together subjects and skills they normally teach separately, subjects and skills such as reading, writing, and social studies. Their rationale is that valuable instructional time is lost when reading lessons and writing lessons do not overlap one another and when, together, they do not overlap social studies lessons.

Children cannot simply read *reading* or write *writing*, these teachers reason, so why not direct their reading and writing toward the content they need also to learn? This is, after all, precisely the content to which children should be learning to apply their developing reading and writing skills. In this way, two things are accomplished. Skills are used to help achieve valued content goals, and the skills themselves are strengthened by being engaged with content. This reasoning stands on firm ground: As research on reading and writing makes abundantly clear, "one does not simply learn to read and write: one learns to read and write about particular things in particular ways."[1]

As most teachers will attest, interdisciplinary education and collaborative unit planning are two of the most popular trends in elementary education. But no clear pattern for either has emerged yet. Some teachers, such as the five mentioned above, are concerned mainly to combine reading and writing instruction with subject matter instruction. Others are interested primarily in integrating social studies with science, mathematics, and the arts. Still others are eager to find powerful themes around

---

[1]Judith A. Langer and Arthur N. Applebee, "Reading and Writing Instruction: Toward a Theory of Teaching and Learning," in *Review of Research in Education*, vol. 13 ed. Ernest Z. Rothkopf (Washington, DC: American Educational Research Association, 1986), 171–94.

which all curricular areas, from reading to math and music appreciation, can be brought together. In this chapter, we present ways the teacher can begin to build experience and a repetoire of strategies for integrated education.

EXEMPLARY INTEGRATED UNITS

We begin with some examples, a gallery of exhibits drawn from actual classroom life. We invite readers, in the spirit of concept formation (chapter 2), to use them to develop a concept of interdisciplinary education.[2]

EXHIBIT A: IN THE YEAR OF THE IMMIGRANT

Three fifth-grade teachers at an urban elementary school joined together to plan an integrated unit on the theme, *immigration.* The gathering of diverse peoples on the North American continent, they believe, is one of the most important ideas treated in the social studies curriculum. Could their eleven-year-old students grapple with the idea in a way that was both engaging and rigorous? These teachers decided they could.

"We tried to give the kids a real feeling for what immigration is like," one teacher said. They provided students with lots of information, some drawn from textbooks and films, and some from literature, helping them all the while to connect that information to personal experiences and prior knowledge. Moreover, the teachers built into the unit plan ample opportunities for children to apply historical information to current immigration events and controversies.

IMMIGRATION UNIT RESOURCES

Films: *Golden Mountain on Mott Street*
                The Girl Who Spelled Freedom

Trade Books: *Immigrant Kids,* Russell Freedman (Dutton, 1980)
                Journey Home, Yoshiko Uchida (Macmillan, 1978)
                In the Year of the Boar and Jackie Robinson, Bette Bao Lord (Harper & Row, 1986)

As students read and dramatized the books and watched the films, they used the information they were gathering to write in their journals about leaving a beloved homeland, anticipating a new life, being welcomed, being turned away, and feeling one's ethnic identity for the first time because one is for the first time *different.* The teachers especially had them write on the themes *coming* (immigration) and *going* (emigration). Several children wrote the following:

---

[2]These examples are based on program descriptions that appeared in Walter C. Parker's "Social Studies Trends" column in *Educational Leadership* in October 1989, November 1987, and March 1987.

Coming to a new language

Away from a place where snow is deep.

Coming to weather that can't make up its mind

Away from soldiers in uniform with tanks and guns.

Coming to streets paved with gold

Away from where the rivers flow.

Coming to cement streets

Away from the people who love me.

Coming to dangerous people.

As well, they wrote advice to children who might immigrate. Some children warned of "really bad gangs like Crips and Bloods." Others told how to find one's way around the local airport. One student was concerned that immigrants from agrarian cultures would not know what to do with a toilet. "In America, there are things that are different," she wrote.

There are toilets that you sit on. You do not have to squat down and get your legs sore. I'll teach you how to flush it. *Flush* means to push a button or handle and the water goes down and clean water comes up.

Working with the school's reading and music specialists, the fifth-grade teachers invited from the community a young composer, actors, and mime artists to help draw all this together into a fifth-grade big event that would culminate the learning. All the writing and reading and discussing would be pulled together in a script, featuring movement, dance, mime, and song. All seventy-five fifth-grade children, they agreed, would have a part. Together they produced a musical drama, "In the Year of the Immigrant." The chorus to the title song went as follows:

Away, away, to have a better home,
for better education,
for better occupations,
together in a nation we shall call home.

Immigrants bring us new perspectives,
moving our world in new directions,
bringing together different ways of life.

Welcome the changing forms of culture,
welcome the changing forms of fashion,
moving in the hope of finding a better way.

The school has one the most diverse populations in the district, with Asian Americans and South Pacific Islanders, African Americans, and European Americans in roughly equal number. One-third of them were classified "at risk." Some spend up to two hours on a bus each day. Not one of the seventy-five children missed any of the daytime or evening performances of "In the Year of the Immigrant."

EXHIBIT B: AN INTERGALACTIC BILL OF RIGHTS

Fifth-grade teacher Tarry Lindquist believes that one of the most powerful ways to plan units is to engage children in meaningful projects. As they participate in a project's tasks—reading, writing, debating, constructing, simulating, dramatizing, and so on—students are required to learn many skills and much content. This is knowledge that a less capable teacher might try to teach outside of such a meaningful project. But incorporated within project activities, the knowledge is more likely to be learned in a way that the learner will remember and later be able to use. Higher-order thinking and the acquisition of knowledge become two sides of one coin.

Mrs. Lindquist received the Teacher of the Year award from the National Council for the Social Studies. In the integrated unit we describe here, one of many extraordinary units she has designed, Mrs. Lindquist practices two powerful principles: First, rather than trying to teach the necessary facts, ideas, and skills before beginning a project, *start* with the project and incorporate the facts, ideas, and skills learning as they are needed. Second, be sure this knowledge is important. Design projects around the knowledge students should be learning, not the other way around.

The Museum of Flight in Seattle, Washington, was about to unveil its new gallery—a huge, glass structure with airplanes on display in every direction. Mrs. Lindquist wanted her students to learn facts about the United States Constitution, but she also want them to grapple with the *concept* of constitution. She also wanted them to develop citizenship skills, especially the sort needed to work with other citizens on difficult public policy issues. Furthermore, she wanted them to learn more about space, extending the astronomy studies they already had begun and building on their fascination with the idea of living beyond our solar system. She embedded this learning in her project.

The year before, with funding provided by a bicentennial celebration organization, Mrs. Lindquist had gathered elementary teachers from around the state to a weekend retreat. The teachers' goal was to create a lesson plan that would have students simulate the decision making that occurred at the Constitutional Convention of 1787, and to situate this learning in a genuine challenge that paralleled the challenge the framers faced in 1787. For the challenge, the teachers decided on the likelihood of space colonization in these students' lifetime, and made the following four assumptions as the project's initial provisions:

High-density population centers will be common because permanent colonies in space will be tremendously expensive.

The trend toward multiethnic crews of both sexes will continue, and probably predicts future populations of space colonies.

As a consequence of prolonged breathing of pure oxygen in controlled environments, humans likely will evolve into a different species. (Mrs. Lindquist called it *homo spatialis*.)

The present system of jurisprudence practiced in the United States may not transfer to civic life in space. For example, light bends differently in space. Eyewitness accounts, taken for granted on earth, could be worth much more, or much less.

Mrs. Lindquist arranged to have fifty fourth-, fifth-, and sixth-grade students from as many classrooms move into the museum's new gallery for an overnight stay

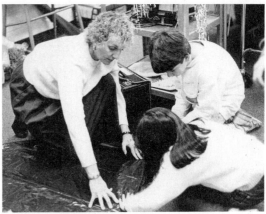

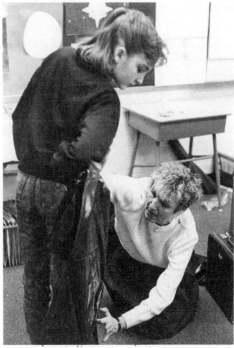

Tarry Lindquist, recipient of the Elementary School Teacher of the Year Award in 1990 from the National Council for the Social Studies, challenges her fifth graders to wrestle with the issues and arguments that dominated the U.S. Constitutional Convention in 1787. She accomplishes this by engaging them in a modern-day simulation involving the colonization of space. The children must develop and sign an intergalactic constitution and bill of rights. The event also requires spaceage formal wear, which the children construct from trash bags.
Photos by Judi Slepyan, parent, Lakeridge Elementary School, Mercer Island, Washington, Public Schools.

before it was opened to the public. Like astronauts, the children were exploring unknown space. And, like the framers of the U.S. Constitution who ventured to Philadelphia in 1787, each student came to this convention as a representative of his or her class. Their job, like the framers 200 years before, was to create a new document, one that did not exist anywhere: an intergalactic bill of rights.

Each of the fifty classrooms that eventually sent representatives to the intergalactic convention first developed a space colony. Students identified its physical size; location (some were on moons, some on space stations); optimal population size, density, and ethnic and gender composition; climate (both controlled and uncontrolled); and natural resources and related products. They also wrestled with space colony culture, making decisions about political life, economy, food, costume, and holidays and traditions.

Shortly after forming their colonies, the children learned that their colony's government had signed an intergalactic constitution with the others that would regulate relations among the fifty colonies. However, signing had been contingent on the framing of a bill of rights. The colonies were afraid that their rights would be lost to an authoritarian central galactic government, or to an overbearing majority that might gain control. The students' task, then, was to frame a draft bill of rights and elect a representative to take it to the intergalactic convention, to be held at the Museum of Flight.

At the convention, representatives were in a bind. They had to balance the wishes of their constituents back home with a healthy concern for the intergalactic *common good*. To do their work, representatives were assigned to "pods" of five, with a high school student who served as senior counselor. Eventually, two pods merged to form a group of ten; these reformed into other groups of ten, and so on—each time encountering different representatives with sometimes unique ideas and arguments, everyone presenting, defending, and rethinking their positions. Finally, agreements were struck and the Bill of Rights signed.

EXHIBIT C: EXPLORE

Explore is an integrated social studies/science curriculum developed by teachers and curriculum specialists in a Colorado school district together with the renowned concept learning and thinking skills expert, Sydelle Seiger-Ehrenberg.[3] This is a K–6 program. Pat Willsey, like Tarry Lindquist, believes deeply in the blending of thinking skills instruction with concept learning. Willsey, a key player in the development of *Explore* and now an elementary school principal in the district, took seriously the admonition of researchers to integrate thinking and knowledge instruction: "There is no choice to be made between a content emphasis and a thinking skills emphasis. No depth in either is possible without the other."[4] Note this blend in *Explore's* outcome statement: "As a result of using thinking strategies and other relevant skills, K–6 students will develop an understanding of the orderliness, diversity, relation-

---

[3]*Explore Curriculum,* developed and written jointly by Sydelle Seiger-Ehrenberg and School District no. 12, Adams County, Northglenn, Colorado, 1990. All material in this section is quoted or adapted from *Explore* curriculum documents.

[4]Lauren B. Resnick and Leopold E. Klopfer, eds. *Toward the Thinking Curriculum: Current Cognitive Research* (Alexandria, VA: Association for Supervision and Curriculum Development, 1989), 6.

ships, and changes that exist/occur and are created in the natural world and in human experience. Further, they will learn to make intelligent, responsible decisions/choices/judgments/plans in light of each understanding."

The curriculum for grades three and four concentrates on the first two conceptual themes respectively. Students are to become proficient in the use of thinking strategies for developing deep and flexible understandings of *orderliness* (consistency, pattern) and *diversity* (variety, uniqueness) that exist or are created:

* in living things
* in the natural environment
* in communities of people and other living things

Further, these third- and fourth-grade children are not expected to develop these understandings only to have them lie dormant in their minds. Rather, they are to learn to *use* them and, through usage, further develop them by making reasoned judgments and plans in light of their understanding. This activity is built directly into the unit plans. Note how this curriculum design, like Mrs. Lindquist's, emphasizes the interdependence of thinking (judging, planning) and knowing (understanding orderliness and diversity in living things, nature, and human communities).

Rounding out the third- and fourth-grade *Explore* curriculum is the study of occupations and avocations in which people use and develop greater understanding of living things, nature, and human communities. Following are four lessons in the first of twelve units. Because our space is limited, we present abridged and slightly revised versions. We begin with the introductory lesson to the grade 3 curriculum.

Introductory Lesson

Intended Learning Outcome: Students will be aware of the general procedures they will be following this year to study science and social studies topics.

Students are told that this year they will be studying science and social studies "as if all of you were scientists." They are then placed in pairs to discuss the question, "From what you know, what does it mean to be a 'scientist?' What does a scientist do?"

As students share their responses, the teacher often asks *verification* questions, especially the central question of science, *How do you know that's true?* This becomes a common question in *Explore* classrooms. Eventually, the teacher presents the following four-step procedure on a chart.

THE SCIENTIFIC WAY OF LEARNING

STEP 1—Question

STEP 2—Hypothesize, Predict

STEP 3—Investigate

STEP 4—Analyze/Evaluate Data, Conclude

The teacher then puts the following list on the board:

SOME THINGS SCIENTISTS INVESTIGATE

What plants need to grow

What the stars and planets are made of

How people in communities get along with each other

What the dinosaurs looked like

How people lived long ago

How people live now

What happens when you mix certain chemicals

How we know about weather and climate

After making sure that the class understands each item on the list, the teacher asks students what they know about each topic *as a result of scientists investigating it.*

The teacher then asks the students to go back over the list and name the kind of scientist that investigates some of these things. For example, "What do people call a scientist who investigates stars and planets? life in human communities? how people lived long ago? dinosaurs?" It is not important that students learn all the names of scientists, but that they realize, first, that there are different types of scientists and, second, that social studies stems from the work of *social* scientists.

To review, the teacher then says, "As you study science and social studies this year, you will be working just like the scientists we have been talking about. What does that mean? What will you be doing? What are the four things we said all scientists do?"

Assessment 1. The teacher displays a list of activities related to airplanes and says to students: "Suppose we were going to study airplanes and how they fly, and I told you that you would be working like real scientists. Which of the things on this list would you expect to be doing?"

   a. Make up a story about airplanes.
   b. Find some facts about airplanes and how they fly.
   c. Ask questions about airplanes and how they fly.
   d. Draw a picture of an airplane.
   e. Describe a trip you took on an airplane.
   f. Try to think of possible answers to your questions about airplanes and how they fly.
   g. Build a model of an airport.
   h. Keep looking for more facts about airplanes to see if the answers to your questions are right.

Assessment 2/ Homework. The teacher reviews the four-step procedure, then shows students a rock, leaf, shell, or similar item, giving them this task: "Suppose you were a scientist and had never seen anything like this before. What would you do to investigate it? Be prepared to tell us what you would do, how, and why."

Unit 1, Lesson 1

Focus Question: (Each lesson begins with a focus question to direct student/teacher attention.) What is true of all living things that distinguishes them from nonliving things?

Intended Learning Outcome: Students will develop a concept of living things in terms of both the characteristics common to all living

things and those that distinguish living things from nonliving things.

Question.   The teacher introduces the lesson: "First we are going to study living things and how they are *alike.* Since we're going to work as *scientists,* what is the first thing we need to do to study living things?" The teacher then reviews the chart, The Scientific Way of Learning, now focusing on the topic, Living Things and How They Are Alike.

Hypothesis.   Student attention is focused on the question, "How do we know whether something is or is not alive?" The teacher points to the second step in the four-step procedure and asks students what they need to do after they have asked a question: come up with possible answers. Then the teacher repeats the question, and students hypothesize. The teacher elicits responses, helping students to explain what they mean, and writes them on a chart:

We *think* something is alive if it has these characteristics:

The teacher emphasizes that students should give the information they *think* is true. Later they will investigate to find out which of their present ideas are correct. After a few characteristics are placed on the chart, students work in pairs to come up with additional responses.

Investigation.   The teacher helps children to move into step 3 of the scientific procedure: "As scientists, what is our next step?" Students should respond that they need to *investigate,* that is, find new information to check the accuracy of what they have put on the chart, and find out what else belongs on it. They may ask, "How can we find the kind of information we need?" At this point *Explore* takes students through a detailed introduction to their textbooks and other references where relevant information might be found. This amounts to teaching students how to *use* their textbooks as an information source. (See chapter 10.)

Once students are familiar with information sources, they are ready to investigate, to test the characteristics they have listed on their charts. *Explore* uses the concept formation strategy, discussed in chapter 2. The teacher says, "To test our ideas, let's investigate several living things and find out whether the things we have listed are true of all of them." Each child is given a data-retrieval chart (see Figure 11-1).

In pairs, using the reference books they just studied, students gather the information each question requires for each living thing on the chart. Pairs then report their work to the whole class, and the teachers uses a class-size retrieval chart to record their work. A transparency of the student chart placed on an overhead projector works well.

Analyzing Data/   The teacher guides students through the concept-formation strategy as a way of
Concluding.   making sense of all the data by drawing it together into a concept. "Let's see what

FIGURE 11-1
Data-Retrieval Chart

RETRIEVAL CHART LIVING THINGS					
List from chart	bird	tree	fish	cactus	person
Moves? How?					
Grows? For how long?					
Changes? In what ways?					
Reproduces others like self?					
Needs food? What kind? From where?					
Needs air?					
Needs water?					

all this information tells us about all living things. First, what do you see is true of some living things but not of others?" Here the teacher is eliciting *differences* among the examples. Then students are directed to focus on *similarities*. "What do you find is true of *all* living things, regardless of what kind?" After this, students are asked to compose a conclusion, or *summary:*

We know something is a living thing if it

_____

_____

Writing a Conclusion.   Students write an informational (expository) paragraph explaining what living things are, giving examples, and telling how they differ from nonliving things.

Classifying.   Continuing the fourth step in "The Scientific Way of Learning," students are helped to push their understanding of the concept still further. The teacher has them test their conclusion and at the same time identify the characteristics that distinguish living from nonliving things by having students inspect a nonliving thing—a cloud, an airplane, popcorn, fire, or a balloon.

The teacher says, "Let's consider something nonliving, like a cloud. What answers do we get to each of the questions on our chart when we ask it about a cloud?"

Later, "Based on the information we now have about a cloud, what about it could make it *seem* like a living thing?" and, "What is true of all living things that is not true of a cloud and proves it is not a living thing even if it moves?"

Labeling.   Students should be introduced to the term scientists use as a synonym for a living thing: organism.

Review.   Students are helped to review *how* they learned what distinguishes living from non-living things.

Assessment.   The teacher prepares a bulletin board with two sections, one marked LIVING THINGS, the other NONLIVING THINGS. Students are directed to bring in a magazine picture or drawing of something that belongs in each section. Each student should be prepared to tell the class the characteristics that make each item belong in one category or another.

Unit 1, Lessons 2 and 3

We briefly sketch here the other two lessons in the first unit of the third-grade *Explore* curriculum. The focus question of Lesson 2 is this: What do all living things need to survive and develop as they should? Here the intended learning outcome is that students develop a concept of the *needs* of all organisms. The concept they develop, again using a data-retrieval chart and the concept-formation strategy, will include these characteristics:

• clean air and water
• nutrition
• sufficient light and warmth
• protection from enemies and disease
• opportunity for the organism to reach its potential

The focus question of Lesson 3 is this: What decisions, choices, judgments, plans, and so on, do people have to make to see to it that living things have what they need to survive and develop? The intended learning outcome is that students develop awareness of and commitment to individual and group *action*, which ensures that living things can meet their needs for survival and development.

This lesson moves children from conceptualizing what living things are, and what they need to thrive, to perceiving reasons for human action on behalf of living things.

living things: attributes ⟶   needs ⟶   action

In this way, this first unit of *Explore* goes to the heart of the most important of the five themes of geography: human–environment interaction (see chapters 1 and 5).

There are two main learning activities in Lesson 3. The first has students consider cases where threatening conditions are putting living things at risk by making it difficult or impossible for them to get what they need. Students are then helped to suggest courses of action that might improve the situation.

Sample situations:

1. There has been a very heavy snowfall. All the food and water for birds and deer has been covered with snow for several days and the animals can't get to any.

2. It has not rained for weeks. The farmers are worried because their crops are not getting enough water.

3. People who picnic near the lake have been throwing junk into it for years. Much of this junk is harmful to the fish, insects, birds, and plants that live in or near the lake.

Students discuss these situations in small groups (three or so) and recommend courses of action. Two focus questions guide their work on each case:

1. Which living things would have trouble surviving if no one did anything to change the situation? Explain why they would have trouble surviving.

2. What could people like you and me do so that the living things in this situation could survive? Explain how each suggestion would help the living things survive.

The second learning activity has children gather data on situations in which the needs of living things are threatened *and* in which people took specific actions that helped living things meet their needs. The teacher assembles reading materials about such people and/or invites them to class from the community. After gathering and recording data about them, students use the concept-formation strategy to compare and contrast these people and their specific actions. Finally, they return to the courses of action they suggested in the first part of the lesson, revising and adding ideas for action based on the information they gathered about real situations.

MAKING SENSE OF INTEGRATED EDUCATION

The exhibits described above suggest just a few of the possibilities available to teachers wanting to integrate social studies education with other disciplines and with instruction on reading, writing, and other skills. These are ambitious projects that may be difficult for the student teacher or beginning teacher to undertake. The first two probably cannot be done by a teacher working alone, at least not in the forms presented here. *Explore* is feasible for a beginning teacher, but it assumes the teacher has a well-developed understanding of the concept-formation strategy and considerable experience with blending instruction on content and thinking. There may be simpler ways for a teacher to begin to develop integrated courses of study, and we look at one of these, learning with biographies, in the next section. First, however, we shall define some terms and anticipate some of the pitfalls of planning interdisciplinary units.

Definitions

To understand integrated or interdisciplinary education, one must first understand the idea of academic disciplines. These are fairly distinct bodies of knowledge, each with its own preferred method of study. Anthropology, for example, is concerned with accumulating a body of knowledge (facts, concepts, generalizations, questions) about culture and customs; anthropologists' preferred method of accumulating this knowledge is ethnographic field work. Biology, sociology, political science, literature, history, and archeology are other distinct bodies of knowledge and method. The school subject called "social studies" is itself an interdisciplinary field. It draws on history and the social sciences—geography, political science, economics, anthropology, sociology, and psychology. The school subject called "science" is also interdisciplinary, drawing on biology, chemistry, physics, physiology, and other natural sciences. "Art," too, is interdisciplinary, combining drawing, painting, sculpting, writing, and other skills.

Interdisciplinary education, however, usually refers not to integrated work *within* these school subjects but *between* and *among* them—between and among social studies, science, literature, art, music, math, and so on. As well, it refers to the development of literacy—reading and writing competence—within these school subjects. Compare these definitions:[5]

Discipline: A specific body of teachable knowledge with its own key concepts and generalizations, methods of inquiry, and special interests.

Interdisciplinary: A knowledge view and curriculum approach that purposefully draws knowledge, perspectives, and methods of inquiry from more than one discipline together to examine a central theme, problem, person, or event.

Under this definition, interdisciplinary education brings several categories of knowledge together for the purpose of helping children more fully understand the object of study. Note that the purpose is not to eliminate the individual disciplines but to use them as tools or resources. Wise teachers do not hide the disciplines from children; instead, they call the disciplines by their proper names and help children to examine them. Recall that the *Explore* curriculum teaches children about the different kinds of science and scientists in its introductory lesson. This is to help children develop a more mature understanding of inquiry itself and an appreciation for diverse *ways* of knowing. Anthropology brings a cultural perspective to a topic, while political science brings questions about power and freedom. Biology brings still different concepts, interests, and questions.

Interdisciplinary education's singular strength, then, is its potential for helping children to get beyond superficial knowledge. It can enable them to develop in-depth, multidimensional understandings on topics that are worth the time and effort. There is little sense in the traditional practice of separating American history and American literature, which in some ways are two dimensions of the same topic. The integration will enrich students' knowledge of each and strengthen their grasp of the whole. Reading, discussing, and dramatizing Esther Forbes's *Johnny Tremain* and Patrick Henry's "Give Me Liberty or Give Me Death" speech—both integral to the

---

[5]Adapted from Heidi Hayes Jacobs, "The Growing Need for Interdisciplinary Curriculum Content," in *Interdisciplinary Curriculum: Design and Implementation*, ed. Heidi Hayes Jacobs (Alexandria, VA: Association for Supervision and Curriculum Development, 1989), 1–12. See also Nathalie J. Gehrke, "Explorations of Teachers' Development of Integrative Curriculums," *Journal of Curriculum and Supervision* 6:2 (Winter 1991): 107–17.

study of the American Revolution—deepens the understanding that will come. We present the following simple integrations in the hope that they will inspire readers to invent their own.

Mrs. Hill has her first-grade children grow corn and potatoes in classroom seed boxes, under grow lamps, while they are learning about Columbus's expeditions. This is their introduction to worldwide ecological changes that were the consequence of the initial contacts between Europeans and Americans. Students keep track of their observations in their science journals.

Mr. Coulter teaches reading and writing to his second graders as a common enterprise called *literacy.* The children's work is published in a classroom newsletter that reports current events, rules, elections of class officers, committee business, field trips, games, and the like.

Ms. Kubota's third-grade children write comparative histories of their own community, Mesa Verde, and the Plymouth colony. These histories are then embedded in plays the children write, in which children from the three communities meet. There are no separate writing lessons.

Mr. Atencio reads stories of courageous people to his kindergartners— stories of Harriet Tubman, Lewis and Clark, and Geronimo. Then the children retell these stories, eventually acting them out. They dictate the "script" to Mr. Atencio, who types it and copies it for the children.

Pitfalls

Skillful teachers manage to avoid most of the pitfalls that inevitably accompany innovations in curriculum and instruction. Interdisciplinary education has its own set of pitfalls and conceptual errors.

Either/Or Thinking ("putting all the eggs in one basket"). This error involves the assumption that either a discipline-based curriculum or an interdisciplinary curriculum is always the right thing to do. Neither is true. Both are needed at different times and for different purposes. It is important to exercise professional judgment, using each when appropriate. This is the eclectic approach, and for thoughtful teachers, it is usually the best course.

Trivializing Learning. While discipline-based education sometimes fragments knowledge, thoughtful teachers recognize that interdisciplinary education can create its own problems. It is particularly susceptible to trivializing the curriculum. This occurs when unimportant content is selected for instruction simply because it easily can be integrated with other content. Meanwhile, important content goes untaught. Just because a learning activity crosses disciplinary boundaries does not make it worthwhile. What makes an activity worthwhile is that students are forming or extending a powerful understanding or skill. (Recall Mrs. Lindquist's second princi-

•••Making Curriculum Connections

Making books can be an effective way to integrate reading and writing with a social studies topic. This page shows the results of young children's efforts to produce a state book, a picture glossary about human-environment interaction, and a simple learning log.

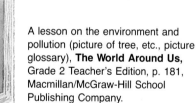

"My Learning Log," **The World Around Us,** Grade 2 Teacher's Edition, p. 276, Macmillan/McGraw-Hill School Publishing Company.

A lesson on the environment and pollution (picture of tree, etc., picture glossary), **The World Around Us,** Grade 2 Teacher's Edition, p. 181, Macmillan/McGraw-Hill School Publishing Company.

A lesson on state symbols (state flag, bird, and flower), **The World Around Us,** Grade 2 Teacher's Edition, p. 156, Macmillan/McGraw-Hill School Publishing Company.

WORKING IN OUR COMMUNITY

Leon got information about places to work in Detroit from the Chamber of Commerce. He also talked to family members to ask them about their jobs.

Third-grade children are producing a book on their community in cooperative learning groups. They gather information from reference books, interviews, and newspapers. Chapters are written individually, with feedback from teammates, then bound together with an introduction and "About the Authors" page.

"Working in Our Community," **The World Around Us,** Grade 3 Student Text, p. 285, Macmillan/McGraw-Hill School Publishing Company.

WORKING IN OUR COMMUNITY

by Leon

Many people in our city, like my dad, work in factories making cars and trucks. Detroit is called the Motor City, because more cars are made here than in any other place in the United States.

There are many other places to work in Detroit. One of my sisters works for an insurance company. My other sister works in a hospital. My mother works in a restaurant, and my brother is a garbage collector. My cousin is a teacher. You can see that there are many different jobs in Detroit.

MOTOR CITY

TRANSPORTATION

Alveto made a chart that showed all the different kinds of transportation found in Detroit. Then he wrote about his favorite kind of transportation.

TRANSPORTATION
by Alveto

Detroit has different kinds of public transportation. Here is a chart showing some of the different kinds. My favorite is the People Mover. It is an elevated train. You can ride it all over the downtown area. Each stop has interesting artwork to look at. I think you'd like riding on the People Mover.

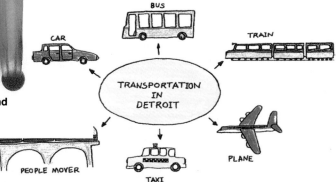

BUS

CAR

TRAIN

TRANSPORTATION IN DETROIT

PEOPLE MOVER

TAXI

PLANE

"Transportation," **The World Around Us,** Grade 3 Student Text, p. 284, Macmillan/McGraw-Hill School Publishing Company.

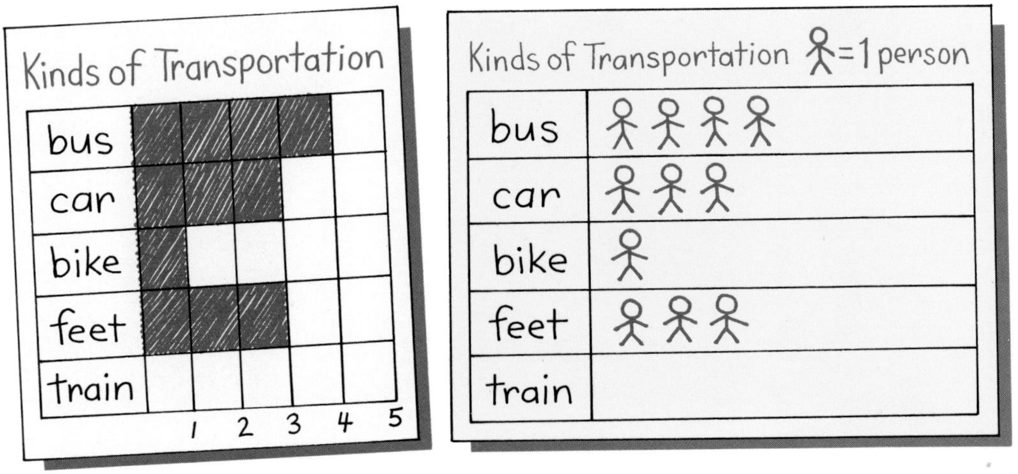

Kinds of Transportation

	1	2	3	4	5
bus	■	■	■	■	
car	■	■	■		
bike	■				
feet	■	■	■		
train					

Kinds of Transportation �persona = 1 person

bus	☺	☺	☺	☺
car	☺	☺	☺	
bike	☺			
feet	☺	☺	☺	
train				

Transportation graphs, **The World Around Us,** Grade 2 Student Text, p. 129, Macmillan/McGraw-Hill School Publishing Company.

Social studies and math converge when children conduct surveys on human behavior. Above, children have gathered data for the building principal. The same data are presented in two forms, a bar graph and a pictograph. The children below hypothesized that hamburgers were the class favorite, but the data show otherwise. Surveys can be conducted and graphs made on many other topics as well, for example, favorite books, political candidates, playground equipment, careers, and holidays.

"Letter to Mrs. Walker" and "Favorite Lunches Graph," **The World Around Us,** Grade 2 Student Text, p. 129, Macmillan/McGraw-Hill School Publishing Company.

Dear Mrs. Walker,

We took a vote on our favorite lunches. We really like your grilled cheese sandwiches. Could we have them more often?

Sincerely,

Mrs. Long's Second Grade

Favorite Lunches

	1	2	3	4	5
Tuna					
Grilled Cheese					
Hamburger					
Soup					
Salad					
Turkey					

ple.) As psychologist Jerome Bruner put it years ago, "The first object of any act of learning, over and beyond the pleasure it may give, is that it should serve us in the future. Learning should not only take us somewhere; it should allow us later to go further more easily."[6] Here is the point: Teachers need to be sure that learning activities are significant and that they contribute to the accomplishment of major curriculum goals.[7]

Confusion. Interdisciplinary education needlessly confuses learners when teachers require them to study simultaneously topics that more fruitfully could be examined separately. Imagine students trying to study three cultures' customs, literature, art, and scientific achievements all at the same time. The loss in analytic clarity and the increased difficulty would not justify the gains hoped for by integrating social studies, literature, art, and science. Experts in any field do not attempt to tackle a problem by focusing their attention on all its parts at once. John Dewey advised, wisely, that we limit a topic for study in such a way as to avoid what he called "the great bad." This is "the mixing of things which need to be kept distinct."[8] Experts limit the problem they are working on; they analyze it, break it into its component parts. They do this to understand the big picture better and, therefore, to know where they most profitably might begin chipping away at the problem.

We should not train students to study a topic by making a jumbled mess of it. Readers may remember the helpful clear plastic illustrations often found in a biology textbook. These made it possible to achieve a sort of layered understanding of the human body. Readers are permitted to focus only on the skeletal system, or only on muscle tissue or major organs, and then to lay these systems on top of one another to examine the whole picture and the interaction of parts.

*Dis*integration, then, can be helpful. It also can be needlessly fragmenting. Knowing how and when to separate topics to discern them and make them meaningful and knowing, on the other hand, when to integrate them is a major achievement of skillful teaching.

Confusion also can result when so-called integrated activities require students to do things they are not prepared to do, such as role playing scenes from Mexico when they have learned nothing about Mexico except its location on a map.[9] Whether in interdisciplinary or disciplinary contexts, instruction should always build carefully on knowledge children already possess, develop in them an awareness of the knowledge they lack, and strategically introduce them to new knowledge.

---

[6]Jerome Bruner, *The Process of Education* (Cambridge, MA: Harvard University Press, 1960), 17.

[7]Jere Brophy and Janet Alleman, "A Caveat: Curriculum Integration Isn't Always A Good Idea," *Educational Leadership* 49: 2 (October 1991): 66.

[8]John Dewey, *The Public and Its Problems* (Chicago: Swallow, 1927).

[9]Brophy and Alleman, "A Caveat," 66.

A Little of This, A Little of That.   Closely related to the pitfall of trivializing learning is what one expert calls "the potpourri problem."[10] This occurs when a unit is composed of bits of information from each discipline. If the subject is the Mayan Civilization, for example, we will find a bit of history, a bit of art, a bit of science, and a bit of math, but not *enough* of any to integrate into a meaningful whole.

Pet Solutions.   The fifth pitfall—the rush to pet solutions—occurs when a potential solution is embraced before alternatives have been carefully considered.[11] Fads often become pet solutions, but so do old habits, as with the teacher who for twenty years has had children choose their own writing topics rather than narrowing their choice for them. Currently a popular pet solution is the idea of "themes" (or phonics or the whole language approach) as the cure-all for elementary school curriculum planning. The essence of any pet solution is that critical thinking is sacrificed to a dearly held belief; professional judgment is replaced with a new habit. There is no substitute for good judgment in teaching. Avoiding each of these pitfalls is a matter of exercising judgment.

WHERE TO BEGIN? THE LITERACY CONNECTION

Thoughtful teachers continually experiment with new approaches to curriculum planning and instruction, trying something different, observing its effects, revising the plan based on these observations, and trying again. Teachers' time and energy are limited, however, so it is best to have a rationale for beginning with this experiment rather than some other one, for beginning here rather than there. Bruner's advice is perhaps the best: Begin with learning that not only takes students somewhere important, but that allows them later to go further more easily.

Recalling this advice, the most significant place to begin interdisciplinary unit planning probably is with the blending of literacy education and social studies education. Both are strengthened as a consequence of being combined, and the combination permits students later to go further more easily with each. By literacy education we mean reading and writing treated as a common enterprise, as discussed in chapter 10. Integrating literacy education with social studies education, returning to the idea with which this chapter began, gives literacy education the kind of context it needs. Strong literacy education cannot take place in a vacuum; it is most successful when situated in the collaborative pursuit of content goals. Like-

---

[10]Jacobs, "The Growing Need," 2.

[11]This is Thomas Roby's term in "Habits Impeding Deliberation," *Journal of Curriculum Studies* 17: 1 (1985): 17–35.

wise, it is through reading and writing that children are engaged with the social studies topics.

An example: Fourth-grade children are developing their reading ability as they are helped to read short stories, newspaper accounts, and expository (textbook) material about two remarkable American reformers, Sojourner Truth and Susan B. Anthony. They are developing their writing ability as they write original biographies of these women in cooperative groups. Moreover, they write the script for a winter play called "Profiles of Great Americans," and read and write poetry on the theme *courage*. The principles realized in this example are simple but powerful:

1. Literacy instruction should overlap instruction on important content. The overlap generally robs neither and it strengthens both. As a rule of thumb, the more overlap, the better.

2. Literacy instruction should be embedded in a rich social environment where high expectations are combined with lots of support, coaching, practice, and feedback. In other words, children need to be *apprenticed* into literacy.[12] Cooperative learning can be a good vehicle for such interaction, as we will see in this chapter and in chapter 13.

With these two principles in hand, we can now present the idea of learning through biography. Drawing on the work of Myra Zarnowski, we detail a strategy for bringing literacy and social studies together in a powerful and exciting way: students writing original biographies of important historical figures.[13]

PRODUCING ORIGINAL BIOGRAPHIES

Sojourner Truth was first "sold" when she was nine years old, probably in the year 1807. She was born a slave in New York State to a Dutch man named Hardenbergh, so that was her name, too—Belle Hardenbergh. When she was nine, John Neely became Belle's new owner. He paid $50 and got both the Dutch-speaking African girl and 100 sheep. Two years later, after learning some English and suffering beatings at the hands of the Neely family, she was sold again, this time for $105 to Martin Schryver, who had a farm near the Hudson River. In 1810, Belle was sold yet again. Her new master, Mr. Dumont, wrote in his ledger, "For $300, Belle, about 13 years old, six feet tall." Years later, with the help of Quakers, Belle won her freedom and took the name Sojourner Truth. It was a good handle for the life she was about to live: a seeker and speaker of truth.

---

[12]Lauren B. Resnick, "Literacy In School and Out,"*Daedalus* 119: 2 (Spring 1990): 169–85.

[13]Myra Zarnowski, *Learning With Biographies: A Reading and Writing Approach* (Washington, DC: National Council for the Social Studies and National Council of Teachers of English, published jointly, 1990).

Her speeches attracted great crowds and are today among schoolchildren's favorites. For example, in May of 1851, she addressed a women's rights convention in Akron, Ohio. Before she or any of the other women could speak, Protestant ministers—all male—dominated the proceedings, deriding the women who wanted social reform. Francis Gage later wrote what happened after the ministers were through:

> Then, slowly from her seat in the corner rose Sojourner Truth, who, till now, had scarcely lifted her head. She moved solemnly to the front, laid her old bonnet at her feet, and turned her great speaking eyes on me.
>
> There was a hissing sound of disapprobation above and below. I rose and announced, "Sojourner Truth," and begged the audience keep silence for a few moments.
>
> The tumult subsided at once, and every eye was fixed on this almost Amazon form, which stood nearly six feet high, head erect and eyes piercing the upper air like one in a dream. At her first word there was a profound hush. She spoke in deep tones, which, though not loud, reached every ear in the house and away through the doors and windows:
>
> "Well, children, where there is so much racket, there must be something out of kilter. That man over there says women need to be helped into carriages and lifted over ditches—and to have the best place everywhere. Nobody ever helps me into carriages or over mud-puddles—or gives me the best place at the table!"
>
> Raising herself to her full height, and lifting her voice to a pitch like rolling thunder, Sojourner asked, "And ain't I a woman? Look at me! Look at my arm!" She bared her right arm to the shoulder, showing her tremendous muscular power. "I have ploughed and planted and gathered into barns, and no man could get ahead of me! And ain't I a woman?
>
> "I could work as much and eat as much as a man—when I could get it—and bear the lash as well! And ain't I a woman?
>
> "My mother bore ten children and saw them sold off to slavery, and when I cried with my mother's grief, none but Jesus heard me! And ain't I a woman?
>
> "Then that little man in black says women can't have as many rights as men. If the first woman God ever made was strong enough to turn the world upside down all alone, these women together" (and she glanced over the platform) "ought to be able to turn it back and get it right side up again! And now that the women are asking to do it, the men better let 'em."
>
> Long cheering greeted this. "I'm obliged to you for hearing me," she concluded, "and now old Sojourner hasn't got nothing more to say."[14]

Sojourner had much more to say. When she wasn't speaking for women's rights, she was speaking against slavery. And after President Lincoln ended slavery, Sojourner worked in Washington DC—"Mr. Lincoln's

---

[14]Francis Gage's account was published in an antislavery journal and reproduced in Edward Beecher Claflin's biography, *Sojourner Truth and the Struggle for Freedom* (New York: Barron, 1987), 81–82.

city"—to overcome the remnants of slavery: racism and deeply entrenched prejudice. She tried to help freed Africans find work and homes, and she worked for a time as a nurse in Freedman's Hospital. These were chaotic, heartbreaking times. The Civil War, in which her son fought in the famous 54th Massachusetts Regiment, became a slaughter on both sides. And just as it ended, Lincoln, whom she had met and much admired, was killed by an assassin.

Still, she was not defeated. Another biographer, Jeri Ferris, writes of yet another of Sojourner's efforts to right wrongs:

> One afternoon as Sojourner walked back to the hospital with an armful of blankets, she was so tired she just couldn't walk any more. Horsedrawn streetcars clanged up and down the road, filled with white folks. Sojourner waited for a car to stop, but none did. Finally, as yet another car passed her, she called out, "I want to ride!" People crowded around, the horses stopped, and Sojourner got on. The conductor was furious and demanded she get off. Sojourner settled back in her seat. "I'm not from the South," she said firmly, "I'm from the Empire State of New York, and I know the law as well as you do."
>
> The next day she tried to ride another streetcar. Again the conductor would not stop. Sojourner ran after the car and caught up with it. When the horses stopped, she jumped on. "What a shame," she panted, "to make a lady run so." The Conductor threatened to throw her off. "If you try," she said, "it will cost you more than your car and horses are worth." He didn't.
>
> The third time Sojourner tried to ride a streetcar, she was with a white friend. "Stand back," shouted the conductor to Sojourner, "and let that lady on."
>
> "*I* am a lady too," said Sojourner, and she stepped aboard with her friend.[15]

We provide this sketch of the life and times of Sojourner Truth to introduce a strategy for helping children to produce original biographies. The creation of an original biography is a splendid way to invite children to read, write, and discuss their way to an in-depth understanding of great citizens such as Sojourner Truth. The names in the following list are a small sample of other persons whose life and times warrant in-depth study by elementary school children. In the spirit of concept formation, teachers can select three or four people who *together* would help children to form the concept of *democratic citizen.* Thus the class could write three or four biographies during a school year, all the while keeping track of the similarities among these people—similarities that make them all examples of democratic citizens:

• They knew that popular sovereignty is the bedrock of democracy, and that this means taking personal responsibility for the health of civic life.
• They took time from their private lives to be active in civic life.

---

[15]Jeri Ferris, *Walking the Road to Freedom: A Story About Sojourner Truth* (Minneapolis: Carolrhoda Books, 1988), 53, 55.

- They understood the difference between complaining and proposing solutions.
- They understood, within the constraints of their times, that democracy means majority rule *and* minority rights.
- They exhibited courage on behalf of these principles.

BIOGRAPHIES OF DEMOCRATIC CITIZENS

James Madison	Abraham Lincoln
Susan B. Anthony	Jane Adams
Thomas Jefferson	Mary McLeod Bethune
Benjamin Franklin	Gordon Hirabayashi
Eleanor Roosevelt	Patrick Henry
George Washington	Martin Luther King, Jr.

Democratic citizen of course is not the only concept around which subjects can be selected for biographies, though it is one of the most important. Other central ideas are *explorers, inventors and scientists, champions of the poor, friends of nature, leaders, dictators, revolutionaries,* and *heroes.* Recall that the discussion of concept learning in chapter 2 emphasized multiple examples. Here this means that a teacher might orchestrate children's biographical studies around one of these themes, having them produce over the year three or four biographies on that theme rather than one each on different themes. This approach should help children to build an in-depth understanding of that theme. On the other hand, teachers might, to cover more ground, mix the kinds of subjects about whom their children write, for example, choosing a hero (Crazy Horse or Harriet Tubman), an inventor (Benjamin Franklin or Eli Whitney), a scientist (Galileo or Newton), and a great citizen (Sojourner Truth or James Madison). Figure 11-2 suggests several themes and related subjects.

Procedure for Writing Biographies

The teacher will need to (a) select the person about whom children will write their biographies, (b) help the children learn about the person and keep track of what they are learning, (c) help children reflect on the person's life and identify key events, (d) orchestrate the cooperative production of biographies in small groups.

Selecting a Subject.   Several criteria guide the selection of subjects for children's biographies. Most important is that the person chosen bring children into contact with powerful ideas of history, government, geography, economics, and/or other social studies disciplines. Individuals who can help children build understandings of one or more of the following seven themes will not only bring children to the heart of social studies but also build firm foundations for further learning:

1. The multicultural nature of societies. North American society, for example, is composed of many ethnicities, all races, men and women, rich and poor.

FIGURE 11-2

Examples of Thematic Clusters of Persons of Prominance Suitable for Biographical Study.

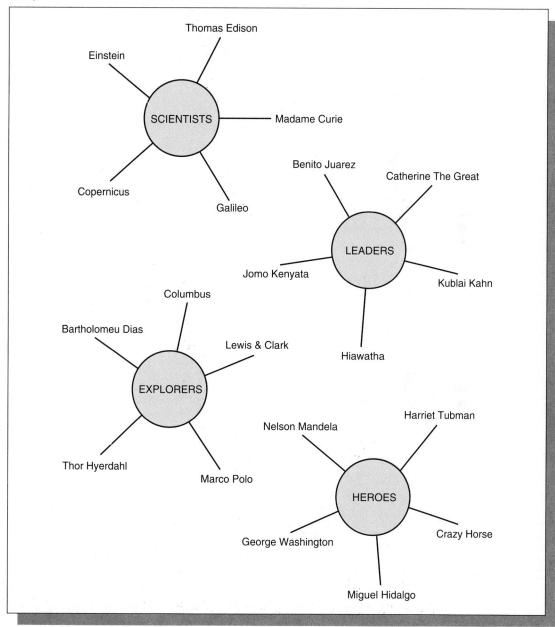

2. The nature of democracies, the conditions that sustain them, and the conditions that undermine them.
3. Human–environment interaction.
4. Great economic transformations—nomadic to agrarian to industrial economies, for example, with the nearly complete cultural change that results.
5. The international system—world geography, area studies, hunger, economic interdependence, development.
6. Participatory citizenship—social responsibility, participation in public problem solving.
7. The enrichment of human life—arts, entertainment, religion.

Another criterion for subject selection is the likelihood that children will be captivated by this life. It may help some children become more interested in the person if information is available on his or her childhood. Ben Franklin's early troubles with his brother James, for example, James Madison's illnesses as a child, and Sojourner Truth's harrowing childhood all seem to fascinate children, broadening them by giving them access to *other* children's lives—lives that are different but reassuringly similar, too. Learning a great deal about a person can itself make that person captivating to the young biographer. As this third-grade student quite wisely reported, one cannot know for certain what makes a subject interesting. He seems to conclude, however, that familiarity breeds interest, not contempt:

> Everyone else was real interested in Hiawatha but I wasn't because, well, the things I knew about him just were boring. But the more I found out, the way they learned to hunt and stuff in the long house, and all the magic, well it got real interesting. Now I know him a lot.

A third key criterion is the availability of materials. The "snapshot biography" method we outline here requires students to learn a great deal about the subject.[16] If the subject is obscure, chances are good that neither the textbook nor the school library will have ample books, primary documents, narrative biographies, or other materials.

Consider how Mr. Brem, a fourth-grade teacher, selects biographical subjects. He has decided to weave a yearlong study of *leadership* through the state history curriculum his school district requires in that grade. He wants his pupils to study and eventually write biographies of three state leaders. He wants the leaders to be culturally diverse, and he wants them to expose students to different historical periods and geographical areas of the state. Now Mr. Brem begins his materials search. A booklet he received last year from the state arm of the League of Women Voters provides information on several civic leaders, and he asks a committee of students to select one of these for the class to study. The social studies education office at the state capital publishes material on the state's governors; Mr. Brem selects the

---

[16]Zarnowski, *Learning with Biographies*, chapter 4.

state's first governor. Now he has selected two of the three subjects he needs. Since they are both European Americans, Mr. Brem wants the third leader to belong to an ethnic minority.

Unaware of who this might be or where materials can be obtained, he appoints another committee of students to go to the school librarian for help. The librarian refers them to information on a civic leader who helped to organize the early Chinese-American community in the state. Now the class has a set of three leaders and is ready for the reading-and-writing approach to biographical study.

Learning About the Subject of a Biography.   Before children can begin to write about a biographical subject, they need to learn something about him or her. Let us be clear, however, that the learning sequence is not read, then write. Rather, it is write a little, drawing on prior experience, then find out a little. Write some, learn a little more, write some more, and so on. One of the major advances in the science of instruction in the past ten years is that teachers do not have to provide all of the facts before asking students to think. The advice instead is to integrate data gathering and reflection. The teacher should concentrate student attention on the higher-order task, in this case production of the biography, which in turn motivates gathering facts about the subject and interpreting his or her life.

So, students begin learning about the subject, let us say Sojourner Truth, by finding out a little something about her. Perhaps the teacher begins by reading aloud for just twenty minutes from Jeri Ferris's book, concentrating on the beginning of the story when Sojourner is taken from her mother and sold to Mr. Neely at the age of nine. Then the teacher asks the children to discuss this passage—the idea of buying and selling persons, in this case a child. She asks them to imagine the feelings of Belle on the auction block and the feelings of her mother and father. She may ask them what they have learned elsewhere about the enslavement of people. Perhaps some of them will talk about the Jews in Egypt in biblical times, maybe some have seen the restored version of the old movie about Spartacus, perhaps some will talk about the Holocaust. Some children may know quite a bit about the capture and subsequent ownership of Africans through books they have read or lessons they have had in prior grades or in church. The discussion will provide the teacher with diagnostic information about children's current knowledge of slavery while activating the students' prior knowledge.

Now the teacher can ask students to bring out their journals and begin to write. She may ask them to write about the same things she previously asked them to talk about, which should be the easiest for them. Then she might ask them to predict what will happen to Sojourner in her new master's home. This should make them want to gather more information. Where will they get it?

The teacher knows that Sojourner's life with Mr. Neely is documented in the textbook. So, the next day she has children take out their journals to remind themselves of the predictions they wrote yesterday. Then, they are given twenty minutes to read the pertinent section in the text and return to their journal to write what really happened. Next, the teacher turns student attention to the map of the Northeast in the textbook and, based on clues given in the passage read aloud yesterday and the text passage today, helps them to find the state where Sojourner first was bought and sold (New York). In their journals, she has them enter the date and sketch a map of New York under the title, Where Sojourner Truth's Story Begins.

Now that they know where the story began (the geographic theme, *location*), students are helped to get a feel for New York (the geographic theme, *place*). Their teacher has them go to their cooperative teams and, working with the textbook, answer these questions:

1. What states, countries, and bodies of water border New York?
2. Is the geography of New York all the same, or are there different land-forms? If so, what are they?
3. If Sojourner was able to fly away from the Neely farm, which route would have the fewest mountains to fly over?

The teacher then tells students to sketch all of this on a blank handout map of New York, including a legend so readers can understand their symbols.

The next day, the teacher reads aloud Virginia Hamilton's retelling of the folk tale, *The People Could Fly.* A wonderfully hopeful tale, though at the same time tragic, it tells of African slaves literally flying from bondage to freedom:

> They say the people could fly. Say that long ago in Africa, some of the people knew magic. And they would walk up on the air like climbin' up on a gate. And they flew like blackbirds over the fields.

But when the people were captured for slavery, we learn in the tale, they shed their wings. The slave ships were too crowded for wings. A few, however, kept the power. Toby did, and he used it to help the others to escape. One day Sarah was hoeing and chopping as fast as she could, a hungry baby on her back, but the baby "started up bawling too loud." The Overseer hollered at Sarah to keep the baby quiet, but Sarah fell under the babe's weight and her own weakness. The Overseer began to whip her. "Get up, you black cow," he called. Sarah looked to Toby: "Now, before it's too late," she panted. "Now." Toby raised his arms and whispered the magic words to her. "Kum . . . yali, kum buba tambe."

> Sarah lifted one foot on the air. Then the other. She flew clumsily at first, with the child now held tightly in her arms. Then she felt the magic, the African mystery. Say she rose just as free as a bird. As light as a feather.[17]

---

[17]From *The People Could Fly*, retold by Virginia Hamilton. In *Cricket* 15: 6 (February 1988): 21–26.

Afterward, students return to their journals to reflect on this new material. The teacher now could highlight the themes *freedom, suffering,* and *survival,* and children could be directed to compare this tale to others they have heard on this theme.

The teacher continues over the next two or three weeks to read aloud from biographies and other accounts of Sojourner Truth, as well as from related stories and reference material. Student committees are sent to the library to gather data on people, places, events, and issues raised in the teacher's readings that students want to find out more about. As well, the teacher assembles some material for the students to read themselves—material in the textbook on Lincoln's decision to free the slaves and material on influential abolitionists: Frederick Douglass, who escaped from slavery in the south; William Lloyd Garrison, who published *The Liberator,* an abolitionist newspaper; and the Grimké sisters, Angelina and Sarah, who moved north after having been raised with captive Africans on a South Carolina plantation. This information helps to elaborate the children's understanding of Sojourner's life, as well as her civic missions, and should lead to their producing much stronger, richer biographies.

For this reason, information on the women's movement of the 1800s needs also to be gathered, such as the Seneca Falls Convention convened by Lucretia Mott and Elizabeth Cady Stanton in 1848. This is the same movement Sojourner jolted with her "Ain't I A Woman" speech, delivered three years later at a second women's rights convention.

The setting for all this information needs also to be grasped; consequently, students should study the geography of New York, Ohio, and Michigan—the three states where Sojourner spent much time working, speaking, and living. In this way, students learn about the subject of their biography and gradually piece together in their minds a model of Sojourner's life and times.

Reflection and Setting Priorities.   After several weeks of reading, writing, and mapping their biographical subject's life, children are ready to reflect on this life and its times and places, and to select key events. A few of these events will become the focal points of the chapters in the book students will write together. The following procedure is recommended.[18]

1. *Opening.* The teacher announces that today is the day the class begins to pull together all that has been learned about the subject, and informs students of what is to come.
2. *Brainstorming.* The teacher asks students to brainstorm all the events in the subject's life that they found interesting, all the events they believe were pivotal in the subject's life, all the events they figure made the subject the most and least proud, and so on. The point here is to get a

---

[18]Adapted from Zarnowski, *Learning with Biographies,* chapter 4.

long list of varied events in the subject's life. Here are just a few of the events in Sojourner's life that students have suggested.

- the time she was separated from her mother
- the second time she was sold
- the third time she was sold
- confronting Mr. Dumont
- rescued by Quakers
- names herself Sojourner Truth
- "Ain't I A Woman?" speech
- meeting President Lincoln
- working as a nurse in Washington, DC
- confronting the trolley conductor
- meetings with Garrison and Douglass

When the brainstorming slows, the teacher has students take a break—go to recess, clean the room, do something physically active. When they return, they open their journals and search for other events to add to the list. They come up with more:

- being born in captivity
- speaking out for women's rights
- becoming an abolitionist
- living in New York
- traveling by buggy in Ohio

3. *Selecting.* Students now are asked to move into cooperative groups of four or five children each. Their first task as a group is to select four or five of the key events brainstormed by the whole class. These might be the four events that interested students the most, or the teacher might direct them to use other criteria. For example, if the teacher previously has worked with children on the meaning of time lines, she or he might have them divide Sojourner's life into four equal segments and choose one event from each segment. Or, the teacher might have them choose one event in each of four categories: meetings with remarkable people, life as a slave, speeches, life as an abolitionist.

   Once the key events have been selected, the children in each cooperative group divide the events among themselves, each choosing one event. Dividing the events—and thus the labor—is crucial to the coming task: producing an original biography.

Writing and Illustrating.   The students are now ready to write and illustrate a biography of their subject. Each cooperative group will produce a biography on the same subject, in this case Sojourner Truth. Some teachers have each group use the same biography title, *The Life and Times of (Sojourner Truth)*. Others let each group create its own variation on this title.

Each person on the team is responsible for one chapter. The chapter's topic is the key event selected before. Groups will have different chapters in their books because each group will choose a different set of four key events. However, if the teacher wishes, he or she can use the cooperative groupwork technique called Jigsaw.[19] In this technique, one member of each small group is working on the same key event as one child on each of the other groups; consequently, these children can meet together to work on their chapter (see chapter 13).

The teacher achieves this by *not* allowing groups to select their own four events. Rather, after the large-group brainstorming of key events, the *large group* also selects four events which will become the chapters in the groups' biographies. Thus, the book my shape up like this:

> title: **THE COURAGE AND CONVICTION OF SOJOURNER TRUTH**
> **chapter 1: "Sold for 50 Dollars!"**
> **chapter 2: "New Name, New Life"**
> **chapter 3: "Ain't I A Woman?"**
> **chapter 4: "The Trolley Incident"**

The child on the team who is responsible for chapter 1 joins with other children from other teams also working on "Sold for 50 Dollars!" Meanwhile, the child on each team responsible for chapter 2 joins with the other "2s," and so on. These are called *expert groups*. Together they discuss what they will write and draw, read one another's drafts, and provide feedback. This is advisable with younger children who are just beginning to write early versions of paragraphs; the group support is helpful, and the teacher can more easily monitor and coach her four expert groups than if every child in the room was writing on a different topic.

Whether the teacher uses the Jigsaw technique or not, the children's work has two parts: They have to write a description of the key event for which they are responsible, and they must draw an accompanying illustration. The least experienced writers may produce only a one- or two-paragraph description, and may fit their illustration on the same page. The teacher may press more experienced writers, however, to produce a two- or three-page description. The illustration is embedded in the text somewhere as in "real" biographies. Skillful teachers are able to boost their children's confidence about both the writing and the drawing by encouraging them to "just get started, get something on paper, pull something together from your journal, whatever; we'll go back and polish it later." (Teachers and children who play the board game, *Pictionary*, understand that illustrating is very different from producing realistic drawings. Virtually anyone can illustrate.)

Each team thus produces the rudiments of a biography: a title page and four chapters. But real biographies have more, and so should these. The following parts of a book make a more complete biography, and they generally can all be done even by the youngest children:

---

[19]Elliot Aronson, *The Jigsaw Classroom* (Beverly Hills, CA: Sage, 1978).

Title Page. Title plus complete publication information, for example: The Life and Times of Sojourner Truth (see Figure 11-3).

Foreword. Written by someone other than the four authors, for example, a parent, another teacher, the mayor, a school board member, a bus driver. Instruct the Foreword writer to write no more than one page and to address two matters:

1. Tell readers some ways you feel you can relate personally to the person about whom the biography was written.
2. Tell readers something about the book.

Introduction with Time Line and Map. The introduction should contain a brief message to readers telling them the subject of the book: Who is its subject? Where and when did he or she live? What, in a nutshell, did he or she do? Why? It is also considerate to tell readers the topic of each chapter. A helpful way to portray the *when* is to sketch a time line of the subject's life. The *where* statement should be illustrated with a map, either physical or political, or both, with a legend to help readers understand the symbols.

FIGURE 11-3
An Example of a Biography Written by Students as a Cooperative Learning Project.

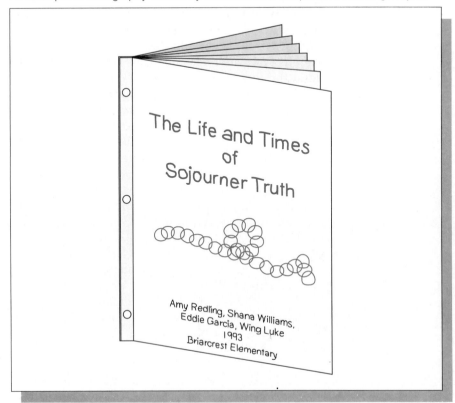

Chapters 1–4.   Each chapter needs a title and author name. Its body is a written description of a key event in the subject's life with an illustration that captures the key event.

About the Authors Page.   Ask each child to write a sentence or paragraph about her- or himself. The teacher might ask each group to decide how long the author statement should be. Children can be prompted to tell readers their full name, the name of the city or town where they live, their age, and something they like to do:

> Wing Luke lives in Denver, Colorado, with his family. He is 9 years old and loves to play soccer. He wrote chapter 4, "The Trolley Incident."

Summing Up: The Biography Approach

The biographical approach we have discussed above has four parts. Here we summarize each. We then give some concluding remarks on the literacy revolution.

1. *Selecting the subject.* Generally this is done by the teacher since he or she knows better than students which historical figures are worth studying—which subjects not only will engage children today but prepare them to go further later.

2. *Learning about the subject.* Writing a biography with one's peers requires much learning about the subject's life and times. In the method outlined above, the learning happens through reading from the textbook and other reference books, reading trade books and folk tales, hearing the teacher and others read aloud, library research, film, interviews, recordings, map study, discussion, and so on. Children need to be apprenticed into the use of a wide variety of information sources to build in-depth understandings. As well, the learning happens though writing itself. Consequently, the writing does not come after all the learning about the subject but is woven into the reading and discussion with the help of journals.

3. *Reflection and setting priorities.* Students reflect back on the life they have been studying and brainstorm key events. Eventually, a handful of events are selected that become the chapters of the biographies.

4. *Writing and illustrating.* Working together and dividing the labor, children write and illustrate a biography of their subject. All groups in the class may be producing biographies of the same subject. The chapters of each of these biographies may be the same, permitting Jigsaw cooperation among children from different groups who are assigned to the same key event, or the chapters may vary from group to group. Another variation has different groups produce different biographies related to a common conceptual theme, such as *leadership.*

Biography writing integrates literacy learning with social studies learning. By embedding literacy instruction in important social studies content

FIGURE 11-4

Literacy Reasearch Emphases

Early Research Emphasis:	Current Research Emphasis:
Reading and writing instruction are separated.	Reading and writing instruction are integrated.
Both are separated from content learning.	Both are developed within content learning.
Reading and writing are fixed abilities that, like muscles, are the same everywhere.	Reading and writing ability evolves like a craft and mirrors the local literacy community.
Reading and writing are finished products.	Reading and writing are complex processes.

and collaborative group work, the teacher creates the kind of social context that can support in-depth learning. Reading comprehension and writing instruction becomes much more than plodding through new vocabulary and learning sentences and paragraphs in a vacuum; literacy comes to mean problem solving, interpretation, competing interpretations, conversation, provocation, writing and rewriting to find out what one thinks is true and what one believes ought to be done, and experimenting with new possibilities that exist now only in the imagination. This is "high" literacy.

THE CHANGING CONCEPT OF LITERACY

The biography-production method we have been discussing is embedded in a conception that sees reading and writing not as fixed abilities that one either has or lacks. Rather, reading and writing are seen as processes—more precisely, as *crafts*—that evolve through trial, error, and support from those more accomplished. This process-oriented notion of literacy learning is different from what research told us only twenty years ago.[20] Then, it was quite common to define literacy as a finished product: You either had it or you didn't; you were "literate" or "illiterate" (see Figure 11-4).

This emphasis on process is changing the way highly skilled teachers orchestrate literacy instruction. They understand that an individual's reading and writing skills grow and change over time. One's literacy is not

---

[20]Glynda Ann Hull, "Building an Understanding of Composing," in *Toward the Thinking Curriculum: Current Cognitive Research*, ed. Lauren B. Resnick and Leopold E. Klopfer, 1989 ASCD Yearbook (Alexandria, VA: Association for Supervision and Curriculum Development, 1989), 104–28.

static; it evolves, and its evolution depends on the individual's social context, that is, his or her "literacy community." All of us belong to one sort of discourse community or another, and that membership functions to socialize us into one or more patterns of using our minds—of reading, writing, and talking. We might be socialized into a literacy community that expects and rewards no more than minimal language use—say, for reading street signs, a ballot, and directions on a medicine label; for "filling out" job applications, "filling out" worksheets, and "completing" credit card applications. This is the vocabulary of low literacy.

It is low because the tasks lack challenge and intellectual rigor. They signal low expectations for students. On the other hand, we might be socialized into a literacy community that has a higher vision of literacy and, consequently, expects and encourages something quite different.[21] Here, language is used in the service of higher-order, important tasks, for example, to plan research on civic problems with an eye toward improving social life, as an avenue to satisfying aesthetic experiences in literature and the arts, and as a means of lively conversation and, hence, conflict resolution and mutual understanding.

When literacy is defined in this more empowering way, literacy instruction cannot remain the same. It, too, needs to change. Now practice and coaching, focused on the *processes* of reading and writing, become the centerpieces of instruction. Learning by doing is the path, and the doing overlaps important content goals. This is the essence of *whole-language learning*. Content, whether the parts of the United States Constitution or the cultures of Asia and Africa, is the landscape on which the path is laid. Continuous feedback and guidance, both from the teacher and from more accomplished peers, makes success possible.

Now, the children do not read a story about rainbows in the morning, then try to write three complete sentences about a story on penguins from the basal reader, and in the afternoon fill in a worksheet on a yet another topic, this time from social studies. Instead, students spend a good part of the day integrating reading, writing, and social studies, and other subjects as well. They do this by working on biographies of someone whose life and times carry them imaginatively and deeply into essential content. The biographical approach is, of course, only one vehicle, but it is a powerful and feasible one. The noted biographer Milton Meltzer observed that the biography approach is

> a vehicle for developing children's natural curiosity about people and the world around them to the point where they themselves investigate a particular life and, through the artful use of language, tell that human story to others.[22]

---

[21]See Carl Bereiter and Marlene Scardamalia, "An Attainable Version of High Literacy: Approaches to Teaching Higher-Order Skills in Reading and Writing," *Curriculum Inquiry* 17: 1 (1987): 9–30.

[22]Milton Meltzer, Foreword to Zarnowski, *Learning About Biographies*, x.

THE CULTURAL CONNECTION
••

We have seen that learning to read and write is best thought of as an apprenticeship, and that this apprenticeship inevitably occurs within a set of expectations. The classrooms of our best teachers are "high" literacy communities: Children are expected to do more than "fill out" this or "complete" that; they are expected instead to develop the crafts of reading and writing and, as they do so, to bring them to the service of important social studies (and science and mathematics) understandings. We now take these notions of high literacy and integrated education one step further by considering the importance of *culture.* (See Figure 11-5.)

Teachers committed to high literacy appreciate two facts. First, classrooms are multicultural places. Students differ from one another and the teacher in one or more of these categories of culture: ethnicity, race, gender, and social class. Second, topics often need to be studied from more than one cultural perspective. Together, these add up to what is called *multicultural education.* We will examine each in turn.

Hospitable Learning Climate

As for the first, skillful teachers create learning communities that genuinely welcome cultural differences among the children gathered there. These teachers are as eager to find out about the cultural backgrounds of their children as they are to discover any other diagnostic information that will help them to individualize learning. Differences are not treated as disadvantages; they are not even perceived that way. Rather, they are perceived and treated as part of the child's experience—his or her prior knowledge—that must be integrated into teaching and learning if desired outcomes are to be reached. This is a tall order. How do these teachers do it?

Perhaps the most helpful thing they do is not implementing a set of techniques but cultivating in themselves an *attitude.* They cultivate in their own professional behavior an anthropologist's perspective on their own cultural roots and those of the children. They recognize that they themselves have been socialized into one or more cultures—that they are not culturally neutral, suspended above ethnicity, race, class, gender, and particular linguistic traditions. Quite the opposite, teachers are thoroughly immersed. Every teacher speaks one or more language and dialect; every teacher belongs to one racial group or another and to one ethnic group, gender, and social class or another.

Skillful teachers do not make much of this fact in overt ways, they don't "advertise" their culture, but they are keenly aware of it and appreciate how profoundly culture influences their point of view and what they do with students. Fundamentally, *this cultural knowledge helps them more clearly to see the cultural tapestry of the classroom—themselves included.* Perceiving clearly the cultural roots of their own speaking, thinking, and behaving

FIGURE 11-5
Schematic Representation of Integrated Education.

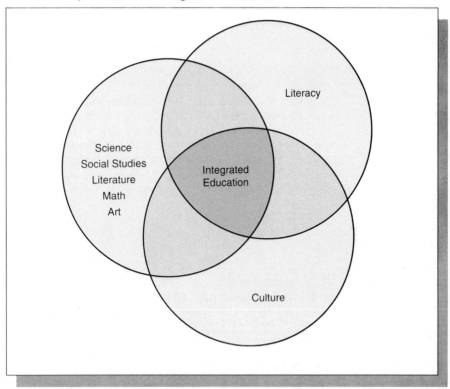

helps them to not ignore the classroom tapestry but instead to pay attention to it, study it, develop expertise on it, and use it. This makes it possible for them to provide what we might call "a hospitable learning climate" for all their students, whatever their cultural backgrounds. It is a learning community that honors diversity. Consider the following case:

Mrs. Carey teaches in the third grade, where the social studies theme is "Communities Now and Then." She has always prided herself on being able to tell both short and long versions of America's story. The long version is the one she tells in her third-grade class, and it takes a whole school year. Her children study European and Asian immigrant communities, both now and long ago. They build replicas of the Plymouth and Jamestown colonies but also St. Augustine, Florida, and Santa Fe, New Mexico. And they study the Chinese men who immigrated to work the railroads, reading Lawrence Yep's *Dragonwings*. Her short version reduces the nine months to a phrase, "We are a nation of immigrants."

This short version, really a title for the yearlong study, indicates the main idea around which Mrs. Carey orchestrates content and instruction.

·················· **EXAMPLE A: AMERICAN REVOLUTION, GRADE 5**

Materials:	Historical fiction. The Collier brothers' *My Brother Sam is Dead* and *War Comes to Willy Freeman.*
Cultural Perspectives:	These two pieces of historical fiction present very different perspectives on the American Revolution. Sam's story is told by his brother Tim. Both Sam and Tim are European American males. Their father is against Sam joining with the American rebels to drive out the British. Younger Tim is torn between his father and Sam. Willy, on the other hand, is a young female who has to disguise herself as a male because she is alone and separated from her family. Soldiers are everywhere. Also, she is African American. It doesn't make much difference to her which side wins. Both enslave Africans. Her father, unlike Tim's, joins with the rebels and, before many pages are turned, is killed defending a rebel fort.
Activity:	Children write in their journals while reading these books. The culminating activity is to write a new story in which Tim and Willy meet and learn of one another's experiences and perspectives on this war.
Note:	These stories should be combined with data gathered from the textbook, maps, and other informational sources so that students are not left only with narrative, fictionalized treatments of the war for independence.

It is the *storyline,* to use a metaphor from literature, and functions powerfully to fashion teaching and learning.

After years of telling this story, Mrs. Carey realized that her own immigrant experience, several generations before, along with her own studies in school of the great European immigration around the year 1900, had unknowingly shaped the storyline. She looked at her Hispanic and African American students and realized they were not part of the "nation of immigrants" storyline. Most of her Hispanic students did not immigrate; rather, the land of their ancestors, once in Mexico, was annexed to the United States after the Mexican-American War. And the ancestors of her black students hardly immigrated; they were forcibly removed from Africa.

She began an effort to change her story. She wanted to do this for the sake of accuracy, but she also felt that the old storyline may have kept some of her students from really going after this material. Maybe they felt that the story, like somebody else's shoes, didn't fit them. For the moment, Mrs. Carey is experimenting with two story lines, "We are a nation of many cultures" and "*E pluribus unum*—out of many, one."

Multiple Perspectives

The second aspect of multicultural education emphasizes a compare-and-contrast approach to the content children are to learn. Teachers make it a

·················   **EXAMPLE B: EUROPEAN/NATIVE AMERICAN ENCOUNTERS, GRADE 1**

Materials: Speare's *Sign of the Beaver* and Bulla's *Squanto: Friend of the Pilgrims.*

Cultural Perspectives: European colonists arriving on the east coast of North America encountered not a new world but a very old one inhabited by millions of people belonging to many different cultures. Children's tendency to stereotype Native Americans—that is, to gloss over the differences among them—can be countered by presenting the differences straightforwardly, using historical fiction. In this activity, the class contrasts two native men: the legendary *Squanto: Friend of the Pilgrims,* and the Indian at the center of Elizabeth George Speare's *Sign of the Beaver.* The latter is neither "savage" nor "friendly," and children learn something of his culture.

Activity: The teacher reads these stories aloud, stopping occasionally to have the children retell what they have heard so far. This lets the teacher diagnose their understanding and watch for what catches their interest. Eventually, students dramatize meetings between the two men in which they share stores of their respective cultures.

Note: Consider using both books as springboards for in-depth study on the two Indian cultures presented. Where exactly did they live? What kind of a place was it? How did they interact with the natural environment? Were they different from other Indian groups in the same geographical regions? What was their language? religion? law? medicine? family structure? shelter? food? education? economy?

point to plan units so that a topic is studied from more than one perspective, and the children must wrestle with their similarities and differences. This strategy has important advantages over the single-perspective approach.

First, any one perspective is prevented from being put forward as neutral (as one teacher put it, "This isn't a perspective, this is the truth!"). Second, children are introduced to the heart of historical thinking: making sense of competing accounts. Third, children are provided learning opportunities that involve comparison across multiple cases. This is strong pedagogy. Research suggests that it increases retention and facilitates students' later *use* of this material when they are working on other things.

Two examples of the multiple-perspective approach are provided on this and the previous pages. Both use children's literature and should help a beginning teacher to build a lasting habit.

With these two examples of the multiple-perspective approach to integrated unit planning, we close this chapter with the emphasis on culture. This is as it should be. Literacy education and interdisciplinary education both are steeped in culture. Both depend on apprenticeships in learning communities that expect great things of all children: high literacy and in-depth knowledge.

DISCUSSION QUESTIONS AND SUGGESTED ACTIVITIES

1. Find instances of the phrases "fill out" and "complete" in curriculum plans and materials. These are presented here as typical examples of *low* literacy. But is this always true? Are the contexts within which you found the phrases typical of low literacy? Discuss with classmates and teachers what you found and what you mean by "low" and "high" literacy.

2. Rank order the three exhibits given in the beginning of the chapter according to the following criteria: (a) student interest, (b) focusing students on essential social studies content, (c) likelihood of producing "peak experiences" (experiences so vivid, exciting, and fulfilling that they stay with a person virtually for a lifetime). Compare your responses to others'.

3. Of these three exhibits, the *Explore* curriculum was described in the greatest detail. Do you think it warranted such treatment? Share it with two or three other educators and ask them their opinion.

4. Review the *Explore* curriculum. Then add a fifth lesson to the four-lesson unit that was described. Select one of the following topics for its focus, then write a *focus question* and an *intended learning outcome* statement.

   • careers involving the study and/or protection of living things
   • international comparison of living things and their needs
   • an organism's "potential"
   • biographies of one or more people studied in Lesson 3
   • community service related to actions suggested in Lesson 3

5. Ask the librarian in two different elementary/middle school libraries to give you a tour of the biography sections. Ask the librarian to identify several of the more popular biographies. As you examine them, consider these questions: (a) What conceptual themes are suggested by these subjects? (b) Could any three or four of them be woven through a school year, all related to a single theme (e.g., leadership)? (c) Which eras of American history are not represented by biographies in either library?

6. Reread the example involving Mr. Atencio's kindergarten class on page 340, and Example B at the end of the chapter involving the two Indian groups. Then, plan a biographical approach with kindergarten children that uses this retelling technique. See Vivian Paley's *Wally's Stories* for ideas.

7. Design an array of biography "book" formats. What forms could kindergartners' books take? How about fifth graders'?

8. In addition to "snapshot" biographies, to what other genres of writing might children be introduced? Plan the lessons that would introduce

them to one of these other genres. For example, plan an introduction to *historical fiction*, then plan the lessons for teaching them to write the sort of historical fiction suggested in the final examples—a story about the meeting of two people from different texts. Finally, sketch unit plans related to other genres (e.g., poetry; plays).

9. Select three eras of United States history and assemble multiple-perspectives curriculum materials for each.

10. Study the diverse cultural identities of a group of children. Use first-hand observation, interviews, and reference books (e.g., ethnic studies textbooks). Take field notes, as an anthropologist would. Pay special attention to the variation within groups. For example, children of European ancestry are not "all alike," nor are children of Asian or African ancestry. Similarly, children whose first language is Spanish differ widely from one another.

SELECTED REFERENCES

Aoki, Elaine M. "Turning the Page: Asian Pacific American Children's Literature." In *Using Multicultural Literature in the Classroom*, edited by Violet J. Harris. Norwood, MA: Christopher-Gordon, in press.

Banks, James A., and Cherry A. McGee Banks. *Multicultural Education: Issues and Perspectives*. Needham Heights, MA: Allyn & Bacon, 1989.

Brown, Rexford. *Schools of Thought*. San Francisco: Jossey-Bass, 1991.

Graves, Donald H. *Writing: Teachers and Children at Work*. Portsmouth, NH: Heineman, 1983.

Heath, Shirley Brice. *Ways with Words*. New York: Cambridge University Press, 1983.

Hull, Glynda Ann. "Building an Understanding of Composing." In *Toward the Thinking Curriculum: Current Cognitive Research*, edited by Lauren B. Resnick and Leopold E. Klopfer, ASCD Yearbook, 104–28. Alexandria, VA: Association for Supervision and Curriculum Development, 1989.

Jacobs, Heidi Hayes. *Interdisciplinary Curriculum: Design and Development*. Alexandria, VA: Association for Supervision and Curriculum Development, 1989.

Langer, Judith A., and Arthur N. Applebee. "Reading and Writing Instruction: Toward a Theory of Teaching and Learning." In *Review of Research in Education*, vol. 13, edited by Ernest Z. Rothkopf, 171–94. Washington, DC: American Educational Research Association, 1986.

Paley, Vivian G. *Wally's Stories*. Cambridge, MA: Harvard University Press, 1981.

Resnick, Lauren B. "Literacy In School and Out." *Daedalus* 119:2 (Spring 1990): 169–85.

Rutherford, F. James, and Andrew Ahlgren. *Science for All Americans*. New York: Oxford University Press, 1990.

Zarnowski, Myra. *Learning with Biographies: A Reading and Writing Approach*. Washington, DC: National Council for the Social Studies and National Council for Teachers of English, published jointly, 1990.

12 Individualizing Instruction in the Social Studies

The increased attention in education to diversity, pluralism, and multiculturalism has resulted in hightened teacher awareness of individual differences among students. Also, the practice of moving children with disabilities out of segregated educational settings and into regular classrooms has had the effect of further sensitizing teachers to learning differences between and among *all* children. If the teacher is required to prepare an Individualized Education Program for a disabled child, it is likely that the teacher will be more observant of the individual learning needs of the child's peers as well. Much of the educational literature published in this century deals with variations in children and their effect on school achievement. Children differ one from another in their capacity to learn; in the rate at which they can learn; in their learning styles; in their methods of work; in their socioethnic, home, and family backgrounds; in their motivation to learn; in their physical fitness; and, indeed, on almost any variable we choose to examine. Some variations are more closely related to school achievement than are others, but the evidence is overwhelming that individual differences among children are so extensive and so pervasive that a group cannot be taught effectively unless some accommodation is made for such differences.

WHAT IT MEANS TO INDIVIDUALIZE INSTRUCTION

To individualize instruction means that each child is provided with personally meaningful learning experiences that are suitable to his or her capabilities, thereby enabling the learner to move in the direction of goals that are believed to be important. *Individualizing instruction does not mean that the teacher always works with individual children in a one-on-one tutorial setting.* Even if the teacher could work with children in a one-to-one relationship, this would not necessarily result in individualized instruction as we are defining it. Unless the teacher is sensitive to the unique learning requirements of each child, tutorial instruction can be just as impersonal and meaningless as whole-class instruction.

For a teacher to have an attitude of sensitivity to and caring about the idiosyncrasies and learning styles of individuals is critical. This means that a key element in the process is *flexibility*. Much of the instruction will, of necessity, take place in group settings. But membership in learning groups does not need to take the form of a permanent placement. Children can be moved from one group to another as is needed to help them learn in their own best way. There is no standard instructional format for individualizing instruction.

The teacher who individualizes instruction sees individual children rather than the class. Much attention is given to the identification of specific learning difficulties of individual children. The program requirements are open ended. Children are neither restricted by so-called grade-level content, nor are they required to achieve grade-level standards. Achievement is assessed in terms of gains made by each individual. Interests and preferences are respected and, insofar as is feasible, are accommodated. Uniform assignments and uniform requirements for the entire class are, as a rule, not given. Learner initiative, independence, and self-direction should be generously rewarded.

Because of the flexibility that should characterize much of individualized instruction, it is easy for the teacher to become careless in setting requirements and standards. Levels of achievement expectations have to be set in terms of their appropriateness for individual children, and, once they are set, learners must be held to them. Records of learner progress must be kept if assessments of achievement are to be made. Children need to be regularly informed of their progress. A knowledge of one's status and progress is a powerful force in motivating improved performance. It is significant that there is hardly any game that human beings play that does not require keeping score. Games in which no score is kept are frequently played carelessly and are less interesting to the players. And although school is not a game, the same principles apply. Teachers will usually get the level of performance they require and expect of children.

OBSTACLES TO INDIVIDUALIZING INSTRUCTION

If individualization is so important to good instruction, why don't more teachers do more of it? The answer to this question is not hard to find. Perhaps most important is the long tradition of whole-group instruction that is reinforced in many practices even today. The way children are grouped in schools often obscures important differences among them. Also, the belief is widely held that if children would just work harder, they could all achieve at the level required. Sometimes administrative and su-

Adult volunteers can be enormously helpful to teachers in providing tutoring for individual children. But the use of volunteer tutors means that the child has to relate to yet another adult in the instructional setting. In this sequence of fascinating photographs, we see the development of a trust relationship emerging as the child relates to the volunteer.
(Photos by Joel Schwarz, Tacoma School District.)

pervisory policies discourage individualization of instruction by mandating that teachers cover specific material. "Covering" the textbooks and teaching for the content of the standardized tests also work against individualizing instruction.

At a more subtle level, the reality of individual differences runs contrary to our social philosophy of equality, that is, the conflict between a recognition of obvious differences among individuals on the one hand and the desire to provide for equality of opportunity on the other. These represent conflicting values, both of which are embraced by this society and, no doubt, by a large number of teachers. We sense a basic unfairness about setting different standards or requirements for different children. Yet we know that unless we do, some children cannot possibly succeed whereas others succeed too easily. Some believe that schools serve a sorting function and that individualization of instruction confounds this process. Others believe that schools *should* teach children how they compare in achievement with their classmates, and this can be accomplished by using the average achievement of the group as the standard for comparison.

There are other practical obstacles to individualization of instruction. There is no doubt it is demanding of teacher time. It necessitates a considerable amount of recordkeeping, requires a skillful teacher to manage it well, and also requires a considerable amount of instructional resources. Some teachers are not able to cope with the flexibility it demands.

good point —

These obstacles to individualization of instruction cannot be swept aside as being unimportant, and we are mindful of the problems they create for the teacher. Nonetheless, it is the teacher's responsibility to make the social studies program vital and relevant for *all* children. Because children come from a wide variety of home and community environments, and because they differ as much as they do in their intellectual abilities and motivations, they cannot possibly benefit equally from identical exposures to educational experiences. If everyone is treated the *same*, we simply institutionalize and perpetuate *inequality* because some individuals and some groups are better able to take advantage of opportunities than the others. Consequently, we would expect all teachers to do as much as they are able to do in reaching each child in the social studies.

APPROACHES TO INDIVIDUALIZATION

Because teachers have their own particular styles and preferences, each will develop ways of individualizing instruction that seem to work best for him or her. Most teachers, however, will find it necessary to use a combination of procedures to attend effectively to the learning needs of individual children.

Management Approaches

Management and instruction are the two basic components of teaching. Consequently, the management aspects of a classroom have a great deal to do with the individualization of instruction. This becomes most apparent in such areas as the room environment, scheduling, the extent of "openness," and the amount and nature of teacher supervision.

Room Environment. If we visit a classroom in which learning is individualized, we are struck by the variety of interesting things children can do there that promote their opportunity to learn. The classroom is a storehouse of learning resources. We see areas of the room arranged for independent, quiet study. Other areas are planned for small-group interaction. We see interesting displays where children can handle and manipulate materials. There are learning centers where they can work at their own pace. There is easy access to books and other media that can be used as needed. There are work areas where children will find art materials, tools of various types, paper, boxes, and other raw materials needed to make things. The room is characterized by disciplined freedom where children can explore intellectually and move about physically. The environment is greatly varied in its appeal to children.

Learner Groups.   In social studies, most groups should be temporary task-oriented clusters of children. Often these groups are formed on the basis of a common interest, as, for example, a group working together on a display, a report, or a small construction project. Other groups are formed on the basis of a common need. For instance, the teacher may work with a small group in reading their text, developing a map skill, or showing them how to use the learning center materials while other children work independently. With the class arranged in this way, it will be possible to group children in many different configurations in accordance with individual needs. What should be avoided are fixed groups that separate children into fast-, medium-, and slow-achieving clusters on a more or less permanent basis.

Scheduling.   In traditional instruction, the time provided for learning is usually thought of as a constant fixed amount that is the same for everyone. Assignments are given on a specific day, and the completed work is due on a specific day. Because learners work at different rates, individualized approaches make time a variable rather than a constant. Within reasonable limits, children are allowed to work at their own pace. This requires careful supervision. Left entirely on their own, some would not make good use of their time, and this would work to the detriment of their learning. Nonetheless, the principle of providing for varying rates of learning is sound. This speaks against the use of rigid time schedules that apply to all, with penalties for "late" work.

Extent of Openness.   We use the term *openness* to mean both intellectual and physical freedom to learn. It suggests an absence of unnecessary and artificially imposed restrictions on what children learn and how they go about learning it. Regimented management procedures, whole-class teaching, and the use of strict *grading* practices tend to reduce the extent of openness in social studies.

The term *grading* has two meanings. The first has to do with placing children in groups called *grades*, usually on the basis of common age; for example, most six-year-olds are in the first *grade*. The second meaning of grades has to do with the awarding of letters or numerical scores to represent a child's level of achievement, for example, an A, B, or C *grade*. The grade concept is often associated with certain curriculum requirements, hence the common expressions "first-grade work," "second-grade work," and so on. There is not now, nor has there ever been, a consensus among teachers and educators as to precisely what constitutes "first-grade, second-grade, or third-grade" work. Nonetheless, it is usually interpreted to mean the average achievement of a child of average intelligence and motivation to do the work prescribed by the curriculum for that grade.

When grade standards are rigidly applied, as they often are, this practice has the effect of restricting learning opportunities. Children who are capable of doing so are discouraged from proceeding beyond what is specified because this would infringe on the curriculum content of the next grade. Meanwhile, the teacher intensifies efforts to get the slower-learning children up to the grade-level standard. Thus, by placing a lid on learning for some children and by requiring unattainable standards for others, the grade standard concept is clearly incompatible with individualized instruction.

These conventional ideas about grades and grade standards must be revised if we are to have the extent of openness needed to individualize instruction. The term *grade* should simply mean the group in which the child is placed and should be disassociated from an expected standard of achievement. That is, to say that a child is in the "third grade" should mean that he or she is in the third year of school. What each child knows or "should" know depends on the individual child. Some will know a great deal; others, very little. Once the issue of grade-level standards is set aside, the teacher can begin looking at the achievement levels of individual children and can set realistic levels of expectation for them.

Teacher Supervision and Guidance.   Fairly early in the school year the teacher will be able to identify the children who are well on the way to self-direction in their study habits, those who need a moderate amount of supervision and guidance, and those who will need to be monitored almost continuously.

In building study habits, the teacher must, on the one hand, remain close enough to the situation to lend direction and support, yet, on the other hand, be far enough away to allow the child to experiment with independence. When five or six first graders are operating the "store" in one corner of the classroom while the teacher is helping four or five others with a mural in another part of the room, it can be expected that help will be needed occasionally in the store to iron out minor problems. The same group as sixth graders could be expected to work through the entire period without help if their tasks were well defined.

Children need supervision and guidance from the teacher in a great variety of ways. In every class some will need special help with reading. These children may be taken singly or in a small group while the remainder read independently. In this reading-study situation the teacher helps the children with word difficulties, helps them get meaning from visual material, calls their attention to picture captions and discusses the pictures, selects certain key passages and singles those out for special teaching, reads to the children short selections of special significance, and tries to build independence in reading. The teacher, through careful guidance, must help children make the best use of reading resources. This type of guidance is not limited to the primary grades but persists throughout the elementary school.

In most classes, too, there will be another group of children who can go much beyond the remainder of the class in their depth of understanding of the topics studied. With these children, the teacher points out possibilities for additional study, challenges them with provocative problems, suggests topics for additional research, helps them secure appropriate reading material, teaches them how to organize their ideas, and gives similar guidance. The teacher can be of most help to these children by suggesting, challenging, and holding them to high standards of achievement and yet expecting much of their study to be done independently.

The teacher's role in guiding and supervising social studies activities may be described, therefore, as a function of the needs of individual children. Children should not be supervised so closely as to discourage independent habits of work. But neither should the teacher fail to offer the kind of constructive help and guidance growing children need. The teacher should be actively involved during the social studies period—moving from group to group and child to child, assisting, encouraging, suggesting, and doing whatever else is needed to help children move in the direction of desired learning goals.

Multimedia Approaches

The intake of new information is an essential requirement of social studies education, and the conventional information sources have been the textbook and the teacher. For years teachers have been urged to expand these classroom information sources to include the many newer learning resources that are now available. The planned use of a generous and varied offering of learning resources greatly enhances the possibility of individualized learning. What is sought is the use of several different learning resources in combination, which is essentially what a multimedia approach does. Providing variation in the information sources available to children is one of the easiest first steps a teacher can take in individualizing the social studies program. Several specific suggestions are offered in this section.

Reading Materials.   The differences in reading ability among individuals are apparent early in the grades and become greater as the children move through school. By the time they are in the fifth and sixth grades, the difference between the least capable and most capable readers is often as much as six to eight years. Accommodating these variations in reading ability is, therefore, critical to social studies instruction.

Usually, the teacher will have little problem in securing appropriate reading material for the more capable readers. Given a minimum of direction, they will be able to handle the textbook on their own. They can then be guided to other sources of information, most of which can be geared to their individual interests related to a topic under study or to individual or small group research projects. School and public libraries provide good selections of books that are relevant to many social studies topics. Additionally, the better readers can make use of special references, pamphlets, newspapers, and magazines. The teacher's role is not so much to assist these children with the reading task itself but to provide stimulating and challenging guidance that will motivate them to do the reading. The teacher should help those children develop advanced skills related to information gathering and processing.

With the less capable readers, the teacher will need to (1) provide direct assistance with the reading and (2) make available less difficult materials that deal with the topic under study. A third option is to provide ways for these learners to get needed information through listening, viewing, direct experience, or some other nonreading resource. In using nonreading resources, however, the teacher must recognize that this further reduces the opportunity for the child to practice using reading skills.

When working with less capable readers, either in small groups or individually, the teacher will want to select only those passages or graphic materials that are particularly vital to understanding the topic. The meanings of essential terms and concepts included in the passage should be developed prior to doing the reading. Carefully structured guide questions should be used to ensure that the reading is done with purpose. That is, children are reading to *find out* specific information. Have these children confirm their responses to literal questions by reading orally the sentence that provides the answer. These reading-study sessions should be kept short (15 to 20 minutes) and should be highly motivated. Additional suggestions relating to reading social studies content are provided in chapter 10.

As one moves lower in the elementary grades, it becomes more difficult to secure simplified reading materials for social studies. There comes a point beyond which it is impossible to simplify the reading task and still have the narrative provide significant information. The teacher can rewrite some passages or create original selections for the slower readers. Because this is time consuming and often difficult, the amount of such original material a teacher can produce is necessarily limited.

Often overlooked as valuable reading sources for social studies are trade books and literary works. Trade books are what children call "library books." Ordinarily such books can be secured from the school library or from the district instructional resources center. Children will use trade books as sources of information as well as reading them for enjoyment. In the middle and upper grades, simplified nontext books are available on many social studies topics. (See chapter 5.)

In addition to making these books available, the teacher must structure the learning environment in ways that will ensure that the children and books are brought together. This can be done by making the books an integral part of a learning center. Although some use can be made of book reports, this procedure can easily become routine, uninteresting, and self-defeating. Teachers can prevent this from happening by devising imaginative ways for children to share what they have read with each other. For example, teachers have made use of such followup activities as these: (1) evaluate the books children have read in terms of specific criteria (What did you like or dislike about the book? What is especially good about the book? What information does it provide? Would you recommend it to a friend? and so forth); (2) make an illustration that conveys some interesting feature of the book; (3) tape record a short review of the book; (4) persuade a classmate to read a book found to be especially interesting or useful; (5) read orally to the class selected passages thought to be particularly relevant to the topic.

Make a note

Learning Kits and Packages.   A learning kit or package is a small collection of relevant materials that children can use on their own in studying a topic, concept, or skill (see Figure 12-1). It will ordinarily contain instructions for use, information source materials (reprints, maps, pictures, pamphlets, or other appropriate resources), along with study guide questions, self-correcting work sheets, or other response formats or a combination of these. Directions must be clear enough to allow children to use the kit or package independently. Learning kits vary in the extent to which they can be used without teacher assistance, but insofar as possible, the kit or package is self-selected by the child; self-directed, self-paced, and self-corrected. Ordinarily such a kit could be contained in a file-size envelope or box. It can be constructed by the teacher or can be purchased from commercial sources.

Learning Centers.   Learning kits, packages, and other self-directed materials can be assembled in a designated place in the classroom called a *learning center.* Usually, a learning center will contain multimedia materials focused on a specific topic, concept, or skill. Children are expected to work in the learning center itself rather than checking out materials that are to be used elsewhere. In a learning center one may find filmstrips and projectors, pictures, printed materials, cassette tape recordings, cartridge-type films, books, learning packets, maps, and other appropriate learning resources. They are designed to be used by children on their own as a means of (1) obtaining basic information, (2) practicing a skill, (3) following up on something taught to the entire class, and (4) enriching and extending basic instruction.

Learning center activities and materials must provide the children with specific and precise directions because they are expected to use the center with a minimum of teacher direction and supervision. If this is to happen, children will also have to be instructed on how to use the center. Children should be provided with some choice in what is to be done and should be allowed to work at their own pace. More than one child should be able to work in the center at the same time, and, in some cases, they may work cooperatively on the same activity.

374

FIGURE 12-1
Components of a Sample Learning Kit.

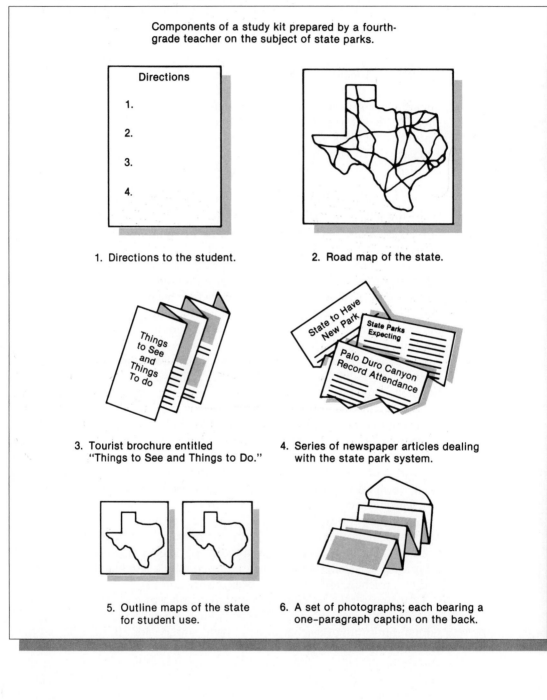

Components of a study kit prepared by a fourth-grade teacher on the subject of state parks.

1. Directions to the student.

2. Road map of the state.

3. Tourist brochure entitled "Things to See and Things to Do."

4. Series of newspaper articles dealing with the state park system.

5. Outline maps of the state for student use.

6. A set of photographs; each bearing a one–paragraph caption on the back.

···············   **EXAMPLE OF THE USE OF MULTIMEDIA IN AN INTERMEDIATE GRADE UNIT**

Activities

In a unit entitled "The Challenge of Change," a fourth- and fifth-grade class used the following resources and activities that were in an activity packet:

1. Write a diary pretending you are in a Conestoga Wagon going from Independence, Missouri, to the Oregon Territory; have at least five entries. Then write a similar diary either for a trip in the present day or what you would imagine a trip would be like in the year 2050. Again include five entries telling of things that you have seen and have done.

2. Research one of the following inventions, or choose a scientific discovery of your own. Be sure to include a discussion of how the invention changed the lives of the people at the time of the invention and how it affects our lives today.

   a. automobile
   b. cotton gin
   c. steam engine
   d. camera
   e. locomotive
   f. telegraph
   g. reaper
   h. phonograph

   i. telephone
   j. electric lights
   k. calculator
   l. computer
   m. airplane
   n. television
   o. satellite
   p. artificial body organs

3. Make a booklet of tools and utensils used by the pioneers; in a second part include tools and utensils that might be used in the daily lives of people today.

4. Interview someone who has immigrated to the United States. Try to find out what changes this made in the person's life. Decide on several (three to six) questions you wish to ask the person, and show them to your teacher prior to the interview.

5. Collect cartoons that deal with people making changes in some way. Perhaps the change might come as the result of some conflict or disagreement, or it might show the results of a changed attitude.

6. Make a collage showing change. Have a theme such as

   a. Changes in My Life
   b. Changes in Our Natural Environment
   c. Inventions That Change Lives
   d. Changes in the Status of Minorities and Women
   e. Changes in Recreation

7. Collect newspaper articles that deal with changes. Choose a theme around which to build your collection, such as political or physical changes in your state, city, or community. Arrange to display your collection.

8. Create a map that shows the places where several (three to six) of your classmates have lived during their lives. Be sure to have a key so you can clearly show which moves were made by which classmate. Your teacher has an outline map for you to use.

Or take a poll to find out how many times each person in your class has moved. Compile your results and show them on a graph.

9. Make a photographic essay showing changes in your community. This could show natural changes or those made by people.

10. Contact a longtime neighborhood resident to find out how the area has changed over time. Use a cassette recorder to tape the oral history interview. Present a report to the class about changes that have taken place, making use of the taped interview.

11. Watch one of the films listed as resources in your packet. Create a poster or a five- or six-frame filmstrip showing the main ideas of the film.

12. Read a fiction book that deals with the changes in the lives of people your own age. Create a way to share your book with the rest of the class. Check the Reading Center for ideas.

Learning Resources

Textbooks	Recordings
Library and other resource books	Slides
Videotapes/TV	Study Prints
Films	Field Trips
Filmstrips	Newspapers
Computer	Magazines
(simulation game, *The Oregon Trail*)	

excellent

It is important to emphasize that the learning center, as a collection of relevant learning resources, is an integral part of the total resources used by the class in studying a topic. *All* children can and should be expected to make some use of it. The learning center should not be perceived only as a "fun" place for those who complete their regular assignment quickly—as a reward for good work. Such restricted use limits the value of the learning center and denies its use to precisely those children who could benefit most from it.

Performance-Based Approaches

In using performance-based approaches to individualizing instruction, careful attention must be given to the specific objectives to be achieved by each child. For example, it is clear that ideas and skills can be handled at varying levels of complexity. Likewise, children vary in their ability to deal with complex ideas. In performance-based teaching, the teacher attempts to match the level of complexity of the objectives with the learner's ability to achieve them. This can be done by using behavioral objectives that are geared to various levels of difficulty, by using instructional material that is self-paced, by using individual contracts, and by assessing learner outcomes actually attained through instruction.

Learner Contracts.   A *learner contract* is defined as a cooperatively developed agreement between an individual and the teacher. The contract specifies precisely what the child will do and when the work is to be completed. Because contracts are individually negotiated, the nature and extent of the work to be completed can be well suited to the ability level and the interests of the child. Some teachers develop and use a contract form that gives the agreement an official appearance. Contracts are signed by both the child and the teacher. Examples of contract forms are provided in Figures 12-2 and 12-3.

The use of contracts has educational values beyond being an interesting assignment format. The children should learn what is involved in a contractual agreement and that there usually are adverse consequences when contracts are not completed as specified. Therefore, it is important that children know what it is they are agreeing to do and what penalties may be attached to the failure to fulfill the conditions of the contract.

Special Assignments.   A teacher may want to make special assignments to accommodate the particular interests or talents of certain children. For example, a child who is intellectually gifted may be assigned to do an independent research project related to a social studies topic. Children who have special talents and abilities in doing art, music, drama, or construction projects should be encouraged to apply these abilities in social studies. Social studies is the ideal area of the curriculum to make adjustments to such special capabilities of learners. Children should not, however, always work on projects for which they have a special talent. Like all other children, they, too, need to have a balanced learning experience.

Individualized Education Program (IEP).   Although the IEP is associated with and required for children with disabilities, such plans can be used with any learner. The use of the IEP requires that the teacher assess the learning needs of individual children and draft a program plan consistent with that assessment. With class sizes being what they are, it is not feasible to think in terms of preparing IEPs for all children unless the teacher is provided considerable assistance. Nonetheless, this procedure may be just what is needed for particular children who have difficulty managing the regular instructional program.

Mastery Learning Based on Behavioral Objectives.   Public concern over the quality of education has required schools to provide more documentary

A Sample Learner Contract Format.

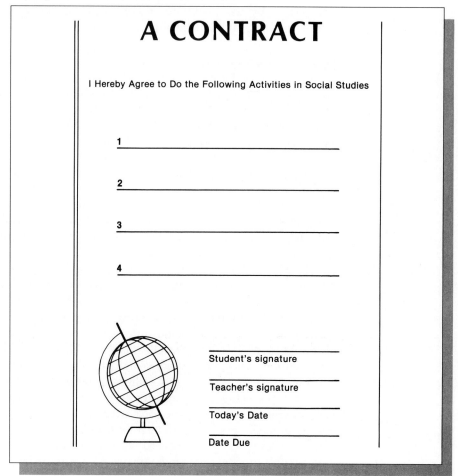

A CONTRACT

I Hereby Agree to Do the Following Activities in Social Studies

1 _____

2 _____

3 _____

4 _____

_____
Student's signature

_____
Teacher's signature

_____
Today's Date

_____
Date Due

evidence of learner achievement than has been the case in the past. In responding to that concern for accountability, schools have turned to the use of minimum competency testing and to "precision teaching," meaning teaching targeted on the achievement of specifically defined objectives. Such "student learning objectives" are usually stated behaviorally and are interpreted as essentials that all children must learn. In other words, of all the potential things that *could* be learned, the teacher or the school authorities have said, "These items must be mastered at certain levels of proficiency by all learners."

Teachers can individualize the achievement of such objectives for children by varying the amount of time from one child to the next, by using

FIGURE 12-3
Other Variations of Learner Contracts.

AN AGREEMENT

As my contribution to the unit, OUR TOWN, I agree to do the project or projects checked:

_____ 1. Interview a person who has lived here a long time.

_____ 2. Conduct a survey of old buildings in our town.

_____ 3. Write a true story about our town.

_____ 4. Write a short play about our town.

_____ 5. Work on a mural with _____

                        (Name other children)

_____ 6. Paint a picture of something in our town.

_____ 7. Prepare a TV program script about our town.

_____ 8. Do an original activity of my own:_____

_____

Today's Date: _____   _____

                                            Student

      Due Date: _____   _____

                                            Teacher

INDIVIDUAL STUDY PLAN

I contract to do the following activities that are described on pages 157–158 of our text, to be completed by November 15:

(Check two)

_____ Using A Time Line   _____ Making History Real

_____ Building Ideas from Words and   _____ Interesting Things To Do
        Pictures

_____ Making an Outline   _____ Things to Think About
                                                      (Write out your answers)

_____ Making a Chart

Date: _____   _____

                                                   Student

                                      _____

                                                   Teacher

different kinds of instructional materials, or by using different presentation modes for different children. What is important is that when the instruction is completed, all learners are able to demonstrate, through *performance*, that they have "mastered" the material.

Performance-based procedures require a close working relationship between individual children and the teacher. This means frequent conferences to monitor performance and progress toward specific objectives. An assessment of the child's status is essential if an individual study program is to be planned. Thus, a system for the diagnosis of learner needs is an essential component of performance-based programs. Much of this can be done informally as the teacher observes the work of individual children. In the middle and upper grades, the teacher can also make use of diagnostic tests.

It is important to stress that independent study, as characterized by performance-based teaching, is not the same as individualized learning. Individualized learning can and often does take place in group settings. Good social studies programs will not result if children constantly work by themselves without the opportunity to interact with others. Some provision must be made for cooperative learning in small and large groups during which time the results of individual study are shared, ideas are discussed, group activities are planned, and new areas of study are explored. This will ensure that the social dimensions of social studies education are not being overlooked.

Creative or Activity-Based Approaches

Much can be done to individualize social studies learning by encouraging children to imagine, to wonder, to act out feelings, to create, and to express their ideas and feelings through art forms and similar creative or activity modes. These approaches must be used in combination with some of the other approaches suggested in this chapter. The difference between this approach and the others is that it individualizes learning at the outgo or expressive level whereas all the others vary the ways children receive ideas or information. The use of creative and expressive activities is discussed in detail in chapter 14.

Social studies activities should be sufficiently varied to appeal to the broad range of interests and capabilities of children. Some activities such as oral and written reports tend to be overused. Activities that are highly correlated with the usual academic skills and abilities are useful, of course, but other options should also be available. Not all children are able to perform these activities well, and consequently their involvement in the social studies program is limited. Most social studies teaching would be improved through the use of a wide range of activities, especially those that require the child to use creative imagination. The suggestions given in chapter 4 illustrate the types of learning activities that should at one time or another be included in social studies instruction.

This section has emphasized the need for taking a broad view of individualizing social studies instruction. Too frequently, individualizing instruction is understood to mean "doing something for the gifted" or "doing something for the slow learners." *The fact is that every child presents the teacher with the challenge of individual differences.* The teacher who accepts this broader concept of individual differences will take into account not only the child's IQ but also the other factors that influence the child's achievement of social studies objectives. This will ensure that some adjustments will be made in the program for the unique needs of every child irrespective of his or her mental ability. But because the problem of providing for exceptional children is a matter of special concern to many teachers, the next section addresses that subject.

INDIVIDUALIZING FOR EXCEPTIONALITY

The Congress of the United States enacted two pieces of legislation during the decade of the 1970s that had a profound effect on the education of persons with disabilities. The first of these was Section 504 of the Vocational Rehabilitation Act of 1973. This law deals largely with the removal of discriminatory practices. Although it is basically a law that protects the civil rights of disabled persons, it has a number of implications for education. It guarantees that an individual may not be denied access to education solely on the basis of a disability. As a result, Section 504 brought some greater extension of employment, training, and promotion opportunities to individuals with disabilities.

Perhaps the most important contribution of Section 504 was its mandate to remove barriers in architecture and in transportation. The law requires that all *activities* (not all areas or spaces) must be accessible to physically disabled participants and spectators. This meant that substantial structural modifications in existing school buildings had to be made to bring them into compliance. New structures must make provisions for these antidiscriminatory requirements in their design. Section 504 was instrumental in establishing "barrier-free" environments in schools.

In 1975 two Congressional Subcommittees held hearings in various parts of the country to determine what, if any, additional legislation was needed to accommodate the educational needs of the disabled. Some of the findings of these hearings were astounding: Over 1.75 million children with disabilities were being excluded *entirely* from receiving a public education solely on the basis of their disability. Over half of the estimated 8 million children were not receiving appropriate services. Many children with disabilities were being placed in inappropriate educational environments because their disabilities had not been detected. As a result of these findings and as a result of concurrent judicial intervention, the 142nd piece of legislation passed by the 94th Congress was the Education for All

What is unusual about the situation in this photograph is that the instruction is being conducted in sign language. Although schools have moved toward a social policy of inclusion, that is, *mainstreaming* of students with disabilities, some specialized instruction is necessary in certain circumstances for school districts to comply with the "least restrictive environment" principle.
(Photo by Carla Anderson, Northshore School District.)

Handicapped Children Act, otherwise known as PL94-142. It passed both Houses of Congress by very wide margins—probably because the issue had already been settled by the courts. The bill was signed into law by President Gerald Ford on November 29, 1975, to go into effect in 1977, with no expiration date.

PL94-142 is one of the most lengthy and complex pieces of legislation ever enacted by Congress. Its main points, however, are easily summarized. The law requires

1. The availability of a free appropriate public education for all children with disabilities between the ages of three and twenty-one, unless inconsistent with state laws; school districts are obliged to search for and identify such children.
2. The maintenance of an Individualized Education Program (IEP) for all disabled children, prepared in cooperation with the parent or guardian, the teacher, and the school principal.

enacted in the 70s but still not practiced

3. The guarantee of complete due process procedures.
4. The provision of special education and related services as needed in the "least restrictive" environment.
5. Nondiscriminatory testing, evaluation, and placement.
6. The placement in regular public school settings with nondisabled peers to the maximum extent appropriate and feasible.

PL94-142 is based on a philosophy of *inclusion* rather than *exclusion*. It embraces the "zero-reject" principle. It frowns on the segregation and labeling of human beings. It shatters long-held assumptions about who is educable.

Teaching Children with Disabilities

Traditionally, elementary school teachers dealt with children with disabilities by referring them to special education classes. As we have seen, this type of arbitrary exclusion is no longer socially or legally acceptable. Today the teacher can expect one or more children with varying types of disabilities to be present in most elementary school classrooms. This practice, known popularly as "mainstreaming," is the school's response to the mandate that such children must be educated with their nondisabled peers to the maximum extent appropriate.

What the teacher can do and will do depends on the nature of the child's disability and the extent of support service provided. It is quite clear that a child who is orthopedically disabled but is intellectually gifted will be handled differently from one who is physically fully functioning but is mildly—or severely—retarded intellectually. In this context, the Individualized Education Program makes good sense because the learning needs of children vary greatly from one to another. Likewise, what the teacher does or does not do will depend on how much technical assistance and support service is available. If the classroom has the services of an interpreter-tutor who can work with the child for part of the time in a one-on-one setting and who works with the teacher on a cooperative basis, it becomes easier for the regular teacher to integrate children with disabilities into the day-to-day life and activities of the classroom.

In the case of a child who is severely disabled, the chances are good that a teacher trained in special education will prepare the Individualized Education Program. The classroom teacher may be responsible for only a small part of the implementation of the IEP. On the other hand, if the teacher has a child in the class with mild mental retardation, that teacher may have full responsibility for the preparation and implementation of the IEP. Even in cases of children who are not severely disabled, the regular classroom teacher may have available the assistance of a special education teacher in preparing the IEP. In those cases in which the child is attending both regular and special education classes, ordinarily the IEP goals and objectives will focus on compensating for the child's disability, and it is the special education teacher who attends the IEP meeting. The regular classroom teacher, the special education teacher, and other support personnel must, of course, work in close cooperation with each other to ensure a coordinated program of instruction for the child.

The Individualized Education Program must take into account the child's present level of attainment or development. In other words, a learning needs assessment must be made, and the current status established. Based on that information, the IEP stipulates the long-range goals that are to be met by the end of the year and the short-term objectives to be achieved in order to attain the long-range goals. The short-term objectives should be listed in the sequence in which they are to be achieved. Although the regular teacher may exercise some initiative in preparing the IEP, the program planning and development *must* include, on a firsthand basis, the principal or other school representative and the child's parent or guardian. Teacher-prepared IEPs that are sent to the child's parent or guardian for signature are not acceptable in terms of the mandate of PL94-142.

The actual format of the IEP will vary from district to district although the substance of what is included will remain pretty much the same. The sample form provided in Figure 12–4 illustrates a standard IEP that includes components required by federal regulations.

Teaching Gifted Children

The term *exceptionality* is used in connection with gifted learners as well as with the disabled. The state education agency or the local school district establishes the criteria for defining giftedness. The criteria are usually derived from a combination of a child's school achievement history, teacher judgment, and scores on so-called "standardized" intelligence tests. Gifted children are those who show evidence of unusual talents or abilities. They ordinarily handle academic learning easily because of their capacity to use symbolic language and to understand abstract relationships. Although giftedness is almost always associated with high intellectual ability and precociousness, there have been some efforts to broaden the scope of the term *intelligence.*[1]

Children who are identified as gifted may qualify for school-funded enrichment programs especially designed for high-ability students. Although federal and state legislation require schools to make provision for disabled learners, such mandates often do not apply to gifted children. Regardless of the availability of special programs for the gifted, the regular classroom teacher will need to make provisions for the learning needs of these students. Social studies is a curriculum area that is ideally suited to make such adjustments because of its open-ended subject matter, and because the variety of possible approaches for studying it is limited only by the teacher's imagination and resources.

---

[1]Tina Blythe and Howard Gardner, "A School for All Intelligences," *Educational Leadership* 47 (April 1990): 33–37.

FIGURE 12-4
Sample IEP Form.

PIEDMONT PUBLIC SCHOOLS
INDIVIDUALIZED EDUCATION PROGRAM

Standard Form

Student _____

Birthdate _____

C.A. _____

Address _____ (include zip)

Lives With _____ Relationship _____ Home Phone _____ Work Phone _____

Home School _____ Grade _____ IEP Conference Date _____ Projected Review Date _____

Teacher _____ Program _____ School _____ Date Enrolled _____ Terminated _____

PLACEMENT OFFICE ONLY:

Date Enrolled _____

Teacher _____

Building _____

Program Assigned _____

I. SUMMARY OF PRESENT LEVELS OF PERFORMANCE
(Include statements of progress in each area from last reporting period)

SCHOLASTIC:

PHYSICAL:

ADJUSTMENT:

II. ANALYSIS OF ASSESSMENT DATA
(Report of significant changes since initial IEP)

ELIGIBILITY CRITERIA:

PROGRAM AND/OR REPLACEMENT CHANGE:

Team Leader: _____ Date: _____
Parent: _____ Date: _____

PROGRAM RECOMMENDATION:

Psychologist: _____ Date: _____
Parent: _____ Date: _____
_____ Date: _____

385

FIGURE 12-4
continued

386

III. STUDENT GOALS & OBJECTIVES

Academic Year _____

Special Classroom Teacher _____

Support Services _____

(Specify Service)

Name of Student	B.D.	Grade	Program	Building	Teacher	Date Enrolled	
						Date Started	Date Completed

Goals:

Initial Objectives:

Evaluation Criteria & Progress Notes (include pre-test, post-test data, and grades)

_____
Signature of person or persons responsible for reporting progress on goals and objectives

_____
Parent Signature

_____
Date

FIGURE 12-4
continued

Student: _____

Projected I.E.P. Review Date _____

IV. RELATED SERVICES

Regular Education Program:	Estimated Time/Week	Anticipated	
		Start	End

Support Services: (C.D.S., P.E., Voc. etc.)

Regular P.E. ☐   Adaptive P.E. ☐

My rights and responsibilities have been explained to me in a manner which I understand.

I have had the opportunity to participate in the development of this Individualized Eduation Program.

I understand all programs and services listed above and give my permission for my child/ward to participate in these programs/services.

I have been informed that the objectives listed on this form are initial objectives and that the person(s) responsible for implementing the objectives will revise and/or add objectives in keeping with the student's progress toward the stated goals.

Parent Signature: _____

Date: _____

V.I.E.P. Committee Members:

Name	Position
_____	_____
_____	_____
_____	_____
_____	_____
_____	_____

The School District shall provide the parent (or the adult student) a copy of the individualized education program.

SUGGESTIONS FOR TEACHING CHILDREN WITH LEARNING DISABILITIES

1. Provide generously for firsthand, concrete experiences. These children learn best by handling, manipulating, sensing, feeling, and doing; and they learn least well by reading, analyzing, generalizing, and finding new solutions to problems.
2. Learning tasks must be specific and simple; learning objectives must be definite, clear-cut, and short-ranged. The children must know precisely what to do and how to do it. Use detailed study guides.
3. Learning experiences should be presented in one small step at a time with successful completion of each step before advancement to the next.
4. Recognize that lessons should be short in duration because of the brevity of the attention span of many children with specific learning disabilities.
5. Expect them to show less initiative and less ability to plan for themselves than nondisabled or gifted children. They are also less able to evaluate their own work, making close supervision and direction by the teacher imperative.
6. Reduce their load of abstract and verbal materials to a level they are able to handle. Work in references, if used at all, must be specific; reading and research must be held to a minimum.
7. Recognize that it will be difficult for them to sense relationships, to make generalizations, or to do inferential thinking. They are more skillful in dealing with *who, what,* and *where* questions than they are with *why* type questions.
8. When teaching crucial items such as those of health, safety, laws or conventions of society, or simple elements of social studies skills, plan to provide for much practice and repetition of the material to be learned.
9. Set realistic levels of expectation for them. Plan in terms of their most pressing needs with a view toward their future life as happy and productive members of society. Try to visualize what knowledge and skills will be most useful to the child in the future.
10. Above all, maintain a patient and encouraging attitude toward them. Help them establish security and status in the classroom. Provide opportunities for a degree of success for them.

SUGGESTIONS FOR TEACHING GIFTED CHILDREN

1. Provide a generous amount of challenging reading material that will allow them to read for informational purposes.
2. Plan learning activities that call for problem solving, making logical associations, making logical deductions, and making generalizations.
3. Give them many opportunities to plan their own work; allow for a considerable amount of individual initiative, commensurate with their degree of maturity.
4. Provide for individual study and research. This should include use of the library and references, as well as note keeping, outlining, summarizing, and reporting.
5. Expect and encourage much originality in self-expression—in discussions, dramatizations, projects, and activities.

6. Recognize that they may have less need for extended firsthand and concrete experiences than do other children because they are able to work with abstractions more easily, see associations and relationships more quickly, and have quick reaction time.

7. Encourage these children to develop self-evaluative skills; they are generally capable of effectively evaluating their own work.

8. Give them many opportunities for leadership responsibilities. Provide opportunities for gifted children to use their talents by tutoring other children. In some schools children of the intermediate grades with high intellectual abilities also work with primary-grade children.

9. Remember that gifted children have many of the common needs of all children. Although it is true that they are ordinarily accelerated in other aspects of their development as well, their physical growth, muscular coordination, social development, and emotional stability cannot be equated with their rate of growth in mental development.

10. The complete acceptance by the teacher of the high intellectual abilities of gifted children is essential to planning an effective program for them. The teacher who sees gifted children as a threat becomes defensive and is unable to work with them satisfactorily.

DISCUSSION QUESTIONS AND SUGGESTED ACTIVITIES

1. Do you believe that a teacher's expectations relate in any way to a child's achievement? Explain.

2. Develop a floor plan of a room environment that would lend itself well to individualizing instruction.

3. How can the teacher ensure that the social values of social studies education are being attained in a program that individualizes instruction?

4. Prepare a small learning kit or package that could be used by children in a grade of your choice.

5. Design a sketch of a classroom learning center for social studies, and show what you would include in it.

6. Develop a learner contract suitable for use in a grade of your choice.

7. What procedures for individualizing instruction might be used in groups that (a) have a high percentage of poor readers; (b) have limited language ability; (c) have a high percentage of high-achieving, capable children; or (d) present difficult management problems?

8. If you visited an elementary school classroom, what would you look for that would suggest that individualizing of instruction is taking place in social studies?

9. What new knowledge and skills does a regular teacher need to have to work effectively with children with disabilities who are assigned to his or her classroom?

10. What differences can you identify between the practice of "mainstreaming" and that of placing children with disabilities in "least restrictive learning environments"?

SELECTED REFERENCES

Brandt, Ronald S., ed. *Educational Leadership* 46 (March 1989). Several authors contribute sixteen articles on students differences.

Butler, Kathleen A. "Learning Styles." *Learning* 88 (November/December 1988): 30–34.

Curtis, Charles K. "Social Studies for Students At-Risk and with Disabilities." In *Handbook of Research on Social Studies Teaching and Learning,* edited by James P. Shaver, 157–74. New York: Macmillan, 1991.

Guild, Pat Burke, and Stephen Garger. *Marching to Different Drummers.* Alexandria, VA: Association for Supervision and Curriculum Development, 1985.

Herlihy, John G., and Myra T. Herlihy, eds. *Mainstreaming in Social Studies.* NCSS Bulletin No. 62. Washington, DC: National Council for the Social Studies, 1980.

Rohrkemper, Mary, and Lyn Corno. "Success and Failure on Classroom Tasks: Adaptive Learning and Classroom Teaching." *The Elementary School Journal* 88 (January 1988): 297–313.

Salend, Spencer J. "Factors Contributing to the Development of Successful Mainstreaming Programs." *Exceptional Children* 50 (February 1984): 409–16.

Shaw, Terry, ed. *Teaching Handicapped Students Social Studies: A Resource Handbook for K–12 Teachers.* Washington, DC: National Education Association, 1981.

13 Cooperative Learning

Societies organized under the democratic ideal place special demands on their school systems. Children in these societies need to be educated to be the kind of citizens who can and will share in popular sovereignty. It is not easy work, and it does not appear to come to us naturally. Indeed, our "primary nature" is egocentric.[1] For this reason, all of us to some degree are tempted to let others look after the common good while we tend to our private affairs—to our friends, families, jobs, hobbies, religions, shopping, entertainment, and so on. But the democratic ideal requires people to extend their caring beyond private life to public life—to share in decision making, to join in efforts to reduce crime and poverty, to fight injustice and work for peace, to help prevent delinquency and substance abuse, create public parks and museums, reduce and repair damage to the natural environment, improve public health, and so on. The list is long. Everyone's help is needed. This is the democratic vision.

Most basically, the work of democracy requires citizens who can work well together in task-oriented groups. These may be study groups, such as parents meeting to study the problem of drug selling near schools, or decision-making groups, or both. These are different from play groups, where there is no task *per se*, and they are different from other settings, such as a baseball game or a church service, where people may be physically near one another and may perhaps share materials. Task-oriented groups have work to do, often problem solving, *and their members are mutually dependent on one another for planning the work and getting it done successfully.*

Can a classroom be such a group? It can and it should. Like it or not, classroom life is a social apprenticeship, and the character of that apprenticeship most likely will be carried with the children into later years, especially the

---

[1] Richard Paul, *Critical Thinking* (Rohnert Park, CA: Sonoma State University, 1991).

work habits that are formed there, the skills and norms of interaction that are fostered, and the attitude toward learning and cooperating that takes shape there. Put differently, children learn by doing, and the kind of doing shapes the kind of learning that will take place. Teachers play the central role in determining the kind of apprenticeship it will be, and there is much they can do help fashion it to be an apprenticeship for cooperation and democracy. This involves structuring tasks that require students to make decisions on their own, to use one another as resources, and to plan and carry out work.

Of course, there are reasons other than democracy why people need to learn to work well together. Consider two. First, the business community in the United States increasingly is demanding employees who can function on teams—together identifying problems worth solving, setting priorities for them, planning, integrating diverse ideas, dividing the work load, and building on one another's contributions. Second, the population of North America is becoming rapidly more diverse ethnically and linguistically. The practice of mainstreaming children with disabilities and busing students from one neighborhood to another has further changed the composition of the classroom. All of this requires contemporary students—students of the 21st century—to overcome initial prejudices rapidly, to learn to appreciate people who are culturally different, and to build healthy, working relationships.

CREATING A POSITIVE CLIMATE FOR HUMAN RELATIONS

The term *group* means more than merely a collection of individuals. Groups develop a solidarity—a unity or cohesiveness—resulting from working and learning together. A fourth-grade class at the beginning of a school year is an aggregate of individual children assigned to a particular room because of their similar chronological ages. This class of individuals may develop into a *group* as the year progresses and the children develop feelings of belonging, identifying with it, developing an esprit de corps, and growing in their concern for the welfare and success of the class *as a whole*. It will be a *group* to the extent that the actions of individuals are influenced by other members and the extent to which the behavior of individual members matter to the group.

An emotionally supportive atmosphere is one that is characterized by trust and by evidence that individuals care about each other. When a child volunteers, "Robin's group had more to do than the rest of us. They should have more time to finish," the observer senses that he or she is in a caring environment. Or when a minor classroom accident results in damage to material or broken equipment and the teacher treats the incident as an accident, one concludes that the teacher values human beings more than things. Teachers who develop comfortable classroom environments are concerned with a broad range of educational outcomes, including those that relate to the emotional and social development of children, in addition to attending to subject matter and skills goals. The classroom conditions that establish the *setting* in which children learn the basics of human relations is sometimes referred to as the *hidden curriculum.*

The most significant characteristic of a desirable classroom climate is the absence of hostility between children and the teacher and among the children themselves. Put positively, a desirable classroom atmosphere is one in which caring, encouragement, and support are amply present and coupled with high expectations for success. This is a powerful combination. It is created not by teachers alone; principals, parents, and central office administrators all play a role. But the example set by the teacher—what that teacher says and does—is perhaps the deciding factor. To illustrate, consider the following eight sets of contrasting teacher behaviors:

DIMENSIONS OF THE HIDDEN CURRICULUM

PRACTICES AND PROCEDURES THAT TEND TO INCREASE HOSTILITY IN A CLASSROOM

1. *Excessively competitive situations*—Fair competition in classrooms is highly desirable. It can stimulate good work, motivate children to do their best, and help children learn the graces associated with winning and losing. It becomes undesirable when it is of the "dog-eat-dog" variety where each child is pitted against every other child whether the competitive situation is fair or unfair.

2. *Negative statements by the teacher*—Ridicule, sarcasm, criticism, and negative and tension-producing statements made by a teacher to children invariably lead to hostility, emotional disturbance, selfishness, fear, and criticism of others. Examples:

"I wish you would start acting like fourth-graders instead of kindergartners."

"Someone is whispering again, and I guess you all know who it is."

PRACTICES AND PROCEDURES THAT TEND TO DECREASE HOSTILITY IN A CLASSROOM

1. *Positive Interdependence*—The teacher often structures learning activities so that "students perceive that they can reach their learning goals if and only if the other students in the learning group also reach their goals."[2] This is the most basic element of cooperative learning, and it helps children learn to care about and support one another's progress.

2. *Positive statements by the teacher*—Friendly, constructive statements by the teacher tend to reduce tension and hostility in the classroom. Examples:

"We will all want to listen carefully in order not to miss anything Sue is going to tell us."

"All of us did our work so well yesterday during our work period. Do you suppose we can do as well today?"

---

[2]David W. Johnson, Roger T. Johnson, Edythe J. Holubec, and Patricia Roy, *Circles of Learning: Cooperation in the Classroom,* (Alexandria, VA: Association for Supervision and Curriculum Development, 1984), 2.

"Most fifth-grade classes could understand this, but I am not sure about you."

"Sit up straight. Don't you have a backbone?"

"Why don't you listen when I give directions? None of you seems to know how to listen."

3. *Disregard for individual differences*—Classrooms where some children are made to feel "this place is not for me" contribute much toward breeding hostility in children. Such rooms are characterized by one level of acceptable performance applied to all, uniform assignments, one system of reward, great emphasis on verbal, intellectual performance.

4. *Rigid schedule and pressure*—A rigid time schedule and constant pressure associated with "hurry up," "finish your work," "you will be late," or stopping lessons exactly on time whether completed or not create insecurity in children that leads to hostility. A class that is always "one jump behind the teacher" is likely to be one in which children blame others for their failure to finish, invent excuses for themselves, and seek scapegoats.

5. *Highly directive teaching practices*—Teachers who must make every decision themselves, give all the assignments, and allow for very little participation on the part of children in the life of the classroom are encouraging feelings of hostility. Such practices usually mean that teachers refer to the class as "my children," or in addressing them, say, "I want you to . . . ," or more subtly, "Miss So-and-so wasn't very proud of her class this morning."

"It is really fun for all of us when you bring such interesting things for sharing."

"It's nice to have Jason and Kendra back with us again. The boys and girls were hoping you would come back today."

3. *Recognition of and response to individual differences*—In such classrooms, all children are challenged at a level commensurate with their abilities. The teacher strives to see *all* children's gifts and talents.

4. *Relaxed, comfortable pace*—Good teachers working with young children maintain a flexible schedule and will not place undue pressures on children. They will have a plan and a schedule, yet will not be compulsive in adhering to it. They will deviate from their plan and schedule now and then in the interest of the needs of the boys and girls they teach. Good teachers recognize that feelings of insecurity are related to hostility and will do everything they can to develop feelings of security in the classroom.

5. *Student involvement in planning and managing the class*—Giving children some opportunity to plan and manage the affairs of the classroom does much to develop feelings of "we-ness," of identification with the group. Children under such circumstances are less inclined to want to think of ways to disrupt Miss So-and-so's orderly room but will work hard to make "our" room a good place to work.

6. *Lack of closeness between teacher and children*—Some teachers feel they must "keep children in their place," meaning they must remain socially distant from them. This leads to a cold objective relationship between the children and teacher, causing the children to feel that the teacher lacks affection and warmth for them. This "holier-than-thou" attitude on the part of the teacher is likely to engender feelings of hostility in some children.

7. *Lack of satisfying emotional experiences*—Some classrooms do not provide opportunities to express positive effect. Everything is deadly serious business—work, work, work. Even the music, art, story time, or dramatic activities are made to seem like work. Little time is spent on teaching children to enjoy one another, feel the inner joy that comes from a good poem or music selection, or express their feelings in some art medium.

8. *Rules are about obeying*—Some teachers have elaborate systems for dealing with violations of classroom rules, but fail to capitalize on them to teach children about caring. Obedience becomes the sole aim, rather than understanding the purpose of the rule.

6. *Warm and friendly relationship between teacher and children*—One of the basic needs of children is that of love and affection. They need it in their homes, in their playgroups, and in their schools. The feeling that children will not respect the teacher who is friendly with them is incorrect. They are likely to respect the teacher more who they feel is a "human being" capable of cordial and warm personal relationships with others. This is a professional relationship, however, and teachers are advised *against* trying to develop a peer relationship with the children they teach.

7. *Many opportunities for pleasurable emotional experiences*—Teachers can reduce tensions that build up in children during the course of classroom life by providing opportunities for the release of these tensions through various emotional experiences. Children have the opportunity to express their feelings orally, in writing, or through art forms. They talk together and enjoy one another's company. They prepare skits, do creative dramatics, and role play situations to help get the feelings of others. All these activities tend to reduce feelings of hostility.

8. *Rules are about caring*—Teachers can use rule violations to help children appreciate that we have rules because we care for one another. We do not call other children names because it hurts their feelings; we don't write on desks and tables out of respect for others who use them; we tell the truth because others deserve sincerity, not lies; we try to be punctual out of care for those who are waiting.

GETTING STARTED WITH COOPERATIVE GROUPS

Committee work or small-group enterprises are effective instructional procedures in the social studies and have many values for children. It is in the
small group that the children get experience with and develop skill in
group processes. These experiences should begin in a limited way even as
early as the kindergarten. In block play, for example, the teacher can let
some children choose the things they wish to build with blocks. Some will
want to build an airport; some, a house; others, a post office; others, a
supermarket; and so on. The teacher can let each of these children choose
two other children to help build the project. The children proceed with the
building and, when it is completed, tell the class or their teacher a story
about their building. Early experiences in such block play will consist
mainly of parallel play—three children may be building an airport but each
is working independently of the other two. As the year progresses, there
will be more evidence of cooperative endeavor. Children become more
conscious of what others in their group are doing and will plan their own
contribution in terms of the other children and the group goal.

A good way to familiarize primary-grade children with small-group
work is to have committees responsible for various housekeeping duties in

Here we see a very practical classroom arrangement for cooperative learning. The
movable furniture makes it possible to convene small groups for a task and then
change the seating pattern again for the next activity. The space between groups
allows the teacher to move easily among them. The teacher's desk is placed so she
may monitor the whole class while assisting an individual student.
(Photo by Robb Mitchell, Lake Washington School District.)

the classroom. José's committee has the responsibility of keeping the library table neat, Paul's committee is in charge of the game shelf, Long's committee is responsible for the care of the aquarium, and Kathy's committee keeps the coat corner orderly. Membership on these committees can be changed from time to time to include all the children in the class. Such experiences will help prepare children for the committee work that is done as a part of the instructional program. Small-group enterprises in the primary grades need careful supervision and direction. The goals or purposes of the group should be well defined, concrete, and easily understood. Materials needed for the group to do its work must be immediately at hand. Rules and responsibilities of working on committees should be discussed, explained, and posted conspicuously in the room. Group-work skills develop slowly and gradually and require practice as do any other skills. The skills of group work can be learned only by working in groups.

In the middle and upper grades, small-group work becomes an increasingly greater part of the social studies instructional program. At these grade levels, each group member can be given an assigned task to help the group achieve its goal. Small groups are used to prepare reports; discuss issues; plan activities; do construction, art, or dramatic activities; write plays, biographies, and short stories; gather resources for the class; interview community resource persons; and so on. Through instruction and experience, children will learn that the success of the group depends on the initiative and cooperation of individuals within the group.

There will be many occasions when the class will be divided into small work groups. These subgroups should be organized in accordance with the ages of the children and the nature of the tasks to be performed. Such subgroups are task oriented; they are formed to do things that really need doing. In this way, group work can avoid artificiality. Groups are not formed merely to have children practice cooperative group work; they are formed to get some sort of work done. Group work therefore can be relatively short lived. A committee may be assigned the task of finding out how tipis are built or to create a map of a nearby river system. When the committee has completed its task and reported to the larger group, it can be dissolved.

When attempting for the first time to organize small-group work, the teacher may find the guidelines on page 398 helpful. Note that it is not necessary to place all students in small groups at the same time, at least not when the teacher is just learning to manage small-group instruction. Instead, we recommend a gradual, diagnostic approach. This permits the teacher and students to "get their feet wet" little by little, all the while observing group dynamics and strengths and weaknesses in the children's cooperative behaviors.

How might these guidelines look in action? In the following example, a teacher appoints a committee to help introduce and question a classroom guest.

·················· FORMING ACADEMIC COMMITTEES

1. Defer small-group work until the management of the class has been well established and until the work habits, interpersonal skills, and special needs of individual children are known.
2. Select children who already have good interpersonal skills for your first academic committee. Keep the group small—never more than five children.
3. Assign the committee an academic task that is simple and well defined, one that the group is certain to accomplish successfully.
4. Have the remainder of the class engage in individual assignments while giving guidance and direction to the smaller group. Either designate a leader for the small group or have the children choose a leader. Explain the nature of their assigned task, and begin to discuss some of their special responsibilities when working in a small group.
5. Have resource materials available for the children. Later on, as they become accustomed to working in groups, they will be able to secure needed materials themselves.
6. Meet with the small group every day for a few minutes before they begin work and again at the end of their work period to make sure things are moving along as planned. If possible, have them make a progress report to the other, larger group during the summary and evaluation that should come at the close of each social studies period.
7. Give students specific help and suggestions in how to organize their work and how to report what they are doing.
8. Have their report to the class be short, concise, and interesting. Have members of the group explain to the class how they did their work as a group. Begin calling attention to some of the responsibilities of persons working collaboratively in small groups.
9. Follow the same procedure with another group of children as soon as possible. Gradually include other children, selecting some who have had previous experience in group work and some who have not. Observe carefully the children who need close supervision and those who are responsible and work well in groups.
10. After all the children have had an opportunity to work in a small group under close supervision, more than one group can work at one time. Eventually, the entire class should be able to work in small groups simultaneously. When this is attempted, it should be preceded by a review of the standards of group work, objectives should be clearly defined beforehand, and a careful evaluation should follow.

The children in Mr. Shigaki's class have been involved in a career awareness study and are going to have resource persons visit their classroom. The children have indicated careers they would like to have included. Mr. Shigaki has asked four children to meet him in the rear of the classroom and is now speaking to them.

"Because the four of you are particularly interested in learning about computer science careers, I am asking that you take responsibility for introducing Ms. Timms tomorrow. You will have to select one person to do the introducing. The others can help by suggesting things that should be said about her in the introduction. Also, all of you should help develop some questions to ask her after her presentation. Remember one of our objectives is to find out what kind of training and skills computer scientists need and what opportunities there are in that field. Is there anything else you think you will need to prepare to be the host group tomorrow?"

One member of the group asks if they were to thank the visitor for coming.

"Yes. Good point! I'm glad you thought of that, Mark. You will need to select someone to thank Ms. Timms. Anything else?" (No further suggestions are offered.)

"I guess you are ready to begin your work then," says Mr. Shigaki. "Lisa, would you act as the group leader and report to me when your group is finished planning?"

Mr. Shigaki then leaves the group to its task and supervises the remainder of the class who have been working on individual assignments.

MANAGING COOPERATIVE GROUP WORK

Let us turn from forming the occasional committee that accomplishes one or more tasks to simultaneous involvement of all children in small group instruction. First, we consider goals, then group size, group composition, and alternative small group structures.

Goals

It would be reasonable to assume that if children are given instruction and have many guided experiences in cooperative groups, that they are likely to develop group interaction skills. But do cooperative learning strategies also affect a child's overall academic achievement? The answer is a confident "Yes": "Results indicate that cooperative learning experiences tend to promote higher achievement than do competitive and individualistic learning experiences."[3] These results apply to all age levels and subject areas, and for all sorts of academic tasks, from simple retention to concept learning and problem solving. Kristin Gruber, a third-grade teacher in Minnesota, tells this success story:

> Andy, a low-achieving student who received LD services, was failing social studies, health, and language early in the year. He needed constant supervision just to stay on task, paid little attention to classroom discussions, and seldom completed assignments. With a cooperative group to support and encourage him, however, Andy completed many assignments during class and brought back homework consistently. . . . By mid-February, he was passing every subject; and he was able to maintain his grades for the rest of the year.[4]

[3]Johnson et al., *Circles of Learning*, 15.
[4]Dianne K. Augustine, Kristin D. Gruber, and Lynda R. Hanson, "Cooperation Works!" *Educational Leadership* 47: 4 (December 1989/January 1990): 4–7.

Why is this so? Researchers provide interesting arguments that center on the main ingredients of cooperative learning: positive interdependence and individual student accountability. Positive interdependence means that group goals cannot be attained unless each member of the group does his or her part; individual accountability means that the group's success depends not only on group members doing their parts but *learning*. Indeed, they will be held accountable for learning: Grades go to individual students, not groups. Add to these another attribute of cooperative learning—discussion. Discussion is a rich stew of face-to-face talking, listening, responding, paraphrasing, and questioning, and positive interdependence makes it necessary. Putting thoughts into words requires students to think about the task at hand and to clarify what they mean; trying to understand what others mean involves still more talking, thinking, and clarifying. Further, discussion often produces disagreements—healthy social and academic conflicts—which, when managed skillfully by the teacher and students, promote deeper levels of both academic learning and interpersonal development. Skillful teachers do not squelch these disagreements, since they foster higher-order thinking and help to make learning exciting.[5] As well, disagreements flourish in democratic civic life; students must therefore learn to deal with them.

Closely related to discussion and controversy is still another reason why cooperative learning improves academic achievement—it promotes what researchers call *engaged time* or *time on task*. Cooperative group work generally helps children to be more engaged in the task (more attentive and involved) than does seatwork. The main drawback of seatwork is that children are working on their own with little or no guidance, and this allows them to drift far from the assigned task or to attempt it without understanding its purpose and without using helpful strategies. This is especially unfortunate when we consider that seatwork often consumes over half the available instructional time in both primary and intermediate grades, and, ironically, is prescribed most often to children who already are doing poorly in school! Elizabeth Cohen sums up this problem:

> Choosing a method of classroom organization that leaves students who rarely succeed in schoolwork quite alone may indeed be the root cause of their disengagement in seatwork settings. Those students are receiving very little information on the purpose of their assignment, on how to complete it successfully, on how well they are doing, or on how they could be more successful. The tasks themselves are rarely sufficiently interesting to hold the students' attention.[6]

Cooperative learning promotes active student involvement in learning and therefore helps teachers to spend wisely the most valuable aid they have—time.

---

[5]David W. Johnson and Roger T. Johnson, "Conflict in the Classroom: Controversy and Learning," *Review of Educational Research* 49 (Spring 1979): 51–70.

[6]Elizabeth G. Cohen, *Designing Groupwork* (New York: Teachers College Press, 1986), 17.

Group Size and Composition

The size of a small group affects its achievement both of academic knowledge and cooperative skills. If groups are too large, there may be duplication of responsibilities, less opportunity for individuals to carry their share of the group effort, difficulty achieving face-to-face interaction, and a tendency for some members to fade out of the group activity. Also, the larger the group, the more skillful group members must be with cooperative behaviors. On the other hand, if groups are too small, there may be insufficient division of labor to warrant group work and too few opportunities to cooperate. In general, however, groups should be kept small—from two to five children, with four to five as the optimal size. When teaching group-work skills, teachers often begin by placing children in pairs to practice particular skills, such as using names, making eye contact with the speaker, and asking for help. Pairs can then be combined into groups of four.

Group size influences the sort of academic work that can be accomplished. Structured Academic Controversy, discussed later in this chapter, requires two pairs of children in groups of four; meanwhile, STAD (also discussed later) has no required group size. The number of students in a Jigsaw group determines the number of topics that can be studied or, when writing original biographies, the number of chapters in the book students produce (see chapter 11).

Our discussion of goals emphasized learning cooperative behaviors and academic achievement. Let us consider a third goal, which bears particularly on group composition: positive intergroup relations among students of different ethnic and racial backgrounds in integrated classrooms. Anyone who has visited a desegregated school knows that friendships across ethnic groups did not automatically follow putting diverse children together in the same school or classroom. To the contrary, especially in the upper grades, children of the same ethnic group, whatever it is, often stay together, playing together at recess and eating together at lunch.

A good deal of research shows that when diverse groups of youngsters work together to attain a group goal, positive feelings obtain: they begin to like and trust one another, more often choose to be with one another during free time, and in general grow in their respect for one another.[7] Of course, a teacher cannot expect these results as a consequence only of placing diverse students together in a small group and structuring a cooperative task for them; rather, students must be prepared for group work. They must learn the skills and norms of cooperation. But placing them in diverse groups is a precondition—it at least provides the *opportunity* to tackle the goal of positive intergroup understanding.

Thus, the cardinal principle of group composition is to achieve the greatest mix possible given the student population. A teacher should achieve

good point

[7]Robert E. Slavin, "Effects of Biracial Learning Teams on Cross-racial Friendships," *Journal of Educational Psychology* 71 (1979): 381–87.

this mix using whatever student variables are available—academic record, interpersonal skill, gender, ethnicity, disability, language, race, and social class. In this way, small groups are as heterogeneous as the whole class. Ability grouping is ruled out because it minimizes rather than maximizes the mix.

The teacher may use one or more of several methods to form heterogeneous student groups:

1. *Work, not play.* Do not allow friends to choose one another for small group work. Friends tend to play rather than work when placed in the same group, and group work should be thought of in terms of work rather than play.[8]

2. *Random assignment.* With a brand-new class, a teacher might randomly assign students to small groups of four to five students each. Forming groups alphabetically is a good way, and it should result in mixed groups. Look over the resulting lists of group members and make any adjustments needed to achieve a greater mix of gender and ethnicity.

3. *Purposeful mixing.* Once a teacher is more familiar with students' work habits, interpersonal skills, and past academic achievement, groups can be purposefully mixed. Some teachers have good success simply by mixing within each group students who are strong and weak on each of these characteristics. Students with poor interpersonal skills and/or poor academic records should not be placed together any more than friends or highly successful students.

4. *Special helper.* A variation on purposeful mixing is to select one or more students for each group who will serve as a special helper. The help needed will depend on the kind of work the teacher has structured for the groups. For example, if groups are to construct a papier-mâché map of the United States, each working on a different region, the teacher might identify students who are good with paper products (mixing, gluing, painting) or at creating map legends. One of these helpers is placed in each small group. If the teacher has decided that groups of four children each are to write historical fiction about Harriet Tubman or James Madison, with each student working on a different "chapter," it will help to have someone who likes to sketch in each group. It will also help to have a strong planner in each group—someone who can help the group decide on four different chapter topics.

In general, social and academic resources that can come in handy are reading, writing, planning, decision making (comparing alternatives), notetaking, brainstorming, operating tape recorders or cameras, observing detail, using the library, creating time lines, using reference books, creative dramatics, assisting students with disabilities, interviewing, building with cardboard, drawing, taking surveys, and so on.

---

[8]Cohen, *Designing Groupwork*, 61.

5. *Index cards.* Write the name of each student on an index card, strip of construction paper, or popcicle stick. Decide on the task to which group work will be devoted and identify the special help that will be needed. Identify the special helpers, putting at least one in each group, and sort the other students into each group aiming for the greatest mix possible with regard to interpersonal skills, ethnicity, language, academic achievement, gender, and so on. (The teacher can use a random method, such as shuffling the deck of name cards, once special helpers have been selected.)[9]

6. *Duration.* A cooperative group exists until the cooperative task is completed. Rather than reforming groups for the next group task, the same group usually remains together for the purpose of further developing its cooperative skills. Groups should stay together long enough to make progress on the interpersonal problems that inevitably arise. While the group remains the same, the task, of course, changes (e.g., from making maps to writing a biography of Thomas Jefferson). A new task is an opportunity for the teacher to select a different set of special helpers. The teacher should keep searching for everyone's special talents so that different helpers can be used on each new task.

Alternative Frameworks For Cooperative Tasks

There are many different ways to structure group work, all with positive interdependence, individual accountability, face-to-face interaction, and discussion. Teachers often invent their own ways and share them with one another. Teachers just beginning to experiment with cooperative learning may prefer STAD (student teams achievement division). When teacher and students are ready, they may want to experiment with Jigsaw or Structured Controversy. We here discuss each in turn.

STAD.   STAD (student teams achievement division) has the students listening to the teacher in standard lecture format—except that a cooperative task is tagged onto the end, thus adding the advantages of cooperative learning to the disadvantages of the teacher talking *at* students.[10] Students are placed in groups before the lesson begins. First, the teacher explains the purpose and rationale of the lesson, then presents needed information. (In a lesson on map legends, for example, the teacher takes thirty minutes or so to display three different maps, explaining the design and function of the legend on each.) Second, the teacher gives the groups one handout with questions and another handout with responses. Each group receives only one copy of each so that group members must share materials. Each group is given twenty minutes to accomplish their task: to understand *why*

---

[9]Cohen, *Designing Groupwork*, 63.

[10]Robert E. Slavin, *Using Student Team Learning* (Baltimore, MD: Johns Hopkins University, 1986).

the answers are correct. Third, students are given a short quiz over the questions and answers, and the group with the highest average score (or that shows the greatest improvement over the last quiz average) is rewarded with special certificates and honorable mention in the class newsletter. This constitutes one round of STAD.

Jigsaw. We encountered Jigsaw in chapter 2 as a method for incorporating cooperative learning into concept formation and again in chapter 11 when children were learning about important people in history by creating original biographies. In both cases, for this is the essence of the Jigsaw method, students are members of two groups—the usual group of four or five students, which in Jigsaw serves as the students' home base, plus an additional "expert group."[11] Typically, the teacher divides the task into four or five parts. In concept formation, each part is an example of the concept children are to form; in biography writing, each part is a chapter in the "book" the group will produce. Or the task might simply be to comprehend a chapter on Native Americans in the textbook, and the parts are the chapter's four lessons. Whatever the task, each member of the home team is assigned to work on one of the four parts, but he or she is not alone. All students assigned to the same part join together to work in expert groups. This may require anywhere from 30 minutes to a week or more, depending on the task. Eventually, experts return to their home teams, where they serve as discussion leaders for their teammates. Following this, student understanding of the *whole* task is assessed, and the teacher rewards the home team that has the highest average score, or that has improved the most, or the one that demonstrated the best use of cooperative skills. This is one round of Jigsaw.

Structured Controversy. We would not want to let the opportunities afforded by cooperative learning to restructure the *ways* we teach social studies cause us to ignore the chance it provides to reconsider *what* we teach in social studies.[12] Structured academic controversy, developed by the Johnson brothers, provides just this chance.[13] It asks teachers to perceive the academic controversy in whatever social studies knowledge they are wanting students to learn and to engage students in that controversy. Rather than teaching about the protection of endangered species, for example, as though the topic were devoid of debate, teachers can help their children to participate in that debate. Other examples are the American Revolution, deciding whether a Bill of Rights was necessary, developing cafeteria rules, deciding who is responsible for making new students feel

---

[11]Elliot Aronson, *The Jigsaw Classroom* (Beverly Hills, CA: Sage, 1978).

[12]Mara Sapon-Shevin and Nancy Schniedewind, "Selling Cooperative Learning Without Selling It Short," *Educational Leadership* 47: 4 (December 1989/January 1990): 63–65.

[13]David W. Johnson and Roger T. Johnson, "Critical Thinking through Structured Controversy," *Educational Leadership* 45: 8 (May 1988): 58–64.

welcome, and current events issues involving public health (such as pl   -
ing nutritional information on food labels) and advertising on children's
television. The study of each of these topics can be designed so that the
disagreements at their center are made the object of study. Doing so boosts
both the intellectual rigor and the excitement of social studies lessons.
Structured Controversy makes such study manageable, even for the beginning teacher and for very young students, and it relies on group work.

First, the teacher helps students gather background information on the
topic, for example the American Revolution. The textbook itself usually
provides at least some of this background. Supplementary resources, such
as primary documents and children's literature, can also be assembled. In
the second phase, each four-person group is divided into two pairs, and
each pair studies one side of the debate. On the American Revolution, one
pair would study the arguments that eventually lead to the colonies de-
claring their independence, the other would learn loyalist arguments.
Third, pairs present their perspectives to one another. Fourth, as a test of
their listening and questionning, the pairs reverse perspectives, giving
now the argument of the other side. In the fifth phase, genuine discussion
begins as the two pairs join together for the purpose of reaching a group
consensus.

IDENTIFYING AND TEACHING COOPERATIVE SKILLS

Teachers who have experimented with small-group instruction and found
it frustrating commonly feel that group work breaks down either because
some children within the groups do most of the work or because the
children waste time and accomplish little or nothing. This is an indication
that the children have not yet developed the prerequisite skills for successful cooperative endeavors. If children are only given the *opportunity* to
work in groups without being prepared to do so, there is little reason to
expect them to function effectively in these groups. Simply dividing the
class into groups, whatever the framework, is not likely to help children
develop the skills needed for cooperative learning.

Children need to be taught how to behave during cooperative group-
work so that they can function reasonably well without the teacher's direct
supervision. Of course, this is not only a matter of teaching the needed
interpersonal skills; group members also need the appropriate academic
skills for completing the assigned task. It would be unwise, for example, to
send a group of fifth graders, even an extremely cooperative group, to the
library to find information on population growth and food distribution if
none of the children knew how to use the library for that purpose. Similarly, if group members are expected to write a report together, they will
require instruction on report writing and have some general writing experience. This instruction does not need to occur in advance; providing it
during the action, when it is needed, can be more effective. In summary,

the nature of the task assigned to a small group should be consistent with the preparation they have received.

In this section, we offer suggestions for which skills need to be taught, and suggest strategies for teaching them. Two kinds of skills are highlighted—skills for getting started as a cooperative group and skills for functioning in a cooperative group.

Getting Started

Tell children both the purpose and rationale for having them learn to work cooperatively in small groups. Teachers have found it helpful to provide examples of real-world situations, both civic and work related, where people need to function well in groups with others who not only are not their friends but may even be strangers, (town meetings, fire departments, fast-food restaurants, hospital emergency rooms, and so on). And whether strangers or not, disagreements are common.

Children typically need to be taught behaviors that help them to do the following:

• move into groups efficiently
• stay with the group during group time
• use quiet voices
• make everyone feel welcome
• state and restate the assignment
• set or call attention to time frame

Functioning

When groups are practicing the skills of getting started, it is especially important that the task be kept short and simple. Once some progress is made in these skills areas, the teacher should instruct the class on some of the behaviors crucial to a group working well together when the task is more complex. These should be posted in the room and referred to often. Examples include:

• plan how best to proceed
• encourage everyone to participate
• use one another's names
• face the speaker and make eye contact
• avoid putdowns
• ask for help when you need it
• ask questions
• be a good sport
• offer to explain, clarify, or summarize
• listen carefully when others are speaking
• paraphrase another's statements
• talk openly about disagreements
• criticize ideas, not people

FIGURE 13-1

A Sample T-chart Used to Help Children Understand a Cooperative Skill.

SKILL: Encouraging Participation	
Looks Like	*Sounds Like*
smiles	"What is your idea?"
eye contact	"Radical!"
thumbs up	"That's a good idea!"
pat on the back	"I'd like to hear what you think."

- cheerfully take the jobs the group wants you to do
- suggest new ideas when the group's motivation is low[14]

Teaching Cooperative Skills

Practicing any cooperative skill requires that learners understand the skill. Otherwise, they are not really practicing anything. A proper understanding of a skill can be developed with the help of the concept learning strategies outlined in chapter 2. Using concept formation, for example, the teacher asks students to observe several examples of the skill, and has them note and summarize the similarities. For example, the teacher might ask a small group that has previously worked together as a committee to model for the class—three or more times—how they move into their group quietly and efficiently. This creates in children's minds a vivid picture of the skill, which they can then attempt to reproduce as they participate in group work.

A variation of List, Group, and Label, the T-chart (Figure 13-1), is also a popular method for helping children understand a cooperative skill.[15] The teacher writes the name of a skill on the chalkboard and creates two columns beneath it, one for a group of adjectives describing what the skill *looks* like, another for phrases that exemplify what the skill *sounds* like. Children are then asked to generate a list for each.

Once a skill is understood well enough to make practice worthwhile, practice should begin in earnest. Some teachers find role playing to be a valuable technique in teaching the skills needed in small-group work. By selecting four to five children to serve as group members, the teacher can demonstrate to the class what it means to "help everyone become a part of the group" or any of the standards that have been discussed. When the role playing is completed, the remainder of the class can analyze the

---

[14]See Johnson et al., *Circles of Learning,* for an elaborate list of skills.

[15]David W. Johnson and Roger T. Johnson, "Social Skills for Successful Group Work," *Educational Leadership* 47: 4 (December 1989/January 1990): 29–33.

situation to determine why the group was functioning well or poorly. It is helpful to have children observe certain specific elements in the situation to be presented. For example, they might try to answer such questions as these:

1. What did individual members do to help the group do its job? What did members do that did not help the group?
2. What did the leader do to help the group get its job done?
3. How did the group find out exactly what it was to do?
4. Did the group use good resources in solving its problems?
5. Did the group seem to be working together as a team? Why or why not?
6. How could the group be helped to do its job better?

Following the role playing, the class can discuss the situation in terms of the specific points being observed. It may then be helpful to replay all or a portion of the situation to help children appreciate the forces at work in group situations. With young children it may be desirable to have an older group demonstrate such things as a domineering leader, an uncooperative group member, a member who wants only the choice tasks, the noncontributor, the irresponsible leader, the member who must always have his or her own way, the member who talks too much, and so on. In teaching group-work skills, the teacher will want to do more than talk about what should or should not be done. Children really need an opportunity to see and experience "how it works" as well as an opportunity to experiment and try their hand at doing productive group work. Role playing can do much to sensitize them to the various subtleties and forces that come into play in small-group situations.

Increasing numbers of schools have videocassette recorders available for classroom use, and this equipment can be useful in teaching collaborative skills. The teacher can videotape a group role playing certain skills needed for productive small-group work. The tape can then be used for study and analysis of the behavior required if small groups are to be effective in their work. The videotape provides a way to demonstrate over and over again the essential characteristics of group work. This teaching procedure is widely used in teaching athletes, and greater use could be made of it in regular classrooms today.

Reward Group Work Appropriately

Part of the reason that group work is at times ineffective is because it is not rewarded as generously as are the academic aspects of the classroom work. This stems from the teacher's attitude toward the value of group activities. If the rewards (recognition, praise, value statements, reports to parents, grades) go only to those who do well in paper-and-pencil activities, children rightly conclude that group activities do not count much in the entire scheme of things. Group work will be enhanced if the teacher regards it as an important part of the instructional program and rewards appropriately the children who have done commendable work in group endeavors.

Debriefing.   While rewarding good skill use is necessary, it is just as important to talk in detail with students about the progress they are making. All groupwork should involve the deliberate practice of one or more cooperative skills; therefore, all groupwork sessions should be followed by a debriefing, in which students are asked to reflect on how often cooperative skills were used, how well they were used, and what skills especially need attention.

TEACHING AND USING DISCUSSION TECHNIQUES

We have seen that discussion is a key ingredient in cooperative learning. Its value lies chiefly in the fact that it represents a type of intellectual teamwork, resting on the principle that the pooled knowledge, ideas, and feelings of several persons have greater merit than those of a single individual. Without discussion a student may never grasp the fact, for example, that there are multiple points of view and opinions on a problem, not just his or her own. Furthermore, this student may never have the opportunity to practice the most fundamental work of popular sovereignty—talking with others about common problems and reaching a decision about what to do. In this section, we look more closely at discussion, concentrating on large-group, roundtable, and panel discussions.

Because the strength of discussion is obtained from the information and viewpoint of many members of the group, it is necessary that most members of the class participate. It is a thinking-together process that breaks down if one member or group dominates it. It is the responsibility of the teacher to encourage the more reluctant children to participate. Although there cannot be a single answer to the question of what to do with the child who dominates the discussion, skillful teachers usually take care of the matter with a statement such as "Jackie, you have given us so many good ideas today, and I know you have many more good suggestions, but we want to find out what some of the others think would be a good way to . . ."

Another strategy for dealing with students who dominate discussions is to use student observers. One or two children are asked to observe the day's discussion. Their task is straightforward—to keep track of who talks and how much. Because student observers learn a good deal about discussion, the domineering student can purposefully be placed in this role. One first-grade teacher placed such a student in the role of student observer, instructing him to gather data without talking.

> He gathered data on who talked and did a good job, noting that one student had done quite a bit of talking in the group while another had talked very

little. The next day when he was back in the group and no longer the observer, he started to talk, clamped his hand over his mouth, and glanced at
the new observer. He knew what behavior was being observed, and he didn't
want to be the only one with marks for talking. The teacher said he may have
listened for the first time all year.[16]

In good class discussions, children should talk freely and voluntarily. There
should be no set pattern of soliciting contributions, nor should letter grades be
given on individual discussion contributions. It will take a while to develop
effective discussions because the needed skills develop gradually.

The physical arrangement of the classroom may either contribute to or
inhibit discussion. For example, it is difficult to interact with someone when
one is not facing the person with whom one is speaking. When classroom
seating is arranged so that all children face the teacher, the pattern of interaction will be *through* the teacher, that is, "child A–teacher–child B–teacher–
child C–teacher." A preferred discussion pattern is to have children interacting
directly with each other; this can be encouraged by having them face one
another. This also can be achieved by arranging the seating in a semicircle for
at least some of the discussion sessions. Through careful and patient teaching,
a teacher can bring the class to a point where they interact courteously with
one another—without always agreeing with each other—and do so without
raising their hands to speak. Such maturity in discussion procedure, however,
requires a considerable amount of good teaching, practice, and time.

If discussions are to have some purpose beyond ordinary conversation,
the participants must have certain skills and attitudes, both of which can be
learned. These skills should be taught through deliberate organized instruction. Skills and attitudes may be stated as standards or guides that
characterize harmonious, productive discussion. For example, one participating in a discussion should

1. Listen attentively when others are speaking.
2. Remain objective and not become emotional.
3. Be open minded, respect and accept the contributions of others, but
   think independently.
4. Assume responsibility for contributing ideas.
5. Prepare adequately for the discussion and be able to support ideas with
   factual evidence.
6. Speak loudly and clearly enough for all to hear.
7. Not be offended when one's ideas or suggestions are not accepted by
   the group.
8. Not dominate the discussion; contributions should be stated concisely
   and briefly.
9. Ask for clarification of ideas that are not understood; ask for evidence
   to substantiate statements.

[16]Johnson et al., *Circles of Learning*, 35.

10. Recognize the problem of semantics in arriving at group decisions or in discussing a controversial issue.
11. Assume responsibility for moving the group toward its goal; help keep the group from becoming sidetracked from the central issue.
12. Have confidence in the ability of the group to come to a satisfactory decision and support the decision of the group once it has been made.

Standards such as the ones listed here are not appropriately stated for use with children, but the ideas can be discussed and understood by them when stated more simply. When communicating standards to children, the T-chart format (see Figure 13-1) can be helpful.

Suggestions for Improving Classroom Discussions

Teach Students to Identify Kinds of Disagreements. Discussion fosters healthy disagreements, which in turn foster more discussion, more higher-order thinking, and more effort to apply what one knows. Consequently, disagreements should not be discouraged; rather, students should be prepared to take advantage of them—to learn more about the topic and one another, and to practice reaching a consensus. An extremely helpful way to teach intermediate-grade students to learn from disagreements is to teach them occasionally to stop for a moment in the middle of a disagreement and to identify the kind of disagreement they are having. Doing so creates some cool distance from the disagreement, provides an opportunity to analyze the issue at hand, and suggests what is to be done. The three most common kinds of disagreements, together with suggested methods for dealing with them, are as follows:

Factual disagreements. Method: gather more data.

Definitional disagreements. Method: get a dictionary; tentatively agree on a definition.

Ethical disagreements. Method: clarify the values at stake; agree to disagree; give reasons for the superiority of one value over another.

Use Questions That Require an Elaborative Response. Discussion questions must be open ended, suggestive of more than one point of view. They should require the respondent to provide an explanation. If questions can be answered by responding "yes" or "no" or with a single word or phrase, there is little to discuss. Questions that call for the reproduction of facts are not good for discussion, either, as for example:

1. By what three routes did people travel to the goldfields of California?
2. What are the Pacific states? Which is the largest? Which is the smallest?
3. Who was John Sutter?
4. Who were the forty-niners?
5. Who was the founder of the California missions?

As these questions are stated, there is nothing to discuss. However, the subject matter of these questions might be used for discussion if the questions were framed differently, as for example:

1. If you had been a gold seeker in 1849, what route would you have taken to the goldfields of California, and why would you have gone that way?

2. Washington, Oregon, and California face the Pacific Ocean. On the east coast of the United States, *fourteen* states occupy the same north–south distance as these three western states. What problems do you suppose are brought about by the size of a state?

3. How might the history of California and the United States have been different if John Sutter had found gold near Los Angeles instead of where he did?

4. How has life in the San Francisco Bay area changed since the days of the forty-niners?

5. What is there about California today that relates directly to the system of missions started by Father Junipero Serra and the Franciscan Fathers?

The two types of questions presented serve different purposes. For a quick check of literal reading comprehension, the first set might be appropriate, but they would not make good discussion questions.

Point Out Inconsistencies and Confusions in the Children's Thinking.
Imagine a class discussing the merits of a law prohibiting smoking in public places such as meeting rooms, auditoriums, elevators, and restaurants. The discussion might proceed as follows:

> CHILD: I think there ought to be such a law because a person has a right not to have to breathe someone else's smoke.
> TEACHER: Is that a right?
> CHILD: Well, if some people have the right to smoke, others should have the right not to smoke.
> TEACHER: Isn't that the way it is now?
> CHILD: Yes . . . but not really . . . when they have to be in the same room or in an elevator, the people who do not smoke do not have any choice, but the people who do smoke do have a choice.
> TEACHER: Then you are talking about choices rather than rights?
> CHILD: Yes, I think so. With smoking in the room, the people who do not smoke and *have* to be there have no choice.

This is an instructive example because it illustrates how the teacher moves the discussion toward a clarification of the main point the child is making.

Keep the Discussion Focused on the Topic.   It is difficult for discussants of any age to stay with the topic, but this is especially so with young children. Almost anything said reminds them of a personal experience that they want to share but that is probably irrelevant to the topic being discussed. When the discussion strays away from the main theme, the teacher must refocus the group's thinking with a comment such as "But let's get back to our main question. . ." or "I wonder if we could look at this problem from another angle. . ."

Maintain a Low Profile in Leading Discussions.   If the object of discussion is to encourage participant talk, the teacher talk should be limited to whatever is needed to keep the discussion moving. Give children time to think about what they want to say. Allow extended periods of silence before calling for a response. Use nonverbal clues generously, such as a nod, an encouraging glance, or some other gesture along with verbal encouragement. Confine your own remarks to probing or clarifying comments or questions and to acknowledging contributions. Avoid having discussions become teacher lectures.

Discussion can be used to encourage children to speculate, to imagine, and to think of alternatives, as in the following example.

> Ms. Fowler's second graders have been making discoveries about changes in their community. To stimulate discussion, Ms. Fowler asked, "If you were a second grader in the year 2050 and lived where you do now, what might you see on your way to school? Don't raise your hand for the next minute; I just want you to think."
>
> After a minute, the children were bursting with ideas. Ms. Fowler was careful to accept all ideas and to try to hear a comment from every child. When a couple of the ideas were silly, she very adeptly brought the discussion back to the main focus by asking these children to clarify what they meant. Ms. Fowler was aware of the children who were too shy to volunteer and called on them, also. She encouraged all children to give evidence for their suggestions.

Many of the same principles and procedures used in group discussions involving the entire class also apply to other forms of discussion procedure. The advantage of smaller groups lies chiefly in allowing for greater participation by individual members. The teacher may find each of the following forms of discussion procedure helpful in social studies instruction.

Roundtable Discussions

A *roundtable discussion* usually involves a small number of persons, perhaps no fewer than three and no more than eight. It requires someone to serve as a moderator to introduce the members of the discussion group, present the problem to be discussed, and keep the discussion moving. The leader's role is one of guiding the group rather than one of dominating it. A permissive atmosphere needs to prevail, and the presentations are conversational rather than oratorical.

Roundtable discussions can be used in the middle and upper grades by having a group of children discuss a problem before the remainder of the class or by dividing the class into several small discussion groups that function without an audience. It is perhaps best to use this procedure with one group at a time, either with or without an audience, until the children have learned how to participate in discussions of this type. It will be necessary for the teacher to introduce the procedure to the class and to explain and demonstrate its purposes and the way it works. Such points as the following need to be emphasized:

1. *Responsibilities of the moderator*—To be informed on the topic to be discussed, introduce the topic, keep the discussion moving, avoid having the group become sidetracked, ask members to explain more fully what they mean, avoid having members argue and quibble over irrelevancies, and summarize and state conclusions.

2. *Responsibilities of members of the discussion group*—To be well informed on the topic to be discussed, especially some phase of it; speak informally while avoiding arguing and quibbling; stay with the topic under discussion; have sources of information available; back up statements with facts; and help the group summarize its conclusions.

3. *Responsibilities of the audience*—To listen attentively, withhold questions until presentation is completed, ask for clarification of ideas, ask for evidence on questionable statements, confine remarks to the topic under discussion, and extend customary audience courtesies to members of the roundtable.

Roundtable discussions may be used for any of the following purposes:

1. To discuss plans for a major class activity.
2. To evaluate the results of a class activity, the merits of a film, school assembly on citizenship, or the decision of a student council.
3. To make specific plans, such as the best way to present the work of the class to the parents.
4. To get facts related to a topic.
5. To discuss current affairs.
6. To present differing views on a community issue or a school problem.
7. To make decisions and recommendations to the class (the student council wants to know how the class feels about a new play schedule. A committee of five children discusses this matter and presents its findings and recommendations to the class).

Panel Discussions

A *panel discussion* is similar to a roundtable discussion in many respects, but there are some important differences. The responsibilities of the moderator are approximately the same as they are for the moderator of the roundtable, as are those of the participants. The procedure is more formal than that of the roundtable. It usually begins with a short statement or presentation by each discussant before the panel is opened for free discussion by members. Panels are usually more audience oriented than roundtables, and frequently some provision is made for audience questions or participation at the end of the panel's presentation. A greater responsibility is placed on participants to prepare themselves well for their particular part on the panel, for each panelist is considered to be more or less an "expert."

One teacher made use of a panel discussion format in the following way.

> The topic for the panel to discuss was a community problem involving the conversion of a military base into a community resource. Various special-interest groups were competing for the use of the newly acquired property. In class the teacher asked children to volunteer to represent one of the following special-interest groups:
>
> 1. city planner
> 2. golf enthusiast
> 3. representative of the local community club
> 4. condominium builder
> 5. representative of a local Indian tribe
> 6. moderator
>
> The children were provided planning time in which to prepare a three- to five-minute statement explaining their point of view regarding the future of this property. Time was allowed for questions to clarify points made in the presentations or to raise other issues.

Buzz Groups for Brainstorming

The following is an example of a "buzz" group in operation.

> The members of Ms. Kryzinski's class were asked to view a television special dealing with energy. The next morning they were anxious to discuss the program and even more anxious to do something about the energy problem.
>
> "What can we do, Ms. K, to help other kids in our school know about some ways to save energy?" a child asked.
>
> "Why don't you decide?" Ms. Kryzinski responded. "You are already arranged in small groups, so why don't you take the next ten minutes and come up with some ideas? Be prepared to give us two or three good ideas that would be possible for us to carry out in our school."
>
> After about ten to fifteen minutes, the children's attention was refocused, and each group presented some ideas. There was no attempt to evaluate suggestions at that time.
>
> All the suggestions were listed on the board and discussed. The class then voted on the list to determine which three they would implement.

We have here a brief description of a *buzz-group* or *brainstorming* technique. It is an informal consideration of ideas or problems where the chief purpose is to solicit the suggestions, feelings, ideas, or consensus of the members participating. In brainstorming for ideas and suggested solutions to problems, it is important *not* to evaluate each one at the time it is offered. If each is discussed, the list will not be very long. The objective of brainstorming is to get as many ideas to the surface as possible, no matter how outlandish they may seem. After the complete list has been generated, time can be taken to evaluate each one and select the best ones by consensus. It is usually best for the group to have a designated leader and recorder.

Talking things over in a buzz session can be helpful in clarifying ideas, getting a wide sampling of opinion and feeling, obtaining suggestions and ideas, and getting children to participate who might be reluctant or fearful in a more structured discussion situation. Likewise, it has some limitations. Buzz sessions can easily get out of hand and become noisy and boisterous where nothing is accomplished except the creation of confusion. There is need, therefore, for the teacher to have firm control of the class before such a procedure is attempted and to establish standards that are clearly understood beforehand.

MAKING USE OF REPORTS

Reports to the class by the children are commonly used in social studies to share information obtained through individual research and study. They serve the purpose of bringing to the group the knowledge and understanding obtained by individuals, as well as teaching children how to organize, plan, and present a report. This suggests a mutual value that accrues to the group as well as to the individual making the report. It also implies a responsibility that each must share if the procedure is to have value.

There is nothing quite so deadly or lacking in instructional value as the elementary schoolchild giving a "report" that has been copied from an encyclopedia. The speaker stumbles over every other word—meanings are not understood, and pronunciation is incorrect. The report lacks continuity and is hard to follow. The listeners become bored or disruptive. Under such a set of circumstances, no one likes to give reports or listen to them. They are a waste of time.

The primary responsibility for good reports rests squarely with the teacher. How to give reports and how to prepare them should be explained. Through discussion, the teacher and the class can establish standards that will be used in the preparation of reports and the evaluation of them after the reports are given. Examples of such standards are these:

RESPONSIBILITIES OF THE SPEAKER

1. Speak in a clear voice.
2. Be well prepared.
3. Speak in your own words.
4. Use charts and pictures to make the report more interesting.
5. Ask for questions at the end of the report.
6. Stick to the topic.

RESPONSIBILITIES OF THE AUDIENCE

1. Listen carefully.
2. Be courteous; do not interrupt the speaker.
3. Ask questions only at the end of the report.

Children can help each other improve the quality of their reports by holding brief evaluative discussions following the presentation. A good practice to follow is to ask for positive statements first—things that were especially well done in the report. Then, the children might offer suggestions concerning the way the report might have been improved. The teacher must set the stage for a positive attitude toward evaluation rather than only pointing out things that were wrong with the report. Care must be exercised so as not to make the evaluations destructively critical of a child's work.

It is the responsibility of the teacher to take an active part in assisting the child with the preparation of the report. This includes helping select a suitable topic, suggesting references, helping with its organization, and suggesting visual devices to use. The teacher should find a few minutes a day or two in advance of the presentation to sit down with the youngster and review what is to be included in the report. Once prepared, the child should be left alone while the report is being given unless help is specifically requested. It is unfair to the child and to the listening group to have the teacher continually interrupting and asking questions. The standards and responsibilities of good listeners apply to the teacher as well as to the children. Of course, when the report is completed the teacher can ask questions, call attention to points that need further clarification, or add pertinent information to the report. Positive comments and concrete suggestions as to how the child might improve future reports should also be offered.

Only a few reports should be scheduled on the same day. It is impossible for children to sustain any degree of interest if they must listen to a dozen or fifteen reports consecutively. A better procedure is to have two or three reports given at a time and to spread the reporting over a period of several days.

A common problem with reports given by children is the tendency for them to be "bookish." Some teachers encourage verbalism by being too rewarding, too complimentary of reports that are well presented but are not given in the child's own words. The dependence of the child on the language of the reference material is probably an indication that the topic is not understood. In order to combat the problem of verbalism in reports, the teacher should

1. Not fully accept bookish presentations that are meaningless to the child and are simply repetitions of what has been read. This usually can be handled by a comment such as "Jackie, I know you spent a lot of time and work preparing your report, but we would have found it much more valuable and interesting if you had told it to us in your own words."

2. Encourage children to make and use visual material in their reports— pictures, charts, diagrams, maps, graphs, the chalkboard, or an overhead projector.

3. Ask children to give concrete examples of what they are describing in words they use in everyday conversation.
4. Encourage children to use more than one source for their information.
5. Be more lavish in praising those who avoid bookish presentations.

Oral and written reports are among the most common ways children share ideas in social studies. In many classrooms these activities are overused and, in some cases, misused. It is important for children to share ideas with each other, however, and if some variation is made in the traditional reporting format, these experiences can be both interesting and informative. For example,

> To culminate a unit in which Ms. Pang's class studied Native North Americans, the children were asked to create an illustrated documentary on a tribe of their choosing.
> Ms. Pang brought in art materials for the children to use in creating their visuals and several cassette tape recorders. The children planned a narration and tape recorded it. They then made illustrations to accompany their narrations and presented their completed "documentaries" to their classmates.

The following are suggested as still other alternatives to the traditional oral and written reports.

Suggestions for Improving Class Reports

1. Dramatize an incident, sequence, or situation relating to the topic and incorporate essential data to be communicated in the dramatization.
2. Use children's own drawn illustrations, charts, and graphs as the basis for a presentation or use illustrations found in newspapers, magazines, or other sources.
3. Pretend to be a tour guide taking the class through the area studied.
4. Use the overhead projector for visual aids in a presentation.
5. Role play the part of a newscaster making an on-the-spot report.
6. Interview a classmate who is role playing the part of someone who is an expert on the topic under study.
7. Collect pictures, arrange them in sequence, and use them as the basis for a report.
8. Write a diary or letter that might have been written by someone in an earlier period.
9. Use artifacts or realia as the basis for a report.
10. Prepare and explain a bulletin board display or diorama.
11. Prepare a narration for a filmstrip.
12. Do an original narration for a film or videotape with sound turned off.
13. Write news stories that might have been appropriate to a particular period or prepare and publish a single issue of a newspaper that might have appeared in some historical period.
14. Tape record a presentation for playback to the class.

DISCUSSION QUESTIONS AND SUGGESTED ACTIVITIES

1. Under what circumstances might a teacher *not* want to clarify in great detail the objectives of a small group?

2. How might a teacher build readiness for small-group activities with a class that has always worked on a whole-class basis?

3. Develop a role-playing exercise designed to teach group-work skills.

4. Select a topic that is appropriate for a grade of your choice, and develop questions that could be used to stimulate a discussion with several factual, definitional, and ethical disagreements.

5. For the same topic you selected in item 4, devise two ways to divide it for Jigsaw. Then, create a question and an answer handout for use in STAD, and devise a two-sided approach to the topic for Structured Controversy.

6. Prepare an informal chart that might be used with children to illustrate points to keep in mind when preparing and making oral reports. Illustrate your chart in a way that you think would appeal to children.

7. In visiting a classroom, what specific things would you look for that would provide an indication of the quality of interaction taking place there?

8. Examine the dimensions of the hidden curriculum given at the beginning of the chapter, and add examples from your own experience that tend to increase or decrease the level of hostility in a classroom.

9. Make a T-chart for several of the skills mentioned in the chapter.

10. Discuss similarities and differences between traditional small-group instruction as used in the teaching of reading, and cooperative learning groups as used in social studies.

SELECTED REFERENCES

ARONSON, ELLIOT. *The Jigsaw Classroom.* Beverly Hills, CA: Sage, 1978.

BRABECK, MARY. *Who Cares? Theory, Research, and Educational Implications of the Ethic of Care.* New York: Praeger, 1989.

COHEN, ELIZABETH G. *Designing Groupwork.* New York: Teachers College Press, 1986.

EDUCATIONAL LEADERSHIP 47:4 (December 1989/January 1990). The entire issue is devoted to cooperative learning.

JOHNSON, DAVID W., AND ROGER T. JOHNSON. *Learning Together and Alone: Cooperative, Competitive, and Individualistic Learning.* Englewood Cliffs, NJ: Prentice-Hall, 1987.

JOHNSON, DAVID W., ROGER T. JOHNSON, EDYTHE J. HOLUBEC, AND PATRICIA ROY. *Circles of Learning: Cooperation in the Classroom.* Alexandria, VA: Association for Supervision and Curriculum Development, 1984.

KAGAN, SPENCER. *Cooperative Learning: Resources for Teachers*. Riverside, CA: University of California, 1988.

KREIDLER, WILLIAM J. *Creative Conflict Resolution*. Chicago: Scott, Foresman, 1984.

OAKES, JEANNIE. *Keeping Track: How Schools Structure Inequality*. New Haven, CT: Yale University Press, 1985.

PAUL, RICHARD. *Critical Thinking*. Rohnert Park, CA: Sonoma State University, 1991.

SLAVIN, ROBERT E. *Student Team Learning: An Overview and Practical Guide*. Washington, DC: National Education Association, 1986.

_____. *Using Student Team Learning*. Baltimore, MD: Johns Hopkins University, 1986.

_____. *Learning to Cooperate, Cooperating to Learn*. New York: Plenum, 1985.

VAN SICKLE, RONALD L. "Practicing What We Teach: Promoting Democratic Education in Schools and Classrooms." Chap. 4 in *Democratic Education in Schools and Classrooms*, edited by Mary A. Hepburn. NCSS Bulletin no. 70. Washington, DC: National Council for the Social Studies, 1983.

14 Learner Involvement Through Activities

I t is a common assumption that when learners are involved in creative activities, less in the way of "real" learning takes place. Traditional attitudes toward learning suggest that it must be accompanied by a hardnosed, joyless discipline. The feeling is widespread that if children enjoy what they are doing in school, the program is not intellectually rigorous. The following narrative describes a parent's attitude on just this point:

At first we were quite concerned when we found out that Lori was to be placed in Mr. Allison's room the next year. His room had such a relaxed atmosphere about it, and he was very popular with the kids. We just assumed, I guess, that a teacher who was so well liked by all the children could not be very effective in maintaining a disciplined environment for learning. I must say this assumption was wholly unfounded.

Mr. Allison was clearly the most creative, imaginative, and overall the most effective teacher Lori had during the seven years she attended that school. He always had the most unusual things going on in that room that would so hook the kids that they spent hours of unsupervised study on what they were doing. Schoolwork seemed to be a sheer delight, strange as that may seem. They analyzed advertising techniques in a unit on consumerism; they simulated law and justice procedures; they studied the effects of immigrant groups on American life and culture; there were art, poetry, music, and dramatic activities galore. Once they constructed a whole set of authentic models of Indian villages representing various tribes that inhabited this part of North America in pre-Columbian times. This involved the children in an incredible amount of research and information gathering in order to do the constructions. There were always games, puzzles, inquiries—tremendous interest grabbers. It was the only time I can recall that children had literally to be told to go home after school. If not, they would stay until dinnertime.

Mr. Allison convinced my husband and me that disciplined learning did not have to give the appearance of rigidity and drudgery. He seemed to embrace the philosophy that a teacher should obtain "maximum learning with minimum effort." But the "minimum effort" only seemed that way because of the tremendous motivating power of the creative activities he used. Actually, I have not seen children work any harder nor be more productive in their efforts than their year with Mr. Allison.[1]

How does a teacher develop this type of stimulating program for students in social studies? In part, this comes from an imaginative teacher who is able to capitalize on the natural interests and curiosities of children. The teacher encourages them to raise questions and to suggest ways of working. These, then, are converted into interesting study activities. In this chapter we will discuss ways that creative and expressive activities can be used in social studies for any or all of the following purposes:

1. to stimulate children's interest
2. to develop various aspects of thinking
3. to give direction and purpose to learning
4. to encourage initiative, exploration, and research
5. to aid in applying factual information obtained through research to concrete situations
6. to provide a setting in which to use socialization and human relations skills
7. to clarify complex procedures
8. to aid in developing an understanding of concepts and generalizations
9. to relate various components of the school program to one another
10. to provide opportunities for thinking, planning, sharing, doing, and evaluating
11. to provide an outlet for creative abilities
12. to provide an opportunity for recognition for the nonverbal, nonacademic child

The shortage of funds has forced cutbacks in the services of special teachers for art, music, drama, and even physical education in many schools. This means that the regular classroom teacher has to assume more responsibility for these subjects if anything at all is to be done with them. This set of circumstances provides the regular teacher with the opportunity to do a considerable amount of meaningful teaching of these subjects and skills within the framework of the social studies curriculum. In those districts where special teachers *are* available in these fields, it is to the regular classroom teacher's advantage to work closely with them in integrating these subjects and skills in the classroom curriculum in social studies.

CONSTRUCTION AND PROCESSING ACTIVITIES
• •

Most children love to make things. They build villages and castles in the sand at the beach; they build boats to float in a nearby pond; they construct

---

[1]An actual case from Minneapolis, Minnesota, reported to one of the authors.

This child is involved in the centuries-old processes of churning and washing butter. Experiences of this type help children appreciate the ingenuity of human beings who lived in earlier times and who had to depend on their own resourcefulness in meeting the challenges of a world without the conveniences that most families enjoy today. *(Photo courtesy of the Southern Oregon Historical Society.)*

birdhouses, model airplanes and cars, and wigwams. These natural sensory-motor play and creative-building activities are valuable for children in and of themselves. They give countless opportunities for thinking and planning as well as for creative expression, use of tools, physical activity, and the development of coordination. Children need many experiences of this type. In social studies, however, these values are only incidental to the chief purpose, which is *to extend and enrich meaning of some aspect of the topic being studied.* The excellence of the final product is, likewise, not a major concern. What is important is the learning that has occurred as a result of the construction activity. This being true, authenticity, genuineness, and truthfulness in the representations are important considerations in conducting construction activities. If constructions are inaccurate, contrary to truth and reality, they may be detrimental to learning because they reinforce incorrect concepts.

It is possible to use construction activities to motivate children's work and to establish more clearly children's purposes for doing things. For example, the teacher of a primary grade conducting a study of the dairy farm might suggest that the class construct a model farm in the classroom. Naturally, the children will want to make their model as authentic as possible; therefore, a considerable amount of research will be necessary as they proceed with the building of the farm. In fact, they cannot even begin unless they know what it is they want to do. This gives them a genuine need for information. The children's purpose in this case may be to learn about the dairy farm to be able to build a classroom model of it. The teacher's purpose, however, is to have children form accurate concepts and understandings of a dairy farm; the construction activity is being used as a vehicle to achieve that goal. Under this arrangement, both learner objectives and teacher objectives will have been achieved.

Selecting Activities

In selecting a construction activity for social studies, the teacher should consider the following criteria.

1. The activity is useful in achieving a definite objective related to social studies.
2. It clarifies, enriches, or extends the meaning of some important concept.
3. It requires children to do careful thinking and planning.
4. It is an accurate and truthful representation.
5. It is within the capabilities of the children.
6. The time and effort expended can be justified by the learnings that occur.
7. It is reasonable in terms of space and expense.
8. The needed materials are available.

There is no limit to the items that children can make in projects related to the social studies. The following have been used successfully by many teachers:

Model furniture

Books

Musical instruments

Simple trucks, airplanes, boats

Puppets and marionettes

Paper bag dolls

"Television" set with paper-roll programs

Looms for weaving

Animal cages

Animals of art materials

Maps (pictorial, product, relief, floor)

Candles

Soap

Baskets, trays, bowls

Preparation of foods (making cookies, jelly, butter, ice cream)

Ships, harbor, cargo

Retail food market and equipment

Scenery and properties for stage, dioramas, panoramas

Holiday decorations

Jewelry

Pottery, vases, dishes, cups

Covered wagons, churns, butter paddles, wooden spoons, and other
   pioneer gear

Post office

Bakery

Fire station

Dairy farm and buildings

Oxcarts

Circus accessories

Playhouses

Model Indian villages

Purses, hot pads, table mats, small rugs

Birdhouses and feeding stations

Seedboxes, planters

Tie-dyeing

Production of visual material needed in the unit, such as pictorial graphs,
   charts, posters, displays, bulletin boards

Block printing

The following suggestions are offered to help the teacher use construction activities in teaching social studies.

Discuss the Purposes of the Activity with the Children. The practice of having children make stores, build boats and covered wagons, or do Indian crafts without knowing why they are performing these activities is open to serious question. Children may not have any idea of the real purpose or significance of the construction. It is suggested, therefore, that at the beginning of such an activity, the reasons for planning it should be discussed and understood by all. The purposes for the construction should be reviewed from time to time during the activity.

Plan the Method of Procedure with the Children. The initial planning will take a considerable amount of time if every detail is to be taken into account. Such extensive planning is not necessary or entirely desirable, for it tends to make children impatient. Decisions must be made, however, as to the basic materials needed, the major responsibilities and who will assume them, the committees needed and who will be on them, where the construction will take place, where needed information may be obtained, and a general overall plan. After the construction project is underway there will be time each day to do additional specific planning. It is best to plan in a general way and get started and leave the details to be worked out at a later time.

Plan Methods of Work with the Children. Construction activities involve working in groups, using tools, perhaps hammering and sawing or other noisy activities, and somewhat more disorder than is usually found in regular classroom work. This means that unless rules and standards concerning the methods of work are established and understood, there is likely to be much noise, commotion, and general confusion. Therefore, it is recommended that the teacher and the children discuss and decide what the rules of work are to be. These might include

1. How to get and return tools and construction materials.
2. Use of tools and equipment, including safe handling.
3. Things to remember during the work period: talking in a conversational voice, good use of materials to avoid waste, sharing tools and materials with others, consideration for others, doing one's share of work, asking for help when needed, and giving everyone a chance to present ideas.
4. Procedures for cleanup time. It is well to establish a "listen" signal to get the attention of the class. It can be playing a chord on the piano, turning off the lights or ringing a small bell. When the listen signal is given, children should learn to stop whatever they are doing, cease talking, and listen to whatever announcement is to be made. In this way, the teacher can stop the work of the class at any time to call their attention

to some detail or get them started at cleanup. Cleanup is one procedure that can be done in a routine way. When the signal is given, all work stops, and the children listen for directions, restore the room to its prior condition, and assemble at the circle or go to their desks.

Provide Plenty of Time Each Day for Planning, Working, Cleaning Up, and Evaluating.   Before work on the construction activity is begun each day, time should be spent in making specific plans. This is to ensure that everyone will have an important job to do and that the children will know their responsibilities. It also is a time when the teacher can go over some of the points the class talked about during its previous day's evaluation. "You remember yesterday we had some problem about which group was to use the tools. Which group has the tools today?" Or "Yesterday our voices became a little loud at times. Perhaps we can be more careful about that today."

During the work period the teacher will want to move from group to group observing, assisting, suggesting new approaches, helping groups in difficulty, clarifying ideas, helping children find materials, and supervising and guiding the work of the class. Children will be identified who need help in getting started, those who are not working well together, those who seem not to be doing anything, or others who may be having difficulty. The teacher will keep an eye on the time and stop the work of the class in time to ensure a thorough cleanup.

An important part of each period is the evaluation that occurs after the work and cleanup. During these times, the teacher will want the class to evaluate the progress it is making on the construction as well as the way children are working with each other.

"Were we able to make progress in building our store today?"

"How do you think we might change the color to make it look more real?"

"Does anyone have any ideas how Steven's group could show more action in their mural?"

"Did anyone see signs of unsafe handling of tools today?"

"I wonder if the mountains aren't too high on Julie's group's map? Did you check that against the picture in your book?"

The precise points discussed in such an evaluation will depend on the class and its work. In any case, some attention should be given to (1) progress on the construction, (2) methods of working together, and (3) problems that need attention the next day.

Make Use of the Construction in Some Way, Relating It to the Unit under Study.   When constructed objects are completed, they should be put to good use. In the primary grades such a project may serve well for dramatic play activities. A market in the classroom, for example, gives the children an opportunity to play customer, grocer, checkout person, or

EXAMPLES OF CONSTRUCTION ACTIVITIES

Primary Grades

After a study of both the urban and rural communities, the class was divided in half. One group was assigned the project of constructing a rural community; the other, an urban community.

Ms. Stillwater planned with each group separately, starting with the development of a list of services and facilities needed in each community. Each child was responsible for constructing at least one part of the community.

For several days before construction was to begin, the children brought in cartons, shoe boxes, and other "building materials" that were to become their communities.

Using paint, construction paper, shellac, and team effort, the children transformed the cartons into urban and rural communities and placed them on butcher paper streets on the floor around the classroom.

Intermediate Grades

Mr. Russo's class had been studying the state's history, and he believed that there was a need for the children to understand better the role that geographical differences had played in the state's development. He thought that the construction of relief maps might be a good method for the children to achieve this understanding.

Because such a construction was too large a project for individual children, he asked them to organize themselves in groups of two or three with whomever they could work best.

Mr. Russo provided the children with a papier-mâché recipe and the necessary construction materials. He encouraged them to be innovative in adding things to their maps that would highlight the significance of relief features.

After he was satisfied that the children understood what they were to do, he had the groups begin planning their maps. He provided a regularly scheduled work period each day and supervised and assisted the groups as needed. The completed relief maps were displayed and discussed in terms of the role of geographic features in the development of the state.

other personnel associated with a market. They read labels and prices, rearrange the material on the shelves, keep the store clean, and so on. In the middle and upper grades, objects made can be examined, discussed, and displayed. A mural can be used for study purposes. A child can explain the way some object is constructed, its main features, how it was used, its history, why it is no longer used, and similar information. In some instances, children can share the information learned and the object they have constructed with other classes in the school. Constructions are of value only insofar as they relate to the work of the class; when they have served this purpose, they should be removed.

Closely related to construction activities are those that help the child understand the various steps or stages in the production of some material item. They deal with the *process* of changing raw materials into finished, usable items and, hence, involve *processing of materials*. These activities help children understand and appreciate the complexities of producing some of the basic material items that most persons use in everyday living. They are commonly used to illustrate the hardships, labor, skill, and ingenuity required of pioneers and early people in a time when it was necessary for them to produce basic materials for themselves. The most common processes used for this purpose are making butter, candles, paper, sugar, salt, bricks, natural dyes, jelly, ink, books, ice cream, soap, and weaving and dyeing cloth.

There are some instructional problems, however, in processing materials in the classroom. For example, is it appropriate to demonstrate the hardships experienced by pioneers in making candles by dipping, by using such modern-day conveniences as an electric hot plate as a source of heat and an aluminum container for the wax? In most classrooms it is, in fact, impossible to duplicate conditions under which candles were made in the seventeenth century. Almost any raw material the class uses in its processing will in all likelihood *already* be semiprocessed. The child may, therefore, leave such an experience with a lack of appreciation of the complexities involved in the process—a misfire of the precise learning the teacher had hoped to put across.

Some processes require extremely careful supervision by the teacher because of physical danger to the children. Candlemaking means heating tallow, wax, or paraffin that can ignite if allowed to become too hot and cause severe burns if dropped accidentally on one's person. Soapmaking calls for the use of lye, always potentially dangerous. These points are mentioned not to discourage the use of construction and processing but to alert the beginner to the real need for careful supervision while such activity is taking place.

MUSIC ACTIVITIES

Music activities make an important contribution to social studies instruction. Through the universal language of music, the child may extend communication to other peoples, races, and cultures, both past and present. Various songs and music forms are associated with periods in our national history, and many songs relate directly to heroes or great historical events. Musical expression is an emotional experience, piercing through everyday inhibitions and extending into the inner reaches of one's personality. Music inspires patriotism, love of country, loyalty, and fidelty. It is for this reason that marching bands are used in holiday parades and between halves at football games. Nation-states have used music effectively in building a feeling of national solidarity. Music has a profound effect on individuals as well as on groups.

Integrating Music in the Classroom

Music educators have worked diligently to break the shackles of the "music period" concept of music education and have consistently recommended a greater integration of music in the total life of the classroom. Music activities, therefore, not only contribute to social studies instruction but support the music program itself. The material that follows suggests some possibilities for the use of singing, rhythmic expression, listening, and creative music activities in social studies units.

Singing. For almost any social studies unit, the teacher will find appropriate and related songs for children to sing. One of the chief values of singing is its affective quality; it gives the child a *feeling* for the material not likely to be obtained in any other way. Through singing, the child senses the loneliness of the voyageur, the gaiety of a frontier housewarming, or the sadness of a displaced people longing for their homeland. Folk songs can be springboards to the study of a period in history, to the contributions of ethnic groups, to the lifestyles of a group, and to many social studies topics. Singing is an experience that can broaden children's appreciation of people everywhere. In the study of communities around the world, the teacher will want to use the songs of various national groups. This provides opportunities to learn more about a culture through the language of music.

Some educators have recognized the rich learning resource folk music provides, and they have promoted the use of folk songs in social studies classrooms.[2] Contemporary folk songs such as "Little Boxes," "We Shall Overcome," "Detroit City," and "Sittin' on the Dock of the Bay" convey powerful social messages. Cowboy songs such as "I Ride an Old Paint," "Colorado Trail," "The Night Herding Song," and "Git Along Little Dogie" have both lyrics and melodies that are hauntingly reminiscent of the lonely life of this American folk group. "The Yellow Rose of Texas," "When Johnny Comes Marching Home Again," and "Over There" are associated with significant conflicts of this nation (Texas Independence, Civil War, and World War I, respectively). Teachers interested in learning more about the use of folk songs in the classroom should write to John W. Scott, P.O. Box 264, Holyoke, MA 01041, or to Diana Palmer, 433 Leadmine Rd., Fiskdale, MA 01518, for information about the newsletter entitled *Folksong in the Classroom*.

Rhythmic Expression. Rhythmic and bodily expression tend to release one from the crust of convention and formality of everyday life and provide a means of self-expression. Through rhythms, bodily expression, and folk dances, the child develops grace and poise and learns the amenities that are characteristic of such social activities. Folk dancing and folk games in

---

[2]Laurence I. Seidman, C.W. Post College, and John Anthony Scott, Rutgers University, have made several presentations at NCSS annual meetings.

themselves are pleasurable and legitimate social activities for children. They provide for teamwork and allow the child to participate in the activity with several other boys and girls. Folk dancing and folk games usually involve eight or more children with a continual shifting of partners. For this reason, folk dancing is well suited for children in the elementary and middle schools.

In social studies, the teacher will want to use the various folk dances and rhythmic activities that are characteristic of many countries, as well as those associated with various periods of our national history. Because ethnic heritage studies have become popular in schools, activities of this type can be particularly meaningful. Far from being solely a recreational activity, rhythmic expression provides a wide range of possibilities for social learnings in general and especially for the social studies.

Creating.   Social studies topics provide many opportunities for the child to create musically. This can be done on an individual basis or as a class project and can be used with almost any topic by any age group. Perhaps it is not used more frequently by teachers because they feel that a considerable amount of technical knowledge of music is necessary. The need for the technical skills of music is greatly overestimated, but if the teacher feels insecure, there will ordinarily be someone available who does have such

Here we see children participating in a folk dance characteristic of early days in the West. This photograph illustrates one of the many instructive and enjoyable activities the teacher can use to make social studies come alive for children.
(Photo courtesy of the Southern Oregon Historical Society.)

skills and can be of assistance. This person might be a music supervisor or teacher, the high school music director, another classroom teacher, or a parent volunteer.

In its simplest form, creative music is a melody or sounds children learn to associate with the topic being studied. For example, the children may make sounds that remind them of a factory, a circus, or a train. Later these sounds can be used in the development of an actual melody. Children commonly produce creative verse to which they may add an appropriate melody. In the middle and upper grades such creative music activities may include the development of words and music for pageants, plays, puppet shows, or simple musicals. These original numbers are frequently of good quality musically and are favorites of the children for years afterward—an indication of the satisfying and long-lasting quality of creative music.

Children can also be encouraged to create their own lyrics for melodies with which they are familiar. Such an activity is especially appropriate when the class is preparing an original play or pageant associated with a topic in social studies. Or, children may find the writing of lyrics to be worthwhile simply as a creative experience. Children can be encouraged to develop lyrics that convey a funny message, or that tell a story about the topic (a ballad), or that speak to the qualities of some person or character, or that use language associated with a particular place or historical period, or for other interesting purposes.

Listening.   Although singing, creating, and rhythmic expression involve *performing* or *doing* aspects of music, listening places the child in the role of a consumer of music. This role deserves more attention than is usually given it because it is the type of musical experience that continues throughout life. Long after most persons stop performing musically, they enjoy listening to music. Relating music listening to the affairs of life and living is, therefore, essential.

Listening to music should be an imaginative experience for children. The teacher can help them learn of mood in music and contrast what is bright, happy, and lively with music that is quiet and restful. Through listening the child learns to identify the use of music by different groups throughout the world—it provides for another direct cultural contact with people of many lands. The teacher will have no difficulty obtaining recordings for the purposes described.

CREATIVE ART ACTIVITIES

Creative art is widely used in social studies instruction because many topics and activities inspire creative expression. A trip to a farm, airport, zoo, post office, or fire station all give impetus to the desire to create. Observing bulldozers, cranes, demolition crews, as well as going on a hike to a nearby

EXAMPLES OF MUSIC ACTIVITIES

Primary Grades

During a unit on the children of Mexico, Ms. Juarez shared some of her own ethnic background with her class. She was able to teach them a few simple folk dances and folk songs she had learned as a child in Mexico.

After learning the words to the songs in Spanish, the children asked her to teach them other words and expressions in Spanish. By the end of the year, many children had developed a fair speaking vocabulary of greetings and commonly used expressions in Spanish.

Intermediate Grades

Mr. Cole's fifth graders were studying the development of the United States. He thought it was important for them to learn how music reflects the mood of the nation at a particular time. He was also able to get examples of popular music from the middle of the nineteenth century to the present time. The lyrics of these songs were analyzed in terms of national events and concerns of the time. Mr. Cole was also able to get recordings of some of these songs and, without telling the class the period from which the song came, asked them to try to determine when the selection was popular.

park or stream, are the types of experiences from which come the creative artwork of children. Through an art medium the child may be able to symbolize experiences, express thoughts, or communicate feelings that cannot be done through the use of conventional language. For a young child in the primary grades, a picture or painting is likely to tell a whole story, and all the action is happening in the picture as it is being shared with others. For example, a first grader's painting may show children playing with a dog while a jet is flying overhead and a police patrol is chasing a speeding motorist. But the action is not stopped at the time the painting was made; it goes on all the time. That is, the children really are playing with the dog, and the airplane is actually flying. Children's artwork tells a story; it can be useful in recording social studies experiences.

Many parallels could be drawn between art experiences and music experiences in social studies. Like music, art provides a cultural link with the many peoples of the world, past and present. It also places the child in the roles of creator and consumer as does music. It deals directly with feelings, emotions, appreciations, and creative abilities of children. In addition to the many desirable outcomes associated with any creative endeavor, creative art experiences have much to offer in stimulating and strengthening learning in the social studies.

In the course of the social studies unit, the teacher might use any of the following art activities:

Preparing murals
Free painting
Making illustrations
Weaving
Block printing
Clay modeling
Potato or stick printing
Chalk, charcoal, and crayon
    drawing
Pencil sketching
Making properties for plays,
    pageants
Making puppets and marionettes
Soap carving
Basket making
Indian beadwork

Poster making
Making models
Making cartoons
Making booklets and books
Crafts related to some locality or
    country
Constructing dioramas to illus-
    trate scenes
Planning and preparing exhibits
Sewing
Making designs and costumes
Wood carving
Toy making
Finger painting
Indian sand painting

Creative art expression as used in social studies may take two forms. The first of these might be described as *personal* and is performed by the children because it expresses an idea or gives personal satisfaction. Having the experience is its own reward, and the child need not share such a piece of art with anyone although children often want to. Artwork of this type is not evaluated in terms of the product produced but in terms of the satisfactions the experience itself gives the learner. Any of the art media can be used for personal expression.

A second type of creative art expression can be thought of as *functional* in that the product is used in connection with some other activity. It might be a mural to be used as the background for a dramatic activity. It might be a model of something that will be used to illustrate an explanation. It could be a visual aid the child plans to use in making a report to the class. In artwork of this type, the representation has to be reasonably accurate and authentic; consequently, the teacher will need to guard against having the children copy exactly the illustrations they find in reference materials.

The poorest of all art experiences are those that are patterned rather than creative. The teacher might, for example, ditto a diagram of a turkey and have children color certain feathers red, others brown, and others black. Children who follow the directions precisely and who can color within the lines are highly rewarded with teacher praise. Then the twenty-five turkeys, all alike, are posted on the bulletin board under the caption "We Do Creative Work." Such conspicuous misuse of art may also take the form of silhouette profiles of Lincoln, hatchets and cherries, covered wagons, or Christmas trees. Teaching of this type tends to depress any creative art ability or interest in art expression that an imaginative child may have, and should be avoided.

······················ **EXAMPLES OF CREATIVE ART ACTIVITIES**

Primary Grades

Third graders peeled and dried apples to make apple-head dolls. They added yarn hair and formed bodies of wire. Each doll was dressed to resemble some well-known historical figure.

Intermediate Grades

In a study of India, fourth graders constructed movable rod puppets. They used the puppets to dramatize folktales from India.

DRAMATIC ACTIVITIES

Dramatic representation in any one of its many forms is a popular activity with children—one in which they have all engaged during their early years. What child has not "been" a fire fighter, a cowhand, a jet pilot, or a doctor during the fanciful and imaginative play of early childhood? Dramatic activities have great value in promoting social studies learnings by helping sharpen the child's power of observation; giving purpose to research activities; giving insight into another's feelings; providing experiences in democratic living; helping create and maintain interest, thereby motivating learning; and affording an excellent opportunity for the teacher to observe the behavior of children.

The most structured dramatic activity is the *dramatization,* which requires a script, staging, rehearsal, and an audience. It may be used to show some historical event, to represent the growth of a movement or idea, to represent life in another period, or to demonstrate some problem of living. Children are usually involved in a considerable amount of creative work in productions of this type. They may plan and prepare costumes, do the artwork necessary for staging and properties, plan a program, send invitations, and make all arrangements attendant to the project. This requires that the children do a great deal of planning, working together, evaluating, and participating.

The least structured dramatic activity is the spontaneous acting out or reliving of situations from the child's world. It is called *dramatic play.* As this activity is used in social studies, the term *dramatic play* is an unfortunate one because it suggests entertainment. Perhaps the terms *creative dramatic representation* or *representative living* would describe more accurately what is involved in the activity. When kindergartners and first graders are playing various roles of mother, father, sister, brother, doctor, and nurse in a corner of the classroom, they are engaging in dramatic play. Free dramatic play is a natural activity for young children, and they participate in it with little or no stimulation from adults. During the periods of free dramatic play, the teacher can learn much about the personalities of individual children—who they identify with, their attitudes toward others, their willingness to share, and their emotional maturity.

As children move into the second and third grades, there is less evidence of spontaneous dramatic play. At this stage of growth, dramatic play usually requires more suggestion and stimulation from the teacher and may be used profitably to help the child understand or appreciate some phase of human relationships. These slightly more structured dramatic activities are referred to as *role playing, sociodrama,* or *creative dramatics.*

Role playing, sociodrama, or creative dramatics is used to present a specific situation for study and discussion. There is no prepared script, it is unrehearsed, speaking parts are not memorized, and properties, if used at all, are held to a minimum. Some small amount of properties may be used simply to help children remain in role. These activities are used to teach or clarify social values, to focus attention on a central idea, to help children organize ideas, to extend vocabulary, and to gain a greater insight into the problems of others by casting themselves in another's role. Because they portray problems in human relationships, they provide an excellent basis for discussion and evaluation. They should be followed by a discussion of questions of this type: "Which character did you like best? Why?" "Which one did you like least? Why?" "How do you suppose the person *felt?*" "If you had been in the wagon master's place, what would you have done?" "Have you ever known anyone like that?"

This final discussion and analysis requires that the situation be cut before the problem has been solved and before the outcome is a certainty. Otherwise, there would be little room left for thoughtful consideration of the problem.

Closely related to creative dramatics is the use of *reaction stories.* Reaction stories are brief, narrative accounts dealing with human relations that are used to uncover various attitudes and emotions. They may be written by the teacher or may be passages selected from published works. They deal with a variety of topics such as sharing, teasing, responsibility, peer pressures, respect for property, and intercultural relations. The story is read to the children, and they are asked to tell their feelings about characters, situations, what they would do under similar circumstances, what alternatives were available to the characters, and other comparable reactions. This critique is similar to the one held at the conclusion of a creative dramatics activity.

SIMULATIONS AND INSTRUCTIONAL GAMES

A fifth-grade class was studying the concept of *assembly-line production* in its unit on the growth of industry in the United States. In the discussion, the children contrasted assembly-line production with custom-made, individ-

················· **EXAMPLES OF DRAMATIC ACTIVITIES**

Primary Grades

Ms. Beatty wanted the children to be able to cope with situations that might arise while they were shopping. She listed situations that could present a problem, such as returning faulty merchandise, knocking over displays, becoming separated from their parent, or inquiring about the location of the restroom. The children added other situations to the list.

Ms. Beatty asked the children to role play the situations. These were discussed in terms of possible and responsible actions in such situations.

Intermediate Grades

Ms. Hall's class had been doing research on the signers of the Declaration of Independence. Each child had been responsible for finding out about at least one of these historical figures.

Ms. Hall then asked various groups of children to reenact the signing of the document. She encouraged them to react as the person they represented might have done.

ually built products. The class listed the strengths and limitations of each method of production:

ASSEMBLY LINE

STRENGTHS	WEAKNESSES
1. It is faster.	1. Sameness makes for an uninteresting product.
2. Every product is the same.	2. Production can be slipshod because no one person is responsible for it.
3. Can be produced at low cost.	3. The sameness of the work makes for a boring job.
4. Because of low production cost, more people can afford to buy the product.	4. A poor worker or a breakdown can stop the whole production.

CUSTOM BUILT

1. "One of a kind" product.	1. Products are more expensive.
2. Higher quality because an individual worker is responsible for it.	2. Buyers cannot be sure of the product's quality because each is different.
3. Product can be made to fit the desires of the buyer.	3. Fewer people can afford to buy the product.

4. Work is less boring to the workers.

4. It takes longer for workers to
become skillful in doing all the
tasks needed to make the product.

The teacher pointed out to the class that each of the items they listed
could serve as a hypothesis that they might be able to test. "Is it really
true," she asked, "that assembly-line production is faster? Do workers on
an assembly line become bored more quickly than those who make the
whole product themselves? Do workers take greater pride in their product
if they do it all themselves and sign their name to it? How could we test the
truth of the statements?" The teacher and the children decided they could
test their hypotheses by using a simple simulation involving the manufacture of envelopes.

The class was divided into two groups: One would be assembly-line
workers; the other groups would be custom workers. The teacher provided
cardboard templates, or patterns, of an outline of an envelope, scissors,
paste, and used ditto paper that would be needed to manufacture envelopes. After the pattern was placed on a piece of paper, its outline could be
traced and could then be cut, folded, and pasted to make the finished
product. The assembly line was arranged according to a division of labor as
follows:

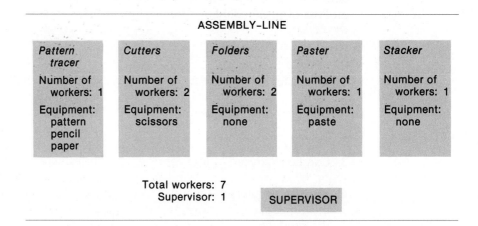

The custom workers consisted of seven individuals (the same number as
on the assembly line) and a supervisor. Each of the seven workers had his
or her own pattern, paper, pencil, scissors, and paste and was required to
do all the steps necessary to make an envelope. These children would be
required to put their own name on each envelope they produced and were
encouraged to personalize their own product.

All children in both groups took turns, and all participated in the activity. The supervisor from each group could make changes and substitutions

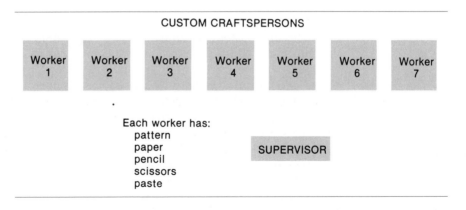

as needed. Three children served as a quality control panel that would accept or reject finished products in terms of quality of workmanship.

When all preparations were completed, the teacher gave the signal to start, and both groups began manufacturing envelopes. After a half hour, the production was stopped, and the debriefing took place. Children were able to test their hypotheses in terms of the data they generated through the simulation.

We have here an example of a simple simulation. It is a strategy designed to reconstruct as closely as possible some of the essential characteristics of the real thing. Simulations and gaming strategies are enthusiastically accepted by those teachers who pursue innovative approaches to social studies teaching. The simulation may be a simple one devised by the teacher, as described here, or it may be one of the growing number of commercially prepared simulations and games now available.

The Nature of Simulations and Games

A *game* may be defined as an activity that involves rules, competition, and players who become winners and losers. The outcome of some games depends entirely on chance, as in the case of tossing dice. In other games, the outcome is determined less by chance and more by the decisions made by the players, as in chess or checkers. Most games involve both elements of chance and skill. It is significant that persons who are involved in a game are called "players." This suggests that games are associated with amusement—they are intended to be enjoyed. When games are used for educational purposes, they are often referred to as *instructional games* in order to avoid creating the impression that they are used only for entertainment. For this reason, too, instructional games frequently are called *simulations.*Instructional games tend to minimize chance and enjoyment aspects although most contain some elements of chance and most are enjoyed by the participants.

A simulation gives the illusion of reality but removes most of the elements that are irrelevant and those that would be dangerous to the participants. In the use of simulators in pilot training or driver training, wrong moves by the trainee do not result in disastrous crashes or collisions. Likewise, in educational simulations, errors of judgment or unwise decisions do not produce disastrous social consequences.

Experts do not agree among themselves about the distinction between games and simulations. Not all games are simulations, as, for example, such games as hopscotch, jacks, or jump rope. Similarly, not all simulations are games, as in the case of astronauts working in a simulated weightless environment. However, in education these activities often take on characteristics of both games and simulations. Consequently, they are popularly, although perhaps not altogether precisely, called *simulation games*.

Values of Simulations and Instructional Games

The values of simulations and instructional games for use with elementary and middle school-age children are not firmly established. Research evidence concerning the effects of simulations and games at the elementary and middle school levels is sparse. Nonetheless, the following points seem to be well grounded on the basis of research and practice.

1. Simulations and games are highly motivating. Children enjoy participating in these activities and do so without much urging from the teacher. The fact that learners show increased interest in the subject when they are involved in simulation games is well documented. One can assume that part of this interest is generated by the reality created by the simulation, by the competitive, gaming aspects of it, and by the fact that there are clearly defined goals to be achieved. Because of their motivating power, it is easy to get children involved in simulation games. Even children who are typically on the fringes of most class activities often become enthusiastically engaged in instructional games and simulations. These activities seem to appeal to the natural inclinations of children to be involved in imaginative play, make believe, and role playing.

2. Simulations and games have been used successfully for instructional purposes outside of school. They have been used in teaching military operations for many years. They are used in training programs in business and industry, in teaching management skills, in the space program, in medicine, law, political science, and many other fields. Computer science has made it possible to develop these simulations and games at a sophisticated level. Because they have proved their usefulness in instructional settings outside of school, it is fair to assume they would have value for in-school instruction as well.

3. There seems to be evidence that simulations and games are effective in dealing with learner attitudes. Wentworth and Lewis cite several studies that report positive learner response after participating in a simulation

or game.[3] Many of these studies have been criticized on technical grounds, making it difficult to generalize their findings. Nevertheless, the impact of games and simulations on learner attitudes is widely reported.

4. There seems to be considerable doubt about the effects of simulations and games on cognitive gain. The research to date does not show that simulations have a clear advantage over other learning resources and procedures in promoting cognitive learning. Perhaps this is because the learners must have the prerequisite skills and must understand the basic concepts before the game is played. That is, the simulation game provides opportunities for the *application of knowledge and skills* rather than breaking new cognitive ground. This might explain, also, why researchers rather consistently report gains in the affective but not the cognitive area.

5. Almost without exception authors and researchers speak to the importance of the postgame or "debriefing" session. It is in these critiques that the major learnings can be identified and discussed. These sessions allow the participants to explore in some detail what choices were available to the players, what decisions were made, and how those decisions contributed to the outcome. In this way, the simulation or game provides the group with a common and shared experience that can be used to extend and enrich learning. From an instructional point of view, the debriefing session must be considered integral to the game itself.

Using Commercially Prepared Simulation Games

Presently there are many commercially prepared simulation games available for elementary school use, most being designed for the middle and upper grades. In the January 1980 issue of *Social Education,* Sharon Pray Muir provides an annotated list of eighty-eight simulation games for elementary school social studies.[4] In preparing this list, she made a thorough search of the field and included only those that are appropriate for use in grades K–6 and that deal directly with social studies concepts and processes. The list includes the title, recommended grade levels, amount of time needed to play the game, number of players, and the cost. She also indicates the social science discipline with which the simulation is associated.

A teacher may use a simulation game strictly in accordance with the instructions provided or may adapt it to suit local needs, learner abilities and interests, and instructional objectives. The teacher must be thoroughly

---

[3]Donald R. Wentworth and Darrell R. Lewis, "A Review of Research on Instructional Games and Simulations in Social Studies Education," *Social Education* 37 (May 1973); 437–38.

[4]Sharon Pray Muir, "Simulation Games for Elementary Social Studies," *Social Education* 44 (January 1980); 35–39, 76.

SELECTED SIMULATION GAMES

Economics   IMPORT, grs. 4–5, 2–4 weeks, 18–35 players, $10. Simulates activities of 6 importing firms in various parts of the world. Each firm buys from several countries. To win, a firm must buy 8 products from 3 countries and sell them at a profit. Simile II; SSSS; EMI

Economics/   ROARING CAMP, grs. 4–7, five 10-minute periods, 18–35 players, $10. Players are
History   given a $600 grubstake with which to file a mining claim and try their luck as prospectors. Each person pays $400 for initial tools, supplies, and equipment and $200 a year thereafter to keep him or her going. Chance selection of plots on which to file claims controls those who hit pay dirt and those who "lose their shirts." Simile II; EMI[5]

[5]Muir, "Simulation Games," 37, 38.

familiar with the game before introducing it to the class. It is advisable for the teacher to play the game with friends or fellow teachers before using it as an instructional tool.

Computer Simulations

The computer can organize and manipulate data with amazing speed, and therefore it is an ideal tool for use for simulations. Once a simulation has been played, students can formulate their own hypothetical propositions in the form of "What if" questions and have the computer respond to them. This kind of creative question asking and decision making is useful in developing thinking skills.

Perhaps the best known of the commercially prepared social studies simulations for the elementary and middle school grades is *The Oregon Trail* developed by the Minnesota Educational Computing Consortium (MECC), 3490 Lexington Avenue North, St. Paul, MN 55126. The story line is that of a wagon train party moving Westward in the 1800s. Along the way the wagon train has to deal with a number of contingencies such as foul weather, sickness, hostile Indians, and dangerous animals. As each is encountered, a decision has to be made, and a poor decision can have disastrous consequences for the entire party. The object is to get the wagon train to Oregon. This is an interesting simulation and one that is well suited for elementary and middle school children.

Popular simulations involving citizenship education are *Decisions, Decisions* (for grades 5 and above), *Choices, Choices* (K–6), and *Our Town Meeting* (5–8), all from Tom Snyder Productions (123 Mt. Auburn St., Cambridge, MA 02138). The first two can be used with an entire classroom and only one computer; the third is designed for use with up to 15 students and one computer. All promote group interaction and community decision making. Another software developer, Focus Media, produces *And If Reelected*, a presidential simulation for grades 7 and up. Students grapple with numerous public policy controversies, such as nuclear waste and budget deficits.

Emphasizing geography is the very popular *Where in the World is Carmen Sandiego?* Produced by Broderbund Software (17 Paul Dr., San Rafael, CA 94903), this exciting game has students play detective as they use geography clues and a reference book *(The World Almanac and Book of Facts)* to solve a crime. Also available are *Where in the U.S.A. is Carmen Sandiego?* and *Where in Europe is Carmen Sandiego?*

Other commercially prepared simulations that have been used with success in elementary and middle school grades are (1) *The Market Place* (grades 3–6) produced by MECC, designed to develop economic concepts and relationships as the player is placed in the role of an entrepreneur; (2) *President-Elect* (grades 8 and above), produced by Learning Arts, P.O. Box 179, Wichita, KS 67201, has to do with variables associated with the election of a president of the United States; (3) *Agent USA*, produced by Scholastic, 730 Broadway, New York, NY 10003, simulates a secret agent traveling around the United States in search of a bomb as students assist in selecting best routes; it is intended to develop map-reading and geography-related skills; and (4) *Stock Market* (grades 4–6) and *Millionaire, The Stock Market Simulation*, both produced by Learning Arts, designed to teach principles of the stock market. These examples illustrate the range of subject matter included in a growing list of simulations and games available for social studies education. The National Council for the Social Studies journal, *Social Education*, provides an update on new simulations and other resources for computer applications to social studies.

Preparing Your Own Game

After some knowledge of, and experience with, simulation games, some teachers have been encouraged to prepare their own games with or without a computer. This is a formidable task, and the teacher may wish to collaborate in such an effort with a colleague. Also, children themselves in the middle and upper grades can assist in creating a simulation game. In any case, the teacher may find the following questions to be of help in constructing a simulation game.

1. What instructional purpose is to be served by the game? That is, what objective or objectives are to be achieved through the use of the simulation game?
2. What real-life situations can be used to illustrate or dramatize the objectives? In most cases, this will call for the preparation of a narrative (referred to as a *scenario*) that establishes the situation and makes explicit the problem, conflict, issue, or process to be simulated.
3. What is to be the sequence of events, and how much time will be required or allowed for each?
4. What players will be involved? How many are there to be? How are they to be grouped?

5. What are the specific objectives of individual or group players? How are success or failure experiences to be recognized and recorded? What resources (votes, play money, political support, food, and so forth) will players have for tradeoffs and bargaining?
6. How do individuals or groups interact to register wins or losses?
7. What is the role of the teacher to be?

SOCIAL PARTICIPATION

The real test of a social studies program comes in the out-of-school lives of children. If the school has provided them with new insights, improved skills, or increased awareness and sensitivity to social affairs, such learning should be apparent in their out-of-school behavior as children and later as adults. The objectives of social studies education, in other words, are tested in the way that learners apply them to social reality in and out of school. In its statement of curriculum guidelines, the National Council for

Visits to places that encourage children to become actively involved in the use of pioneer technology make a unique contribution to social studies education. Experiences of this type are important not only for the knowledge gained but for giving today's children a sense of what it felt like to have lived in these earlier times.
(Photo courtesy of the Southern Oregon Historical Society.)

the Social Studies speaks of *social participation* as one of the four essential components of social studies education.[6]

To be socially active does not mean that young children have to be concerned with the great social issues of our time. But they can and should be involved in experiences that bridge the gap between what is learned in school and the world in which they live. They can and should practice skills and apply knowledge that prepares them for intelligent and responsible involvement in social affairs of the society of which they are a part.

Of course, children are not going to be able to be socially active without some help and encouragement from their teacher. The following are a few examples of activities that teachers have used successfully with elementary and middle school-age children.

1. Middle graders formed a volunteer Good Neighbor Club to help elderly residents in the neighborhood with yard work, errands, and other assistance as needed.

2. A class interviewed parents, school personnel, and adult friends and neighbors to determine the ethnic background of people living in the area. They used the data to prepare an exhibit entitled "Living and Working Together—Our Ethnic Heritages" to be displayed in a local store window. This included maps, photographs, and artifacts secured from the neighborhood.

3. A group organized a food gathering campaign for the Neighbors in Need Program.

4. On a walk around the school neighborhood, a second-grade class noticed that a main sidewalk was so badly damaged that children on their way to and from school had to walk into the street to avoid it. The class wrote a letter to the City Council asking that the sidewalk be repaired. They received a letter from the president of the City Council thanking them for their concern and assuring them that it would be repaired. He also commended them for their display of civic responsibility. The sidewalk was repaired.

5. A group in a rural area organized a "Clean Up Our Hill Saturday," during which time the children picked up litter in the public areas of the neighborhood. They encouraged and assisted adult residents to do the same. Children were able to secure litterbags, decals for trash cans, litterbags for cars, antilitter bumper stickers, and antilitter literature from the local Department of Ecology. These materials were distributed by the children to the local residents.

[6]National Council for the Social Studies, "Revision of the Social Studies Curriculum Guidelines," *Social Education* 43 (April 1979); 266. The other three components are *knowledge, abilities* (skills), and *valuing.*

6. A class developed a working relationship with a nearby retirement home. Residents who were able to were invited and came to school activities. The children also put on programs for the retirees at the home. As the project developed, parents of the children also became involved. Some of the parents invited residents to their homes for dinner and took them to church and for Sunday drives. The senior citizens had skills and hobbies that they shared with the children.

7. Elementary schoolchildren made tray favors for a local convalescent home for each of the major holidays during the school year.

8. Sixth graders collected and refurbished used toys and donated them to Goodwill Industries for redistribution.

9. Children collected books in the neighborhood for the local library's used-book sale.

10. A class made a survey of their homes to look for safety hazards or fire dangers and corrected them.

11. A social studies class sponsored a bicycle safety program in the school.

12. Upper graders volunteered to do free babysitting for mothers on Election Day.

DISCUSSION QUESTIONS AND SUGGESTED ACTIVITIES

1. Select a unit topic for a grade in which you have a special interest. Suggest ways that the activities discussed in this chapter could be incorporated in such a unit.

2. Criticize or defend the following statement: Social studies for young children should be more activity oriented than subject-matter centered.

3. When you visit an elementary school classroom, observe the type of construction activities underway. Are they accurate and authentic representations? What purposes was the teacher hoping to accomplish through the use of construction?

4. Demonstrate to your peers how you would proceed with a processing activity of some type (i.e., making butter, dipping candles, weaving a basket, and so forth). Indicate the concepts being developed in the activity.

5. Obtain or write an unfinished, open-ended story that could be used as a role-playing activity for children. Put the characters in a social problem situation. What alternatives are open to the major characters in the story?

6. Suggest situations that might be developed into a simulation game. With the help of two or three peers, develop a simple simulation game.

7. Develop plans for a social participation project for a grade of your choice. Have your plans critiqued by your peers.

8. The use of song lyrics was discussed in the text. What possibilities can you suggest for the use of song lyrics in learning about the period in which a song was written?

SELECTED REFERENCES

AKENSON, JAMES E. "Linkages of Art and Social Studies: Focus Upon Modern Dance/Movement." *Theory and Research in Social Education* 19 (Winter 1991): 95–108.

ASSOCIATION FOR SUPERVISION AND CURRICULUM DEVELOPMENT. *Educational Leadership* 48 (November 1990). This issue is devoted to the theme "social responsibility."

BRAUN, JOSEPH A. *Microcomputers and the Social Studies: A Resource Guide for the Middle and Secondary Grades.* New York: Garland, 1986.

FOWLER, CHARLES. "The Arts Are Essential to Education." *Educational Leadership* 47 (November 1989): 60–63.

KATZ, LILLIAN G., AND SYLVIA C. CHARD. *Engaging Children's Minds: The Project Approach.* Norwood, NJ: Ablex, 1991.

LEWIS, BARBARA A. "Today's Kids Care about Social Action." *Educational Leadership* 49 (September 1991): 47–49.

MCCLURE, AMY A., AND CONNIE S. ZITLOW. "Not Just the Facts: Aesthetic Response in Elementary Content Area Studies." *Language Arts* 68 (January 1991): 27–33.

NELLI, ELIZABETH. "Mirror of a People: Folktales and Social Studies." *Social Education* 49 (February 1980): 155–58.

SINGER, DOROTHY G., AND JEROME L. SINGER. *Make Believe: Games and Activities to Foster Imaginative Play in Young Children.* Glenview, IL: Scott, Foresman, 1985.

SUNAL, CYNTHIA SZYMANSKI. "Studying Another Culture Through Children's Games." *The Social Studies* 79 (September/October 1988): 232–38.

TURNER, THOMAS N. " 'And What Do You Think He Saw?' Using Chain Songs and Rounds." *Social Studies and the Young Learner* 1 (September/October 1988): 22–24.

WENTZEL, KATHRYN R. "Social Competence at School: Relation Between Social Responsibility and Academic Achievement." *Review of Educational Research* 61 (Spring 1991); 1–24.

WHARTON-BOYD, LINDA F. "The Significance of Black American Children's Singing Games in an Educational Setting." *Journal of Negro Education* 52 (Winter 1983); 46–56.

15 | Assessing and Evaluating Learning in Social Studies

Evaluation is an indispensable part of teaching because (1) it helps learners know what is important to learn; (2) it informs children of their progress or lack of it; (3) it informs learners if and how they are deficient so that they can improve; and (4) it helps teachers know how well desired objectives have been achieved so they may plan subsequent instruction. Additionally, evaluation is essential in reporting the progress of children to their parents and informing the public about the effectiveness of school programs. But to *evaluate* student learning, the teacher must first make use of sound *assessment* procedures.

Assessing learning involves finding out what children are learning and comparing that with what we want them to be learning. The "finding out" part is, technically speaking, *assessment*, while the comparison part is *evaluation*. Assessment is a neutral process. Like a detective trying to get the facts, assessment's emphasis is on observation of what is happening *now*. Evaluation, however, involves value judgment, comparing what *is*—the facts about the learner's present understanding—with what *ought* to be—the desired outcome of instruction. Actually, this distinction is often blurred. When teachers assess children's present understanding of *democracy*, they do so with a desired level of understanding in mind. Indeed, assessment and evaluation usually occur in one breath. In this chapter, we will follow common practice, and use the terms almost interchangeably, though we will make the distinction where necessary for clarity.

Let us stress immediately that the desired outcome of instruction must be conceptualized with great care, for it powerfully influences the nature of assessment as well as the whole process of teaching and learning. Often called the *objective* of instruction, the desired outcome is the target at which teaching and learning are aimed and against which the learner's progress is judged. Unless we can define and set priorities for what we want children to learn, it will not matter whether we devise effective ways of assessing learning. Just as good instruction is no victory if the subject matter is not important, good assessment practices are irrelevant if the outcome is of little consequence.

This chapter begins by considering five principles for developing desired outcomes or objectives of instruction. We follow this with a discussion of minimum competency testing and examples of informal assessment techniques and teacher-made tests. We close the chapter with a discussion of standardized tests.

DESIRED OUTCOMES

A growing number of educators in the early 1990s began to notice that something was missing in schools: exemplary targets for learning and instruction. There was much testing going on, to be sure, but to what ends? To what desired outcome? The minimum competency movement of the 1980s had established *minimal* outcomes such as balancing a checkbook, filling out job applications, reading a prescription, and other tasks that, while necessary, failed to capture the hopes and dreams we have for our children. Quite the opposite, they captured our fears. They were aimed at the bottom of the learning ladder, not the top. Consequently, minimum competencies gave no hint of the kinds of targets toward which students and teachers should marshal their skills and put forth their very best efforts.[1] We here present five principles to guide those who wish to develop such outcomes. The first can be summarized as *essential learnings,* the second as *authentic exhibitions,* the third as *high standards,* the fourth as *clarify the targets early,* and the fifth as *don't go it alone.*

Essential Learnings

Desired outcomes generally should be concerned with a relatively small number of *essential* subject matters or skills. Key themes of citizenship, history, and geography were discussed in chapters 1 and 5, and the teacher should direct assessment in social studies primarily to these. It is more important, for example, to develop outcome statements related to ideas such as democracy, cultural pluralism, and human–environment interaction than it is to spend time listing crops produced in Latin America, Civil War battlefields, and home towns of U.S. presidents. Of course, these latter subjects may have their place in a well-conceived curriculum, but *school time is precious.* Skillful teachers spend most of their assessment energies on the learnings that matter the most.

---

[1] Grant Wiggins, "Teaching to the Authentic Test," *Educational Leadership* 46 (April 1989): 41–47; Dennie Palmer Wolf, "Portfolio Assessment: Sampling Student Work," *Educational Leadership* 46 (April 1989): 4–10; and Theodore R. Sizer, *Horace's School* (Boston: Houghton Mifflin, 1992).

Authentic Exhibitions

Teachers should plan exhibitions to match essential learnings. Once they have grappled with the question of which subjects and skills are most important, teachers need to plan ways for children to exhibit or demonstrate their grasp of these learnings. Built into these exhibitions is the requirement that learners demonstrate their ability to *use* what they have learned to accomplish some task. Rather than merely reproducing knowledge, children analyze, manipulate, or interpret it in some way or ways required by the exhibition. In this way, higher-order thinking is incorporated into the assessment program. By observing the exhibition task, the teacher can determine whether the student understands the material well enough to use it, and judge the quality of that usage as well.

Many common forms of assessment, such as circling a letter on a multiple-choice test item, do not embody this principle. While they surely have their place in a total program of assessment, they are not tasks that require the application of one's knowledge. They are not exhibitions of knowledge-in-use. For this reason, they should be only one part of an assessment program.

Some teachers ask their students to help plan the exhibitions. One group suggested that teamwork on biography writing (see chapter 11) would be a good way to exhibit several essential learnings at once—cooperative skills, the writing process, and the life and times of whoever the biography was about. The production of the biography is a task that the teacher can easily observe to assess children's understanding of all three learnings.

Exhibitions do not need to be this elaborate. Recall the discussion of concept learning in chapter 2: classifying is a task that requires children to exhibit their understanding of a particular idea (e.g., democracy) while *using* the understanding to distinguish among examples and nonexamples, produce new examples, or correct nonexamples. When the concept is *democracy*, students who understand it can distinguish between the governments of Canada and Iraq, or they can create a fictional society with a democratic political system. As well, they can specify the changes needed in Iraq's government to make it a democracy.

High Standards

Exhibitions should require students to aim for and demonstrate a high degree of competence. Minimum competencies place in the learner's mind a low standard of knowing. This is unfortunate because the outcomes desired actually are much more ambitious than this. Knowing the century in which Geronimo lived, for example, is a far cry from collaboratively writing a biography of his life and times. Knowing the date the U.S. Constitution was signed and the names of those who signed it falls woefully short of the high standard of knowing what democracy requires of citizens; knowing why the Constitution has the content it does; comprehending its several parts; understanding how this document functions in their daily lives; and grasping the principles on which it relies, such as popular sovereignty, civil liberties, loyal opposition, and limited government. We need citizens who so deeply "know" the Constitution that they could themselves write a similar constitution—not so much from memory as from a creative application of the principles that undergird it.

This is a *standard-setting* level of understanding. It functions to inform children and teachers alike of what it means to have learned the topic not minimally but optimally. It thus encourages them to aim high.

Clarify Targets Early

Teachers should clarify the desired outcome early in the learning process. If teachers want children to develop their skills and knowledge to a standard-setting level, the children must know the target well in advance. Good teachers always clarify the goals of instruction *at the beginning of the year,* and state specific objectives *at the beginning of a unit.* This is the essence of the fourth principle.

For example, Ms. Paley's kindergartners know in advance that their dramatizations of historical events must be rich in detail. Consequently, each time she repeats to them the story of Rosa Parks's bus ride or of Squanto, the Pilgrims' friend, it is with the expectation that their retellings of the story will evolve. And they do.[2] Likewise, Mr. Smith tells his seventh-grade class in September that by June they will draw a world map beautifully from memory on a blank piece of tag board. "When they arrive here, I tell them they'll end up with 150 countries, and they tell me, 'No way.'" But they do, confidently. "I used to hear about countries on television and think they were over there somewhere," admitted one student. "I hadn't heard of half of them. Now I can figure out better what's going on in the world. I'll always know that Angola is in Africa and not just over there somewhere."[3]

Teachers like Ms. Paley and Mr. Smith wisely make clear for children the targets for what Theodore Sizer calls the "destinations" of their efforts.[4] They then assess continuously, in large and small ways, formally and informally, collecting samples of students' work, using teacher-made as well as standardized tests. Such teachers can provide additional instruction and experiences as needed, calibrating them to student progress toward the outcomes.

Don't Go It Alone

Teachers should engage in discussion and advanced study to improve their ability to develop desired outcomes that incorporate these principles. Ca-

---

[2]Vivian Paley, *Wally's Stories* (Cambridge, MA: Harvard University Press, 1981).

[3]Sam Allis, "Quick! Name Togo's Capital," *Time,* July 16, 1990, p. 53.

[4]Sizer, *Horace's School,* 86.

pable teachers routinely rethink the targets they have set for children's schoolwork. Their judgment as to which understandings are essential will change from year to year, along with their ideas about how those understandings should be exhibited and what standards should be expected.

Regular discussion with colleagues about these matters is probably the most important form of continuing education for the teacher. The play of competing viewpoints that discussion affords will stimulate new insights. Indeed, a leading indicator of a healthy, growing, renewing school climate is that the faculty frequently can be seen engaged in such discussions. Faculty meetings are not spent solely on "administrivia." Time is reserved to consider substantive topics, such as the following:

- A committee of teachers is proposing that a small number of essential learnings be woven through the curriculum of each grade level. To get the conversation rolling, the committee suggests a set of five learnings and related exhibitions. They are careful not to single out reading or writing as distinct learnings, but to integrate them with the content knowledge on which children should be using these skills.
- The fourth-grade teachers display samples of their students' work. These are impressive biographies of Indian chiefs who once lived in the region where the school is located. The narrative of each chief is rich with detail about the natural environment as well as the culture of that chief's society. The teachers' point is that history, geography, and literacy education can be integrated. They propose that the whole faculty experiment with this approach in the following year. They volunteer to serve on a steering committee.

Teachers must also continue their own education. Advanced reading in educational theory and in specific subject areas, usually through graduate work at a college or university, is essential if one's professional judgment is to thrive. Teachers also should read professional journals regularly, and even submit an occasional article. It is through this sort of study and sharing, and the reflection that writing demands, that teachers hone their sense of essential learnings and update their knowledge of instructional practices and corresponding assessment techniques.

A desired outcome, to summarize, describes an exhibition of learning. It shows students and teachers what it looks like to learn important material deeply. It lets children know in a straightforward way what it means to do their schoolwork well. Figure 15-1 shows a summary of the principles used to develop desired outcomes. It should be clear that a threefold relationship exists among outcomes, instruction, and assessment. Compatibility must be maintained in the relationship. For example, it is inconsistent, and unfair to students, to establish targets that exhibit higher-order thinking and cooperative learning skills and at the same time fail to provide instruction to develop them, or to evaluate only content knowledge. Teaching methods and assessment procedures must be in harmony with the desired outcomes.

FIGURE 15-1
Principles for Developing Desired Outcomes

1. Assessment should be directed to *essential learnings.*
2. Outcomes generally should be *exhibitions of knowledge-in-use.*
3. Outcomes should establish *standard-setting* targets for learning.
4. Outcomes should be *known to learners well in advance* of instruction and assessment.
5. The art of developing desired outcomes evolves through *continued discussion* with colleagues and other educators.

MINIMUM COMPETENCY TESTING IN THE SOCIAL STUDIES

For several years there has been a growing concern about the level of academic competence of youngsters who have completed school programs. This concern focused initially on the so-called basic skills—meaning reading, writing, and mathematics skills—but has now been extended to other areas of the curriculum, including social studies. To ensure that school graduates attain a level of functional competence, states and school districts have instituted testing policies that require students to achieve specified levels as a condition of promotion from one grade to the next or for graduation from high school. It is one form of holding schools accountable for what they do; it is also a measure intended to enhance the quality of education.

Intended or not, the scores children earn on competency tests reflect on the teacher's competence. Consequently, teachers, quite understandably, focus the greatest intensity of the instructional effort on those subjects and skills that are included in the competency test battery. This is clearly one reason for the diminished attention given to the arts, science, and social studies in recent years. Teachers give the greatest attention to the basic skills and, in some instances, teach directly for the test. Social studies educators, therefore, have argued for the inclusion of social studies on such competency test batteries, for they know that if social studies education is not included, it will suffer from neglect.

Competency tests can be regular standardized tests produced by commercial publishers (standardized tests are discussed later in this chapter), but more often they are tests constructed at the state or local level. Locally produced tests are sometimes hastily prepared and are wanting in technical quality. In the case of social studies, these instruments lean heavily on testing for easily measured outcomes such as history, geography, or civics information and skills.

Teachers are obliged to familiarize themselves with local policies regarding competency testing and to work within those policies. But competency testing should represent only one part of the assessment program that a teacher uses. The day-to-day assessment of children's work—much of it informal, much of it relying on careful observation, and much of it diagnostic—is essential if the teacher is to assess learner progress and determine whether instruction has been effective. What follows, therefore, is a discussion of assessment techniques and procedures that can be used to provide a balanced assessment of the attainment of a broad range of outcomes that should characterize social studies instruction.

INFORMAL ASSESSMENT TECHNIQUES

Much of the evaluation of learning in social studies is done informally by the teacher. Many times each day the teacher observes learners and makes a judgment about the quality of their work. The teacher notices what problems individual children are encountering or what kind of help they need in order to progress. Teachers find themselves spending a considerable amount of time assessing the status of individual children and groups. The teacher then makes decisions concerning what deficiencies are apparent in children's work, whether the instruction is proceeding too rapidly or too slowly, what materials are required, how well concepts have been understood, or how proficient children are in their use of skills. Of course, formal tests have a place in this process, but most of the assessments a teacher does involve informal methods and observation. This means that careful records must be kept if the progress of each child is to be reported accurately. Some of the more commonly used assessment techniques and devices are described on the pages that follow.

Group Discussion

Group discussion can be used to appraise the progress of the children in terms of previously established plans and standards. Discussion will activate self-evaluative thinking; it helps clarify and remind children of learning objectives; it is useful in establishing an attitude of looking forward to progress and successful achievement. The teacher should reserve some time near the end of every social studies period for the class to discuss its progress and to make plans for the next day's work. As was noted earlier, this helps children's thinking, helps identify concepts needing further study, and reminds them of the things they are learning in social studies. In addition to the daily discussions of the progress of the class, this technique can also be used in a variety of other situations:

1. As a followup of a major class activity such as a field trip, a social action project, a dramatization.
2. As a method of evaluating group reports, unit projects, and creative dramatics activities.
3. As a means of improving small-group endeavors.

4. As a means of evaluating behavior of the class at a school assembly, in the lunchroom, or on the playground.
5. As a method of working out some problem of human relations within the classroom.
6. As a means of bringing to light attitudes that may be held by children.
7. As a means of verifying information obtained through individual study.

The use of discussion as an assessment technique necessitates the identification of standards to be attained and a knowledge of what is expected on the part of the learners. This means that in most cases the teacher and the class will have to decide on standards that apply in a given situation. For example, if a class is about to engage in an activity calling for small committees, the following standards may be agreed on:

1. Work quietly, so that others may work too.
2. Know where the materials are.
3. Arrange with other groups to borrow materials.
4. Speak quietly to other committee members.
5. Stop work as soon as the bell rings.
6. Arrange and clean up the area after work.

Specific work standards of this type should be posted on a chart and referred to when the work of the class is being evaluated through discussion. Verbal agreement on standards is not sufficient for young children — they forget from day to day just what the standards are. Posting the standards and discussing them without "harping" on them help remind children of their responsibilities and enhance their learning. Knowledge of progress is a strong force in the motivation of learning, and a knowledge of areas in which improvement is needed helps give direction to learning. The use of class discussion as an assessment technique can serve both of these purposes.

Observation

Observation is among the best techniques the teacher can use in learning about children, appraising their progress, and sensing their needs for improvement. Although all teachers use this method of learner appraisal, not all teachers are skillful in its application. Much of what is called observation might properly be described as an unorganized set of impressions the teacher obtains during the course of instruction, essentially on a catch-as-catch-can basis. The teacher who makes the most of observation knows what he or she is looking for, systematizes observations, and makes an attempt to objectify the information so obtained. To this end it is suggested that the teacher

1. Spell out exactly the traits to be evaluated and state evidences of these traits in terms of child behavior. For example, if the teacher desires to observe whether there is evidence of progress in *consideration for others*, the following would be appropriate:

Does the child
a. show respect for the ideas and feelings of classmates?
b. abstain from causing disturbances that make it impossible for others to do their best work?
c. carry a fair share of the work load in a small group?
d. enjoy giving a classmate an "assist" when needed?
e. display sensitivity to injustices that may occur in the course of life in and out of the classroom?
f. return borrowed materials? Obtain permission to use materials that belong to others?
g. observe rules established by the group?
h. fulfill responsibilities on time? Avoid doing things that hold up the progress of the class?

2. Select certain children for intensive observation and study rather than observing "in general." This intensive observation might be limited to certain specific situations. For example, just what happens to David when he is placed on a committee to do some project in connection with a social studies unit? How can the situation be changed to help him develop more responsible habits of work in a group situation? The purpose of observations of this type is to gain insight into the child's behavior in the context of a specific set of circumstances.

3. Record observations in writing and do not depend on memory. Keep a written record of information obtained through observation, and maintain this record over a period of time to establish a definite pattern in the child's behavior. At best, observation is a highly unreliable method of evaluating learner progress, and without a record of the observations, it is of little value indeed. The written record may take the form of anecdotal accounts, a checklist, or a rating device. Information of this type is helpful to the teacher in interpreting and reporting the progress of children to their parents.

Checklists

Checklists may be constructed from previously established specific objectives and can be used either by the teacher or by the children themselves to assess progress. It is a good practice for classes to work out short checklists cooperatively and apply them to their work individually. The checklists may be used when children are giving reports or short talks to call attention to clarity of speaking, new information presented, use of visual material, extent of preparedness, and other responsibilities of the speaker. A similar checklist can be devised to cover the responsibilities of the audience. An example of a self-assessment sheet developed by a teacher with a class is reproduced in part in Figure 15-2.

In addition to the checklists developed and used by the children for self-appraisal, the teacher can devise similar checklists for use in recording observations. As previously noted, this procedure adds objectivity and reliability to the teacher's observation. The specific points to be checked

FIGURE 15-2
Student Self-Assessment Checklist.

SELF-ASSESSMENT CHECKLIST

DATE _____ NAME _____

In this unit I was able to	Super-well	Good	Okay	Needed more help
choose appropriate activities				
use my work time efficiently				
work cooperatively with another person				
use materials from the Resource Center				
keep my work area clean				
use the suggestion that others gave me				

Remarks:

would be the behavior characteristics that provide evidence either of the presence or absence of the trait under study. Commercially prepared behavior-rating scales may be used for this purpose.

Conferences

Conferences with children should teach them how to assess their own work, thereby leading to increased self-direction. The teacher–learner conference can be of help in discovering particular learning problems and difficulties that children may be having, gaining insight into their feelings about schoolwork, and becoming aware of special personal–social problems the children may be having, as well as being a method of assisting every child individually in a personal way. Teachers need to budget their time to allow regular ten-minute conferences with individual children. Children need the personal contact with their teacher that a conference can give.

A conference will be of little value if the teacher does all the talking and the child all the listening. A friendly, helpful approach is needed, one that results in greater feelings of personal worth on the part of the child along with some constructive and concrete helps for improvement. This close working relationship with children is critical to good education, especially in the social studies.

ANECDOTAL RECORD

Sara Larsen

9/24   Difficulty in getting going in independent choice work; ignored all sugges-
        tions of activities. . . . "It's boring."

9/26   Found a fiction book related to unit for Sara. Read during work time. Took it
        home today.

9/27   Finished book . . . took suggestion to make a poster showing main charac-
        ters.

10/1   Asked for time to show class the poster and to tell about the story.

10/2   Showed work. Talented artist. Received lots of compliments/support from
        classmates.

10/3   Sara asked for another book; suggested biography to her, plus suggested
        she do a map showing the area in which the person lived.

Anecdotal Records

An *anecdotal record* is a description of some incident or situation in the life of the child. A collection of such descriptions of learner behavior kept over a period of time, therefore, provides the teacher with a documentary account of changes of behavior that have occurred or are in progress. It is another way of systematically recording observations. Anecdotal records should indicate the date and time of the incident, the circumstances under which it occurred, and an objective description of the situation. If an interpretation is made of the incident, it should be kept separate from the description of the actual happening. Above are six entries in one teacher's anecdotal record on a child.

Because this is a time-consuming procedure, the teacher will want to limit its use to those particular children who seem to be exhibiting behavior that the teacher believes requires in-depth study.

Work Samples, Portfolios, and Exhibits

The practice of saving samples of children's work in a portfolio has become popular in recent years.[5] In many schools, it has become the primary means of assessing children's progress both through a single school year and across several years. This practice is similar to that of the parent who cuts notches on the inside of a closet door recording the height of a child at various ages. Both the parent and the teacher know that changes are occurring, but, because of their continuous, day-to-day contact with the child, changes are imperceptible. They need, therefore, a specific example of the child's status at one point to compare with his or her status at a

---

[5]Wolf, "Portfolio Assessment"; Valencia, Sheila, "A Portfolio Approach to Classroom Reading Assessment: The Whys, Whats, and Hows," *The Reading Teacher* 44 (January 1990): 338–40.

subsequent time. The greater the time interval between the two samples, the greater should be the evidence of change.

Work samples that are saved for this purpose are usually written material and may include a report, a story, a classroom test, an explanation, a booklet, or a research project. The teacher might also want to save a child's map work, artwork done in connection with the social studies, or a small construction project. The tape recorder can also be used to obtain a sample of the child's oral language. For example, children find it revealing and profitable to hear reports privately that they have made to the class at various times during the school year. The same device can be used by the entire class to evaluate their progress in discussions, dramatizations, and similar speaking situations. Care must be taken that the work samples saved are closely related to essential learnings and desired social studies outcomes. There is no need to clutter the portfolio with relatively unimportant work when there are so many learning outcomes that are critically important and in need of continuous assessment.

The portfolio of the child's work can be useful during parent conferences at the regular reporting periods during the school year. Additionally, some teachers send samples of the child's work home from time to time simply to keep the parents informed of the child's progress in school. To make sure the parent has received the material, teachers may want to use a message sheet that asks the parent to comment, sign, and return to the teacher.

Experience Summaries

Experience summaries are ordinarily constructed cooperatively by the teacher and the class and are used to record and assess a single or specific experience. For example, when the group returns from its trip to the airport, the children can summarize some of the important things they have learned as a result of the trip and place these on a chart. The chart may then be used to evaluate the extent to which they found out the things they set out to learn. The following is an example of an experience summary.

·············· EXPERIENCE SUMMARY

What We Learned at the Food Distribution Center:

1. How food is sent to grocery stores.
2. That food we eat comes from all over the world.
3. Certain foods must be kept in temperature-controlled rooms so they do not spoil.
4. It takes many people to handle the food before we see it in our stores.
5. Food is sent by railroad cars, ships, trucks, and sometimes planes before it reaches the store.
6. Grocery stores order the amounts they need each week before it is sent to them.

FIGURE 15-3
Sample Diary/Log

Date _____   Name _____
Today—
I learned a new fact: _____
I tried something new: _____
I worked with: _____
I was best at: _____
I spent most of my time: _____

Diaries and Logs

Diaries and logs are similar to experience summaries except that they are kept on a continuing basis. Each day the class can summarize its progress and record it on a chart or in a notebook. This provides a running account of work in the unit and can be used to review and check on previous plans and decisions as the unit progresses. In the final phases of the unit, the class, by referring to its log, can recall many details of its work that would otherwise be overlooked or forgotten. In the primary grades, the teacher will have to assume much of the responsibility for recording the material to be placed in the log although children can and should assist in deciding *what* is to be recorded. In the middle and upper grades, individual children or committees can assume this responsibility if they are given some help and guidance by the teacher. A form such as the one shown in Figure 15-3 can be used to record diary or log entries.

TEACHER-MADE TESTS

Classroom tests constructed by the teacher usually are used to assess the child's progress in the more tangible information and skill outcomes of social studies instruction. Even though paper-and-pencil tests can be used successfully with primary-grade children, their value increases as the child moves into the middle and upper grades. These tests are of greater value when they test understanding of basic concepts and generalizations rather than only facts. Too frequently questions dealing with *who, what, when, where,* and *how many* take precedence over more reflective and penetrating items such as those that call for knowing *why, for what reason,* and *how do we know,* mainly because they are easier to construct. An important require-ment of any good test is that it should enhance and encourage desirable study habits. Overemphasis on recall of minutiae and inconsequential details inevitably leads to rote memory of facts without understanding their significance or without relating them to the basic and underlying key ideas. When conventional objective-type test items such as multiple choice, alternate response, completion, recall, and matching are used, their construction should be technically correct. Many of the standard works on measurement and evaluation discuss in detail the advantages and limitations of various objective-type test items and offer suggestions for their construction.[6]

Teacher-made tests are essential in assessing the children's achievement of social studies skills. Tests designed to measure the child's skill in using a map—locating places, identifying map symbols, reading the legend, understanding scale, interpreting map data, recognizing landforms—are a necessary part of instruction in the use of maps. An example of this type of teacher-made test appears in Figure 15-8. Similarly, short tests can be designed to evaluate the child's ability to use reference material, to read social studies materials, to understand the vocabulary of social studies, to evaluate news stories, to distinguish between fact and opinion, and other social studies skills. Examples of teacher-made tests are provided in Figures 15-4 through 15-15.

In constructing specific items to evaluate certain kinds of learnings, the teacher may find the suggestions of Maxine Dunfee helpful:

To test for *factual information*—

Arranging in order the steps in a process

Matching events with periods of time

Supplying key words missing in statements of essential facts

Matching vocabulary and definition

Placing events or persons on a time line

To test for *understandings*—

Matching causes and effects

Supplying a generalization to be drawn from a given set of facts

Stating the most important ideas learned

Selecting a conclusion to be drawn from a chart, diagram, or graph

To obtain insights into *attitudes*—

Responding to statements in terms of strength of belief, feeling, or opinion by indicating degree—always, sometimes, never

---

[6]See, for example, Norman E. Gronlund and Robert L. Linn, *Measurement and Evaluation in Teaching*, 6th ed. (New York: Macmillan, 1990). Chapters 5, 6, and 7 provide excellent practical and technical information regarding the construction of objective test items for teacher-made classroom tests.

FIGURE 15-4

COMPARING HEATING FUELS

This is a test to see how well you can get information from your textbook. Give each of the four fuels a rating of 1, 2, 3, or 4, with 1 being *best* and 4 being *poorest,* on each of the points listed. Also, write the page or pages of your text on which you found the information.

	Text page	Coal	Gas	Oil	Electricity
1. Availability					
2. Cost					
3. Cleanliness in the home					
4. Effect on environment					
5. Consumer satisfaction					
6. Reliable source					

Responding to statements that imply prejudice or lack of prejudice by indicating state of agreement—I agree, I disagree, I am uncertain

Matching attitudes with likely resultant actions

Writing endings to stories that describe problem situations

To test for *skills*—

Interpreting an imaginary map, locating physical and cultural features and answering questions calling for interpretation of information provided

Supplying a missing step in directions for doing something that involves a skill

Demonstrating how to conduct a meeting, how to give a good report, and so on

Using a table of contents or index to locate specified information[7]

The figures show examples of teacher-made tests that could be used for evaluating social studies outcomes.

---

[7]Maxine Dunfee, "Evaluating Understandings, Attitudes, Skills, and Behaviors in Elementary School Social Studies," *Evaluation in Social Studies,* 35th Yearbook, Chap. 8 (Washington, DC: National Council for the Social Studies, 1965), 165–67.

FIGURE 15-5

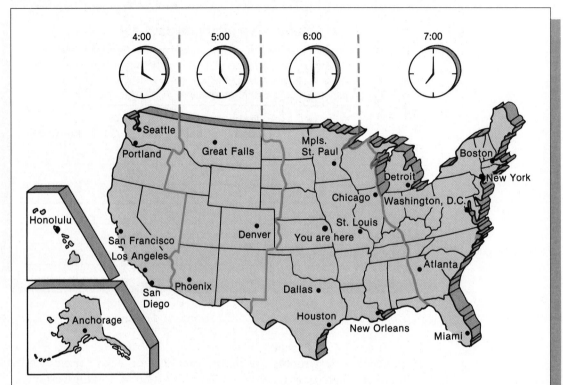

FINDING YOUR WAY AROUND

Use the map above to answer these questions.

1. If you were to go from where you are (on the map) to Boston, what direction would you have to travel? _____

2. If you were going to travel from where you are (on the map) to Anchorage, Alaska, what is the *last* city through which you would pass? _____

3. What large city on the map could you get to *only* by boat or airplane? _____

4. If you travel by car from where you are (on the map) to San Diego, through which large city are you likely to pass? _____

5. The map shows Washington and New York. Between those two cities are two other large cities. Place them on the map where they belong and label them. Write their names here. _____

6. You fly from where you are (on the map) to Great Falls. The flight takes exactly one hour. It is six o'clock when you leave. What time is it when you arrive in Great Falls? _____

FIGURE 15-6

UNDERSTANDING WORD MEANINGS

One example is given for each of the terms listed. Your job is to write down *another* example.

1. Raw material   *Wood* is a raw material for making furniture;
           another raw material is _____
           Used in making _____

2. Fuel   *Oil* is a fuel used for heating; another fuel is _____
           Used for _____

3. Grain   *Corn* is a grain used for feed; another example
           of a grain is _____
           Used for _____

4. Industry   *Dressmaking* is an industry; another example
           of an industry is _____
           that makes _____

5. Natural resource   *Water* is a natural resource necessary for life;
           another natural resource is _____
           Used for _____

6. Continent   *Africa* is a continent in the Eastern Hemisphere; another continent in
           the Eastern Hemisphere is _____
           In the Western Hemisphere? _____

7. Manufactured product   A *typewriter* is a manufactured product used
           for printing; another example of a manufactured
           product is _____
           Used for _____

FIGURE 15-7

MATCHING CAUSE AND EFFECT

Directions: Each of the events listed in the first column was the cause of an event listed in the second column. In the space provided at the left, place the letter of the result that matches each cause.

____1. Expanding factories needed many workers.

____2. Automobiles were mass produced at low cost.

____3. Trains and trolleys were built to take people to their jobs.

____4. Workers needed to live close to their jobs.

a. People with average income could buy their own cars.

b. Immigrant workers came in large numbers.

c. Laws were passed to prevent child labor.

d. Workers lived in crowded and congested conditions.

e. People could have their homes farther from where they worked.

FIGURE 15-8

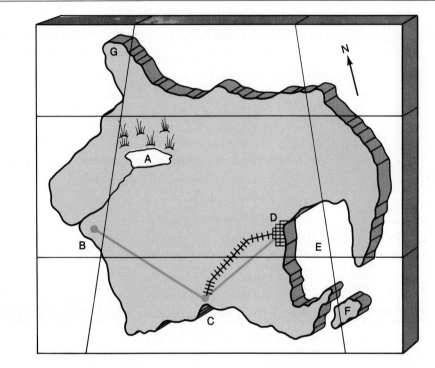

USING MAP SYMBOLS AND KNOWING DIRECTIONS

Use the map above to decide the correct answers. Then underline the correct answers.

1. The land north of A is (a swamp), (a desert), (mountainous).
2. The mouth of a river is located near letter (A), (B), (C).
3. The city at D is perhaps a (capital), (seaport), (mining town).
4. The river flows (from southwest to northeast), (from northeast to southwest), (from east to west).
5. An island is marked by the letter (A), (B), (F).
6. A railroad runs between (B and C), (D and B), (D and C).
7. The letter E marks (a bay), (a peninsula), (an island).
8. A peninsula is shown on this map at (B), (G), (C).
9. A delta might be found just north of (C), (A), (B).
10. The letter G is due north of (C), (A), (B).

FIGURE 15-9

KNOWING THEIR MEANING

Directions: The phrases in the right-hand column explain the words or terms listed in the left-hand column. In the space to the left of each phrase, place the letter of the word or term that matches the description.

a. Blimp
b. Drill
c. Mohair
d. Derrick
e. Raw sugar
f. Helium
g. Gusher
h. Sulfur
i. Refinery
j. Flowing well

____ 1. An oil well from which the oil shoots high into the air.

____ 2. A building in which raw materials are changed into finished products.

____ 3. The brown crystals that form when the juice of sugar cane is boiled and allowed to cool.

____ 4. The framework that supports the machinery used to drill an oil well.

____ 5. The tool used to bore holes into the earth.

____ 6. An airship that floats in the air when filled with a light gas.

____ 7. Cloth made from goat hair.

____ 8. A very light gas.

____ 9. A well from which a steady stream of oil flows without having to be pumped.

____10. A yellow mineral.

FIGURE 15-10

WHAT DID YOU LIKE BEST?

Directions: In the space to the left of each activity, write a letter "L" if you liked it and a "D" if you did not like it. Place a star (*) next to the two you liked best of all.

____1. Making individual booklets on the unit.

____2. Working in committees.

____3. Dramatizing important events.

____4. Writing summaries.

____5. Doing map work.

____6. Seeing films and filmstrips.

____7. Reading different books.

____ 8. Collecting pictures.

____ 9. Taking the field trip.

____10. Hearing the resource people.

____11. Making a mural.

____12. Preparing the exhibit.

____13. Preparing the report.

____14. Doing the simulation.

____15. Working in the learning center.

FIGURE 15-11

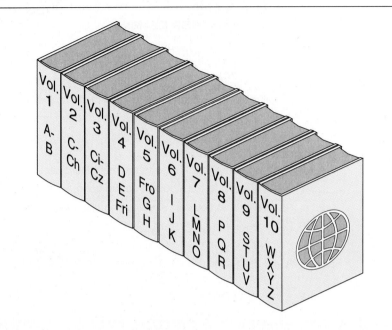

USING THE ENCYCLOPEDIA

Directions: Using the ten-volume *Our Own Encyclopedia* shown in this diagram, select the number of the volume in which you would find information about each of the items listed below. Write the number of the volume you select in the spaces on the left side of the sheet. Then list the volume number of *World Book* in which the same items are found in the spaces on the right side of the sheet.

Our Own		*World Book*
_____	1. *Earthquakes in Guatemala*	1. _____
_____	2. *The French writer Crèvecoeur*	2. _____
_____	3. *The history of rocketry*	3. _____
_____	4. *The People's Republic of China*	4. _____
_____	5. *Russia*	5. _____
_____	6. *Apple-growing in Washington State*	6. _____
_____	7. *Jet aircraft*	7. _____
_____	8. *Countries that are members of the United Nations*	8. _____
_____	9. *Unidentified flying objects*	9. _____
_____	10. *The history of Czechoslovakia*	10. _____

FIGURE 15-12

TRUE OR FALSE

Directions: The following list contains some statements that are true and some that are not true. Read each one and decide whether it is or is not true. If it is true, place a "T" in the space just to the left of the statement. If it is false, place an "F" in the space, and *rewrite* the statement on the line below it to make it true.

_____ 1. Some of the dry land in Arizona and New Mexico is irrigated and produces fine crops.

_____

_____ 2. Colorado and Nevada were settled by people moving east.

_____

_____ 3. The Mormons settled at Great Salt Lake in a region then owned by California.

_____

_____ 4. Gold was discovered in the Comstock Lode in the state of Nevada.

_____

_____ 5. The large area in the Rockies that is lower than the surrounding mountains is called the Continental Divide.

_____

_____ 6. The Indian house used by the Navajos is called a hogan.

_____

_____ 7. The Plains Indians lived in villages called pueblos.

_____

_____ 8. An early mission was established in what is now the state of Arizona by Father Kino.

_____

FIGURE 15-13

CHECKLIST FOR DISCUSSION

(Middle Grades)	Always	Usually	Seldom	Rarely
1. States problems clearly				
2. Sticks to the point				
3. Shows respect for ideas of others				
4. Contributes regularly				
5. Raises questions on issues				
6. Helps in making decisions				
7. Uses evidence to back up points				
8. Helps in summarizing				

FIGURE 15-14

WHAT'S GOING ON HERE?

Directions: Read each paragraph carefully; then write a sentence telling what the paragraph is describing.

Situation 1.   It was the first Tuesday in November. On this day the fire station had the United States flag flying just outside the entrance. All day long people were going in and out of the fire station. A sign in the window said "Polling Place."
What was going on at the fire station?

_____

Situation 2.   A large number of people are in the room. At the front of the room, sitting behind a large desk up on a platform is a man dressed in a black robe who seems to be in charge of things. As we watch, two men face each other in front of the man in the black robe. One man seems to be holding a Bible. He says to the other man, "Raise your right hand. Do you swear to tell the truth, the whole truth, and nothing but the truth, so help you God?"
What is going on in this room?

_____

Situation 3.   A large crowd of people is in a huge room. There are signs and banners all over the place. There is much noise and confusion. People speak to the crowd, but many are not listening. The person who is now speaking has just said, "I yield five minutes to the delegate from the great State of Virginia."
What is going on here?

_____

Situation 4.   People are scurrying around all over the place. Everyone seems to be in a hurry. Over the loudspeaker, a voice is saying, "The East Concourse is now open."
Where is all this taking place?

_____

FIGURE 15-15

<table>
<tr><td colspan="4" align="center">**CHECKLIST FOR DISCUSSION**</td></tr>
<tr><td>**(Primary Grades)**</td><td align="center">Always</td><td align="center">Sometimes</td><td align="center">Not Often</td></tr>
<tr><td>1. Helps make plans</td><td></td><td></td><td></td></tr>
<tr><td>2. Listens to what is said</td><td></td><td></td><td></td></tr>
<tr><td>3. Takes turns</td><td></td><td></td><td></td></tr>
<tr><td>4. Gives own ideas</td><td></td><td></td><td></td></tr>
<tr><td>5. Considers what others have said</td><td></td><td></td><td></td></tr>
</table>

STANDARDIZED AND CRITERION-REFERENCED TESTS

We close this chapter with a brief word about standardized and criterion-referenced tests. Standardized tests are *norm-referenced* tests. A child's performance is evaluated in terms of the performance of a large sample of other children of the same age and grade (the norming population). The teacher can compare, therefore, the achievement of the class to other children. This is different from *criterion-referenced* tests, in which the child is evaluated in terms of the degree of his or her progress toward the attainment of specific outcomes. Criterion-referenced assessment often is associated with the "mastery" of certain learnings, meaning that the child continues to work on the material until a certain expected level of competence *(criterion level)* has been achieved, that is, until the desired outcome has been exhibited.

Criterion-referenced tests have gained considerable attention in recent years for two reasons. First, there is growing dissatisfaction with the validity of standardized tests. A school district may be proud that its average student scores higher on, for example, the California Achievement Test, than the average student in a neighboring school district. But what does this mean? Does it mean that this students is able to exhibit standard-setting levels of understanding of cultural pluralism or democratic government? Probably not, because the test does not require it. Instead, according to critics, the test requires a display of factual recall, reading ability, and knowledge of how to take such tests.[8] Criterion-referenced tests more easily can be geared to desired outcomes and authentic exhibitions of knowledge.

Second, the chief obstacle to the wise use of standardized tests is that teachers and school administrators have been inclined to regard the grade

---

[8]Wiggins, "Teaching to the Authentic Test." See also Lauren B. Resnick and Daniel P. Resnick, "Assessing the Thinking Curriculum: New Tools for Educational Reform," in *Changing Assessments: Alternative Views of Aptitude, Achievement, and Instruction,* ed. B. R. Gifford and M. O-'Conner, 38–76 (Boston: Kluwer, 1991).

norm as a high standard that all must achieve if their progress is to be regarded as satisfactory. In other words, teachers believe that all children must attain a grade score on the test equal to their present grade status. *This is an erroneous approach to the use of standardized tests* because the grade norm represents an average performance. For many children this level of achievement expectation will be too low; for others it will be too high. The teacher can reasonably expect the range of achievement of groups in which children have been randomly selected to range from two to four grades below, to two to four grades above the grade norm. This range will be less in the lower grades but becomes wider as the children move into the higher grades. Just what constitutes an adequate and satisfactory performance on the test will depend on individual children. Standards or levels of achievement expectation, therefore, should properly be established in terms of the capabilities of individual children and should not be dictated by the norms of a standardized test.

Knowing the results of a standardized achievement test, the teacher may set limited achievement expectations for a child, thus producing the effect of a self-fulfilling prophecy. There is no way of overcoming this problem entirely except to sensitize teachers to it and to stress the need for data from a variety of sources before making a judgment about an appropriate level of achievement expectation for individual children. Because social studies achievement tests are so closely related to reading ability, the teacher should be especially suspicious of the validity of social studies test scores of children who are poor readers.

Published tests in the social studies differ in the extent to which they emphasize various social studies outcomes. Some are almost entirely subject-matter tests. These tests can be of value only if the content of the test and the content of the social studies curriculum are consistent. The test will lack validity to the extent that it lacks congruity with the curriculum. For example, if the teacher were administering a test that was heavily loaded with items about life in early America, the children would not do well on it unless the material had actually been taught. It would be inconsistent and improper to use such a test if the class had been studying their home state all year. It should be emphasized that decisions on the curriculum content should come first and that the selection of the test should come second, although that is often difficult to do. In selecting a test, the person making the selection should ascertain that its content is compatible with the curriculum in the particular school in which it is to be used.

To sidestep the issue of building a social studies test to fit the diverse programs operating throughout the country, some test makers have placed emphasis on *skills* rather than on subject matter. Because administrators typically want teachers to "teach to the test," there has been an increase in skills teaching throughout this nation. Unfortunately, the teaching of important knowledge, such as the themes of history and geography presented in chapter 5, has decreased. For this reason, we reiterate the point made earlier: Standardized testing, including minimum competency testing, should be only one part of an assessment program. In the long run, a

FIGURE 15-16
Student Achievement Profile

SOCIAL STUDIES ACHIEVEMENT PROFILE

Child's Name _____ Grade _____ Reporting Period _____ Teacher _____

This profile represents a comprehensive report of this child's achievement in social studies during the reporting period indicated. Teachers may wish to add items in each of the categories under the space labeled "Other." Narrative comments can be made on the reverse side of this sheet.

	Outstanding	Satisfactory	Needs Improvement	Does not apply

Knowledge Gain

1. Is developing a background of information related to the curriculum content of the grade.
2. Understands social studies concepts appropriate to age and grade level.
3. Demonstrates understanding of relationships among ideas such as cause and effect, sequence of events, predicting outcomes.
4. Uses social studies vocabulary with understanding.
5. Is able to cite examples of out-of-school applications of ideas studied.
6. Applies what is learned to new (other similar) situations.

Other:

Skill Development

1. Reads well enough to secure needed information.
2. Is able to express ideas orally and in writing:
   Orally
   In writing
3. Is able to work independently on study projects, doing assigned work.
4. Is able to work with others on collaborative assignments and projects as a leader:
   As a group member
5. Is able to gain information through attentive listening.

(continued)

more important part is the day-to-day assessment, often quite informal, that establishes and clarifies standard-setting targets and measures children's progress toward them.

FIGURE 15-16

Continued

SOCIAL STUDIES ACHIEVEMENT PROFILE	Outstanding	Satisfactory	Needs Improvement	Does not apply
6. Is able to use references (other than the textbook) to gain needed information.				
7. Is able to read and use maps appropriate to age and grade level.				
8. Is able to arrange information in useable forms: take notes, make an outline, prepare a summary, keep records.				
9. Shows evidence of the ability to do critical thinking and problem solving.				
Other:				
Values and Attitudes				
1. Shows interest in social studies.				
2. Shows respect for the ideas and feelings of others.				
3. Is developing a sensitivity to the rights of others.				
4. Is developing a respect for the ideals, the heritages, and the institutions of this nation.				
5. Is developing a commitment to those common values shared by all Americans: justice, equality, responsibility, rule of law, freedom, diversity, privacy, human dignity.				
6. Is maturing in responsibility for personal behavior through increased self-direction and independence (completion of work on time, conduct in unsupervised situations, punctuality, and so on).				
Other:				
Standardized Test Score Data:				

DISCUSSION QUESTIONS AND SUGGESTED ACTIVITIES

1. Why is assessment essential to good social studies instruction? What is the role of establishing desired outcomes and why is it important?

2. Select a unit for a grade of your choice, and develop two or three outcome exhibitions. Choose one of these and develop standards for distinguishing the best from good and fair performances.

3. Do you think that it is a good idea to evaluate teacher effectiveness by the increase in achievement of children during a year? What do you see as the relationship between teacher effectiveness and learner achievement?

4. The text mentions that a teacher's knowledge of scores on achievement tests may produce the effects of a self-fulfilling prophecy. Explain how this could happen. What other teaching practices in social studies might also result in a self-fulfilling prophecy?

5. Refer to the list of major goals for the social studies in chapter 1. Which goals lend themselves to formal evaluation through paper-and-pencil tests? Which goals require the use of other techniques? Which goals require the evaluator to observe the behavior of the learner on a first-hand basis? Which goals are most frequently evaluated? Why?

6. What advantages and disadvantages can you see in using statewide or even nationwide achievement examinations in social studies?

7. Select a child in a regular classroom, and, with the assistance of the teacher, prepare a social studies achievement profile using the form given in Figure 15-16.

8. Secure a basic social studies textbook for a grade in which you have a special interest, and examine the methods of evaluation it suggests and recommends. Do you regard these methods as sound? Why or why not? Is there a good balance in emphasis given to the evaluation of knowledge, values and attitudes, and skills objectives?

9. Suggest specific techniques you might use to evaluate each of the following:
   a. Ability to apply knowledge or a skill.
   b. Ability to generalize.
   c. Ability to detect bias in a news story.
   d. Knowing where to look for something in a reference book.
   e. Degree of acceptance of a child by other children in the class.
   f. Ability to detect sex-role or racial stereotyping.

10. What different purposes are served through the use of standardized achievement tests, teacher-made tests, and informal assessment procedures?

SELECTED REFERENCES

Au, Kathryn H., Judith A. Scheu, Alice Kawakami, and Patricia A. Herman. "Assessment and Accountability in a Whole Literacy Curriculum." *The Reading Teacher* 44 (April 1990): 574–78.

Berthoff, Ann E. *The Sense of Learning.* Portsmouth, NH: Heinemann, 1990.

Brophy, Jere E. "How Teachers Influence What Is Taught and Learned in Classrooms." *The Elementary School Journal* 83 (September 1982): 1–13.

Larkins, Guy. "Minimum Competency Testing: A Negative View." Chap. 7 in *The Social Studies,* edited by Howard D. Mehlinger and O. L. Davis, Jr., NSSE Yearbook 80, part 2. Chicago: University of Chicago Press, 1981.

Lipson, Marjorie Y., and Karen K. Wixson. *Assessment and Instruction of Reading Disability.* New York: HarperCollins, 1991.

Perrone, Vito, ed. *Expanding Student Assessment.* Alexandria, VA: Association for Supervision and Curriculum Development, 1991.

Resnick, Lauren B. and Daniel P. Resnick. "Assessing the Thinking Curriculum: New Tools for Educational Reform." In *Changing Assessments: Alternative Views of Aptitude, Achievement, and Instruction,* edited by B. R. Gifford and M. O'Conner, 38–76. Boston: Kluwer, 1991.

Sizer, Theodore R. *Horace's School.* Boston: Houghton Mifflin, 1992.

Valencia, Sheila. "A Portfolio Approach to Classroom Reading Assessment: The Whys, Whats, and Hows." *The Reading Teacher* 44 (January 1990): 338–40.

Wiggins, Grant. "Teaching to the Authentic Test." *Educational Leadership* 46 (April 1989): 41–47.

Wolf, Dennie Palmer. "Portfolio Assessment: Sampling Student Work." *Educational Leadership* 46 (April 1989): 35–39.

Index